Management and Cost Accounting

Students' Manual

COLIN DRURY

Management and Cost Accounting

REVISED
FOURTH EDITION

Students' Manual

INTERNATIONAL THOMSON BUSINESS PRESS
I ⓉP An International Thomson Publishing Company

London • Bonn • Johannesburg • Madrid • Melbourne • Mexico City • New York • Paris
Singapore • Tokyo • Toronto • Albany, NY • Belmont, CA • Cincinnati, OH • Detroit, MI

Management and Cost Accounting: Students' Manual

Copyright © 1985, 1988, 1992, 1996 J. C. Drury

 A division of International Thomson Publishing
The ITP logo is a trademark under licence

British Library Cataloguing-in-Publication Data
A catalogue record for this book is available from the British Library

First edition published by Chapman & Hall 1985
Reprinted 1986 (twice), 1987 (twice), 1988
Second edition published by Chapman & Hall 1988
Reprinted 1990, 1991
Third edition published by Chapman & Hall 1992
Reprinted 1993, 1994, 1995
Fourth edition published by International Thomson Business Press 1996
Reprinted 1997, 1998 and 1999 (revised)

Typeset by Columns Design Ltd, Reading, Berkshire
Printed by TJ International, Padstow, Cornwall

ISBN 1-86152-510-9

International Thomson Business Press
Berkshire House
168–173 High Holborn
London WC1V 7AA
UK

http://www.itbp.com

Contents

Preface   vii

Cost and revenue classification   1
Accounting for materials and labour   7
Accounting for overhead expenditure   15
Accounting for a job costing system   31
Process costing   45
Joint product and by-product costing   56
Absorption costing and variable costing   67
Cost–volume–profit analysis   76
Measuring costs and benefits for decision-making   92
Activity-based costing   107
Accounting information for pricing decisions   113
Decision-making under conditions of uncertainty   125
Capital investment decisions: 1   139
Capital investment decisions: 2   152
The budgeting process   168
Operational control, management control and performance measurement   180
Standard costing and variance analysis: 1   192
Standard costing: 2 Further aspects   208
Behavioural aspects of accounting control systems   233
Mathematical approaches to cost estimation   241
Quantitative models for the planning and control of stocks   253
The application of linear programming to management accounting   268
Measuring divisional profitability   283
Transfer pricing in divisionalized companies   299
Past, current and future developments in management accounting practice   314
New questions for 1999   318
New ACCA questions   402

Preface

This manual is complementary to the main textbook, *Management and Cost Accounting*. Throughout the main book I have kept the illustrations simple to enable the reader to understand the principles involved in designing and evaluating management and cost accounting systems. More complex problems are provided at the end of each chapter so that the student can pursue certain topics in more depth, and concentrate on the application of principles. The objective of this manual is to provide solutions to the problems which have an asterisk beside the question number and, where necessary, to supplement the main text with a discussion of the additional issues raised by the questions.

The solutions given in this manual are my own and not the approved solutions of the professional body setting the question. Where an essay question is asked and a full answer requires undue repetition of the book, either references are made to the appropriate sections of the main book, or an answer guide or outline is provided. You should note that there will be no 'ideal' answer to questions which are not strictly numerical. Answers are provided which, it is felt, would be generally acceptable in most contexts.

Where possible the questions are arranged in ascending order of difficulty. A short description of each question is given at the beginning of each chapter of this manual. The reader should select questions which are appropriate to the course which is being pursued. As a general rule questions designated as ACCA Level 1, ACCA Foundation, CIMA Cost Accounting 1 and 2 and AAT are appropriate for a first year course. These questions are mainly concerned with cost accounting which is covered in Part II of the main text. Questions designated as CIMA Management Accounting, ICAEW Management Accounting, ACCA Level II Management Accounting and ACCA Professional Two Management Accounting are appropriate for a second year course.

Finally I would like to thank, once again, the Association of Accounting Technicians, the Institute of Chartered Accountants in England and Wales, the Chartered Association of Certified Accountants and the Chartered Institute of Management Accountants for permission to reproduce questions which have appeared in past examinations.

Cost and revenue classification

Solutions to Chapter 3 questions

Question 3.1

See the description of cost behaviour in the sections in Chapter 3 on classification of costs for decision-making and classification of costs for control for the answer to these questions. In particular the answer should provide graphs for fixed costs, variable costs, semi-fixed costs and semi-variable costs.

Question 3.2

You will find the answer to this question in Chapter 3. In particular the answer should describe the classification of costs for stock valuation and profit measurement; classification for decision-making and planning; classification for control. In addition the answer should illustrate methods of classification (see Chapter 3 for examples) within the above categories and describe the benefits arising from classifying costs in the manner illustrated.

Question 3.3

See Chapter 3 for the answer to this question.

Question 3.4

(a) See 'The role of the management accountant in the management process' in Chapter 1 for the answer to this question. In particular your answer should stress that the cost accountant provides financial information for stock valuation purposes and also presents relevant information to management for decision-making and planning and cost control purposes. For example, the cost accountant provides information on the costs and revenues of alternative courses of action to assist management in selecting the course of action which will maximize future cash flows. By coordinating plans together in the form of budgets and comparing actual performance with plans the accountant can pinpoint those activities which are not proceeding according to plan.

(b) (i) Direct costs are those costs which can be traced to a cost objective. If the cost objective is a sales territory then *fixed* salaries of salesmen will be a direct cost. Therefore the statement is incorrect.

(ii) Whether a cost is controllable depends on the level of authority and time span being considered. For example, a departmental foreman may have no control over the number of supervisors employed in his department but this decision may be made by his superior. In the long term such costs are controllable.

(iii) This statement is correct. See 'Sunk costs' in Chapter 3 for an explanation of why this statement is correct.

Question 3.5 See Chapter 3 for the answer to this question.

Question 3.6 Cost information is required for the following purposes:

(a) costs for stock valuation and profit measurement;
(b) costs for decision-making;
(c) costs for planning and control.

For the alternative measures of cost that might be appropriate for each of the above purposes see Chapter 3.

Question 3.7 (i) See Chapter 3 for a definition of opportunity cost and sunk cost.

(ii) *Opportunity cost*: If scarce resources such as machine hours are required for a special contract then the cost of the contract should include the lost profit that would have been earned on the next best alternative. This should be recovered in the contract price.

Sunk cost: The original cost of equipment used for a contract is a sunk cost and should be ignored. The change in the resale value resulting from the use of the equipment represents the relevant cost of using the equipment.

(iii) The significance of opportunity cost is that relevant costs do not consist only of future cash outflows associated directly with a particular course of action. Imputed costs must also be included.

The significance of sunk costs is that past costs are not relevant for decision-making.

Question 3.8 Total fixed costs will remain unchanged in the short term (within the relevant range) and variable costs are constant per unit. If output declines fixed costs per unit will increase. The correct answer is Option A, since total variable costs should decline if output is less than the original budget.

Question 3.9 See Chapter 3 for the answer to this question.

Question 3.12 (a) A large proportion of non-manufacturing costs are of a discretionary nature. In respect of such costs, management has some significant range of discretion as to the amount it will budget for the particular activity in question. Examples of discretionary costs (sometimes called *managed* or *programmed costs*) include advertising, research and development, and training costs. There is no optimum relationship between inputs (as measured by the costs) and outputs (as measured by revenues or some other objective function) for these costs. Furthermore, they are not predetermined by some previous commitment. In effect, management can determine what quantity of service it wishes to purchase. For example, it can choose to spend small or large amounts on research and development or advertising. The great difficulty in controlling such costs is that there is no established method for determining the appropriate amount to be spent in particular periods.

For a description of fixed and variable costs see Chapter 3. Examples of fixed costs include depreciation of the factory building, supervisors' salaries and leasing charges. Examples of variable costs include direct materials, power and sales commissions.

(b) The £500 000 is a sunk cost and cannot be avoided. It is therefore not a relevant cost for decision-making purposes. The project should be continued because the incremented/relevant benefits exceed the incremental/relevant costs:

	(£000)
Incremental benefits	350
Incremental costs	200
Net incremental benefit	150

(c) An opportunity cost is a cost that measures the opportunity lost or sacrificed when the choice of one course of action requires that an alternative course of action be given up. The following are examples of opportunity costs:

(i) If scarce resources such as machine hours are required for a special contract then the opportunity cost represents the lost profit that would have been earned from the alternative use of the machine hours.

(ii) If an employee is paid £5 per hour and is charged out at £11 per hour for committed work then, if that employee is redirected to other work, the lost contribution of £6 per hour represents the opportunity cost of the employee's time.

The CIMA terminology defines a notional cost as: 'A hypothetical cost taken into account in a particular situation to represent a benefit enjoyed by an entity in respect of which no actual cost is incurred.' The following are examples of notional costs:

(i) interest on capital to represent the notional cost of using an asset rather than investing the capital elsewhere;

(ii) including rent as a cost for premises owned by the company so as to represent the lost rent income resulting from using the premises for business purposes.

(a) (i)

Question 3.13

Schedule of annual mileage costs

	5000 miles (£)	10 000 miles (£)	15 000 miles (£)	30 000 miles (£)
Variable costs:				
Spares	100	200	300	600
Petrol	380	760	1140	2280
Total variable cost	480	960	1440	2880
Variable cost per mile	0.096	0.096	0.096	0.096
Fixed costs				
Depreciation[a]	2000	2000	2000	2000
Maintenance	120	120	120	120
Vehicle licence	80	80	80	80
Insurance	150	150	150	150
Tyres[b]	–	–	75	150
	2350	2350	2425	2500
Fixed cost per mile	0.47	0.235	0.162	0.083
Total cost	2830	3310	3865	5380
Total cost per mile	0.566	0.331	0.258	0.179

Notes

[a] Annual depreciation $= \dfrac{£5500\ (\text{cost}) - £1500\ (\text{trade-in price})}{2\ \text{years}} = £2000$

[b] At 15 000 miles per annum tyres will be replaced once during the two-year period at a cost of £150.

The average cost per year is £75. At 30 000 miles per annum tyres will be replaced once each year.

Comments

Tyres are a semi-fixed cost. In the above calculations they have been regarded as a step fixed cost. An alternative approach would be to regard the semi-fixed cost as a variable cost by dividing £150 tyre replacement by 25 000 miles. This results in a variable cost per mile of £0.006. For a discussion of the alternative treatment of semi-fixed costs see Chapter 3.

Depreciation and maintenance cost have been classified as fixed costs. They are likely to be semi-variable costs, but in the absence of any additional information they have been classified as fixed costs.

(ii) See Figure Q3.13.

(iii) The respective costs can be obtained from the vertical dashed lines in the graph. (Figure Q3.13).

(b) The *cost per mile* declines as activity increases. This is because the majority of costs are fixed and do not increase when mileage increases. However, *total cost* will increase with increases in mileage.

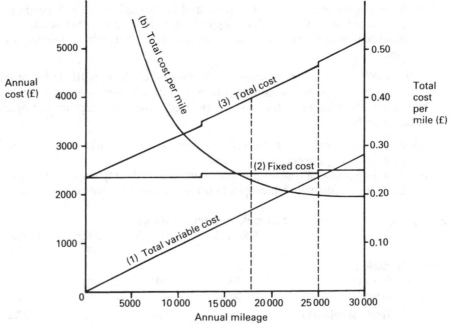

Figure Q3.13 *The step increase in fixed cost is assumed to occur at an annual mileage of 12 500 miles and 25 000 miles, because tyres are assumed to be replaced at this mileage.*

Question 3.14 (a) See Figure Q3.14 (a).

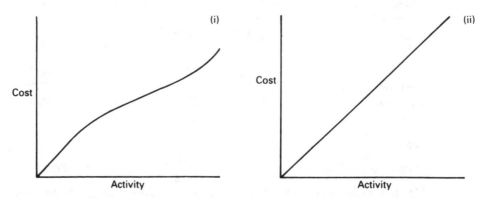

Figure Q3.14(a) *(i) A curvilinear cost. (ii) A linear variable cost.*

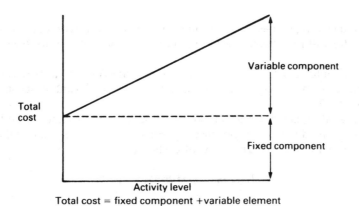

Activity level

Total cost = fixed component +variable element

Figure Q3.14(b)

(b) See Chapter 3 for an explanation of a semi-variable cost and a step fixed cost. An example of a semi-variable cost is machine maintenance, where part of the cost consists of a fixed element (preventive maintenance) and a variable element that varies according to the intensity of use. Supervision is an example of a stepped fixed cost. See Figure 3.5 in Chapter 3 for a diagram of a step fixed cost. A diagram of a semi-variable cost is shown in Figure Q3.14(b).

(c) (i) With the production unit method of depreciation, the original cost of the asset is divided by the estimated number of units produced during its life. The depreciation charge for a period is

number of units produced × depreciation rate per unit

The production unit method might be used for machinery or motor vehicles, provided that the decline in value of these assets is related to usage.

(ii) Depreciation does not provide funds for asset replacement. If a firm wishes to ensure that funds are provided, an amount of cash that will accumulate to the replacement value of the asset must be invested.

Question 3.17

(a) (i) For an explanation of sunk and opportunity costs see Chapter 3. The down payment of £5000 represents a sunk cost. The lost profit from subletting the shop of £1600 p.a. ((£550 × 12) − £5000) is an example of an opportunity cost. Note that only the £5000 additional rental is included in the opportunity cost calculation. (The £5000 sunk cost is excluded from the calculation.)

(ii) The relevant information for running the shop is:

	(£)
Net sales	100 000
Costs (£87 000 − £5000 sunk cost)	82 000
	18 000
Less opportunity cost from subletting	1 600
Profit	16 400

The above indicates that £16 400 additional profits will be obtained from using the shop for the sale of clothing. It is assumed that Mrs Johnson will not suffer any other loss of income if she devotes half her time to running the shop.

(b) The CIMA terminology defines a notional cost as 'A hypothetical cost taken into account in a particular situation to represent a benefit enjoyed by an entity in respect of which no actual expense is incurred.' Examples of notional cost include:

(i) Interest on capital to represent the notional cost of using an asset rather than investing the capital elsewhere.

(ii) Including rent as a cost for premises owned by the company so as to represent the lost rent income resulting from using the premises for business purposes.

Question 3.18 (a) See Chapter 3 for a description of opportunity costs. Out of pocket cost can be viewed as being equivalent to incremental or relevant costs as described in Chapter 3.

(b) Depreciation is not a relevant cost since it will be the same for both alternatives. It is assumed that tyres and miscellaneous represent the additional costs incurred in travelling to work. The relevant costs are:

Using the car to travel to work:

	£
Petrol	128
Tyres and miscellaneous	52
	180
Contribution from passenger	120
Relevant cost	60

Using the train:

Relevant cost	£188

(c)

	£000	£000	%
Sales		2560.0	100
Direct materials	819.2		32
Direct wages	460.8		18
Variable production overhead	153.6		6
Variable administration/selling	76.8		3
Total variable cost		1510.4	59
Contribution		1049.6	41
Fixed production overhead^a	768		30
Fixed administration/selling^b	224		8.75
		992	
Profit		57.6	2.25

Notes
^{a}100/80 × £2,560,000 × 0.24
^{b}100/80 × £2,560,000 × 0.07

Accounting for materials and labour

Solutions to Chapter 4 questions

Question summary

4.1–4.7   Various essay problems on topics related to Chapter 4.

4.8–4.10   Computations for various stores pricing problems. Question 4.9 also requires the calculation of the economic order quantity (EOQ). Question 4.10 is the most difficult one and requires that output be expressed in terms of equivalent units. It will therefore by necessary to refer to Chapter 7 for an explanation of this term.

4.11   This consists of two parts: stores pricing and labour cost accounting.

4.12   A simple problem that is useful for illustrating some of the problems to be considered when introducing an incentive scheme.

4.13   Calculations of wages based on hourly rate, piecework and bonus systems.

4.14   Accounting treatment of holiday pay and overtime plus a computation and evaluation of a time rate and incentive payment system.

4.15   Calculation of labour turnover percentage and efficiency ratio and a discussion of how labour turnover can be reduced.

4.16, 4.17   These are more difficult problems, focusing on the effects of introducing incentive schemes.

4.18   A discussion of problems associated with operating a manual materials control system and an explanation of how a computerized system can solve some of these problems.

Question 4.2

Your reply should indicate that there is a need to verify that actual stocks should agree with the computerized records. It is likely that computerized records will be more reliable than a clerical recording system. Nevertheless, errors may still exist. In addition there is the problem of theft and wastage. It is therefore important that physical stocks be checked periodically with the computerized records. Your answer should stress that a continuous system of stocktaking is preferable to the alternative of a complete periodic system of stocktaking.

Question 4.4

(a) With a computer-based system orders for receipts, issues and returns of materials can be input usually with more speed and accuracy than a manual system. Stock issue prices and balances will be automatically determined by the computer program. For each item of stock, control levels, such as minimum and maximum stock levels and the reorder level, can be set-up. The computer-based system will automatically highlight those stock items which are outside the control levels and this will minimize stockouts and overstocking. With a computerized system purchase requisitions are automatically generated when stocks reach their reorder point.

(b) The answer should describe goods received notes, stores requisitions and purchase requisitions. See Chapter 4 for a description of these items.

Question 4.5 (a) The managing director's conclusions are incorrect because:
   (i) Purchases may be in excess of materials used to produce goods for sale. In other words, raw material stocks may have increased.
   (ii) Material prices might have increased but the quantity of materials purchased or used remains unchanged.
   (iii) Stocks of WIP and finished goods may have increased, thus requiring more purchases.
   (iv) The actual selling price may have been lower than expected.

(b) Material losses may have occurred because of the following:
   (i) Purchase of inferior quality materials resulting in excessive wastage. This might be overcome by setting standards indicating the qualities required. If certain suppliers are known for the higher quality materials a list of such suppliers should be kept. Close cooperation is essential between the production departments and the purchasing department, and the reporting system should be designed so that the purchasing department is immediately informed when inferior quality materials are purchased so that steps can be taken to avoid this occurring again in the future.
   (ii) Use of inefficient and unskilled labour. This might be overcome by improving training.
   (iii) Obsolete stocks. This can be reduced by setting maximum, minimum and reorder stock levels and regularly checking on the frequency of issues. A report on obsolete stocks should be prepared for management at frequent intervals, indicating the reasons for the obsolescence. All purchase requisitions should be initiated only by the storekeeper, who should check the stock levels prior to completing the purchase requisition.

Question 4.10 (a)

Stores ledger account: Timber (LIFO basis)

	(£)		(£)
Opening balance (40 000 at	56 000	12 April (80 000 units at £1.50)[a]	120 000
£1.40)		26 April (70 000 units at £1.70)[b]	119 000
5 April (125 000 units at £1.50)	187 500	(30 000 units at £1.50)	45 000
19 April (70 000 units at £1.70)	119 000	Balance:	
		55 000 units $\begin{pmatrix} 15\ 000 \text{ at } £1.50 \\ 40\ 000 \text{ at } £1.40 \end{pmatrix}$	78 500
	362 500		362 500

Notes
[a] On a LIFO basis issues will be at £1.50. Therefore 80 000 units are issued (£120 000/£1.50).
[b] On a LIFO basis 70 000 units will be issued at £1.70 = £119 000. The remaining issues will be at £1.50 per unit. Total issues are £164 000. Therefore the number of units issued at £1.50 per unit will be:

$$\frac{£164\ 000 - £119\ 000}{£1.50 \text{ per unit}} = 30\ 000 \text{ units}$$

Stores ledger account: Varnish (FIFO basis)

	(£)			(£)
Opening balance (1600 litres at		12 April[a] (1000 litres at		
£1.20)	1920	£1.20)		1200
5 April (400 litres at £1.10)	440	26 April[b] (600 litres at £1.20)	720	
19 April (1800 litres at £1.30)	2340	(400 litres at £1.10)	440	
		(300 litres at £1.30)	390	1550
		Balance (1500 litres at £1.30)		1950
	4700			4700

Notes

[a]On a FIFO basis issues will be at £1.20 per litre. Therefore 1000 litres are issued (£1200/£1.20).

[b]On a FIFO basis the total issues will add to £1550, consisting of:

> 600 litres at £1.20 (Unused opening balance)
> 400 litres at £1.10 (5 April purchase)

The balance of £390 (£1550 − £1160) will be issued at £1.30. This will result in 300 litres being issued at £1.30 (£390/£1.30).

Comparison of book-stock and physical stocks:

	Timber (units)	Varnish (litres)
Physical stock	55 000	700
Book-stock	55 000	1500
Difference	—	800

(b) The calculation of the number of desks *completed* during the period is as follows:

Quantity sold	4600
Closing stock	925
Total output	5525
Less opening stock	650
Completed desks	4875

Comparison of material that should have been consumed and material actually consumed

	Timber		Varnish	
Desks completed	4875		4875	
Less opening WIP equivalent production[a]	200	($\frac{2}{3} \times 300$)	75	($300 \times \frac{1}{4}$)
	4675		4800	
Add closing WIP equivalent production[a]	120	($\frac{3}{4} \times 160$)	60	($37\frac{1}{2}\% \times 160$)
Equivalent production[a]	4795		4860	
Consumption per desk	30 sq. ft		0.47 litres	
Total estimated consumption	143 850 sq. ft		2284 litres	
Actual consumption[b]	180 000 sq. ft		3100 litres	($\begin{matrix}2300 \text{ issues plus}\\800 \text{ stock loss}\end{matrix}$)
Excess usage	36 150 sq. ft		816 litres	

Notes

[a]The objective is to ascertain the material that should have been used for production in the *current period*. Therefore opening stock equivalent production is deducted to ascertain production in the *current period*.

[b]Physical quantity issued per stores ledger account plus 800 litres stock loss for varnish.

(c) It appears that stores records for timber are accurate, but the consumption of material once it has been issued is not adequately controlled since actual consumption is approximately 25% greater than estimated consumption. There is a stock loss of 800 litres for varnish, suggesting that the storekeeping for this material is not under control. However, the consumption of varnish is under control once it has been issued from store. The possible reasons for the differences are as follows:

<table>
<tr><td align="center">Timber</td><td align="center">Varnish</td></tr>
<tr><td>Inaccurate usage estimates</td><td>Inaccurate stock records of</td></tr>
<tr><td>Excess waste/scrap</td><td>receipts and issues</td></tr>
<tr><td>Pilfering in factory</td><td>Inaccurate stock counts</td></tr>
<tr><td>Inaccurate estimate of degree of completion</td><td>Pilferage in stores</td></tr>
<tr><td>Inaccurate record of stock of finished goods</td><td></td></tr>
</table>

Question 4.11 (a) (i) *FIFO*: Because the units contained in the closing stock are less than the most recent purchase quantity, the value of the closing stock will be based on the price per unit of the most recent purchase. Therefore the value of the closing stock is £123.20, consisting of 44 units at £2.80 per unit.

(ii) *LIFO*:

	Receipts	Issues
Opening stock	35 at £2.00	
2.11.81		25 at £2
5.11.81	40 at £2.25	
10.11.81		38 at £2.25
13.11.81	30 at £2.50	
23.11.81	50 at £2.80	
24.11.81		48 at £2.80

From the above schedule we can see that the closing stock consists of the following purchases:

	(£)
Opening stock (10 at £2)	20.00
5 November purchase (2 at £2.25)	4.50
13 November purchase (30 at £2.50)	75.00
23 November purchase (2 at £2.80)	5.60
Closing stock	105.10

(b) The value of material issued on 24 November is £125.76 and is calculated as follows:

	Receipts			Issues			Closing balance		
	Quantity	Price (£)	Value (£)	Quantity	Price (£)	Value (£)	Quantity	Price (£)	Value (£)
1.11.81	—	—	—	—	—	—	35	2.00	70.00
2.11.81	—	—	—	25	2.00	50.00	10	2.00	20.00
5.11.81	40	2.25	90	—	—	—	50	2.20	110.00
10.11.81	—	—	—	38	2.20	83.60	12	2.20	26.40
13.11.81	30	2.50	75	—	—	—	42	2.41	101.40
23.11.81	50	2.80	140	—	—	—	92	2.62	241.40
24.11.81	—	—	—	48	2.62	125.76	44	2.62	115.64

The cost of the 10 units issued to replace those previously damaged should be charged (debited) to a scrap account and the stores ledger control account should be reduced (credited). The issue cost represents abnormal scrap, which should not be included in the stock valuation. Therefore cost of the scrap should be written off as a period cost. If the scrap was considered to be a normal unavoidable cost inherent in the production process then it would be reasonable to charge the cost of the normal scrap to the job. For a discussion of the treatment of normal and abnormal losses see Chapter 7.

(c) *Calculation of total hours worked*

	Hours
Normal hours (£4800/£3 per hour)	1600
Overtime hours (£1440/£4.50 per hour)	320
	1920

Allocation of wages cost   (£)

    Capital expenditure (60 hours at £3)   180

    Non-productive time (280 hours at £3)   840

    Productive time (balance of £1580 hours (1920 − 340 at £3)   4740

    Overtime premium (320 hours at £1.50)   480

    Shift premium   360

                                                                6600

The journal entries are as follows:

	Dr	Cr
Wages control account	6600	
Cost ledger control account[a]		6600
Work in progress account	4740	
Capital equipment account	180	
Production overhead account (840 + 480 + 360)	1680	
Wages control account		6600

Note

[a]For an explanation of this account see 'Interlocking accounting' in Chapter 5.

Question 4.13

(a) *Advantages.*

  (i) Both the firm and the employee should benefit from the introduction of an incentive scheme. Employees should receive an increase in wages arising from the increased production. The firm should benefit from a reduction in the fixed overhead per unit and an increase in sales volume.

  (ii) The opportunity to earn higher wages may encourage efficient workers to join the company.

  (iii) Morale may be improved if extra effort is rewarded.

Disadvantages:

  (i) Incentive schemes can be complex and difficult to administer.

  (ii) Establishing performance levels leads to frequent and continuing disputes.

  (iii) The quality of the output may decline.

(b)

	(i) Hourly rate	(ii) Piecework
Employee A	38 × £3 = £114	(42 × £0.30) + (72 × £0.45) + (92 × £0.75) = £114
Employee B	36 × £2 = £72	(120 × £0.30) + (76 × £0.45) = £70.20
Employee C	40 × £2.50 = £100	(50 × £0.75) = £37.50
Employee D	34 × £3.60 = £122.40	(120 × £0.30) + (270 × £0.45) = £157.50

Note that with the piecework system the employees are paid an agreed rate per unit produced. The piece rates are £0.30 per unit of x (6 minutes × £0.05), £0.45 for y (9 × £0.05) and £0.75 for z (15 × £0.05). Only employee C earns less than 75% of basic pay. Therefore C will receive a gross wage of £75. The piece rate wages should be charged directly to the products and the difference between the guaranteed minimum wage of £75 and the piecework wage of £37.50 for employee C should be charged to an appropriate overhead account.

    With a bonus scheme, a set time is allowed for each job and a bonus is paid based on the proportion of time saved. The calculations for each employee are:

Time allowed (hours)		Time saved (hours)	Bonus (£)	Total wages (£)
A (42 × 6/60) + (72 × 9/60) + (92 × 15/60)	= 38	0	0	114
B (120 × 6/60) + (76 × 9/60)	= 23.4	0	0	72
C (50 × 15/60)	= 12.5	0	0	100
D (120 × 6/60) + (270 × 9/60)	= 52.5	18.5	$\frac{2}{3}$ × 18.5 × £3.60 = £44.40	£122.40 + £44.40

Employees A, B and C do not earn a bonus, because the time taken is in excess of time allowed.

Question 4.14 (a) For the answer to this question you should refer to 'Elements of manufacturing cost' in Chapter 3 and 'Accounting treatment of various labour cost items' in Chapter 4.

(b) *Current system*

Total weekly wages	£960 (6 × £160)
Weekly wage per employee	£160 (£960/6 employees)
Average output per employee	1000 units (6000 units/6)
Labour cost per unit of output	16p (£960/6000 units)

New system

Average output per employee	1000 units (6600 units/6)
Weekly wage per employee	£180 (800 × 16p) + (200 × 17p) + (100 × 18p)
Total weekly wages	£1080 (£180 × 6)
Labour cost per unit of output	16.36p (£1080/6600 units)

Note that the above calculations are based on the assumption that each individual produces the average output of 1100 units per week. If this is not the case then total wages will differ slightly from the above figure.

With time-based remuneration systems, workers are paid for the number of hours attended at the basic wage rate. An additional premium over the base rate is paid for overtime. The merits of time-based systems are that they are simple to administer and easy to understand. The weekly wage is known in advance and does not fluctuate with changes in output. Time rate systems have a number of disadvantages. In particular, there is no motivation to increase output, and this can result in a greater need for supervision. Time-based systems are most appropriate where the quality of the output is particularly important or where the workers have little influence over the volume of production.

With individual performance-based remuneration systems, wages paid are related to output. The merits of performance-based systems are that effort and efficiency are rewarded, and this generally results in higher wages, improved morale and the ability to attract efficient workers. In the above illustration, on average, each employee's wage increases by £20 per week (a 12.5% increase). The employer gains from increased production, higher sales revenue and a decrease in unit fixed costs. Labour cost per unit has increased in the above illustration, but it is likely that this will be compensated for by a lower fixed overhead cost per unit and additional sales revenue.

Individual performance-based remuneration systems suffer from the following disadvantages:

(i) Some workers may suffer a decline in wages. For example, a worker who produces 900 units per week would receive a weekly wage of £145 (800 × 16p plus 100 × 17p), a decline of £15 per week.

(ii) Performance-based systems are more complex and expensive to administer, and can result in complex negotiations and frequent disputes.

(iii) Quality of output might suffer.

Question 4.15 (a) Labour turnover percentage

$$\frac{\text{Number of employees leaving during the period (7)}}{\text{Average total number of employees for the period (42)}} \times 100$$

$$= 16.7\%$$

(b) Possible reasons for the labour turnover include:

(i) Promotion either within or outside the firm.

(ii) Personal circumstances such as moving from the area, retirement, pregnancy.

(iii) Dissatisfaction with pay or working conditions.

The costs of labour turnover include leaving, recruitment and training costs. Leaving costs include the costs associated with completing the appropriate documentation and lost production if the employees cannot be immediately replaced. Recruitment costs result from the advertising, selection and engagement of new staff. Training costs include costs associated with lost production when training is being given, defective work and low productivity during the training period.

Labour turnover and associated costs can be reduced by ensuring that:

(i) pay and working conditions are satisfactory and comparable with alternative employers;
(ii) adequate training is provided;
(iii) an appropriate career structure exists.

(c) The time allowed for 114 268 units is 5194 hours (114 268/22)

Efficiency ratio = Time allowed (standard hours)/actual hours
$$= 5194 \text{ hours}/4900 \text{ hours}$$
$$= 106\%$$

Therefore the labour rate is £4.738 per hour (£4.60 × 103/100)
Standard cost = £23 892 (5194 hours at £4.60)
Actual cost   = £23 216 (4900 hours at £4.738)
Variance   =   £676 Favourable

Question 4.16

(i) Current average maximum production = 30 × 55 hrs × 6 units = 9 900 units
    Proposed maximum production   = 30 × 55 hrs × 8 units = 13 200 units

Existing payment system

Output levels (units)	7 000	9 600	9 900
	(£)	(£)	(£)
Sales value (£10 per unit)	70 000	96 000	99 000
Pre-finishing VC	56 000	76 800	79 200
Direct labour:			
Guaranteed	3 600	3 600	3 600
Overtime (W1)	—	1 800	2 025
Variable overhead (W2)	560	768	792
Fixed overhead	9 000	9 000	9 000
Total cost	69 160	91 968	94 617
Profit	840	4 032	4 383

Proposed scheme

Output levels (units)	7 000	9 600	9 900	12 000
	(£)	(£)	(£)	(£)
Sales value	70 000	96 000	99 000	120 000
Pre-finishing VC	56 000	76 800	79 200	96 000
Direct labour at				
£0.55 per unit	3 850	5 280	5 445	6 600
Variable overhead (W3)	420	576	594	720
Fixed overhead	9 000	9 000	9 000	9 000
Total cost	69 270	91 656	94 239	112 320
Profit	730	4 344	4 761	7 680

Working

(W1) 9600 units requires 1600 hrs (9600/6), ∴ Overtime = 400 hrs × 4.50
     9900 units requires 1650 hrs (9900/6), ∴ Overtime = 450 hrs × £4.50
     Basic hours = 1200 hrs

(W2)   7000 units = 7000/6 × £0.48, 9600 units = 9600/6 × £0.48, 9900 units
                   = 9900/6 × £0.48
(W3)   7000 units = 7000/8 × £0.48, 9600 units = 9600/8 × £0.48, 9900 units
                   = 9900/8 × £0.48
       12 000 units = 12 000/8 × £0.48

(ii) At low output levels the average wage rate per unit is £0.50 (£3/6 hrs), compared with £0.55 with the incentive scheme. However, once overtime is worked, the wage rate per unit of output is £0.75 (£4.50/6), compared with £0.55 per unit under the incentive scheme. Overtime starts at 7200 units (1200 hrs × 6 units). Hence savings will increase with the incentive scheme beyond 7200 units.

Variable overheads vary with productive hours. Therefore variable overhead per unit will be £0.08 (£0.48/6) under the old scheme and £0.06 per unit under the new scheme (£0.48/8).

The proposed incentive scheme will also enable the maximum output level to be achieved, thus enabling maximum sales demand to be achieved.

Accounting for overhead expenditure

Solutions to Chapter 5 questions

Question summary

5.1–5.3   Discussion questions relating to Chapter 5.

5.5–5.8   Problems that require the apportionment of overheads, the preparation of overhead analysis statements and the calculation of departmental overhead rates. Questions 5.5, 5.6 and 5.8 also require the calculation of product costs. Part (b) of 5.8 requires the preparation of an overhead control account.

5.9   Calculation of budgeted machine hours and from incomplete data.

5.10–5.16   Calculation and discussion of different overhead rates. Questions 5.11–5.13 and 5.15 and 5.16 require the calculation of the under/over recovery of overheads. In addition, Question 5.13 also requires an analysis of the under/over recovery of overheads. Question 5.16 requires a separation of fixed and variable overheads using the high–low method.

5.17–5.22   Reapportionment of service department costs. Question 5.18 also requires the calculation of a product cost and selection of the most suitable method of recovering overheads. Question 5.21 requires a comparison of three different methods of reapportioning service department costs, and 5.22 requires a discussion of the usefulness of fully allocated costs.

5.23   An explanation of the calculation of a product cost using the principles explained in Chapters 4 and 5. This question is particularly useful for reinforcing the cost accounting treatment of labour, materials and overheads.

5.24   An excellent question for providing a consolidation of Chapter 5. Part (a) requires the calculation of overhead absorption rates and includes the reciprocal allocation of service department overheads. Part (b) requires the provision of relevant cost information (including the abstraction of variable overheads) for decision-making. This question provides a useful introduction to decision-making.

(a) Calculation of department overhead rates

Question 5.5

	Department P (£)	Department Q (£)	Department R (£)
Repairs and maintenance	42 000	10 000	10 000
Depreciation	17 000[a]	14 000	9 000
Consumable supplies	4 500[b]	2 700	1 800
Wage related costs	48 250	26 250	12 500
Indirect labour	45 000	27 000	18 000

Canteen/rest/smoke room	15 000[c]	9 000	6 000
Business rates and insurance	13 000[d]	10 400	2 600
	184 750	99 350	55 900
Direct labour hours	50 000	30 000	20 000
Overhead absorption rate	£3.70	£3.31	£3.00

Notes

The calculations for Department P are:

[a]Depreciation = £170 000/£400 000 × £40 000.

[b]Consumable supplies = 50 000/100 000 × £9000.

[c]Canteen = 25/50 × £30 000.

[d]Business rates insurance = 5000/10 000 × £26 000.

(b) Job 976: Sample quotation

		(£)	(£)
Direct materials			800.00
Direct labour	P (30 × £7.72[a])	231.60	
	Q (10 × £7.00[b])	70.00	
	R (5 × £5.00[c])	25.00	326.60
Overhead absorbed	P (30 × £3.70)	111.00	
	Q (10 × £3.31)	33.10	
	R (5 × £3.00)	15.00	159.10
Production cost			1285.70
Selling, distribution and administration costs (20% × £1,285.70)			257.14
Total cost			1542.84
Profit margin (20% of selling price)			385.71
Selling price (£1542.84 × 100/800)			1928.55

Notes

[a]£386 000/50 000.

[b]£210 000/30 000.

[c]£100 000/20 000.

(c)

	(£)
Direct materials	800.00
Direct labour	326.60
Prime cost	1126.60
Overhead applied (125%)	1408.25
Total cost	2534.85

The auditor's system results in a higher cost for this quotation. However, other jobs will be overcosted with the previous system. the auditor's system will result in the reporting of more accurate job costs with some job costs being higher, and others being lower, than the present system. For a more detailed answer see 'Blanket Overhead Rates' in Chapter 5.

Question 5.6 (a)

	Total	A	B	C	X	Y
	(£)	(£)	(£)	(£)	(£)	(£)
Rent and rates[a]	12 800	6 000	3 600	1 200	1200	800
Machine insurance[b]	6 000	3 000	1 250	1 000	500	250
Telephone charges[c]	3 200	1 500	900	300	300	200
Depreciation[b]	18 000	9 000	3 750	3 000	1500	750
Supervisors' salaries[d]	24 000	12 800	7 200	4 000		

		6 400	3 000		1 800		600		600	400
Heat and light[a]										
		70 400								
Allocated			2 800		1 700		1 200		800	600
			38 100		20 200		11 300		4900	3000
Reapportionment of X			2450 (50%)	1 225 (25%)		1 225 (25%)		(4900)	
Reapportionment of Y			600 (20%)	900 (30%)		1 500 (50%)			(3000)
			£41 150		£22 325		£14 025			
Budgeted D.L. hours[e]			3 200		1 800		1 000			
Absorption rates			£12.86		£12.40		£14.02			

Notes
[a] Apportioned on the basis of floor area.
[b] Apportioned on the basis of machine value.
[c] Should be apportioned on the basis of the number of telephone points or estimated usage. This information is not given and an alternative arbitrary method of apportionment should be chosen. In the above analysis telephone charges have been apportioned on the basis of floor area.
[d] Apportioned on the basis of direct labour hours.
[e] Machine hours are not given but direct labour hours are. It is assumed that the examiner requires absorption to be on the basis of direct labour hours.

(b)

	Job 123 (£)	Job 124 (£)
Direct material	154.00	108.00
Direct labour:		
Department A	76.00	60.80
Department B	42.00	35.00
Department C	34.00	47.60
Total direct cost	306.00	251.40
Overhead:		
Department A	257.20	205.76
Department B	148.80	124.00
Department C	140.20	196.28
Total cost	852.20	777.44
Profit	284.07	259.15
(c) Listed selling price	1136.27	1036.59

Note
Let SP represent selling price.
Cost + 0.25SP = SP
Job 123: £852.20 + 0.25SP = 1SP
0.75 SP = £852.20
Hence SP = £1136.27
For Job 124: 0.75SP = £777.44
Hence SP £1036.59

(d) For the answer to this question see section on material control procedure in Chapter 4.

(a) Overhead analysis sheet for ABC Limited for the year ending 31 December 1995 **Question 5.8**

Expense	Machining (£000)	Assembly (£000)	Finishing (£000)	Maintenance (£000)	Total (£000)	Basis of apportionment
Indirect wages	10	6	8	30	54	Allocation
Indirect material	15	4	8	20	47	Allocation
Power	80	10	12	—	102	Machine hours

Light and heat	5	2	1.5	1.5	10	Area
Depreciation	4	1.6	0.6	0.8	7	Book value
Rent and rates	12.5	5	3.75	3.75	25	Area
Personnel	18	12	24	9	63	No. of employees
	144.5	40.6	57.85	65.05	308	
Reallotment of maintenance	39.03	13.01	13.01	(65.05)	—	
	183.53	53.61	70.86	—	308	

(b)

Machining $\dfrac{£183\,530}{40\,000 \text{ hours}}$ £4.59 per machine hour

Assembly $\dfrac{£53\,610}{8\,000 \text{ hours}}$ £6.70 per direct labour hour

Finishing $\dfrac{£70\,860}{16\,000 \text{ hours}}$ £4.43 per direct labour hour

Note that assembly and Finishing Department overheads are recovered on the basis of direct labour hours, since direct labour hours represent the predominant activity. In the Machining Department overheads are likely to be most closely related to machine hours.

(c) Cost estimate:

			(£)	(£)
Direct material (2500 + 400 + 200)				3100
Direct labour:	Machining $\left(800 \text{ hrs} \times \dfrac{£60\,000}{12\,000 \text{ hours}}\right)$		4000	
	Assembly $\left(350 \text{ hrs} \times \dfrac{£32\,000}{8000 \text{ hours}}\right)$		1400	
	Finishing $\left(140 \text{ hrs} \times \dfrac{£72\,000}{16\,000 \text{ hours}}\right)$		630	6030
Production overheads:				
	Machining	1400 × 4.59	6426	
	Assembly	350 × 6.70	2345	
	Finishing	140 × 4.43	620.20	9391.20
				18 521.20

(d) Machining department – fixed production overhead control account

	(£)		(£)
Creditors	128 000	WIP[a]	179 010
Profit & Loss A/C (Over-recovery of overheads)	51 010		
	179 010		179 010

Note
[a]39 000 machine hours × £4.59 per hour = £179 010.

(e)

	(£)	
Expenditure	55 530 favourable	[Budgeted cost (£183 530 − actual cost £128 000)]
Volume	4 520 adverse	(Balancing figure)
	51 010 favourable	

Overhead recovery rate $\quad$ = £714 000/119 000 machine hours
$\qquad\qquad\qquad\qquad$ = £6 per machine hour

Budgeted machine hours $\quad = \dfrac{\text{Budgeted overhead (£720 000)}}{\text{Overhead recovery rate (£6)}}$

$\qquad\qquad\qquad\qquad$ = 120 000 machine hours

$\therefore$ Answer = (c)

(a) Percentage of direct material cost = $\dfrac{£250\ 000}{£100\ 000} \times 100 = 250\%$

Direct labour hour rate = £250 000/50 000 hours = £5 per hour
(b) Percentage material cost = 250% × £7000 = £17 500
Direct labour cost $\qquad$ = 800 × £5 = £4000
(c) Overhead incurred £350 000
Overhead absorbed £275 000 (55 000 × £5)
Under absorption of overhead £75 000
The under absorption of overhead should be regarded as a period cost and charged to the profit and loss account.
(d) The answer should stress the limitations of the percentage of direct material cost method and justify why the direct labour hour method is the most frequently used method in non-machine paced environments. See Appendix 5.2 for a more detailed answer to this question.

(a) *Year 1*

(1)	Budgeted machine hours	132 500
(2)	Budgeted fixed overheads	£2 411 500 (132 500 × £18.20)
(3)	Actual machine hours	134 200 (£2 442 440/£18.20)
(4)	Fixed overheads absorbed	£2 442 440
(5)	Actual fixed overheads incurred	£2 317 461
	Over-absorption of fixed overheads	£124 979 (5 − 4)

The section on 'Under- and over-recovery of fixed overheads' in Chapter 5 indicates that an under- or over-recovery will arise whenever actual activity or expenditure differs from budgeted activity or expenditure. Actual activity was 1700 hours in excess of budget and this will result in an over-recovery of fixed overheads of £30 940. Actual overheads incurred were £94 039 (£2 317 461 − £2 411 500) less than budget and this is the second factor explaining the over-absorption of fixed overheads.

Summary	(£)
Over-recovery due to actual expenditure being less than budgeted expenditure	94 039
Over-recovery due to actual activity exceeding budgeted activity	30 940
Total over-recovery of overhead for year 1	124 979

Year 2		
(1)	Budgeted machine hours (134 200 × 1.05)	140 910
(2)	Budgeted fixed overheads	£2 620 926
(3)	Fixed overhead rate (£2 620 926/140 900 hours)	£18.60
(4)	Actual fixed overheads incurred	£2 695 721
(5)	Fixed overheads absorbed (139 260 × £18.60)	£2 590 236
(6)	Under-recovery of overhead for year 2 (4 − 5)	£105 485

Analysis of under-recovery of overhead   (£)

Under-recovery due to actual activity
being less than budgeted activity (139 260 − 140 910) × £18.60   30 690

Under-recovery due to actual expenditure being greater
than budgeted expenditure (£2 695 721 − £2 620 926   <u>74 795</u>

Total under-recovery for the year   <u>105 485</u>

Change in the overhead rate
Change in the rate (£18.60 − £18.20)/£18.20   = + 2.198%
This can be analysed as follows:
Increase in budgeted
expenditure (£2 620 926 − £2 411 500)/£2 411 500   = + 8.684%
Increase in budgeted
activity (140 910 hours − 132 500 hrs)/132 500   = + 6.347%

The increase of 2.198% in the absorption rate is due to an expenditure increase of 8.684% in budgeted expenditure partly offset by an increase in budgeted activity of 6.347% over the 2 years.

Proof
(1.08684/1.06347) − 1 = 0.02198 (2.198%)

(b) See 'Blanket and departmental overhead rates' and 'Pre-determined overhead rates' in Chapter 5 for the answers to these questions.

Question 5.16 (a) (i) and (ii) An activity increase of 150 hours (1650 − 1500) results in an increase in total overheads of £675. It is assumed that the increase in total overheads is due entirely to the increase in variable overheads arising from an increase in activity. Therefore the variable overhead rate is £4.50 (£675/150 hours) per machine hour. The cost structure is as follows:

1. Activity level (hours)	1500	1650	2000
2. Variable overheads at £4.50 per hour	£6750	£7425	£9000
3. Total overheads	£25 650	£26 325	£27 900
4. Fixed overheads (3 − 2)	£18 900	£18 900	£18 900

(iii) The fixed overhead rate is £10.50 (£15 − £4.50 variable rate)

normal activity = fixed overheads (£18 900)/fixed overhead rate (£10.50)
= 1800 machine hours

(iv) Under-absorption = 100 machine hours (1800 − 1700) at £10.50 = £1050

(b) (i) A machine hour rate is recommended for the machine department because most of the overheads (e.g. depreciation and maintenance) are likely to be related to machine hours. For non-machine labour-intensive departments, such as the finishing department, overheads are likely to be related to direct labour hours rather than machine hours. Overheads are therefore charged to jobs performed in the finishing department using the direct labour hour method of recovery.

Calculation of overhead rates

	Machining department	Finishing department
Production overhead	£35 280	£12 480
Machine hours	11 200	
Direct labour hours		7800
Machine hour overhead rate	£3.15	
Direct labour hour overhead rate		£1.60

		Machining department (£)	Finishing department (£)
(ii)			
Direct materials			
(189 × 1.1 × £2.35/0.9)		542.85	–
Direct labour[a]			
25 hours × £4		100.00	
28 hours × £4			112.00
Production overhead			
46 machine hours at £3.15		144.90	
28 direct labour hours at £1.60			44.80
		787.75	156.80

Total cost of job = £944.55 (£787.75 + £156.80)

Note
[a]Overtime premiums are charged to overheads, and are therefore not included in the above job cost.

Question 5.17

(a) The service department cost should be reallocated using the following bases:
Canteen: Number of employees
Engineering shop: Number of service hours
Stores: Number of stores orders
The canteen does not receive any services from the other service departments. Therefore the canteen should be reallocated first. The Engineering Shop receives services from the other two service departments and should be reallocated last.

Overhead allocation

Dept.	Basis	M/C	Assemb	Paint shop	Eng shop	Stores	Canteen
		(£)	(£)	(£)	(£)	(£)	(£)
Allocation		180 000	160 000	130 000	84 000	52 000	75 000
Canteen	Employees	27 000	17 000	13 000	10 000	8 000	(75 000)
Stores	Orders	24 000	18 000	12 000	6 000	(60 000)	
Eng. shop	Service hrs	45 000	30 000	25 000	(100 000)		
Total overhead		276 000	225 000	180 000			
Machine hours		9200					
Direct labour hours			11 250				
Labour cost				£45 000			
Machine hour rate		£30					
Direct labour hour rate		£20					
Direct labour cost rate		400% of direct labour cost					

(b) Overhead absorption statement

	M/C (£)	Assembly (£)	Paint shop (£)
Overhead absorbed[a]	300 000	156 000	140 000
Actual overhead	290 000	167 000	155 000
(Under-)		11 000	15 000
Over-absorption	10 000		

Notes
[a]10,000 machine hours × £30 per hour.
7,800 Direct labour hours at £20 per hour.
400% of direct labour cost of £35 000.

(c) See 'Predetermined overhead rates' in Chapter 5 for an explanation of why overheads should be absorbed using predetermined bases. The second part of the question relates to whether or not volume allocation base (i.e. machine hours and direct labour hours or cost) are appropriate, particularly when direct labour is a small proportion of total cost. The answers should discuss the need for developing non-volume-based cost driver rates using activity-based costing systems. Activity-based costing is described in Chapter 12.

Question 5.18 (a) To calculate product cost, we must calculate overhead absorption rates for the production departments. You can see from the question that the service departments serve each other, and it is therefore necessary to use the repeated distribution method or the simultaneous equation method to reallocate the service department costs. Both methods are illustrated below:

	Cutting (£)	Machining (£)	Pressing (£)	Engineering (£)	Personnel (£)
Allocation per question	154 482	64 316	58 452	56 000	34 000
Engineering reallocation	11 200(20%)	25 200(45%)	14 000(25%)	(56 000)	5 600(10%)
Personnel reallocation	21 780(55%)	3 960(10%)	7 920(20%)	5 940(15%)	(39 600)
Engineering reallocation	1 188(20%)	2 673(45%)	1 485(25%)	(5940)	594(10%)
Personnel reallocation	327(55%)	59(10%)	119(20%)	89(15%)	(594)
Engineering reallocation[a]	20	44	25	(89)	
	188 997	96 252	82 001	—	—

Note
[a]The costs are so small that any further apportionments are not justified. Consequently a return charge of 15% is not made to the engineering department and the costs are apportioned in the ratio 55:10:20.
Simultaneous equation method

Let
E = total overhead allocated to engineering department
and
P = total overhead allocated to personnel department
Then
$E = 56\,000 + 0.15P$
$P = 34\,000 + 0.10E$

Rearranging the above equations,

$$E - 0.15P = 56\,000 \tag{1}$$

$$-0.10E + P = 34\,000 \tag{2}$$

Multiplying equation (2) by 0.15 and equation (1) by 1,

$$E - 0.15P = 56\,000$$
$$-0.015E + 0.15P = 5100$$

Adding these equations,

$$0.985E = 61\,100$$
and so $$E = £62\,030$$

Substituting for E in equation (1),

$$62\,030 - 0.15P = 56\,000$$
$$6030 = 0.15P$$
and so $$P = 40\,200$$

We now apportion the values of E and P to the production departments in the agreed percentages:

	Cutting (£)	Machining (£)	Pressing (£)
Allocation per question	154 482	64 316	58 452
Allocation of engineering	12 408(20%)	27 914(45%)	15 508(25%)
Allocation of personnel	22 110(55%)	4 020(10%)	8 040(20%)
	189 000	96 250	82 000

Overhead absorption rates

A comparison of the machine and direct labour hours in the machine department indicates that machine hours are the dominant activity. Therefore a machine hour rate should be used. A direct labour hour rate is appropriate for the cutting and pressing departments. Note that unequal wage rates apply in the cutting department, but equal wage rates apply in the pressing department. The direct wages percentage and the direct labour hour methods will therefore result in identical overhead charges to products passing through the pressing department, and either method can be used. Because of the unequal wage rates in the cutting department, the direct wages percentage method is inappropriate.

The calculation of the overhead absorption rates are as follows:

		(hours)
Cutting:	Product A (4000 × 9 hours)	36 000
	Product B (3000 × 6 hours)	18 000
	Product C (6000 × 5 hours)	30 000
	Total	84 000

$$\text{Absorption rate} = \frac{£189\,000}{84\,000} = £2.25 \text{ per direct labour hour}$$

Machining:	Product A (4000 × 2)	8 000
	Product B (3000 × $1\frac{1}{2}$)	4 500
	Product C (6000 × $2\frac{1}{2}$)	15 000
		27 500

$$\text{Absorption rate} = \frac{£96\,250}{27\,500} = £3.50 \text{ per machine hour}$$

Pressing:	Product A (4000 × 2)	8 000
	Product B (3000 × 3)	9 000
	Product C (6000 × 4)	24 000
		41 000

$$\text{Absorption rate} = \frac{£82\,000}{41\,000} = £2 \text{ per direct labour hour}$$

Product cost calculations

	A (fully complete) (£)	B (partly complete) (£)
Direct materials	7.00	4.00
Direct labour: Cutting (Skilled)	12.00 (3 × £4)	20.00 (5 × £4)
(Unskilled)	15.00 (6 × £2.50)	2.50 (1 × £2.50)
Machining	1.50 ($\frac{1}{2}$ × £3)	0.75 ($\frac{1}{4}$ × £3)
Pressing	6.00 (2 × £3)	—

Prime cost	41.50			27.25	
Overhead: Cutting	20.25 (9 × £2.25)			13.50 (6 × £2.25)	
Machining	7.00 (2 × £3.50)			5.25 ($1\frac{1}{2}$ × £3.50)	
Pressing	4.00 (2 × £2)			—	
	72.75			46.00	
	a(i)			a(ii)	

(b) The accounting entries for overheads are presented in Chapter 6. You will find when you read this chapter that a credit balance in the overhead control account represents an over recovery of overheads. Possible reasons for this include:

(i) actual overhead expenditure was less than budgeted expenditure;
(ii) actual production activity was greater than budgeted production activity.

Question 5.21 (a) With the direct method of allocation inter-service department apportionments are ignored, service department costs are reapportioned to *production* departments only.

	Personnel and Administration (£000)	Maintenance (£000)	Stores (£000)	Moulding (£000)	Extrusion (£000)	Finishing (£000)
Materials	36	23		330	170	20
Labour	155	25	18.72	168.75	115.2	81
Variable overhead				71.25	151.8	30
Fixed overhead	15	15	17.28	449.30	371.7	67
	206	63	36	1019.3	808.7	198
Personnel[a]	(206)			100.98	64.63	40.39
Maintenance reallocation[b]		(63)		18	36	9
Stores reallocation[c]			(36)	8	12	16
Total cost				£1146.28	£921.33	£263.39

Notes

[a]Personnel costs are reapportioned on the basis of the number of employees in each production department. For example, 25/51 of the personnel department costs of £206 000 are apportioned to the moulding department.

[b]Maintenance costs are reapportioned in proportion to the total maintenance hours worked in each department.

[c]Stores costs are reapportioned in proportion to stores floorspace.

(b) This method is the specified order of closing described in Appendix 5.1. There the service department that provided the largest proportion of services for other service departments was closed first. In this answer the service department providing the largest value of cost input to other service departments (namely the personnel department) is closed first, and the department providing the second largest value of cost input to other service departments is closed next. Return charges are not made.

	Personnel and Administration (£000)	Maintenance (£000)	Stores (£000)	Moulding (£000)	Extrusion (£000)	Finishing (£000)
Original allocation	206	63	36	1019.3	808.7	198
Personnel reallocation	(206)	14.21(4/58)	10.65(3/58)	88.79(25/58)	56.83(16/58)	35.52(10/58)
Maintenance reallocation		(77.21)	13.63(15/85)	18.17(20/85)	36.33(40/85)	9.08(10/85)

					Stores reallocation					

Stores
  reallocation   (60.28)   13.4 (20/90)   20.09(30/90)   26.79(40/90)

Total cost   £1139.66   £921.95   £269.39

(c) The reciprocal method incorporates all inter-servicing relationships. Let

P = total cost of personnel and administration
M = total cost of maintenance
S = total cost of stores

The total costs that will be transferred to the service departments can be expressed as:

$$P = 206 + 0.0556M \ (W1)$$
$$M = 63 + 0.0690P \ (W2) + 0.15 \ (W3)$$
$$S = 36 + 0.166M \ (W4) + 0.0517P \ (W5)$$

The total costs of the production department will be:

Moulding (£000) $1019.3 + 0.431P \ (W6) + 0.22M \ (W7) + 0.2S \ (W8)$
Extrusion (£000) $808.7 + 0.276P \ (W9) + 0.44M \ (W10) + 0.3S \ (W11)$
Finishing (£000) $198.0 + 0.172P \ (W12) + 0.11M \ (W13) + 0.4S \ (W14)$

Workings

(W1) M coefficient = 5/90   (W8) S coefficient = 20/100
(W2) P coefficient = 4/58   (W9) P coefficient = 16/58
(W3) S coefficient = 10/100   (W10) P coefficient = 40/90
(W4) M coefficient = 15/90   (W11) S coefficient = 30/100
(W5) P coefficient = 3/58   (W12) P coefficient = 10/58
(W6) P coefficient = 25/58   (W13) M coefficient = 10/90
(W7) M coefficient = 20/90   (W14) S coefficient = 40/100

(d) The direct method is the simplest, but ignores inter-service department apportionments. If there is a significant proportion of inter-servicing apportionments, this method is likely to result in inaccurate calculations.

The step-down method gives partial recognition to inter-department servicing, and does not involve time-consuming apportionments. The reciprocal method takes full account of inter-department servicing, and is the only method that will yield accurate results.

The choice of method will depend on cost behaviour. If a significant proportion of costs are variable then service department reallocations will be important for decision-making and cost control. In this situation the reciprocal method should be used. However, if the vast majority of costs are fixed, the cost allocations should not be used for cost control and decision-making, and here is a case for using the direct or step-down method.

(e) The answer to this question should include a discussion of cost-plus pricing. See 'Limitations of cost-plus pricing' and 'Reasons for using cost-based pricing formulae' in Chapter 13 for the answer to this question.

(a) (i) *Direct apportionment*   **Question 5.22**

	Heat (£000)	Maintenance (£000)	Steam (£000)	Processing (£000)	Assembly (£000)	Total (£000)
Allocation	90	300	240			630
Heat (4 : 5)	(90)			40	50	—
Maintenance (1 : 2)		(300)		100	200	—
Steam (2 : 1)			(240)	160	80	—
				300	330	630

With the direct method of allocation, inter-service department apportionments are ignored; service department costs are reapportioned to *production* departments only.

(ii) *Step-down method*

This method is the specified order of closing described in Appendix 5.1. There the service department that provided the largest proportion of services for other services was closed first. In this answer the service department providing the largest value of cost inputs to other service departments (namely the maintenance department) is closed first, and the department providing the second largest value of cost input to other service departments (namely steam) is closed next. Return charges are not made.

	Heat (£000)	Maintenance (£000)	Steam (£000)	Processing (£000)	Assembly (£000)	Total (£000)
Allocation	90	300	240			630
Maintenance[a]	30	(300)	45	75	150	
Steam[a]	60		(285)	150	75	
Heat[a]	(180)			80	100	
				305	325	630

Note

[a]Proportions allocated to each department:
Maintenance = 3/30, 4.5/30, 7.5/30, 15/30
Steam = 192/912, 480/912, 240/912
Heat = 4/9, 5/9.

(iii) *Reciprocal method*

Either the algebraic method or the repeated distribution method can be used to take account of reciprocal service arrangements. Both are illustrated in this answer.

Algebraic method

Let
h = total cost of heating
m = total cost of maintenance
s = total cost of steam
Then
$h = 90 + (3/30)m + (192/960)s$
$m = 300 + (5/100)h + (48/960)s$
$s = 240 + (5/100)h + (4.5/30)m$

Expressing these equations in decimal form, we get:

$$h = 90 + 0.10m + 0.2s \tag{1}$$
$$m = 300 + 0.05h + 0.05s \tag{2}$$
$$s = 240 + 0.05h + 0.15m \tag{3}$$

Substituting for s,

$$h = 90 + 0.10m + 0.2(240 + 0.05h + 0.15m)$$
$$m = 300 + 0.05h + 0.05(240 + 0.05h + 0.15m)$$

Expanding these equations gives:

$$h = 90 + 0.10m + 48 + 0.01h + 0.03m$$
$$m = 300 + 0.05h + 12 + 0.0025h + 0.0075m$$

Rearranging,

$$0.99h = 138 + 0.13m \tag{4}$$
$$0.9925m = 312 + 0.0525h \tag{5}$$

Substituting in equation (4) for m,

$$0.99h = 138 + 0.13\frac{(312 + 0.0525h)}{0.9925}$$

$$0.99h = 138 + 40.866 + 0.0069h$$

$$h = \frac{138 + 40.866}{0.99 - 0.0069} = 181.941$$

Substituting for h in equation (5),

$$0.9925m = 312 + 0.0525(181.941)$$

$$m = \frac{312 + 0.0525(181.941)}{0.9925} = 324.165$$

Substituting into equation (3),

$$s = 240 + 0.05(181.941) + 0.15(324.165) = 297.722$$

We now apportion the values of h, m and s to the production departments according to the basis of allocation specified:

	Processing (£000)	Assembly (£000)
Heat (181.941)	72.776 (40/100)	90.970 (50/100)
Maintenance (324.165)	81.041 (7.5/30)	162.082 (15/30)
Steam (297.722)	148.861 (480/960)	74.431 (240/960)
	302.678	327.483

Repeated distribution method

	Heat (£000)	Maintenance (£000)	Steam (£000)	Processing (£000)	Assembly (£000)
Allocation per question	90.00	300.00	240.00		
Heat reallocation	(90.00)	4.50(5%)	4.50(5%)	36.00(40%)	45.00(50%)
Maintenance reallocation	30.45(10%)	(304.50)	45.67(15%)	76.13(25%)	152.25(50%)
Steam reallocation	58.03(20%)	14.51(5%)	(290.17)	145.09(50%)	72.54(25%)
Heat reallocation	(88.48)	4.42(5%)	4.42(5%)	35.40(40%)	44.24(50%)
Maintenance reallocation	1.89(10%)	(18.93)	2.84(15%)	4.73(25%)	9.47(50%)
Steam reallocation	1.45(20%)	0.36(5%)	(7.26)	3.63(50%)	1.82(25%)
Heat reallocation	(3.34)	0.16(5%)	0.17(5%)	1.34(40%)	1.67(50%)
Maintenance reallocation[a]		(0.52)		0.17	0.35
Steam[a]			(0.17)	0.11	0.06
				302.6	327.4

Note
[a]At this stage the costs are so small that no further reallocations between service departments are justified. The costs of the maintenance department are reapportioned in the ratio 7.5 : 15, while those of the steam department are reapportioned in the ratio 480 : 240.

(b) The main problems encountered are as follows:
    (i) The costs allocated to the service departments are the result of arbitrary apportionments. The costs are then reallocated from the service to production departments using further arbitrary allocations. Consequently, the associated costs attached to products will be arbitrary and dependent upon the selected apportionment methods.
    (ii) If a substantial part of the service department costs are fixed and costs are allocated to production departments on the basis of usage, there is a danger that the resulting unit product costs will fail to distinguish between the fixed and variable cost categories. This could result in misleading information being used for short-term decisions.
    (iii) If the responsibility accounting system allocates the actual costs of the service departments to the production departments, the production departments will be accountable for the inefficiencies arising in the service departments. Consequently, the production managers will be demotivated and the service department managers will not be motivated to be efficient because they will always be able to recover their costs.

    Possible solutions include the following:
    (i) Avoid the use of arbitrary apportionments and identify appropriate cost drivers for the main activities undertaken by the service/support departments using an activity-based costing (ABC) system. See Chapter 12 for an explanation of an ABC system.
    (ii) Separate fixed and variable costs when reallocating service department costs to production departments.
    (iii) Charge service department costs to production departments on the basis of actual usage at standard cost. If the production managers have no control over the usage of the service, the service department costs should be regarded as uncontrollable (see 'Guidelines for reporting' in Chapter 18 for a discussion of this point). The service department managers will be motivated to control costs if they are accountable for the difference between actual and standard usage multiplied by the standard cost.

(c) The answer should include a discussion of the following points:
    (i) In today's production environment an increasing proportion of total costs are fixed, and short-term variable costs do not provide a useful measure of the cost of producing a product. Managers require an estimate of long-run product costs. The allocation of fixed costs to products provides a rough guide of a product's long-run cost. The answer should draw attention to the criticisms that Kaplan and Cooper (see Chapter 12) have made of traditional cost allocation methods and explain that an ABC system is an approach that has been recommended to overcome the problems of arbitrary overhead allocations.
    (ii) It is a tradition in some industries (e.g. Government contracts) for selling prices to be based on full product costs plus a percentage profit margin.
    (iii) Total manufacturing costs are required for stock valuation (SSAP 9) for external reporting. However, it is questionable whether costs computed for stock valuation ought to be used for decision-making.
    (iv) It is sometimes claimed that fixed costs should be allocated to managers in order to draw their attention to those costs that the company incurs to support their activities. This is because the manager may be able to indirectly influence these costs, and should therefore be made aware of the sums which are involved. If this approach is adopted, controllable and non-controllable costs ought to be distinguished in the performance reports.

Question 5.23 (a) *Cost of Job 123*

Direct materials:	(£)	(£)
Y (*W1*) (400 kg × £0.505)	202.00	
Z (*W2*) (265 kg × £1.45)	384.25	586.25

Direct labour:

Department A (*W3*) (76 hrs × £4.50)	342.00	
Department B (*W4*) (110 hrs × £4)	440.00	782.00

Overhead (*W5*):

Department A (76 hrs × £2.70)	205.20	
Department B (110 hrs × £2.25)	247.50	452.70
		1820.95

Workings and comments

(*W1*)

$$\frac{(£529.75) + (600 × £0.50) + (500 × £0.50) + (400 × £0.52)}{1050 + 600 + 500 + 400} = £0.505 \text{ weighted average price}$$

400 kg issued to job 123 is a direct cost

(*W2*)

$$\frac{£9946.50 + (16\,000 × £1.46)}{6970 + 16\,000} = £1.45 \text{ weighted average price.}$$

Direct issues to the job are 270 kg (300 − 30), but 5 kg were damaged and destroyed. It is unlikely that the materials are a direct consequence of the job, and therefore it is incorrect to regard the 5 kg as a direct cost to the job. If such losses are expected to occur from time to time, the cost of the lost materials should be charged to departmental overheads and included in the departmental overhead rate calculation. If such losses are abnormal (as indicated in the question), they should not be charged as product costs. Instead, they should be charged to an abnormal losses account (see Chapter 7) and written off to profit and loss account as a period cost.

(*W3*) 76 hours have been directly identified to the job at the hourly rate of £4.50. Six hours were overtime, resulting in excess payments. As these hours are likely to be due to the general high level of production, the overtime premium is included in the overhead rate and shared out amongst all jobs. An additional 3 hours rectification were spent on the job, but such work is a *normal* part of the work *generally* undertaken by the department. The cost of rectification is therefore charged to overheads and included in the overhead absorption rate. See 'Defective units' in Chapter 8 for the accounting treatment of the cost of rectification.

(*W4*) 110 hours are charged to the job. Of these, 30 hours were overtime, but this was a direct result of a customer's requirement on another job. Therefore the overtime premium is not charged to the job.

(*W5*) All direct items can be ignored when calculating overhead rates, but direct materials include scrapped materials and direct labour includes rectification work. However, scrapped materials are to be regarded as abnormal costs, but 20 hours rectification should be charged to overheads. Department A overtime premium is part of the overhead cost, but the overtime premium for Department B is charged directly to another customer.

Calculation of overhead rates	Department A (£)	Department B (£)
Rectification (20 × £4.50)	90	—
Indirect labour	2420	2960
Overtime premium	450	—
Lubricants	520	680
Maintenance	720	510
Other	1200	2150
	5400	6300

Direct labour hours	$2000 \left(\dfrac{\text{£}9000^{a}}{\text{£}4.50} \right)$	$2800 \left(\dfrac{\text{£}11\,200}{\text{£}4} \right)$
Direct labour hour overhead rate	£2.70	£2.25

Note
^{a}£9000 − £90 rectification cost.

(b) Information on the cost of individual jobs can be used as follows:
    (i) for stock valuation of partly completed and completed jobs;
    (ii) to determine the selling price of a product where no established market price exists;
    (iii) as an assessment of the profitability of a job when the selling price is market determined.

Note that the job cost calculation may be inappropriate for decision-making purposes. The major objective is to use the cost for stock valuation purposes.

Accounting for a job costing system

Solutions to Chapter 6 questions

Question summary

6.1, 6.2	Preparation of ledger accounts for an integrated accounting system.
6.3, 6.4	Preparation of ledger accounts for an interlocking accounting system. Question 6.3 also includes a reconciliation of the cost accounts with the financial accounts.
6.5	Preparation of cost ledger accounts when extracts from financial accounts and the reconciliation of the costing and financial accounting profit are given in the question.
6.6	Preparation of ledger accounts from incomplete information so as to estimate the cost of closing stock of

	materials destroyed by fire.
6.7	Stores pricing on a weighted average basis and preparation of raw materials and finished goods accounts.
6.8	Preparation of journal entries for payroll and labour cost accounting.
6.9	Preparation of wages control account plus an evaluation of the impact of a proposed piecework system.
6.10	Preparation of a production overhead account including the measurement of output in standard hours.
6.11–6.15	Preparation of contract accounts.

Question 6.1

(a) The opening WIP balance indicates that overheads are absorbed as follows:

Process 1 = Production overhead (125)/Direct wages (50) = 250% of direct wages
Process 2 = Production overhead (105)/Direct wages (70) = 150% of direct wages

(b) NB Limited accounts (All figures in £000)

Building account

	(£)		(£)
Balance	800		

Plant account

	(£)		(£)
Balance	480		

Provision for depreciation – plant account

	(£)		(£)
Balance c/fwd	108	Balance b/fwd	100
		Production overhead control (96/12 months)	8
	108	Balance b/fwd	108
			108

Raw material stocks account

	(£)		(£)
Balance b/fwd	400	Creditors	10
Creditors	210	Work in progress 1	136
		Work in progress 2	44
		Balance c/fwd	420
	610		610
Balance b/fwd	420		

Work in Progress 1 account

	(£)		(£)
Balance b/fwd	246	Abnormal loss[a]	20
Raw material stock	136	Work in progress 2[b]	483
Production overhead control	210	Balance c/fwd	173
(£84 × 250%)			
Direct wages	84		
	676		676
Balance b/fwd	173		

Work in Progress 2 account

	(£)		(£)
Balance b/fwd	302	Finished goods[b]	908
Raw material stock	44	Abnormal loss[a]	33
Direct wages	130	Balance c/fwd	213
Production overhead control	195		
(£130 × 150%)			
Work in progress 1	483		
	1154		1154
Balance b/fwd	213		

Finished goods account

	(£)		(£)
Balance b/fwd	60	Cost of sales	844
Work in progress 2	908	Balance c/fwd	124
	968		968
Balance b/fwd	124		

Debtors account

	(£)		(£)
Balance b/fwd	1120	Bank	1140
Sales	1100	Balance c/fwd	1080
	2220		2220
Balance b/fwd	1080		

Capital account

	(£)		(£)
		Balance b/fwd	2200

Retained profit account

	(£)		(£)
		Balance	220

Creditors account

	(£)		(£)
Raw material stocks	10	Balance b/fwd	300
Bank	330	Raw material stocks	210
Balance c/fwd	170		
	510		510
		Balance c/fwd	170

Bank account

	(£)		(£)
Debtors	1140	Balance b/fwd	464
Balance c/fwd	466	Direct wages	200
		Production overhead control	170
		Production overhead control	250
		Creditors	330
		Administration overhead	108
		Selling/distribution overhead	84
	1606		1606
		Balance b/fwd	466

Sales account

	(£)		(£)
Balance c/fwd	2300	Balance b/fwd	1200
		Debtors	1100
	2300		2300
		Balance c/fwd	2300

Cost of sales account

	(£)		(£)
Balance b/fwd	888	Balance c/fwd	1732
Finished goods	844		
	1732		1732
Balance b/fwd	1732		

Abnormal loss account

	(£)		(£)
Balance b/fwd	9	Balance c/fwd	62
Work in progress 1[a]	20		
Work in progress 2[a]	33		
	62		62
Balance b/fwd	62		

Production overhead control account

	(£)		(£)
Bank	170		
Bank	250	Work in progress 1	210
Provision for depreciation	8	Work in progress 2	195
		Production overhead	
		under/over-absorbed (Balance)	23
	428		428

Production overhead over/under absorbed account

	(£)		(£)
Production overhead control	23	Balance b/fwd	21
		Balance c/fwd	2
	23		23
Balance b/fwd	2		

Admininstration overhead account

	(£)		(£)
Balance b/fwd	120	Balance c/fwd	228
Bank	108		
	228		228
Balance b/fwd	228		

Selling and distribution overhead account

	(£)		(£)
Balance b/fwd	80	Balance c/fwd	164
Bank	84		
	164		164
Balance b/fwd	164		

Wages account

	(£)		(£)
Bank	200	Work in progress 1	84
Balance c/fwd	14	Work in progress 2	130
	214		214
		Balance b/fwd	14

Notes

[a]The total cost of the abnormal losses are:

	Process 1	Process 2
	(£)	(£)
Direct materials	6	18
Direct wages	4	6
Production overhead	10 (250% × £4)	9 (150% × £6)
	20	33

[b]WIP transfers are:

	From WIP1 to WIP2	From WIP2 to Finished goods
	(£)	(£)
Direct materials	154	558
Direct wages	94	140
Production overhead	235 (250% × £94)	210 (150% × 140)
	483	908

(c) See 'Normal and Abnormal losses' in Chapter 7 for an explanation and possible reasons for abnormal losses.

(a)

Question 6.3

Raw materials stores account

	(£)		(£)
Balance b/d	49 500	Work in progress	104 800
Purchases	108 800	Loss due to flood to P&L a/c	2 400
		Balance c/d	51 100
	£158 300		£158 300
Balance b/d	51 100		

Work in progress control account

	(£)		(£)
Balance b/d	60 100	Finished goods	222 500
Raw materials	104 800	Balance c/d	56 970
Direct wages	40 200		
Production overhead	74 370		
	£279 470		£279 470
Balance b/d	56 970		

Finished goods control account

	(£)		(£)
Balance b/d	115 400	Cost of sales	212 100
Work in progress	222 500	Balance c/d	125 800
	£337 900		£337 900
Balance b/d	125 800		

Production overhead

	(£)		(£)
General ledger control	60 900	Work in progress	
Notional rent (3 × £4000)	12 000	(185% × £40 200)	74 370
Overhead over absorbed	1470		
	£74 370		£74 370

General ledger control account

	(£)		(£)
Sales	440 000	Balance b/d	
Balance c/d	233 870	(49 500 + 60 100 + 115 400)	225 000
		Purchases	108 800
		Direct wages	40 200
		Production overhead	60 900
		Notional rent	12 000
		P & L a/c	226 970
		(profit for period: see (b))	
	673 870		673 870

(b) *Calculation of profit in cost accounts*

	(£)	(£)
Sales		440 000
Cost of sales	212 100	
Loss of stores	2 400	
	214 500	
Less overhead over absorbed		
Profit	1 470	213 030
		226 970

Reconciliation statement[a]

	(£)	(£)	(£)
Profit as per cost accounts			226 970
Differences in stock values:			
Raw materials opening stock	1500		
Raw materials closing stock	900		
WIP closing stock	1030	3 430	
WIP opening stock	3900		
Finished goods opening stock	4600		
Finished goods closing stock	3900	(12 400)	(8 970)
Add items not included in financial accounts:			
Notional rent			12 000
Profit as per financial accounts			230 000

Note

[a] Stock valuations in the financial accounts may differ from the valuation in the cost accounts. For example, raw materials may be valued on a LIFO basis in the cost accounts, whereas FIFO or weighted average may be used in the financial accounts. WIP and finished stock may be valued on a marginal (variable costing) basis in the cost accounts, but the valuation may be based on an absorption costing basis in the financial accounts. To reconcile the profits, you should start with the profit from the cost accounts and consider what the impact would be on the profit calculation if the financial accounting stock valuations were used. If the opening stock valuation in the financial accounts exceeds the valuation in the cost accounts then adopting the financial accounting stock valuation will reduce the profits. If the closing stock valuation in the financial accounts exceeds the valuation in the cost accounts then adopting the financial accounting stock valuation will increase profits. Note that the notional rent is not included in the financial accounts and should therefore be deducted from the costing profit in the reconciliation statement.

(c) The over recovery of overhead could be apportioned between cost of goods sold for the current period and closing stocks. The justification for this is based on the assumption that the under/over recovery is due to incorrect estimates of activity and overhead expenditure, which leads to incorrect allocations being made to the cost of sales and closing stock accounts. The proposed adjustment is an attempt to rectify this incorrect allocation.

The alternative treatment is for the full amount of the under/over recovery to be written off to the cost accounting profit and loss account in the current period as a period cost. This is the treatment recommended by SSAP 9.

Question 6.5 (a) (i)

Raw materials stock account

	(£)		(£)
Opening stock (110 − 7)	103	Issues (difference)	578
Purchases	640	Returns (to supplier)	20
		Closing stock (130 + 15)	145
	743		743

(ii)

Work in progress account

	(£)		(£)
Opening stock (25 + 3)	28	Finished goods a/c (difference)	984
Raw materials a/c	578	Closing stock (27 − 5)	22
Direct labour (220 + 20)	240		
Production overhead absorbed			
(240 at 66⅔%)	160		
	1006		1006

(iii)

Finished goods account

	(£)		(£)
Opening stock (82 − 9)	73	Cost of sales a/c (difference)	989
Work in progress a/c	984	Closing stock (72 − 4)	68
	1057		1057

(iv)

Profit and loss account

	(£)		(£)
Sales returns a/c	30	Sales a/c	1530
Cost of sales a/c	989		
Gross profit c/d	511		
	1530		1530
Production overheads under		Gross profit b/d	511
absorbed	2		
Administration expenses	200		
Net profit	309		
	511		511

The reconciliation statement indicates that discounts, selling expenses and debenture interest are not included in the cost accounts. Therefore these items are not included in the costing profit and loss account.

(b) Interest on capital tied up in stocks should be taken into account for decision-making and cost control purposes. This is because the interest on capital tied up in stocks represents an opportunity cost (in terms of the lost interest) which would have been earned if the money tied up in stocks had been invested.

Interest on capital tied up in stocks should not be included in product costs for stock valuation purposes per SSAP 9. Therefore the cost accumulation system will not include notional costs for stock valuation purposes. Nevertheless it is essential that all *relevant* costs (including opportunity costs) are included in cost statements for the purpose of decision-making and cost control.

(a) The closing stock of raw materials is found by preparing the appropriate control accounts (starting with Finished goods) and ascertaining WIP transfer and material issues as follows: **Question 6.6**

Finished goods stock account

	(£)		(£)
Opening balance	5 490	Variable cost of sales[a]	57 600

Work in progress account (difference)	60 880	Closing balance (given)	8 770
	66 370		66 370

Work in progress account

	(£)		(£)
Opening balance (given)	17 500	Transfer to finished goods	
Direct wages (given)	16 200	account	60 880
Overhead control account[b]	12 960	Closing balance (given)	22 160
Material issued to WIP			
(difference)	36 380		
	83 040		83 040

Stores control account

	(£)		(£)
Opening balance (given)	16 740	Materials issued per WIP a/c	36 380
Purchases	44 390	Closing balance (difference)[c]	24 750
	61 130		61 130

Notes

[a]Sales = $166\frac{2}{3}$% of variable cost of sales

∴. variable cost of sales = $\dfrac{£96\,000 \times 100}{166\frac{2}{3}}$ = £57 600

[b]Overhead charged to production = 80% of direct wages
= 80% × £16 200 = £12 960

[c]The question states all material issues are charged to production. Therefore the stores control account will not include any issue of indirect materials. Consequently, the balance of the control account represents the closing stock of materials destroyed by fire.

(b) (i) The original purchase price is a sunk and irrelevant cost. The cost of the fire is not the purchase price of the stock destroyed but the cost of placing the company back into the position it occupied before the fire; to do this requires purchasing materials at current replacement costs.

(ii) For a discussion of the implications of charging material issues to production using replacement costs see 'Pricing the issues of raw materials' in Chapter 4.

(c) For a discussion of the implications of valuing work in progress and finished goods using the variable cost approach see Chapter 9.

Question 6.7 (a)

Stores ledger card

Date		Kilos	Total value (£)	Average price per kilo (£)	
	Opening balance	21 600	28 944	1.34	
1	Issue	(7 270)	(9 742)	1.34	
7	Purchase	17 400	23 490		
		31 730	42 692	1.3455	(£42 692/31 730)
8	Issue	(8 120)	(10 925)	1.3455	
15	Issue	(8 080)	(10 872)	1.3455	
20	Purchase	19 800	26 730		
		35 330	47 625	1.348	(£47 625/35 330)
22	Issue	(9 115)	(12 287)	1.348	
	Closing balance	26 215	35 338	1.348	

Summary of transactions

	(£)
Opening balance	28 944
Purchases	50 220
Issues	(43 826)
Closing balance	35 338

Raw material stock control account

	(£)		(£)
Opening balance	28 944	WIP	43 826
Purchases	50 220	Closing balance	35 338
	79 164		79 164

Production costs for the period:	(£)
Raw materials	43 826
Labour and overhead	35 407
	79 233
Cost per unit (£79 233/17 150 units)	£4.62

Units sold = opening stock (16 960) + production (17 150)
— closing stock (17 080) = 17 030 units

Finished goods stock control account

	(£)		(£)
Opening balance	77 168	Cost of sales	
Raw materials	43 826	(difference/balancing figure)	77 491
Labour and overhead	35 407	Closing balance	
		(17 080 × £4.62)	78 910
	156 401		156 401

(b) The financial ledger control account is sometimes described as a cost control account or a general ledger adjustment account. For an explanation of the purpose of this account see 'Interlocking accounting' in Chapter 6.

(c) Budgeted production (units):

Sales	206 000	
Add closing stock	18 128	(206 000 × 1.10 × 20/250)
Less opening stock	(17 080)	
	207 048	units

For month 12 the raw material usage is 1.90 kilos per unit of output:

(7270 + 8120 + 8080 + 9115 = 32 585 kg used)/17 150 units produced
∴ Budgeted material usage = 207 048 units × 1.9 kg per unit
= 393 391 kg

Budgeted material purchases

Budgeted usage	393 391 kg	
Add closing stock	22 230	(11 700 × 1.9)
Less opening stock	(26 215)	
	389 406 kg	

Question 6.8 (a) A wages control account is a summary account which records total wages payable including employers' national insurance contributions. The account is cleared by a credit and corresponding debits in respect of total wages costs charged to WIP and the overhead control account. The detail which supports the control account is maintained in subsidiary payroll records.

(b) (i)

	Dr (£)	Cr (£)
Wages control	122 300	
Bank		122 300
Wages control	58 160	
Employees' National Insurance		14 120
Employees' pension fund contributions		7 200
Income tax		27 800
Court order retentions		1 840
Trade union subscriptions		1 200
Private health plans		6 000
	180 460	180 460
Production overhead control Dr	18 770	
Employer's National Insurance		18 770
	18 770	18 770

(ii)

	Dr	Cr
Work-in-progress control:		
Wages	77 460	
Overtime wages – direct	16 800	
Production overhead control:		
Overtime premium	9 000	
Shift premium	13 000	
Indirect wages	38 400	
Overtime wage – indirect	10 200	
Warehouse construction account	2 300	
Statutory sick pay	9 000	
Idle time	4 300	
Wages control		180 460
	180 460	180 460

Question 6.11 (a) (i) Examples of long-term contract work include road building, civil engineering, ship building and building of schools and hospitals.
(ii) Characteristics include:
1. location of work may be remote from the contractor's main office;
2. high level of direct costs;
3. the price of the contract may be fixed in advance.
(b) (i) For the answer to this question see the third paragraph of the section headed 'Contract costing' in Chapter 6.
(ii) Attributable profit is that part of total profit which reflects the profit attributable to that part of the work carried out at the accounting date. Attributable profit should only be taken when the outcome of the contract can be estimated with reasonable certainty. No profit should be taken in the early stage of the contract because the outcome cannot be foreseen with reasonable certainty.
(iii) All of the anticipated loss should be recognized in accordance with the prudence concept.

(c)

Contract Account

	(£)		(£)
Materials issued from stores	600 000	Materials returned to stores	50 000
Wages paid	250 000	Materials on site c/fwd	20 000
Wages accrued	30 000	Value of plant c/fwd	60 000
Sub-contractors' charges	25 000	Cost of sales/work certified	
Plant purchased at cost	100 000	(balance) c/fwd	900 000
Overheads	25 000		
	1 030 000		1 030 000
Cost of sales b/fwd	900 000	Attributable sales revenue	1 150 000
Profit and loss a/c (profit taken)	250 000		
	1 150 000		1 150 000
Materials on site b/fwd	20 000	Wages accrued b/fwd	30 000
Value of plant b/fwd	60 000		

Contractee's account

	(£)		(£)
Value of work certified	1 200 000	Cash/bank	1 000 000
		Balance c/fwd	200 000
	1 200 000		1 200 000

Note that the second section of the Contract account represents the contract profit and loss account. Attributable sales revenue is computed bv adding the profit taken to the cost of sales. The attributable profit taken is calculated as follows:

$$\frac{\text{Cash received to date (£1 000 000)}}{\text{Contract price (£1 140 000)}} \times \text{Estimated profit from the contract (£350 000)}$$
$$= £250\ 000$$

Alternative more prudent approaches are possible for determining attributable profit. The estimated profit from the contract is calculated as follows:

	(£)	(£)
Value of contract		1 400 000
Costs to date	900 000	
Costs to completion	150 000	1 050 000
Anticipated profit		£350 000

(d) (i) Under the old SSAP rules, work in progress was valued as follows: costs to date, plus attributable profits, less progress payments received and receivable.

(ii) Under the new rules, work in progress is valued by deducting the cost of work certified (cost of sales) from the cost to date.

(a) (i)

Question 6.12

Contract account

	(£000)		(£000)
Plant	8 000	Plant c/fwd	3 500
Planning and survey fees	2 000	Materials returns	500
Materials	15 000	Materials c/fwd	400
Labour	8 000		
Labour on cost	1 000	Cost of work certified b/d	
Plant hire	3 500	(cost of sales)	37 065

Site costs:		
Rent and rates	156	
Salaries	1 200	
Head Office costs	750	
Direct expenses	1 804	
Labour c/fwd	55	
	41 465	41 465
Costs of sales c/d	37 065	Attributable sales revenue 50 000
Profit taken	12 935	
	50 000	50 000
Plant b/fwd	3 500	
Materials b/fwd	400	

(ii) The contract is approximately half complete and the budgeted profit is £27 m. Therefore the estimated share of the profit *to date* is approximately £13.23 m (50/102 × £27 m). However, the profit *to date* as per the above account is £12.935 m, and it is considered prudent to incorporate a profit of £12.935 m in the accounts. It is assumed that no retention money has been retained. Consequently, it is inappropriate to reduce the profit based on the formula illustrated in Chapter 6.

(iii) In view of the fact that the contract is only 50% complete, the prudence concept may be applied and only a proportion of the profit taken. Applying the formula illustrated in Chapter 6, the profit taken could be as follows:

$$\frac{2}{3} \times \text{estimated profit (£27 000)} \times \frac{\text{value of work certified (£50 000)}}{\text{value of contract (£102 000)}} = £8824$$

Other alternative approaches are appropriate for applying the prudence concept.

(b) Because of the considerable length of time that is taken to complete a contract, it is necessary to determine the profit to be attributed to each accounting period. Financial accounting normally recognizes revenue when the goods are delivered, but such an approach is inappropriate for long-term contracts, since profits on large contracts would not be reported until they were completed. The profit and loss account would not reflect a fair view of the profitability of the company during the year, but would show only the results of contracts that had been completed before the year end. To overcome this problem, it is preferable to take credit for ascertainable profit while contracts are in progress.

It is difficult to estimate accurately the total profit on the contract or the proportion of profit to date. SSAP 9 recommends that in determining the proportion of profit taken to date the judgement involved should be exercised with prudence, and caution should be applied so that the profit on the contract to date is not overstated.

Question 6.13 (a)

Contract accounts (for the previous year)

	MNO (£000)	PQR (£000)	STU (£000)		MNO (£000)	PQR (£000)	STU (£000)
Cost of contract to data b/fwd		190	370	Wages accrued b/fwd		2	
Materials on site b/fwd			25	Plant Control a/c		8	
Plant on site b/fwd		35	170	Materials on site c/fwd	8		
Materials control a/c	40	99	180	Plant on site c/fwd	70		110
Wages control a/c	20	47	110	Prepayment c/fwd			15
Subcontractors a/c			35	Cost of work not certified			
Salaries	6	20	25	c/fwd			26
Plant control a/c	90	15		Cost of work certified			
Wages accrued c/fwd		5		(balance)	82	411	786
Apportionment of construction services[a]	4	10	22				
	160	421	937		160	421	937

Cost of work certified b/fwd	82	411	786	Value of work certified		90	390	950
Profit taken this period[b]			114	Loss taken[b]			21	
Profit taken previous periods[b]			15					
Profit not taken	8		35					
	90	411	950			90	411	950
Cost of work not certified b/fwd			26	Wages accrued b/fwd			5	
Materials on site b/fwd	8							
Plant on site b/fwd	70		110					
Prepayment b/fwd			15					

Notes

[a]Costs incurred by construction services department:

	(£000)
Plant depreciation $(12 - 5)$	7
Salaries	21
Wages paid	8
	36

Wages incurred by each department are:

	(£000)
MNO	20
PQR	50 $(47 + 5 - 2)$
STU	110
	180

The costs apportioned to each contract are:

	(£000)
MNO	$4 \left(\dfrac{20}{180} \times £36 \right)$
PQR	$10 \left(\dfrac{50}{180} \times £36 \right)$
STU	$\dfrac{22}{36} \left(\dfrac{110}{180} \times £36 \right)$

See (b) (i) for calculation.

(b) (i) *Contract MNO*: Nil.
   Contract PQR:

	(£)
Cost of contract to date (see part (a))	411 000
Value of work certified	390 000
Recommended loss to be written off	21 000

Contract STU:

	(£)
Cost of work certified	786 000
Cost of work not yet certified	26 000
Estimated costs to complete	138 000
Estimated cost of contract	950 000
Contract price	1 100 000
Anticipated profit	150 000

The profit taken to date is calculated using the following formula:

$$\frac{\text{cash received to date } (\pounds 950\,000)}{\text{contract price } (\pounds 1\,100\,000)} \times \text{estimated profit from the contract } (\pounds 150\,000)$$

$= \pounds 129\,545$ (say $\pounds 129\,000$)

The profit taken for the current period is £114 000, consisting of the profit to date of £129 000 less the profit previously transferred to the profit and loss account of £15 000.

(ii) *Contract MNO*: This contract is at a very early stage, and it is unlikely that the outcome can be reasonably foreseen. It is therefore prudent not to anticipate any profit at this stage.

Contract PQR: This contract has incurred a loss, and, applying the prudence concept, this loss should be written off as soon as it is incurred.

Contract STU: Applying the prudence concept, a proportion of the profit

$$\frac{\text{cash received to date}}{\text{contract price}}$$

is recognized in this period. The proportion of profit that is recognized is arbitrary and very much a matter of opinion. Alternative apportionments applying the concept of prudence could have been applied.

Process costing

Solutions to Chapter 7 questions

Question summary

7.1–7.5   An explanation of the accounting for normal and abnormal losses. Preparation of process accounts when there is no opening or closing WIP. Consequently the problem of equivalent production does not arise.

7.6–7.7   Preparation of process accounts requiring the calculation of equivalent production and cost per equivalent unit using the weighted average basis. Neither problem includes any normal or abnormal losses.

7.8–7.9   Calculation of equivalent production and cost per equivalent unit using the weighted average basis. Both problems include normal losses in process that are charged only to completed production.

7.10–7.15 Problems similar to 7.8–7.9, with losses in process apportioned between work in progress and completed production. Questions 7.11 and 7.12 involves a loss in process which

generates sales revenues. Question 7–15 assumes that losses occur part way through the process

7.16   Preparation of process accounts with normal and abnormal losses not requiring equivalent production calculations plus a description of weighted average and FIFO methods of stock valuation.

7.17–7.21 Calculation of the cost per equivalent unit using the FIFO basis. Question 7.20 is the most difficult. Question 7.21 also includes aspects of standard costing and cost information for pricing decisions.

7.22   Comparison of FIFO and weighted average methods and a discussion of alternative methods of stock valuation.

7.23   Cost control problem requiring the preparation of a performance report using equivalent production calculations.

(a) (i)

Question 7.5

Process A account

	(kg)	(£)		(kg)	(£)	(£)
Direct material	2 000	10 000	Normal loss	400	0.50	200
Direct labour		7 200	Process B	1400	18.575	26 005
Process costs		8 400	Abnormal loss	200	18.575	3 715
Overhead		4 320				
	2000	29 920		2000		29 920

Unit cost = (£29 920 − £200)/1600 = £18.575

(ii)

Process B account

	(kg	(£)		(kg)	(£)	(£)
Process A	1400	26 005	Finished goods	2620	21.75	56 989
Direct material	1400	16 800	Normal loss	280	1.825	511
Direct labour		4 200	(10% × 2800)			
Overhead		2 520				

		5 800			
		55 325			
Abnormal gain	100	2175			
	2900	57 000		2900	57 500

Unit cost = (£55 325 − £511)/(2800 − 280) = £21.75

(iii)

Normal loss/gain account

	(kg)	(£)		(kg)	(£)
Process A	400	200	Bank (A)	400	200
Process B	280	511	Abnormal gain (B)	100	182.5
			Bank (B)	180	328.5
	680	711		680	711

(iv)

Abnormal loss/gain

	(£)		(£)
Process A	3715	Process B	2175
Normal loss/gain (B)	182.5	Bank	100
		Profit & Loss	1622.5
	3897.5		3897.5

(v)

Finished goods

	(£)		(£)
Process B	56 989		

(iv)

Profit and loss account (extract)

	(£)		(£)
Abnormal loss/gain	1622.5		

Question 7.6 (a)   Units completed = 8250 − Closing WIP (1600) = 6650

Calculation of number of equivalent units produced

	Completed units	Closing WIP	Total equivalent units
Previous process	6650	1600	8250
Materials	6650	1600	8250
Labour and overhead	6650	960 (60%)	7610

(b)

	(£)	Total equivalent units	Cost per unit (£)
Previous process cost	453 750	8250	55
Materials	24 750	8250	3
Labour and overheads	350 060	7610	46
			104

(c)

Process account

	Units	(£)		Units	(£)
Input from previous process	8250	453 750	Finished goods[a]	6650	691 600
			Closing WIP[b]	1600	136 960
Materials		24 750			
Labour and overheads		350 060			
	8250	828 560		8250	828 560

Note
[a]Cost of completed production = 6650 units × £104 = £691 600

b

	(£)
Closing WIP: Previous process cost (1600 × £55) =	88 000
Materials (1600 × £3) =	4 800
Labour and overhead (960 × £46) =	44 160
	136 960

(d) See the introduction to Chapter 8 and 'Accounting for by-products' in Chapter 8 for the answer to this question.

(a)   Cleansing agent process account

	(kg)	(£)		(kg)	(£)
Ingredient A	2 000	1 600	Completed production	8 600	9 460
B	3 000	1 500	WIP c/fwd (1170 + 516)	2 400	1 686
C	6 000	2 400			
Wages		3 764			
Overheads		1 882			
	11 000	11 146		11 000	11 146

Calculation of cost per unit

	Total cost (£)	Completed units	Equivalent WIP(1)	Equivalent WIP(2)	Total equivalent units	Cost per unit (£)
Materials	5 500	8 600	600	1800	11 000	0.50
Labour	3 764	8600	360	450	9 410	0.40
Overheads	1 882	8600	360	450	9 410	0.20
	11 146					1.10

			(£)
WIP(1):	Materials	600 × £0.50 = 300	
	Labour	360 × £0.40 = 144	
	Overheads	360 × £0.20 = 72	516
WIP(2):	Materials	1800 × £0.50 = 900	
	Labour	450 × £0.40 = 180	
	Overheads	450 × £0.20 = 90	1 170
Completed units: 8600 × £1.10			9 460
			11 146

Note that 11 000 kg were put into the process and 8600 kg were completed. Therefore the WIP is 2400 kg consisting of two batches – one of 600 units 60% complete and the second of 1800 units 25% complete.

(b) See Chapter 7 for definitions and an explanation of the accounting treatment of abnormal gains and equivalent units. See Chapter 8 for a definition of by-products. Note that income from by-products should be credited to the process account from which the by-product emerges.

(a) *Production statement*

Input		Output	
Opening stock	3 400	Finished stock	36 000
Input	37 000	WIP	3 200
		Normal loss	1 200
	40 400		40 400

PROCESS COSTING ■■ 47

Cost statement

	Opening stock (£)	Current cost (£)	Total cost (£)	Completed units (£)	Normal loss (£)	WIP equivalent units (£)	Total equivalent units	Cost per unit (£)	WIP (£)
Materials	25 500	276 340	301 840	36 000	1200	3200	40 400	7.47	23 904
Conversion cost	30 600	336 000	366 600	36 000	1200	1600	38 800	9.45	15 120
			668 440					16.92	39 024

Normal loss (1200 × £16.92)	20 304	
Completed units (36 000 × £16.92)	609 112	629 416
		668 440

The question does not indicate at what stage in the production process the normal loss is detected. It is assumed that the normal loss is detected at the end of the production process, consequently it is not allocated to WIP. Therefore the total cost of production transferred to finished stock is £629 416.

If the short-cut method described in Chapter 7 is adopted and the normal loss equivalent units are excluded from the above unit cost calculations, the closing WIP valuation is £40 240 and the value of completed production is £628 200. This is equivalent to the following calculation, which apportions the normal loss between completed production and WIP on the basis of equivalent production (and not completed units as recommended in Chapter 7):

	Completed production (£)	WIP (£)
Materials normal loss		
(1200 × £7.47 = £8964)	8 232 (36 000/39 200)	732 (3200/39 200)
Conversion cost normal loss		
(1200 × £9.45 = £11 340)	10 857 (36 000/37 600)	483 (1600/37 600)
Normal loss allocation	19 089	1215
WIP per cost statement		39 024
Completed production	609 112	
	628 201	40 239

(b) The following characteristics distinguish process costing from job costing:
  (i) The cost per unit of output with a process costing system is the average cost per unit, whereas job costing traces the actual cost to each individual unit of output.
  (ii) Job costing requires that a separate order and job number be used to collect the cost of each individual job.
  (iii) With a process costing system, each unit of output is similar, whereas with a job costing system each unit of output is unique and requires different amounts of labour, material and overheads.
  (iv) With a job costing system, costs are accumulated for each order and WIP is calculated by ascertaining the costs that have been accumulated within the accounting period. With a process costing system, costs are not accumulated for each order and it is necessary to use the equivalent production concept to value WIP.
  (v) With a process costing system, the allocation of costs to cost of goods sold and closing stocks is not as accurate, because each cost unit is not separately identifiable. Consequently WIP is estimated using the equivalent production concept.

Statement of input and output (units)

Input		(£)	Output	(£)
Opening WIP		1200	Completed and transferred to	
Transferred in		4000	finished stock	3200
			Normal loss	520
			WIP (completed units)	500
			Uncompleted WIP (balance)	980
		5200		5200

It is not clear from the question at what point in the process the loss occurs. It is assumed that the WIP has just passed the inspection point and should be charged with a share of normal loss. By adopting the short-cut method and making no entry for normal losses in the cost per unit calculations, the normal loss is automatically apportioned between completed units and WIP. It is not possible to adopt the approach suggested in Chapter 7, which is to calculate the value of the normal loss and apportion this loss between completed units and WIP in the ratio of completed and uncompleted units. This is because the question does not indicate the stage at which the normal loss occurs. You could have also assumed that the loss was detected when the goods were completed and charge all of the loss to completed production. If the question does not specify when the loss occurs, you should assume that it occurs either at the end of the process or that the WIP has just passed the inspection point. It is assumed that additional materials are added at the start of the process.

Statement of cost per unit

	Opening WIP (£)	Current cost (£)	Total cost (£)	Completed units (W1)	Equivalent uncompleted WIP	Equivalent total units	Cost per unit (£)
Materials (W2)	10 800	34 830	45 630	3700	980	4680	9.75
Conversion cost	14 040	68 503	82 543	3700	490	4190	19.70
			128 173				29.45

	(£)
WIP: Completed units (500 × £29.45)	14 725
Uncompleted units: Materials (980 × £9.75)	9 555
Conversion cost (490 × £19.70)	9 653
	33 933
Completed units transferred to finished stock (3200 × £29.45)	94 240
	128 173

(W1) Completed units = 3200 + 500 (Completed WIP)
(W2) Materials include previous process cost (4000 units at £7.50 each is included in the current cost column).

Process account

	Units	(£)		Units	(£)
WIP b/fwd:	1200		Normal loss	520	—
Materials		10 800	Transferred to		
Conversion cost		14 040	finished stock	3 200	94 240
Transferred from			Completed		
previous process	4000	30 000	WIP c/fwd	500	14 725
Materials		4 830	Uncompleted		
Direct wages		32 965	WIP c/fwd	980	19 208
Overhead		35 538			
	5200	128 173		5200	128 173

Question 7.15 The physical input and output to the process is as follows:

	Units
Input:	
Opening WIP	3 000
Introduced during period	20 000
	23 000
Output:	
Completed production	15 000
Closing WIP	4 000
Abnormal loss (Opening WIP)	3 000
	22 000
Difference = normal loss	1 000
	23 000

The cost per unit (CPU) is calculated as follows:

Cost element	OP WIP (£)	Current cost (£)	Total cost (£)	Completed units	CL. WIP	Normal loss[a]	Abnormal loss[b]	Total equivalent (£)	CPU (£)	WIP
A	12 600	84 000	96 600	15 000	4000	1000	3000	23000	4.20	16 800
B	2 400	16 000	18 400	15 000	4000	1000	3000	23 000	0.80	3 200
C	—	19 200	19 200	15 000	—	1000	—	16 000	1.20	—
Conversion cost	2 880	88 800	91 680	15 000	2000	900	1200	19 100	4.80	9 600
	17 880	208 000	225 880						11.00	29 600

Notes

[a]All of the material will have been added at the 90% stage. Therefore materials are 100% complete as regards normal loss.

[b]The opening WIP that is spoilt is 40% complete. Material C is not added until the 60% stage, but materials A and B will already have been added.

			(£)	(£)
Closing WIP				29 600
Completed production	15 000 × 11.00 =		165 000	
Normal loss	1 000 × 4.20 =	4 200		
	1 000 × 0.80 =	800		
	1 000 × 1.20 =	1 200		
	900 × 4.80 =	4 320	10 520	175 520
Abnormal loss:				
A	3 000 × 4.20 =	12 600		
B	3 000 × 0.80 =	2 400		
Conversion cost	1 200 × 4.80 =	5 760		20 760
				£225 880

Process account

	(£)		(£)
Opening WIP	17 880	Completed production	175 520
A	84 000	Abnormal loss	20 760
B	16 000	Closing WIP	29 600
C	19 200		
Conversion cost	88 800		
	£225 880		£225 880

(a) Expected output from an input of 39 300 sheets: 3 144 000 cans (39 300 × 80)
Less 1% rejects — 31 440 cans
Expected output after rejects — 3 112 560 cans

The normal loss arising from the rejects (31 440 cans) is sold at £0.26 per kg. It is therefore necessary to express the rejects in terms of kilos of metal. Each sheet weighs 2 kilos but wastage in the form of offcuts is 2% of input. Therefore the total weight of 80 cans is 1.96 kg (0.98 × 2 kg) and the weight of each can is 0.0245 kilos (1.96 kg/80 cans). The weight of the normal loss arising from the rejects is 770.28 kg (31 440 × 0.0245 kg). The normal loss resulting from the offcuts is 1572 kg (39 300 × 2 kg × 0.02). Hence the total weight of the normal loss is 2342.28 kilos (1572 kg + 770.28 kg), with an expected sales value of £609 (2342.28 kg × £0.26).

Process account

	(£)		(£)
Direct materials		Finished goods	
(39 300 × £2.50)	98 250	(3 100 760 cans × £0.042[a])	130 232
		Normal loss	609
Direct labour and		Abnormal loss	
overheads	33 087	(11 800 kg[b] at £0.042[a])	496
	131 337		131 337

Abnormal loss account

	(£)		(£)
Process account	496	Sale proceeds[c]	75
		Profit and loss account	421
	496		496

Notes

[a] Cost per unit $= \dfrac{£98\,250 + £33\,087 - £609}{\text{expected output (3 112 560 cans)}} = £0.042$ per can

[a] Expected output (3 112 560) − actual output (3 100 760 cans) = 11 800 cans

[c] Abnormal loss = 11 800 cans (3 112 560 − 3 100 760)
This will yield 289.1 kilos (11 800 × 0.0245 kilos) of metal with a sales value of £75 (289.1 × £0.26).

(b) (i) See 'Opening and closing work in progress' in Chapter 7 for the answer to this question.
(ii) See 'Weighted average method' and 'First in, first out method' in Chapter 7 for the answer to this question.

(a)

Production statement	
Input:	Units
Opening WIP	20 000
Transfer from previous process	180 000
	200 000
Output:	
Closing WIP	18 000
Abnormal loss	60
Completed units (balance)	181 940
	200 000

Statement of equivalent production and calculation of cost of completed production and WIP

	Current costs (£)	Completed units less opening WIP equivalent units	Abnormal loss	Closing WIP equivalent units	Current total equivalent units	Cost per unit (£)
Previous process cost	394 200	161 940	60	18 000	180 000	2.19
Materials	110 520	167 940	60	16 200	184 200	0.60
Conversion cost	76 506	173 940	60	12 600	186 600	0.41
	581 226					3.20

	(£)	(£)
Cost of completed production:		
Opening WIP (given)	55 160	
Previous process cost (161 940 × £2.19)	354 649	
Materials (167 940 × £0.60)	100 764	
Conversion costs (173 940 × £0.41)	71 315	581 888
Cost of closing WIP:		
Previous process cost (18 000 × £2.19)	39 420	
Materials (16 200 × £0.60)	9 720	
Conversion costs (12 600 × £0.41)	5 166	54 306
Value of abnormal loss (60 × £3.20)		192
		636 386

Process 3 account

	(£)		(£)
Opening WIP	55 160	Transfer to finished goods	
Transfer from process 2	394 200	stock	581 888
Materials	110 520	Abnormal loss	192
Conversion costs	76 506	Closing WIP	54 306
	636 386		636 386

(b) Normal losses are unavoidable losses that are expected to occur under efficient operating conditions. They are an expected production cost and should be absorbed by the completed production whereas abnormal losses are not included in the process costs but are removed from the appropriate process account and reported separately as an abnormal loss. See 'Equivalent production and normal losses' in Chapter 7 for a more detailed explanation of the treatment of normal losses.

(c) If the weighted average method is used, both the units and value of WIP are merged with current period costs and production to calculate the average cost per unit. The wejghted average cost per unit is then applied to all completed units, any abnormal losses and closing WIP equivalent units. In contrast, with the FIFO method the opening WIP is assumed to be the first group of units completed during the current period. The opening WIP is charged separately to completed production, and the cost per unit is based only on current costs and production for the period. The closing WIP is assumed to come from the new units that have been started during the period.

Question 7.19 (a) It is assumed that the normal loss occurs at the start of the process and should be allocated to completed production and closing WIP. It is also assumed that process 2 conversion costs are not incurred when losses occur. Therefore losses should not be allocated to conversion costs.

Statement of input and output (units)

	Input		Output
Opening WIP	1 200	Completed output	105 400
Transferred from Process 1	112 000	WIP	1 600
		Normal loss (5% × 112,000)	5 600
		Abnormal loss (balance)	600
	113 200		113 200

Since the loss occurs at the start of the process it should be allocated over all units that have reached this point. Thus the normal loss should be allocated to all units of output. This can be achieved by adopting the short-cut method described in Chapter 7 whereby the normal loss is not included in the unit cost statement.

Calculation of cost per unit and cost of completed production (FIFO method)

	Current costs (£)	Completed units less opening WIP equiv. units	Abnormal loss	Closing WIP equiv. units	Current total equiv. units	Cost per unit (£)
Previous process cost	187 704					
Materials	47 972					
	235 676	104 200(105 400 − 1200)	600	1600	106 400	2.215
Conversion costs	63 176	104 800(105 400 − 600)	–	1200	106 000	0.596
	298 852					2.811

Cost of completed production:	(£)	(£)
Opening WIP (given)	3 009	
Previous process cost and materials (104 200 × £2.215)	230 803	
Conversion cost (104 800 × £0.596)	62 461	296 273
Abnormal Loss (600 × £2.215)		1 329
Closing WIP:		
Previous process cost and materials (1600 × £2.215)	3 544	
Conversion costs (1200 × £0.596)	715	4 259
		301,861

Process 2 account

	(£)		(£)
Opening WIP	3 009	Transfer to finished goods	296 273
Transfers from Process 1	187 704	Abnormal loss	1 329
Raw materials	47 972	Closing WIP	4 259
Conversion costs	63 176		
	301 861		301 861

(b) If the loss occurs at the end of the process then the normal loss should only be charged to those units that have reached the end of the process. In other words, the cost of normal losses should not be allocated to closing WIP. To meet this requirement a separate column for normal losses is incorporated into the unit cost statement and the normal loss equivalent units are included in the calculation of total equivalent units. The cost of the normal loss should be calculated and added to the cost of completed production. For an illustration of the approach see 'Equivalent production and normal losses' in Chapter 7.

Question 7.21 The physical input and output to the process are as follows:

Input:	Rolls	Output:	Rolls
Opening WIP	1000	Spoiled	550
Started from new	5650	Closing WIP	800
Reworked	500	Completed (balance)	5800
	7150		7150

The 5800 rolls will include the reworked output of 500 rolls, which is assumed to be completed during the period. Therefore the un-reworked output is 5300 rolls. It is assumed that the normal loss is 10% of the un-reworked output of 5300 units. Hence the abnormal loss is 20 rolls (550 − 530 rolls).

(a) *Schedule of completed production and cost per roll*

	Current cost (£)	Un-reworked completed rolls less opening WIP equivalent rolls	Reworked equivalent rolls[a]	Normal loss	Abnormal loss	Closing WIP equivalent rolls	Total equivalent rolls	Cost per roll (£)
Materials	72 085	4300	300	530	20	640	5790	12.4499
Labour	11 718	4700	250	530	20	320	5820	2.0134
Overheads[b]	41 013	4700	250	530	20	320	5820	7.0469
	124 816							21.5102

Notes
[a] Reworked equivalent rolls refers to production for the current period only. Previous period costs are not included in the cost per unit calculation when the FIFO method is used.
[b] Note that overheads are charged to production at the rate of £3.50 per £1 of labour.

(b) *Allocation of costs*

Completed units:
	(£)
Un-reworked completed rolls	
[(4300 × £12.4499) + (4700 × £2.0134) + (4700 × £7.0469)]	96 118
Reworked rolls	
[(300 × £12.4499) + (250 × £2.0134) + (250 × £7.0469)]	6 000
Cost of normal spoilage (530 × £21.5102)	11 400
Opening WIP (£12 000 + £4620 + £16 170[a])]	32 790
	146 308

Value of closing WIP	
[(640 × £12.4499) + (320 × £2.0134) + (320 × £7.0469)]	10 868
Cost of abnormal spoilage (20 × £21.5102)	430
	157 606

Note
[a] Overhead costs at the rate of £3.50 per £1 of labour should be added to the value of the opening WIP.

(c) The advantages of converting to a standard costing system are as follows:
   (i) Calculations of *actual* costs per unit for each period will not be required. Completed production and stocks can be valued at standard costs per unit for each element of cost.
   (ii) Targets can be established and a detailed analysis of the variances can be presented. This process should enable costs to be more effectively controlled.

(d) Actual costs computed in (a) and (b) imply that cost-plus pricing is used. Possible disadvantages of this approach include:
  (i) Prices based solely on costs ignore demand and the prices that competitors charge.
  (ii) Overheads will include fixed overheads, which are arbitrarily apportioned and may distort the pricing decision.
  (iii) Replacement costs are preferable to historic costs for pricing decisions. Standard costs represent future target costs and are therefore more suitable for decision-making than historic costs based on a FIFO system.
  For additional comments see 'Limitations of cost-plus pricing' in Chapter 13.
(e) The implications are:
  (i) Replacement costs should be used for management accounting, but they will have to be adjusted for external reporting (see 'Pricing of stores issues' in Chapter 4 for a discussion).
  (ii) Practical difficulties in using replacement costs. For example, it is necessary to constantly monitor the current market price for all stock items.
  (iii) The benefits from the use of replacement costs will depend upon the rate of inflation. The higher the rate of inflation, the greater the benefits.

Question 7.23

(a)

Cost element	Opening WIP value (£)	Current cost (£)	Total cost (£)	Completed units	WIP equivalent units	Total equivalent units	Cost per unit (£)	WIP value (£)
Direct materials	17 400	162 600	180 000	8200	800	9000	20	16 000
Conversion	10 000	173 920	183 920	8200	160	8360	22	3 520
			363 920				42	19 520

Completed units 8200 × £42 = 344 400
Total cost 363 920

Process account

	Units	(£)		Units	(£)
Opening WIP	1000	27 400	Process B	8200	344 400
Materials	8000	162 600	Closing WIP c/d	800	19 520
Conversion cost		173 920			
		363 920			363 920

(b) *Calculation of equivalent production produced during current period*

	Total equivalent units	Opening WIP equivalent units	Equivalent units produced during period
Materials	9000	1000	8000
Conversion cost	8360	400	7960

Performance report

	Standard cost (£)	Actual cost (£)	Difference (£)
Materials	160 000 (8000 × £20)	162 600	2600 A
Conversion cost	183 080 (7960 × £23)	173 920	9160 F
			6560 F

Joint product and by-product costing

Solutions to Chapter 8 questions

Question summary

8.1–8.3   Discussion problems on joint and by-products.

8.4–8.6   Preparation of process accounts and apportionment of joint costs to products. Question 8.6 is also concerned with the accounting treatment of by-products.

8.7   Preparation of a flow chart for joint and by-products and calculation of cost per unit.

8.8–8.12   Apportionment of joint costs and decisions on whether or not joint products should be further processed.

8.13–8.18   Questions set at advanced level requiring the apportionment of joint costs and the presentation of cost information for decision-making. Question 8.13 is not too difficult, and is appropriate for a first year course. Questions 8.17 and 8.18 are similar. They are the most difficult questions in the chapter, requiring approximately two hours' preparation.

Question 8.4 (a)

Process 1 account

	(kg)	(£)		(kg)	(£)
Materials	7000	3500	Normal loss (W2)	700	280
Labour and overhead		4340	Transferred to		
Abnormal gain (W3)	130	156	process 2 (W1)	6430	7716
	7130	7996		7130	7996

Workings

(W1)

$$\text{Cost per unit} = \frac{\text{cost of production (£7840)} - \text{scrap value of normal loss (£280)}}{\text{expected output (6300 kg)}}$$

$$= £1.20 \text{ per kg}$$

(W2) Normal loss is 10% of *total* output, which in this case is equivalent to total input [therefore normal loss = (10% × (6430 + 570))].

(W3)   Abnormal gain = actual output (6430) − expected output (6300)

Normal loss account				Abnormal gain account	
(£)		(£)		(£)	
Process 1		Abnormal		Normal loss	Process 1 156
(700 × 40p) 280		gain a/c		(130 × 40p) 52	
		(130 × 40p) 52	P & L a/c 104		

Cash

(570 × 40p) 228

280		280	156		156

Process 2 account

	(kg)	(£)		(kg)	(£)
Previous process cost	6430	7 716	By-product net income	430	645
Labour and overhead		12 129	Output to be account for		19 200
			E	2000	
			F	4000	
	6430	19 845		6430	19 845

The allocation of £19 200 to E and F depends on the apportionment method used.

(i) *Physical output method*

	E (£)	F (£)
1. Total output cost	$6400 \left(\dfrac{2000}{6000} \times £19\,200 \right)$	$12\,800 \left(\dfrac{4000}{6000} \times £19\,200 \right)$
2. Closing stock	$2880 \left(\dfrac{2000 - 1100}{2000} \times £6400 \right)$	$2\,560 \left(\dfrac{4000 - 3200}{4000} \times £12\,800 \right)$
3. Cost of sales	$3520 \left(\dfrac{1100}{2000} \times £6400 \right)$	$10\,240 \left(\dfrac{3200}{4000} \times £12\,800 \right)$
4. Sales revenue	7700 (1100 × £7)	8 000 (3200 × £2.50)
5. Profit (4 − 3)	4180	(2 240)

(ii) *Market value of output method*

	E (£)	F (£)
1. Market value of output	14 000 (2000 × £7)	10 000 (4000 × £2.50)
2. Cost of output	$11\,200 \left(\dfrac{14}{24} \times £19\,200 \right)$	$8\,000 \left(\dfrac{10}{24} \times £19\,200 \right)$
3. Closing stock	$5\,040 \left(\dfrac{900}{2000} \times £11\,200 \right)$	$1\,600 \left(\dfrac{800}{4000} \times £8\,000 \right)$
4. Cost of sales	$6\,160 \left(\dfrac{1100}{2000} \times £11\,200 \right)$	$6\,400 \left(\dfrac{3200}{4000} \times £8\,000 \right)$
5. Sales revenue	7700	8 000
6. Profit (5 − 4)	1 540	1 600

(c) See Chapter 8 for the answer to this question. In particular, the answer should stress that joint cost apportionments are necessary for stock valuation, but such apportionments are inappropriate for decision-making. For decision-making relevant costs should be used. It can be seen from the answer to part (b) that one method of apportionment implies that F makes a loss whereas the other indicates that F makes a profit. Product F should only be deleted if the costs saved from deleting it exceed the revenues lost.

Question 8.7 (a) See Figure Q8.7

Workings
(W1)   (4000 + 2600 − 300)/900 = £7
(W2)   (2100 + 3300)/300 = £18

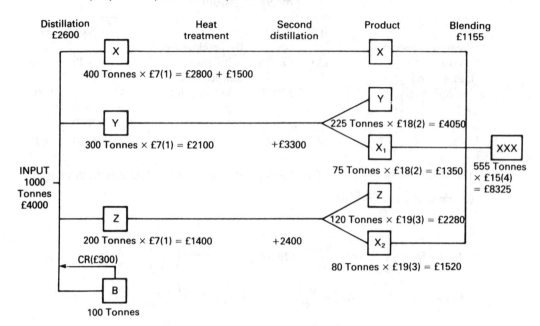

Figure Q8.7

(W3)   (1400 + 2400)/200 = £19
(W4)   (2800 + 1500 + 1155 + 1350 + 1520)/555 = £15

(b)

Product	Output (tonnes)	Total cost (£)	Cost per tonne (£)
XXX	555	8325	15
Y	225	4050	18
Z	120	2280	19

(c) An alternative treatment is to credit the income direct to the profit and loss account rather than crediting the proceeds to the process from which the by-product was derived.

Question 8.8 (a)

	B (£)	K (£)	C (£)	Total (£)
Revenue	35 000	50 000	60 000	
Pre-separation joint costs (1)	17 500	12 500	10 000	
Post separation costs	20 000	10 000	22 500	
Profit/(loss)	(2 500)	27 500	27 500	52 500

(b)				
Incremental costs	20 000	10 000	22 500	
Incremental revenue	14 000	30 000	42 000	
Incremental benefit	(6 000)	20 000	19 500	

Therefore profit will increase by £6000 if B is sold at split off point and the revised profit statements will be:

Revenue	21 000	50 000	60 000	
Pre-separation costs[a]	17 500	12 500	10 000	
Post separation costs	—	10 000	22 500	
Profit	3 500	27 500	27 500	58 500

Note
[a]B = 3500/8000 × £40 000; K = 2500/8000 × £40 000; C = 2000/8000 × £40 000.

(a) You can see from the question that the input is 240 000 kg and the output is **Question 8.11**
190 000 kg. It is assumed that the difference of 50 000 kg is a normal loss in output which occurs at the start of processing. Therefore the loss should be charged to the completed production and WIP. By making no entry for normal losses in the cost per unit calculation the normal loss is automatically apportioned between completed units and WIP.

	Opening WIP (£)	Current cost (£)	Total cost (£)	Completed units	Closing WIP	Total equivalent units	Cost per unit (£)	WIP value (£)
Materials	20 000	75 000	95 000	160 000	30 000	190 000	0.50	15 000
Processing costs	12 000	96 000	108 000	160 000	20 000	180 000	0.60	12 000
			203 000				1.10	27 000
				Completed units (160 000 units × £1.10)				176 000
								203 000

(b) This question requires a comparison of incremental revenues and incremental costs. Note that the costs of process 1 are irrelevant to the decision since they will remain the same whichever of the two alternatives are selected. You should also note that further processing 120 000 kg of the compound results in 240 000 kg of Starcomp.

Incremental sales revenue:

	(£)	(£)
Starcomp (120 000 × 2 kg × £2)	480 000	
Compound (120 000 × £1.60)	192 000	288 000
Incremental costs:		
Materials	120 000	
Processing costs	120 000	240 000
Incremental profits		48 000

It is therefore worthwhile further processing the compound.
(c) The sales revenue should cover the additional costs of further processing the 40 000 kg compound and the lost sales revenue from the 40 000 kg compound if it is sold without further processing.
Additional processing costs:

	(£)
Materials (£160 000 − £120 000)	40 000
Processing costs (£140 000 − £120 000)	20 000
Lost compound sales revenue (40 000 × £1.60)	64 000
	124 000

$$\text{Minimum selling price per kg of Starcomp} = \frac{£124\,000}{40\,000\,\text{kg} \times 2}$$

$$= £1.55$$

Question 8.12 (a) *Profit and loss account*

	W (£)	X (£)	Z (£)	Total (£)
Opening stock	–	–	8 640	8 640
Production cost	189 060	228 790	108 750	526 600
Less closing stock	(14 385)	(15 070)	(15 010)	(44 465)
Cost of sales	174 675	213 720	102 380	490 775
Selling and administration costs	24 098	27 768	10 011	61 877
Total costs	198 773	241 488	112 391	552 652
Sales	240 975	277 680	100 110	618 765
Profit/(loss)	42 202	36 192	(12 281)	66 113

Workings
Joint process cost per kilo of output = £0.685 per kg (£509 640/744 000 kg)
Production cost for products W, X and Y:

$$\text{Product W } (276\,000 \text{ kg} \times £0.685) = £189\,060$$
$$X \ (334\,000 \text{ kg} \times £0.685) = £228\,790$$
$$Y \ (134\,000 \text{ kg} \times £0.685) = £91\,790$$

Closing stocks for products W and X:

$$\text{Product W } (21\,000 \text{ kg} \times £0.685) = £14\,385$$
$$X \ (22\,000 \text{ kg} \times £0.685) = £15\,070$$

Cost per kilo of product Z:

	(£)
Product Y (128 000 kg × £0.685) =	87 680
Further processing costs	17 920
Less by-product sales (8000 × £0.12) =	(960)
	104 640
Cost per kilo (£104 640/96 000 kg)	£1.09

Closing stock of product Z (10 000 kg × £1.09) = £10 900
Add closing stock of input Y (6000 × £0.685) = £4 110
Closing stock relating to product Z £15 010

Production cost relating to final product Z:

	(£)
Product Y (134 000 kg × £0.685) =	91 790
Further processing costs	17 920
Less by-product costs	(960)
	108 750

(b) The joint costs are common and unavoidable to both alternatives, and are therefore not relevant for the decision under consideration. Further processing from an input of 128 000 kg of Y has resulted in an output of 96 000 kg of Z. Thus it requires 1.33 kg of Y to produce 1 kg of Z (128/96).

	(£)
Revenue per kilo for product Z	1.065 (£100 110/94 000 kg)
Sale proceeds at split-off point (1.33 × £0.62)	0.823
Incremental revenue per kg from further processing	0.242

Incremental costs of further processing   0.177 [(£17 920 − £960)/96 000]
Incremental profit from further processing   0.065

It is assumed that selling and administration costs are fixed and will be unaffected by which alternative is selected. The company should therefore process Y further into product Z and not accept the offer from the other company to purchase the entire output of product Y.

(c) See 'Methods of apportioning joint costs to joint products' in Chapter 8 for the answer to this question.

(a) Figure Q8.13 indicates that the relative sales value of each product is as follows: **Question 8.13**

	Boddie (£000)	Soull (£000)	Total (£000)
Total sales	8400	36 000	44 400
Plus NRV of Threekeys		2 170 *(W1)*	2 170
	8400	38 170	46 570

Workings
(W1)   (280 000 litres × £8) − £70 000 delivery costs

Allocation of joint costs:

$$\text{Boddie} = £840\,000 \left(\frac{8400}{46\,570} \times £4\,657\,000 \right)$$

$$\text{Soull} = \frac{£3\,817\,000}{4\,657\,000} \left(\frac{38\,170}{46\,570} \times £4\,657\,000 \right)$$

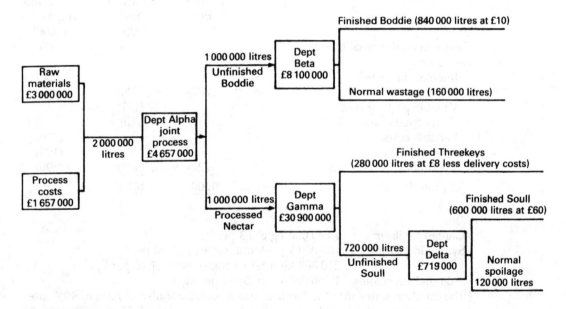

Figure Q8.13 *Diagram of joint cost system.*

(b) *Profit and loss statement*

	Boddie (£000)	Soull (£000)	Threekeys (£000)	Total (£000)
Sales	8400	36 000	2240	46 640
Less specifically attributable costs:				
Department Beta	8100			

Department Gamma		30 900		
Department Delta		719		
Delivery costs			70	
Contribution to joint costs	300	4 381	2170	6 851
Less apportioned joint costs	840	3 817	–	4 657
Profit/(loss)	(540)	564	2170	2 194

(c) The incremental revenues are in excess of the incremental costs for all three products. In other words, each product provides a contribution towards the joint costs. Consequently, all three products should be produced.

Question 8.16 (a) *Preliminary workings*

The joint production process results in the production of garden fertilizer and synthetic fuel consisting of 80% fertilizer and 20% synthetic fuel. The question indicates that 1 600 000 kg of fertilizer are produced. Therefore total output is 2 000 000 kg, and synthetic fuel accounts for 20% (400 000 kg) of this output. The question also states that a wholesaler bought 160 000 kg of the synthetic fuel, and the remaining fuel (400 000 kg − 160 000 kg = 240 000 kg) was used to heat the company greenhouses. The greenhouses produce 5 kg of fruit and vegetables per kg of fuel. Therefore 1 200 000 kg of fruit and vegetables were produced during the period.

Summary profit statements

	Garden fertilizer (£000)	Synthetic fuel (£000)	Fruit and vegetables (£000)
Sales revenue/internal transfers[a]	4800	560	600
Less costs:			
Internal transfers[a]			(336)
Joint costs[b]	(2880)	(720)	
Variable packing costs		(192)	
Direct fixed costs		(40)	
Variable costs			(420)
Fixed labour costs			(100)
Apportioned fixed costs	(720)	(18)	(90)
Net profit/(Loss)	1200	(410)	(346)

Notes

[a] Garden fertilizer: 1 600 000 kg at £3 per kg

Synthetic fuel: 160 000 kg external sales at £1.40 per kg

240 000 kg internal transfers at £1.40 per kg

Fruit and vegetables: 1 200 000 kg at £0.50 per kg

[b] The question states that the fertilizer has a contribution/sales ratio of 40% after the apportionment of joint costs. Therefore joint costs of £2 880 000 (60% × £4 800 000 sales) will be apportioned to fertilizers. Joint costs are apportioned on a weight basis, and synthetic fuel represents 20% of the total weight. Thus £2 880 000 joint costs apportioned to fertilizers represents 80% of the joint costs. The remaining 20% represents the joint costs apportioned to synthetic fuel. Joint costs of £720 000 [20% × (100/80) × £2 880 000] will therefore be apportioned to synthetic fuel.

(b) Apportioned joint and fixed costs are not relevant costs since they will still continue if the activity ceases. The relevant revenues and costs are as follows:

	(£)
Relevant revenues	224 000 (160 000 kg at £1.40)
Less packing costs	(192 000)
avoidable fixed costs	(40 000)
Net benefit to company	(8 000)

The percentage reduction in avoidable fixed costs before the relevant revenues would be sufficient to cover these costs is 20% (£8000/£40 000).

(c) The notional cost for internal transfers and the apportioned fixed costs would still continue if the fruit and vegetables activity were eliminated. These costs are therefore not relevant in determining the net benefit arising from fruit and vegetables. The calculation of the net benefit is as follows:

	(£)
Relevant revenues	600 000
Less variable costs	(420 000)
avoidable fixed labour costs	(100 000)
Net benefit	80 000

(d) Proposed output of synthetic fuel is 400 000 kg, but there is a contracted requirement to supply a minimum of 100 000 kg to the wholesaler. Consequently, the maximum output of fruit and vegetables is 1 500 000 kg (300 000 kg of synthetic fuel × 5 kg). In determining the optimum price/output level the fixed costs will remain unchanged whatever price/output combination is selected. Internal transfers are a notional cost and do not represent any change in company cash outflows arising from the price/output decision. The price/output decision should be based on a comparison of the relevant revenues less incremental costs (variable costs) for each potential output level. In addition, using synthetic fuel for fruit and vegetable production results in a loss of contribution of £0.20 per kg (£1.40 − £1.20 packing) of synthetic fuel used. This opportunity cost is a relevant cost which should be included in the analysis. The net contributions for the relevant output levels are as follows:

Sales (000kg)	Contribution per kg[a] (£)	Total contribution (£)	Contribution foregone on fuel sales (£)	Net contribution (£)
1200	0.15	180 000	0[b]	180 000
1300	0.145	188 500	4 000[c]	184 500
1400	0.135	189 000	8 000[d]	181 000
1500	0.125	187 500	12 000[e]	175 500

The optimum output level is to sell 1 300 000 kg of fruit and vegetables. This will require 260 000 kg of synthetic fuel. Sales of synthetic fuel to the wholesaler will be restricted to 140 000 kg.

Notes
[a] Average selling price less variable cost of fruit and vegetable production (£420 000/1 200 000 kg = £0.35 per kg).
[b] 240 000 kg of synthetic fuel used, resulting in 160 000 kg being sold to the wholesaler. Therefore existing sales to the wholesaler of 160 000 kg will be maintained.
[c] 260 000 kg of synthetic fuel used, resulting in 140 000 kg being sold to the wholesaler. Therefore sales will decline by 20 000 kg and the lost contribution will be £4000 (20 000 kg × £0.20 per kg).
[d] 280 000 kg of synthetic fuel used, resulting in 120 000 kg being sold to the wholesaler. Therefore lost contribution is £8000 (40 000 kg × £0.20).
[e] 300 000 kg used, resulting in 100 000 kg being sold to the wholesaler. Therefore the lost contribution is £12 000 (60 000 kg × £0.20).

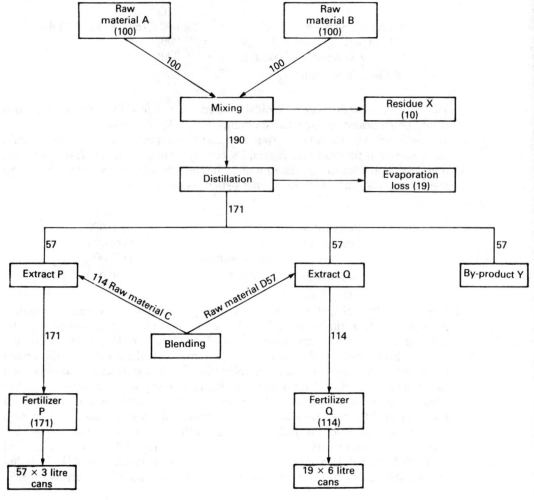

Figure Q8.17 *Flowchart for an input of 100 litres of raw materials A and B.*

(a) Figure Q8.17 shows a flowchart for an input of 100 litres of raw material A and 100 litres of raw material B. The variable costs for an input of 100 litres of raw materials for each product are shown below:

Raw materials:			Fertilizer P	Fertilizer Q
	(£)	(£)	(£)	(£)
100 litres of A at £25 per 100 litres	25.00			
100 litres of B at £12 per 100 litres	12.00	37.00		
Mixing:				
200 litres at £3.75 per 100 litres	7.50			
Residue X (10 litres at £0.03)	(0.30)	7.20		
Distilling:				
190 litres at £5 per 100 litres	9.50			
By-product Y (57 litres × £0.04)	(2.28)	7.22		
Total joint costs		51.42	25.71[a]	25.71[a]
Raw material C (114 litres at £20 per 100 litres)			22.80	
Raw material D (57 litres at £55 per 100 litres)				31.35
Blending:				
P (171 litres at £7 per 100 litres)			11.97	

Q (114 litres at £7 per 100 litres)		7.98
Cans:		
P (57 cans at £0.32 per can)	18.24	
Q (19 cans at £0.50 per can)		9.50
Labels:		
P (57 cans at £3.33 per 1000 cans)	0.19	
Variable cost from 100 litres input of		
each raw material	78.91	74.54

Output is restricted to 570 000 litres of Q. An input of 100 litres of raw materials A and B yields an output of 114 litres of Q. Therefore an input of 500 000 litres [570 000/(114/110)] of each raw material will yield an output of 570 000 litres of Q. An input to the joint process of 500 000 litres of each raw material will yield an output of 855 000 litres (171 × 5000) of P. The total manufacturing cost based on an input of 500 000 litres of each raw material is shown below:

	Fertilizer P (£)	Fertilizer Q (£)
Total variable cost: 5000 × £78.91	394 550	
5000 × £74.54		372 700
Mixing and distilling fixed costs	13 000[a]	13 000[a]
Blending fixed costs	19 950[b]	13 300[b]
(i) *Total manufacturing cost*	427 500	399 000

Notes
[a]Joint costs are apportioned to the main products on the basis of the output from each process. The mixing and distilling processes yield identical outputs for each product. Therefore 50% of the costs are apportioned to each product.
[b]Apportioned on the basis of an output of 171 litres of P and 114 litres of Q.

(ii) *Manufacturing cost per litre*

$$\text{Fertilizer P} = £0.50 \ (£427 \ 500/855 \ 000 \text{ litres})$$
$$\text{Fertilizer Q} = £0.70 \ (£399 \ 000/570 \ 000 \text{ litres})$$

(iii) *List price per litre*
Costs and profit as a percentage of list price are:

	(%)
List price	100
Net selling price	75
Profit (20% × 75%)	15
Total cost (75% − 15%)	60
Selling and distribution (13.33% × 75%)	10
Manufacturing cost (60% − 10%)	50

List price per litre is, therefore, twice the manufacturing cost per litre:

$$P = £1.00$$
$$Q = £1.40$$

(iv) *Profit for the year*

$$P = £128 \ 250 \ (15\% \text{ of } £1) \times 855 \ 000 \text{ litres}$$
$$Q = £119 \ 700 \ (15\% \text{ of } £1.40) \times 570 \ 000 \text{ litres}$$

(b) Manufacturing joint product Q will also result in an additional output of P. The break-even point will depend on whether or not P is sold at split-off point as scrap or further processed and sold at the normal market price. The following analysis assumes that P is further processed and sold at the normal market price:

	(£)
Variable cost of producing 50 000 litres of Q	
[(50 000 × £372 700)/570 000]	32 693
Variable selling costs of Q	2000
	34 693
Contribution from sale of 75 000 litres of P:	16 500
75 000 litres × £0.22[a]	
Net cost	18 193

The selling price should at least cover the net cost per litre of £0.364 (£18 193/50 000 litres). Therefore the break-even selling price is £0.364 per litre.

Note
[a] Output of P is 1.5 times the output of Q (see the Flowchart). Therefore output of P is 75 000 litres (50 000 × 1.5)
Variable manufacturing cost per litre of P = £0.46
(394 500/855 000 litres)
Variable selling cost per litre of P = £0.07
[0.7 × (13.33% of £0.75)]
Selling price per litre = £0.75
Contribution per litre = £0.22

(c) There is no specific answer to this question. The recommendation should be based on price/demand relationships and the state of competition. The normal mark-up is 25% on cost (20% of selling price equals 25% mark-up on cost).

Selling price based on normal mark-up = [1.25 (£18 193)]/50 000 litres
= £0.455

The above price assumes that the additional output of P can be sold at the normal market price. If P cannot be sold then the following costs will be incurred:

	(£)
Variable costs of Q	34 693
Pre-separation variable costs previously apportioned to P:	
5000 at £25.71 per 100 = £128 550 (for 570 000 output)	
Pre-separation variable costs for an output of 50 000 litres	
[(£128 550/570 000) × 50 000]	11 276
	45 969

Minimum selling price = £0.919 (£45 969/50 000)
Note that pre-separation variable costs previously allocated to P will still be incurred if P is not produced. The recommended price will depend on the circumstances, competition, demand and the company's pricing policy.

Absorption costing and variable costing

Solutions to Chapter 9 questions

Question summary

9.1, 9.2   Essay questions relating to Chapter 9.

9.3–9.11   These questions are appropriate for a first-year course and require absorption costing and variable costing profit calculations and stock valuations. Questions 9.10 and 9.11 are the most difficult, and include an explanation of the difference between variable and absorption costing profit calculations. Question 9.5 also involves CVP analysis.

9.12–9.15   Questions set at advanced level on variable and absorption costing. Question 9.15 requires a knowledge of variance analysis.

Question 9.4

(a) *Calculation of unit costs*

Direct material cost	10.00
Direct wages cost	4.00
Variable overhead cost	2.50
Variable manufacturing cost	16.50
Fixed manufacturing overhead (£400 000/320 000 units)	1.25
Total manufacturing cost	17.75

Profit statements

(i) Marginal costing

	January–March (£000)		April–June (£000)	
Opening stock	Nil		165	
Production costs:				
variable	1 155	(70 000 × £16.50)	1 650	(100 000 × £16.50)
Closing stock	(165)	(10 000 × £16.50)	(330)	(20 000 × £16.50)
	990		1 485	
Selling and distribution costs: variable	90		135	
	1,080		1 620	
Revenue from sales	2,700		4 050	
Contribution	1,620		2 430	
Fixed production costs	(100)		(100)	
Fixed selling and distribution costs	(20)		(20)	
Fixed administration costs	(30)		(30)	
Budgeted profit	1,470		2 280	

(ii) Absorption costing

	(£000)		(£000)	
Opening stock	Nil		177.5	
Total production costs	1 242.5	(70 000 × £17.75)	1 775.0	(100 000 × £17.75)
	1 242.5		1 952.5	

Closing stock	(177.5) (10 000 × £17.75)	(355.0) (20 000 × £17.75)
	1 065.0	1 597.5
Add under absorption of production overhead (10 000 × 1.25)	12.5	–
Less over absorption of production overhead (20 000 × 1.25)	–	(25.0)
Total selling and distribution costs	110.0	155.0
Administration costs	30.0	30.0
	1 217.5	1 757.5
Revenue from sales	2 700.0	4 050.0
Budgeted profit	1 482.5	2 292.5

(b) The difference in profits of £12 500 is due to the fact that part of the fixed production overheads (10 000 units at £1.25 per unit) are included in the closing stock valuation and not recorded as an expense during the current period. With the marginal costing system all of the fixed manufacturing costs incurred during a period are recorded as an expense of the current period.

(c) It is assumed that the question requires the production overhead account to be written up only in respect of fixed production overhead.

Fixed production overhead control account

	(£)		(£)
Actual expenditure	102 400	WIP A/c (74 000 × £1.25)	92 500
		Under-absorption transferred to P & L a/c	9 900
	102 400		102 400

(d) See 'Some arguments in support of variable costing' for the answer to this question.

Question 9.6 (a) Variable cost per unit:

	(£)
Variable production cost	49
Variable non-manufacturing costs (20% off sales value)	28
	77
Manufacturing absorption cost per unit	69

Fixed costs for the period (£20 × 16 000 units)   £320 000 per annum
(£160 000 per six months)

(i) *Marginal costing profit statements*

	March 1993 (£)		September 1993 (£)	
Opening stock	–		73 500	(1500 × £49)
Variable production costs	416 500	(8500 × £49)	343 000	(7000 × £49)
Less closing stock	(73 500)	(1500 × £49)	(24 500)	(500 × £49)
	343 000		392 000	
Variable non-manufacturing costs	196 000	(7000 × £28)	224 000	(8000 × £28)
	539 000		616 000	
Sales	980 000	(7000 × £140)	1 120 000	(8000 × £140)
Contribution	441 000		504 000	
Fixed costs				
(£160 000 + £180 000/2)	250 000		250 000	
Profit	191 000		254 000	

(ii)   *Absorption costing profit statements*

	March 1993 (£)		September 1993 (£)	
Opening stock	–		103 500	(1 500 × £69)
Production cost	586 500	(8500 × £69)	483 000	(7000 × £69)
Less closing stock	(103 500)	(1500 × £69)	(34 500)	(500 × £69)
	483 000		552 000	
Under- (over-) recovery of fixed overheads	(10 000)	(500 × £20)	20 000	(1000 × £20)
	473 000		572 000	
Variable non-manufacturing costs	196 000	(7000 × £28)	224 000	(8000 × £28)
Fixed non-manufacturing costs	90 000		90 000	
	759 000		886 000	
Sales	980 000		1 120 000	
Profit	221 000		234 000	

(b) With a marginal costing system all of the fixed manufacturing overhead incurred during a period is charged as an expense whereas fixed overheads are included in the stock valuations with the absorption costing system. In the first period fixed overheads of £30 000 (1500 × £20) are included in the closing stock valuation and not charged as an expense of the current period. Therefore the absorption costing profits exceed the marginal costing profits by £30 000. In the second period stocks increase by 1000 units and the absorption costing statement includes £20 000 (1000 × £20) in the stock movements. This results in absorption costing profits being £20 000 less than the marginal costing profits. The following is a reconciliation of the profit statements:

	31st March (£)	30th September (£)
Marginal costing profits	191 000	254 000
Fixed production overheads included in increases/(decreases) in stock movements	30 000	(20 000)
	221 000	234 000

(c) For an explanation of those situations where marginal costing may be beneficial in making decisions you should refer to Chapter 11 in respect of the following situations:
   (i) deleting a segment;
   (ii) make or buy decisions;
   (iii) pricing decisions;
   (iv) product mix decisions where limiting factors exist;
   (v) equipment replacement decisions.

Question 9.8

(a) See sections on some arguments in support of variable costing and some arguments in support of absorption costing in Chapter 9 for the answer to this question.

(b) (i)

	(£)	
Fixed production overhead per unit	= 0.60	(£144 000/240 000 units)
Variable production cost per unit	= 1.30	(£312 000/240 000 units)
Variable selling and administration overhead per unit	= 0.10	(£24 000/240 000 units)
Fixed selling and administration overhead per unit	= 0.40	(£96 000/240 000 units)
	2.40	
Selling price	3.00	
Profit	0.60	

	(£)
Fixed production overhead incurred	144 000
Fixed production overhead absorbed (260 000 × £0.60)	156 000
Over-recovery	£12 000

(ii) *Absorption costing profit:*

	(£)
Opening stock (40 000 × £1.90)	76 000
Production cost (260 000 × £1.90)	494 000
	570 000
Less closing stock (70 000 × £1.90)	133 000
Cost of sales (230 000 × £1.90)	437 000
Less over recovery of fixed production overhead	12 000
	425 000

Selling and administration overhead:	
Variable (230 000 × £0.10)	23 000
Fixed	96 000
Total cost	544 000
Sales (230 000 × £3)	690 000
Profit	£146 000

Marginal costing profit:

	(£)
Contribution (230 000 × (£3 − £1.40))	368 000
Less fixed costs (£144 000 + £96 000)	240 000
Profit	£128 000

(iii)

	(£)
Absorption costing profit	146 000
Fixed overhead included in stock increase (30 000 × £0.60)	18 000
Marginal costing profit	£128 000

(iv) The profit figure will be the same with both systems whenever production equals sales and therefore opening stock equals closing stock.

Question 9.9 (a)

Cost element	Total cost (£)	Completed units	WIP equivalent units	Total equivalent units	Cost per unit (£)	WIP (£)
Materials	714 000	98 000	4000	102 000	7.00	28 000
Labour	400 000	98 000	2000	100 000	4.00	8 000
Variable overhead	100 000	98 000	2000	100 000	1.00	2 000
Fixed overhead	350 000	98 000	2000	100 000	3.50	7 000
	1 564 000				15.50	45 000

(b) *Absorption costing profit statement*:

	(£)	(£)
Sales		1 800 000
Production cost	1 564 000	
Closing WIP	(45 000)	
Closing finished goods stock (8000 × £15.50)	(124 000)	1 395 000
Gross profit		405 000

Less: Variable selling and administration
costs (£1.60 × 90 000) (144 000)
Fixed selling and administration costs (250 000)
Net profit £11 000

(c) *Marginal costing profit statement*:

	(£)	(£)
Sales		1 800 000
Variable cost of production	1 214 000	
Closing WIP	(38 000)	
Closing finished goods stock (8000 × £12)	(96 000)	
Variable cost of sales	1 080 000	
Variable selling and administration costs	144 000	1 224 000
Contribution		576 000
Less: Fixed costs (350 + 200 + 50)		(600 000)
Net loss		£(24 000)

(d) The absorption costing statement shows a profit of £11 000 whereas the marginal costing statement shows a net loss of £24 000. The difference of £35 000 is due to the fact that the closing stock valuation includes £35 000 fixed overhead (£7000 WIP and £28 000 finished goods) whereas the fixed overheads are not included in the stock valuation when the marginal costing approach is used. Instead, *all* the fixed overheads are charged as a period cost. With the absorption costing system, the fixed overheads of £35 000 that are included in the stock valuation will be recorded as an expense when the stocks are sold. Consequently, the absorption costing method shows £35 000 greater profits than the marginal costing method. For a detailed discussion of a comparison of the impact on profits of the two methods see Chapter 9.

For internal profit measurement purposes both methods are acceptable, but for external reporting SSAP 9 requires that stocks should be valued on an absorption costing basis.

Question 9.10

(a)
$$\text{Break-even point} = \frac{\text{fixed costs (£180 000)}}{\text{unit contribution (£10} - \text{£6)}} = 45\,000 \text{ units per period}$$

(b)

	Period 1 (£000)	Period 2 (£000)	Period 3 (£000)
Opening stock	—	180	—
Production cost at £9 per unit (*W1*)	630 (70 × £9)	360 (40 × £9)	540 (60 × £9)
	630	540	540
Less closing stock	180 (20 × £9)	—	180 (20 × £9)
	450	540	360
Under/(cover) recovery of fixed overheads (*W2*)	(30)	60	—
Variable overhead expenditure variance (*W3*)	(2)	5	—
Total cost	418	605	360
Sales	500	600	400
Profit/(loss)	82	(5)	40

Workings

		(£)	
(*W1*)	Variable cost per unit	6	
	Fixed costs per unit	3	(£180 000/60 000 units)
		9	

(W2) Period 1 10 000 units at £3
2 20 000 units at £3
3 Actual production = normal activity

(W3) Actual variable cost is compared with budgeted variable costs for actual production, and the difference represents under/over spending

Period 1 (70 000 × £1) − £68 000 = £2000 Favourable variance
2 (40 000 × £1) − £45 000 = £5000 Adverse variance
3 (60 000 × £1) − £60 000 = 0

(c)

	Period 1 (£000)	Period 2 (£000)	Period 3 (£000)
Contribution from output differing from break-even point (W1)	+20	+60	−20
Fixed overhead included in stock changes (W2)	+60	−60	+60
Variable overhead expenditure variance	+ 2	− 5	0
Profit for period	82	− 5	+40

Workings
(W1)	(50 − 45) × £4	(60 − 45) × £4	(40 − 45) × £4
(W2)	(+20 × £3)	(−20 × £3)	(+20 × £3)

In period 1 sales volume was 5000 units in excess of the break-even sales volume, and at a contribution of £5 per unit a profit of £20 000 would result if calculated on a marginal costing basis. However, actual profit was £82 000. There are two reasons for this. First, absorption costing has been used and £60 000 (20 000 units × £3) fixed overheads has been carried forward in fixed overheads and thus deferred as an expense. The break-even point calculation assumes a marginal costing system with fixed overheads of £180 000 per period being regarded as a period cost. Secondly, the break-even analysis and stock valuations assume variable overheads will be £1 per unit of output. In period 1 output was 70 000 units and expected variable overhead expenditure was £70 000. Actual expenditure was £68 000, thus resulting in an increase in profits of £2000.

Similar comments apply to periods 2 and 3, but note that the opening stock exceeds closing stock by 20 000 units in period 2. Consequently, £60 000 fixed overheads (20 000 units × £3) are included as an expense in the opening stock, but since closing stock is zero no fixed overheads are deferred as an expense until period 3. Therefore the total fixed overhead charged for period 2 is £240 000 (£180 000 + £60 000 included in the opening stock).

Question 9.12 (a) It is assumed that opening stock valuation in 1982 was determined on the basis of the old overhead rate of £2.10 per hour. The closing stock valuation for 1982 and the opening and closing valuations for 1983 are calculated on the basis of the new overhead rate of £3.60 per hour. In order to compare the 1982 and 1983 profits, it is necessary to restate the 1982 opening stock on the same basis as that which was used for 1983 stock valuations.

We are informed that the 1983 closing stock will be at the same physical level as the 1981 opening stock valuation. It should also be noted that the 1982 opening stock was twice as much as the 1981 equivalent. The 1981 valuation on the revised basis would have been £130 000, resulting in a 1982 revised valuation of £260 000. Consequently, the 1982 profits will be £60 000 (£260 000 − £200 000) lower when calculated on the revised basis.

From the 1982 estimate you can see that stocks increase and then decline in 1983. It appears that the company has over-produced in 1982 thus resulting in large opening stocks at the start of 1983. The effect of this is that more of the sales demand is met from opening stocks in 1983. Therefore production declines in 1983, thus resulting in an under recovery of £300 000 fixed overheads, which is charged as a period cost. On the other hand, the under recovery for 1982 is expected to be £150 000.

The reconciliation of 1982 and 1983 profits is as follows:

	(£)
1982 profits	128 750
Difference in opening stock valuation for 1982	(60 000)
Additional under recovery in 1983	(150 000)
Budgeted loss for 1983	(81 250)

(b) To prepare the profit and loss accounts on a marginal cost basis, it is necessary to analyse the production costs into the fixed and variable elements. The calculations are:

	1981 (£)	1982 (£)	1983 (£)
Total fixed overheads incurred	600 000	600 000	600 000
Less under recovery	300 000	150 000	300 000
Fixed overheads charged to production	300 000	450 000	300 000
Total production cost	1 000 000	975 000	650 000
Proportion fixed	3/10	6/13 (450/975)	6/13
Proportion variable (balance)	7/10	7/13	7/13

Profit and loss accounts (marginal cost basis)

	Actual 1981 (£)	(£)	Estimated 1982 (£)	(£)	Budget 1983 (£)	(£)
Sales		1 350 000		1 316 250		1 316 250
Opening finished goods stock at marginal cost	70 000[a]		140 000[a]		192 500[b]	
Variable factory cost	700 000[a]		525 000[b]		350 000[b]	
	770 000		665 000		542 500	
Closing finished goods stock at marginal cost	140 000[a]	630 000	192 500[b]	472 500	70 000[b]	472 500
		720 000		843 750		843 750
Fixed factory cost	600 000		600 000		600 000	
Administrative and financial costs	220 000		220 000		220 000	
		820 000		820 000		820 000
Profit/(loss)		(£100 000)		£23 750		£23 750

Notes
[a] 7/10 × absorption cost figures given in the question.
[b] 7/13 × absorption cost figures given in the question.

(c) The under absorption of overhead may be due to the fact that the firm is operating at a low level of activity. This may be due to a low demand for the firm's products. The increase in the overhead rate will cause the product costs to increase. When cost-plus pricing is used the selling price will also be increased. An increase in selling price may result in a further decline in demand. Cost-plus pricing ignores price/demand relationships. For a more detailed discussion of the answer required to this question see section on 'Limitations of cost-plus pricing' in Chapter 13.

(d) For an answer to this question see section on 'Reasons for using cost-based pricing formulae' in Chapter 13 and 'Some arguments in favour of absorption costing' in Chapter 9. Note that SSAP 9 requires that absorption costing (full costing) be used for external reporting.

Question 9.13 (a) Sales for the second six-monthly period have increased for department A, but profit has declined, whereas sales for department B have declined and profit has increased. This situation arises because stocks are valued on an absorption cost basis. With an absorption costing system, fixed overheads are included in the stock valuations, and this can result in the amount of fixed overhead charged as an expense being different from the amount of fixed overhead incurred during a period. The effect of including fixed overheads in the stock valuation is shown below:

	1 July–31 December 1984 Department A (£000)	1 July–31 December 1984 Department B (£000)	1 January–30 June 1985 Department A (£000)	1 January–30 June 1985 Department B (£000)
Fixed overheads brought forward in opening stock of finished goods[a]	36	112	72	96
Fixed overheads carried forward in closing stock of goods[b]	72	96	12	160
Profit increased by	36			64
Profit reduced by		16	60	
Net profit as per absorption costing profit and loss account	94	50	53	83
Profit prior to stock adjustment	58	66	113	19

Notes

[a] Stocks are valued at factory cost with an absorption costing system. The opening stock valuation for department A for the first six months is £60 000 based on a product cost of £20 per unit. Therefore opening stock comprises 3000 units. Fixed manufacturing overheads are charged to the product made in department A at £12 per unit. Consequently, the stock valuation includes £36 000 for fixed overheads. The same approach is used to calculate the fixed overheads included in the opening stock valuation for the second period and department B.

[b] Closing stock for department B (first period) = 6000 units (£120 000/£20). Fixed overheads included in closing stock valuation = £72 000 (6000 units × £12).

The same approach is used to calculate fixed overheads included in the remaining stock valuations.

Comments

During the first six months for department A, stocks are increasing so that the stock adjustment results in a reduction of the fixed overhead charge for the period of £36 000. Fixed manufacturing overheads of £132 000 have been incurred during the period. Therefore the total fixed manufacturing overhead charge for the period is £96 000. In the first period for department B stocks are declining and the stock adjustment will result in an additional £16 000 fixed manufacturing overheads being included in the stock valuation. Consequently, the fixed manufacturing overhead charge for the period is £320 000 (£304 000 + £16 000). When stocks are increasing, the stock adjustment will have a favourable impact on profits (department A, period 1), and when stocks are declining, the stock adjustment will have an adverse impact on profits (department B, period 1).

In the second period stocks decline in department A and the stock adjustment will have an adverse impact on profits, whereas in department B stocks increase and this has a favourable impact on profit. When the two periods are compared, the stock adjustment has an adverse impact on the profits of department A and a favourable impact on the profits of department B. With an absorption costing system, profit is a function of sales and stock movements, and these stock movements can have an adverse impact on profits even when sales are increasing.

(b) *Departmental profit and loss accounts (marginal costing basis)*

	1 July–31 December 1984 Department A (£000)	1 July–31 December 1984 Department B (£000)	1 January–30 June 1985 Department A (£000)	1 January–30 June 1985 Department B (£000)
Sales revenue	300	750	375	675
Variable manufacturing costs:				
Direct material	52	114	30	132
Direct labour	26	76	15	88
Variable overheads	26	76	15	88
Variable factory cost of production	104	266	60	308
Add opening stock of finished goods	24	98	48	84
	128	364	108	392
Less closing stock of finished goods	48	84	8	140
Variable factory cost of goods sold	80	280	100	252
Total contribution	£220	£470	£275	£423
Less:				
Fixed factory overheads	132	304	132	304
Fixed administrative and selling costs	30	100	30	100
Net profit	58	66	113	19

Cost–volume–profit analysis

Solutions to Chapter 10 questions

Question summary

10.1–10.4   Discussion questions on CVP analysis.

10.5–10.10   Construction of break-even or profit–volume graphs. Question 10.6 requires the calculation of variable costs using the high–low method of analysing fixed and variable costs. Question 10.7 includes a change in sales mix, and 10.9 and 10.10 include an increase in fixed costs.

10.11–10.13   Introductory CVP analysis questions involving a non-graphical approach.

10.14   Muti-choice style question requiring the calculation of break-even point based on a planned sales mix.

10.15–10.17   Calculation of break-even points

based on different sales mix assumptions. Question 10.17 also involves a product abandonment decision.

10.18–10.21   Variety of CVP analysis questions involving a non-graphical approach. Question 10.20 introduces CVP analysis under conditions of uncertainty.

10.22–10.27   More advanced CVP analysis questions. Question 10.23 includes a discussion as to whether direct labour is a fixed or variable cost and an illustration as to how direct labour cost behaviour affects the break-even point. Question 10.27 focuses on changes in product mix.

Question 10.5   (a) See Figure Q10.5.

(b) See Chapter 10 for the answer to this question.

(c) The major limitations are:

    (i) Costs and revenue may only be linear within a certain output range.

    (ii) In practice, it is difficult to separate fixed and variable costs, and the calculations will represent an approximation.

    (iii) It is assumed that profits are calculated on a variable costing basis.

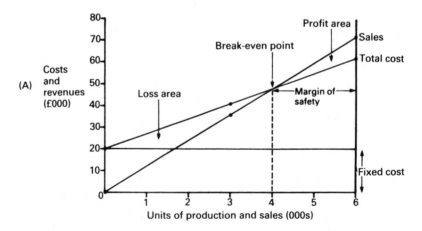

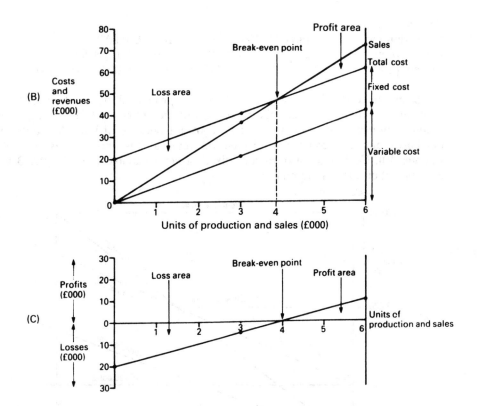

Figures Q10.5 (A) Break-even chart. (B) Contribution graph. (C) Profit–volume graph.

    (iv) Analysis assumes a single product is sold or a constant sales mix is maintained.
(d) The advantages are:
    (i) The information can be absorbed at a glance without the need for detailed figures.
    (ii) Essential features are emphasised.
    (iii) The graphical presentation can be easily understood by non-accountants.

Question 10.6

(a) This question requires the separtion of total cost into the fixed and variable elements using the high–low method.

	Low (£)	High (£)
Sales at £30 000 per unit	480 000 (16 × £30 000)	900 000 (30 × £30 000)
Profit	40 000	250 000
Total costs (difference)	440 000	650 000

An increase in output of 14 units results in an increase in total costs of £210 000. Assuming that fixed costs are constant for all activity levels the variable costs per unit is £15 000 (£210 000/14 units). At 30 units activity the variable costs will be £450 000 and monthly fixed costs are £200 000 (£650 000 − £450,000). Over a six-month period total fixed costs are £1 200 000.

    Break-even point = Fixed costs (£1,200,000)/unit contribution (£15,000)
                  = 80 units

See Figure Q10.6 for graph.
(b) Revised unit
    contribution   £10 000

Revised total
 contribution   £143 000 (130 units × £1.10 × £10 000)
Revised profit   £230 000 (£1 430 000 − £1 200 000 fixed costs)
Current profit   £750 000 (130 × £15 000 − £1 200 000 fixed costs)

The selling price should not be reduced because profits will decline by £520 000.

(c) Costs may not be variable and fixed throughout the entire production range. For example, unit variable cost may not be constant because of bulk discounts on purchases and increasing and decreasing returns (see 'Economists' model', Chapter 10). Costs may also be semi-fixed or semi-variable (see Chapter 3 for an explanation of these terms).

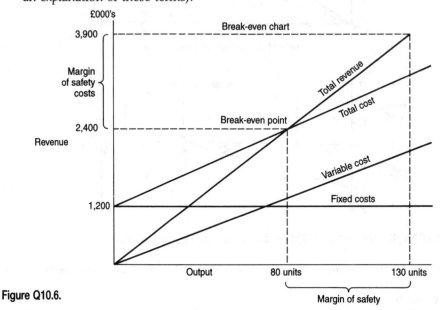

Figure Q10.6.

Question 10.7 (a) $\text{Break-even point} = \dfrac{\text{fixed costs (£1 212 000)}}{\text{average contribution per £ of sales (£0.505)}} = \text{£2 400 000}$

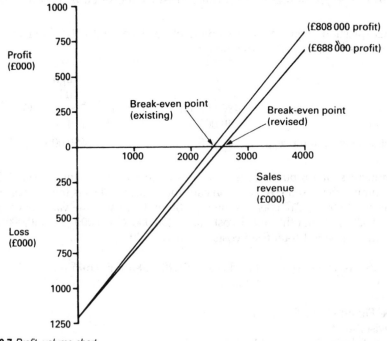

Figure Q10.7 *Profit–volume chart.*

Average contribution per £ of sales = $[0.7 \times (£1 - £0.45)] + [0.3 \times (£1 - £0.6)]$

(b) The graph (Figure Q10.7) is based on the following calculations:

Zero activity: loss = £1 212 000 (fixed costs)
£4 m existing sales: $(£4m \times £0.505) - £1\,212\,000 = £808\,000$ profit
£4 m revised sales: $(£4m \times £0.475) - £1\,212\,000 = £688\,000$ profit
Existing break-even point: £2 400 000
Revised break-even point: £2 551 579 (£1 212 000/£0.475)
Revised contribution per £ of sales: $(0.5 \times £0.55) + (0.5 \times £0.40) = £0.475$

(c) $\dfrac{\text{Required contribution}}{\text{Contribution per £ of sales}} = \dfrac{£455\,000 + £700\,000}{£0.55} = £2\,100\,000$

(a) See Figures Q10.10(A) and Q10.10(B) for the break-even charts.

Question 10.10

(b) Both charts indicate that each product has three break-even points. With the Standard quality, profits are earned on sales from 80 000 to 99 999 units and above 140 000 units; whereas with the De Luxe quality, profits are earned on sales from 71 429 − 99 999 units and above 114 286 units. The charts therefore provide guidance regarding the level of sales at which to aim.

(c) *Expected unit sales*
Standard: $(172\,000 \times 0.1) + (160\,000 \times 0.7) + (148\,000 \times 0.2) = 158\,800$
De Luxe: $(195\,500 \times 0.3) + (156\,500 \times 0.5) + (109\,500 \times 0.2) = 158\,800$

Expected profits

	Standard (£)	De Luxe (£)
Total contribution	397 000 (158 800 × £2.50)	555 800 (158 800 × £3.50)
Fixed costs	350 000	400 000
Profit	47 000	155 800

Margin of safety

Standard: expected sales volume (158 800) − break-even point (140 000)
= 18 800 units
De Luxe: expected sales volume (158 800) − break-even point (114 286)
= 44 514 units

(d) The profit probability distributions for the products are:

	Standard			De Luxe	
Demand	probability	Profits (£)	Demand	Probability	Profits/(loss) (£)
172 000	0.1	80 000	195 500	0.3	284 250
160 000	0.7	50 000	156 500	0.5	147 750
148 000	0.2	20 000	109 500	0.2	(16 750)

The De Luxe model has the higher expected profit, but is also more risky than the Standard product. There is a 0.2 probability that the De Luxe model will make a loss, whereas there is a zero probability that the Standard product will make a loss. The decision as to which product to produce will depend upon management's attitude towards risk and the future profitability from its other products. If the company is currently making a loss it may be inappropriate to choose the product that could make a loss. On the other hand, the rewards from the De Luxe model are much higher, and, if the company can survive if the worst outcome occurs, there is a strong argument for producing the De Luxe product.

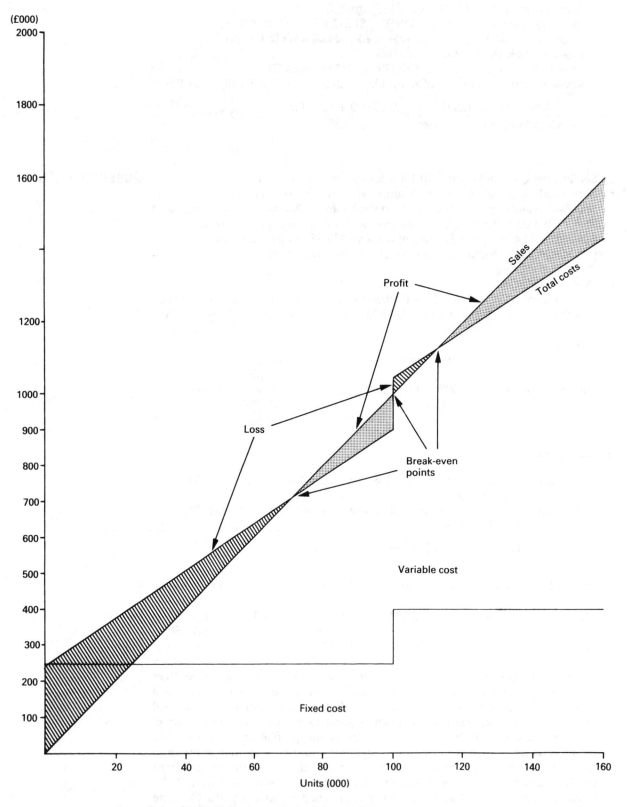

Figure Q10.10 *(A) Break-even chart – Deluxe quality.*

COST–VOLUME–PROFIT ANALYSIS

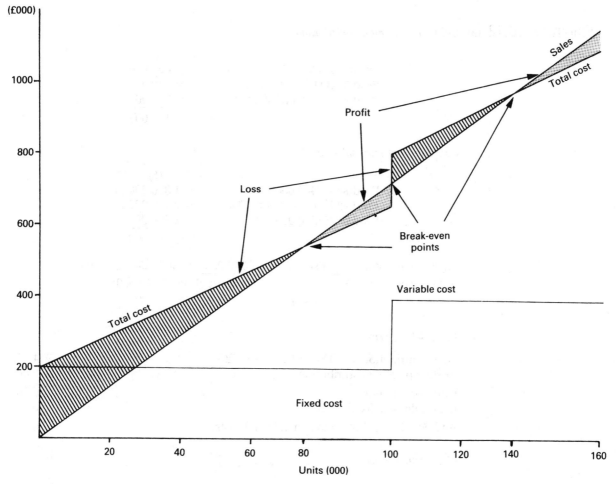

Figure Q10.10 *(B) Break-even chart – standard quality.*

(a)

Question 10.11

With promotion

Unit variable cost	=	£1.54 (55% × £2.80)
Promotional selling price	=	£2.24 (80% × £2.80)
Promotional contribution per unit	=	£0.70
Contribution for 4 week promotion period	=	£16 800 (6000 × 4 weeks × £0.70)
Less incremental fixed costs	=	£5 400
		£11 400

Without promotion

Normal contribution per unit	=	£1.26 (£2.80 × 45%)
Contribution for 4 week period	=	£12 096 (£1.26 × 2400 × 4 weeks)

Therefore the promotion results in a reduction in profits of £696.

(b)

Required contribution	=	£17 496 (£12 096 + £5400 fixed costs)
Required sales volume in units	=	24 994 (£17 496/£0.70 unit contribution)
Required weekly sales volume	=	6249 units (24 994/4 weeks)
Sales multiplier required	=	2.6 (6249/2400)

(c) Other factors to be considered are:
1. The effect of the promotion on sales after the promotion period.
2. Impact of the promotion on sales of other products during and after the promotion.

Question 10.12 (a) *Calculation of total contribution*

	(£)
Product A (460 000 × £1.80)	= 828 000
Product B (1 000 000 × £0.78)	= 780 000
Product C (380 000 × £1.40)	= 532 000
	2 140 000

Calculation of total sales revenue

	(£)
Product A (460 000 × £3)	= 1 380 000
Product B (1 000 000 × £2.45)	= 2 450 000
Product C (380 000 × £4)	= 1 520 000
	5 350 000

$$\text{Break-even point (sales revenue basis)} = \frac{\text{fixed costs (£1 710 000)} \times \text{total sales (£5 350 000)}}{\text{total contribution (2 140 000)}}$$

$$= £4\ 275\ 000$$

(b) *£2.75 selling price*

Total contribution 590 000 × (£2.75 − £1.20)	914 500
Existing planned contribution	828 000
Extra contribution	86 500
Less additional fixed costs	60 000
Additional contribution to general fixed costs	26 500

£2.55 selling price

	(£)
Total contribution 650 000 × (£2.55 − £1.20)	877 500
Existing planned contribution	828 000
Extra contribution	49 500
Less additional fixed costs	60 000
Contribution to general fixed costs	(10 500)

It is worthwhile incurring the expenditure on advertising and sales promotion at a selling price of £2.75.

(c) Required contribution = existing contribution (£828 000)
+ additional fixed costs (£60 000)
= £888 000

The required sales volume at a selling price of £2.75 that will generate a total contribution of £888 000 is 572 903 units (£888 000/£1.55 unit contribution).

(d) See 'Margin of safety' in Chapter 10 for the answer to this question. At the existing selling price for product A, the margin of safety for Z Ltd is £1 075 000 (£5 350 000 sales revenue − £4 275 000 break-even point) of sales revenue. This is 20.1% of the current level of sales. If Z Ltd incurs the advertising and promotion expenditure and reduces the selling price to £2.75 for product A, the break-even point will increase to £4 446 000 and total sales revenue will increase to £5 593 000. This will result in a margin of safety of £1 147 000 or 20.5% of sales.

Question 10.14

	Product X	Product Y	Total
Unit contribution	(£4)	(£5)	
Sales (units)	8 000	2 000	
Total contribution	£32 000	£10 000	£42 000
Total sales revenue	£96 000	£16 000	£112 000

Average contribution per unit sold = £42 000/10 000 units = £4.20
Average selling price   = £112 000/10 000 units = £11.20
Break-even point (units) = Fixed costs/average contribution per unit
                         = £27 300/£4.20
                         = 6500 units
Break-even point (sales revenue) = 6500 units × average selling price of
                         £11.20
                         = £72 800

Question 10.15

Break-even point	$\dfrac{\text{fixed costs}}{\text{contribution per unit}}$
Product X	25 000 units (£100 000/£4)
Product Y	25 000 units (£200 000/£8)
Company as a whole	57 692 units (£300 000/£5.20[a])

Note

[a]Average contribution per unit $= \dfrac{(70\ 000 \times £4) + (30\ 000 \times £8)}{100\ 000\ \text{units}}$

            $= £5.20$

The sum of the product break-even points is less than the break-even point for the company as a whole. It is incorrect to add the product break-even points because the sales mix will be different from the planned sales mix. The sum of the product break-even points assumes a sales mix of 50% to X and 50% to Y. The break-even point for the company as a whole assumes a planned sales mix of 70% to X and 30% to Y. CVP analysis will yield correct results only if the planned sales mix is equal to the actual sales mix.

(a) (i)

Question 10.17

Products	1	2	3	Total
1. Unit contribution	£1.31	£0.63	£1.87	
2. Specific fixed costs per unit	£0.49	£0.35	£0.62	
3. General fixed costs per unit	£0.46	£0.46	£0.46	
4. Sales volume (000s units)	98.2	42.1	111.8	252.1
5. Total contribution (1 × 4)	£128.642	£26.523	£209.066	£364.231
6. Total specific fixed costs (2 × 4)	£48.118	£14.735	£69.316	£132.169
7. Total general fixed costs (3 × 4)	£45.172	£19.366	£51.428	£115.966
8. Unit selling price	£2.92	£1.35	£2.83	
9. Total sales revenue (8 × 4)	£286.744	£56.835	£316.394	£659.973

Average contribution per unit = Total contribution (£364.231)/sales volume
                                 (252.1)
                                 = £1.4448
Average selling price per unit = Total sales revenue (£659.973)/sales
                                 volume (252.1)
                                 = £2.6179

Break-even point (units) $= \dfrac{\text{Total fixed costs}}{\text{Average contribution per unit}}$

                                 = (£132.169 + £115.966)/£1.4448
                                 = 171.743 units
Break-even point (sales value) = 171.743 units × average selling price
                                 (£2.6179)
                                 = £449.606

Alternatively, the break-even point (sales value) can be calculated using the following formula:

$$\text{Break-even point} = \frac{\text{Fixed costs } (132.169 + £115.966)}{\text{Total contribution } (£364.231)} \times \text{Total sales } (£659.973)$$

$$= £449.606$$

It is assumed that the question requires the calculation of the break-even point to cover both general and specific fixed costs. An alternative answer would have been to present details ot the break-even point to cover only specific fixed costs.

(ii) The planned sales mix for Product 2 that was used to calculate the break-even point in (i) is 42.1/252.1 Therefore the number of units of Product 2 at the break-even point is:

$$42.1/252.1 \times 171\ 743 \text{ units} = 28\ 681$$

(b) At the forecast sales volume the profit/contributions are as follows:

	(£000s)
Contributions to all fixed costs	26.523
Less specific fixed costs	14.735
Contribution to general fixed costs	11.788
Less share of general fixed costs	19.366
Net loss	7.578

Product 2 provides a contribution of £11 788 towards general fixed costs and, unless savings in general fixed costs in excess of £11 788 can be made if Product 2 is abandoned, it is still viable to produce Product 2. If the company ceases production of Product 2 it will lose a contribution of £11 788 and total profits will decline by £11 788. The company should investigate whether a greater contribution than £11 788 can be generated from the resources. If this is not possible the company should continue production of Product 2.

Question 10.19 (a) *Analysis of semi-variable costs*[a]

$$\text{Method A: variable element} = \frac{\text{increase in costs}}{\text{increase in activity}} = \frac{£10\ 000}{100\ 000\ \text{copies}}$$

$$= £0.10 \text{ per copy}$$

fixed element = total semi-variable cost (£55 000) − variable cost (£35 000) at an activity level of 350 000 copies

Therefore   fixed element = £20 000

$$\text{Method B: variable element} = \frac{\text{increase in costs}}{\text{increase in activity}} = \frac{£5000}{100\ 000\ \text{copies}}$$

$$= £0.05 \text{ per copy}$$

fixed element = total semi-variable cost (£47 500) − variable costs (£17 500) at an activity level of 350 000 copies

Therefore   fixed element = £30 000

Note
[a]The analysis is based on a comparison of total costs and activity levels at 350 000 and 450 000 copies per year.

Contribution per copy of new magazine

	Method A	Method B
	(£)	(£)
Selling price	1.00	1.00
Variable cost (given)	(0.55)	(0.50)
Variable element of semi-variable cost	(0.10)	(0.05)

	Lost contribution from existing magazine	(0.05)	(0.05)
	Contribution	0.30	0.40

Calculation of net increase in company profits

	Method A			Method B		
Copies sold	500 000	400 000	600 000	500 000	400 000	600 000
Contribution per copy	30 p	30 p	30 p	40 p	40 p	40 p
Total contribution	£150 000	£120 000	£180 000	£200 000	£160 000	£240 000
Fixed costs[a]	£100 000	£100 000	£100 000	£150 000	£150 000	£150 000
Net increase in profit	£50 000	£20 000	£80 000	£50 000	£10 000	£90 000

Note

[a]Method A = specific fixed costs (£80 000) + semi-variable element (£20 000)
$\qquad$ = £100 000

$\quad$ Method B = specific fixed costs (£120 000) + semi-variable element (£30 000)
$\qquad$ = £150 000

(b) $$\text{Break-even point} = \frac{\text{fixed costs}}{\text{contributlon per unit}}$$

$\qquad$ Method A = £100 000/0.30 = 333 333 copies
$\qquad$ Method B = £150 000/0.40 = 375 000 copies

The margin of safety is the difference between the anticipated sales and the break-even point sales:

$\qquad$ Method A = 500 000 − 333 333 = 166 667 copies
$\qquad$ Method B = 500 000 − 375 000 = 125 000 copies

(c) Method B has a higher break-even point and a higher contribution per copy sold. This implies that profits from Method B are more vulnerable to a decline in sales volume. However, higher profits are obtained with Method B when sales are high (see 600 000 copies in (B)).

$\quad$ The break-even point from the sale of the existing magazine is 160 000 copies (£80 000/£0.50) and the current level of monthly sales is 220 000 copies. Therefore sales can drop by 60 000 copies before break-even point is reached. For every 10 copies sold of the new publication, sales of the existing publication will be reduced by one copy. Consequently, if more than 600 000 copies of the new publication are sold, the existing magazine will make a loss. If sales of the new magazine are expected to consistently exceed 600 000 copies then the viability of the existing magazine must be questioned.

(a) (i) The opportunity costs of producing cassettes are the salary forgone of £1000 per month and the rental forgone of £400 per month. **Question 10.20**
$\quad$ (ii) The consultant's fees and development costs represent sunk costs.
(b) The following information can be obtained from the report.

	£10 selling price	£9 selling price
Sales quantity	7500–10 000 units	12 000–18 000 units
Fixed costs[a]	£13 525	£17 525
Profit at maximum sales[b]	£3975	£4975
Profit/(loss) at minimum sales[c]	(£400)	(£2525)
Break-even point[d]	7729 units	14 020 units
Margin of safety:		
$\quad$ Below maximum	2271 units	3980 units
$\quad$ Above minimum	229 units	2020 units

Notes
[a]Fixed production cost + £1400 opportunity cost

^{b}(10 000 units × £1.75 contribution) − £13 525 fixed costs = £3975 profit
(18 000 units × £1.25 contribution) − £17 525 fixed costs = £4975 profit
^{c}(7 500 units × £1.75 contribution) − £13 525 fixed costs = £400 loss
(12 000 units × £1.25 contribution) − £17 525 fixed costs = £2525 loss
^{d}Fixed costs/contribution per unit

Conclusions
  (i) The £10 selling price is less risky than the £9 selling price. With the £10 selling price, the maximum loss is lower and the break-even point is only 3% above minimum sales (compared with 17% for a £9 selling price).
 (ii) The £9 selling price will yield the higher profits if maximum sales quantity is achieved.
(iii) In order to earn £3975 profits at a £9 selling price, we must sell 17 200 units (required contribution of 17 525 fixed costs plus £3975 divided by a contribution per unit of £1.25).

Additional information required
  (i) Details of capital employed for each selling price.
 (ii) Details of additional finance required to finance the working capital and the relevant interest cost so as to determine the cost of financing the working capital.
(iii) Estimated probability of units sold at different selling prices.
(iv) How long will the project remain viable?
 (v) Details of range of possible costs. Are the cost figures given in the question certain?

Question 10.22 (a) *Impact of stitching elimination*
Loss of contribution from 10% sales reduction

(£300 000 × 10% × £4.50)	£135 000
Productlon cost reduction (270 000 × £0.60)	£162 000
Net gain from the stitching elimination	£27 000

Note
Contribution per unit − Fixed cost per unit (£1.50) = Net profit per unit (£3). Therefore contribution per unit = £4.50.

Use of plastic eyes
The reduction in sales volume arising from the stitching elimination also applies to the evaluation of the proposals for the change in type of eye and change in filling.
Glass eyes required for production = £540 000 (270 000 × 2)

Input required to allow for 5% input losses (540 000/0.95 × £0.20) =	£113 684
Plastic eyes required to allow for 10% input losses	
(540 000/0.90 × £0.15) =	£90 000
Net saving from plastic eyes	£23 684

Use of scrap fabric for filling

Cost of synthetic filling (270 000/2000 × £80)	£10 800
Additional production cost of scrap fabric (270,000 × £0.05)	£13 500
Net increase in cost from use of scrap fabric	£2 700

The overall net increase in annual net profit arising from the implementation of the three proposals is £47 984 − (£27 000 + £23 684 − £2700)
(b) Additional contribution from all three changes

(£162 000 + £23 684 − £2700)/ 270 000 =	£0.678
Existing contribution	£4.50
Revised contribution per unit	£5.178

Number of toys required to give the same contribution prior to the changes:
($£4.50 \times 300\,000$)/£5.178 = 260 718 toys
Therefore the reduction in sales required to leave net profit unchanged
= (300 000 − 260 718)/300 000
= 13.1%

(c) The report should indicate that answers to the following questions should be obtained before a final decision is taken:
  (i) How accurate is the estimate of demand? Demand is predicted to fall by 10% but the answer to (b) indicates that if demand falls by more than 13%, profit will be lower if the changes are implemented.
  (ii) Have all alternative courses of action been considered? For example, would a price reduction, or advertising and a sales promotion, stimulate demand and profits?
  (iii) Will the change to using scrap fabric result in a loss of revenues from the sale of scrap?
  (iv) Will the elimination of stitching result in redundancy payments and possible industrial action?
  (v) Consideration should be given to eliminating stitching and using plastic eyes but not using scrap fabric for filling.

Question 10.25

(a) *Budgeted ROCE*

	Sales (£000)	Gross profit (£000)
Accommodation	1350 (45%)	945 (70%)
Restaurant	1050 (35%)	210 (20%)
Bar	600 (20%)	180 (30%)
	3000	1335
Less fixed costs		565
Profit before tax		770

ROCE 770/7000 × 100 = 11%

(b) (i) Required additional profits = £280 000 (4% × £7 million)
Contribution per two-night holiday:

		Sales (£)	Gross profit % margin (£)	Contribution (£)
Accommodation	(2 × £25)	50	70	35
Restaurant	(40 % × £50)	20	20	4
Bar	(20% × £50)	10	30	3
				42

Number of holidays required to provide a contribution of £280 000 = 6667
(£280 000/42)
Number of holidays per week in three off-peak quarters = 171 (6667/39)

	(£000)
(ii) Required additional contribution	280

Contribution arising from increases in selling prices from:

Restaurant (10% × £1 050 000)	105	
Bar (5% × £600 000)	30	135
Required additional contribution from accommodation		145

Percentage required increase in accommodation prices = 145/1350 × 100
= 10.74%

To achieve the desired increase in ROCE, accommodation prices would have to increase by 10.74%. It is assumed that demand would be unaffected by a price increase of this magnitude.

(c) The major problems arising are:
    (i) *Two-flight cheap holidays*
        1. Avoiding an increase in fixed costs. For 9 months, the proposal would require 171 additional customers staying at the hotel each week. Will this increased demand cause an increase in fixed costs (e.g. reception and maintenance staff)?
        2. The calculations in (a) assume that variable costs vary with sales revenue rather than the number of customers. It is assumed that the gross margin percentage will be the same on cheaper holidays. This implies that the variable costs as a percentage of sales revenue will be reduced. It is therefore important that the assumptions made in (a) regarding variable costs being a function of sales revenue are appropriate. An alternative assumption, such as variable costs being a function of the number of guest days, would result in a different answer.
        3. Will the introduction of cheap holidays affect the sales volume relating to normal business?
    (ii) *Increasing prices*
        1. An increase in selling prices may lead to a reduction in demand.
        2. With this proposal, it is also assumed that variable costs are a function of sales revenue. If variable costs per guest night were to remain unchanged, the gross profit percentage margin would increase if prices were increased.
        3. There is a need to obtain more information before increasing prices. For example, when were the prices last increased, how does the price increase compare with current levels of inflation, how do the hotel prices compare with competitors' prices?

Recommendation
The assumptions in (a) regarding the percentage reduction in variable costs and no increase in fixed costs are questionable. Also, a large number of holidays would need to be sold in order to achieve the target ROCE. In contrast, a modest price increase of 10% seems possible without adversely affecting demand. On the basis of the information given, it is recommended that the second alternative be chosen.

Question 10.26 (a)

	Estimated variable cost per unit	
	Normal materials	Cheaper-grade materials
	(£)	(£)
Direct material	36.00	31.25
Direct labour	10.50	10.50
Variable overheads	10.50	10.50
	57.00	52.25
Wastage (5/95 × £52.25)		2.75
	57.00	55.00

Contribution from using normal grade of materials

Selling price (£)	80	84	88	90	92	96	100
Variable cost (£)	57	57	57	57	57	57	57
Unit contribution (£)	23	27	31	33	35	39	43
Demand (000)	25	23	21	20	19	17	15
Contribution to general fixed costs (£000)	575	621	651	660	665	663	645

Contribution from using cheaper grade of materials

Selling price (£)	80	84	88	90	92	96	100
Variable cost	55	55	55	55	55	55	55
Unit contribution	25	29	33	35	37	41	45
Demand (000)	25	23	21	20	19	17	15

Contribution to specific fixed costs (£000)	625	667	693	700	703	697	675
Specific fixed costs (£000)	30	30	30	30	30	30	30
Contribution to general fixed costs (£000)	595	637	663	670	673	667	645

The selling price that maximizes profit is £92 and the optimum output is 19 000 units. For all levels of demand (other than 15 000 units), profits are higher for the cheaper-grade material. At 15 000 units, profits are identical for both grades of materials.

If the reject rate for the cheaper grade of materials increased from 5% to 6% then at the optimum output level higher profits would be earned from using the normal grade of materials. Fixed inspection costs can increase by 10%, and profits will still be higher with the cheaper-grade materials for all output levels other than 15 000 units. As long as demand is in excess of 15 000 units (£30 000 inspection costs/£2 variable cost saving), it is preferable to use the cheaper-grade materials. Profits are not very sensitive to selling prices within the range £90–£96.

(b) Total revenues and total costs are required to construct a cost–volume–profit graph (Figure Q10.26).

Demand (000)	25	23	21	20	19	17	15
Total revenue (£000)	2000	1932	1848	1800	1748	1632	1500
Total variable cost (£000) (normal grade)	1425	1311	1197	1140	1083	969	855
Total variable cost plus £30 000 inspection cost (cheaper grade)	1405	1295	1185	1130	1075	965	855

The above costs and revenues are plotted on the CVP diagram, and optimum output is determined at the point where the difference between the total cost and revenue line is the greatest. This occurs at an output level of 19 000 units. The selling price with a demand of 19 000 units is £92.

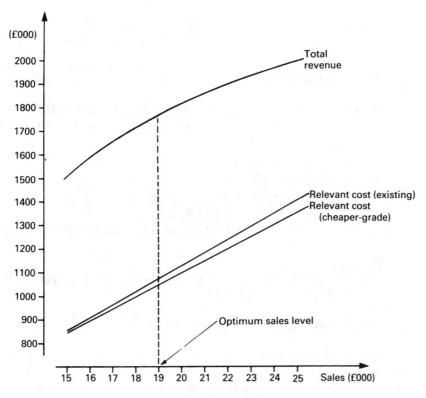

Figure Q10.26

Question 10.27 (a)

| | Manual production | | Computer-aided | |
	Thingone (£)	Thingtwo (£)	Thingone (£)	Thingtwo (£)
Selling price	20	50	20.00	50.00
Variable production costs	(15)	(31)	(12.75)	(26.35)
Bad debts[a]	—	(2)	—	(2.00)
Finance cost[b]		(3)	—	(3.00)
Contribution	5	14	7.25	18.65
Fixed costs per month	£31 500		£43 500	

Notes
[a] 4% of selling price
[b] 2% × £50 × 3 months

(i) *Thingone only is sold*
Manual process break-even point = 6300 units (£31 500/£5)
                 = £126 000 sales revenue
Computer-aided break-even point = 6000 units (£43 500/£7.25)
                 = £120 000 sales revenue

Point of indifference:
Let x = point of indifference
Then indifference point is where:

$$5x - 31\ 500 = 7.25x - 43\ 500$$
$$= 5333.33 \text{ units}$$
$$= £106\ 667 \text{ sales revenue}$$

(ii) *Sales of Thingone and Thingtwo in the ratio 4 : 1*
Manual process:

average contribution per unit $= \dfrac{(4 \times £5) + (1 \times £14)}{5} = £6.80$

break-even point   = 4632.35 units (£31 500/£6.80)
                 = £120 441 sales revenue (4632.35 × £26 (*W1*))

Computer-aided process:
average contribution per unit $= \dfrac{(4 \times £7.25) + (1 \times £18.65)}{5} = £9.53$

break-even point   = 4564.53 units (£43 500/£9.53)
                 = £118 678 sales revenue (4564.53 × £26 (*W1*))

Indifferent point:
Let x = point of indifference
Then indifference point is where:

$$6.80x - 31\ 500 = 9.53x - 43\ 500$$
$$= 4395.60 \text{ units}$$
$$= £114\ 286 \text{ sales revenue} (4395.60 \times £26\ (W1))$$

Workings
(W1) Break-even point (sales revenue) = break-even point in units × average
     selling price per unit sold

Therefore, average sales revenue per unit $= \dfrac{(4 \times £20) + (1 \times £50)}{5} = £26$

(b) If Thingone alone is sold, budgeted sales are 4000 units, and break-even sales
are 6000 units (computer-aided process) and 6300 units (manual process). Hence
there is little point producing Thingone on its own. Even if the two products are
substitutes, total budgeted sales are 6000 units, and Thingone is still not worth

selling on its own. Only if sales are limited to £180 000 (budgeted sales revenue) is Thingone worth selling on its own. However, the assumption that the products are perfect substitutes and £180 000 sales can be generated is likely to be over-optimistic. In other words, the single-product policy is very risky.

Assuming that Thingone and Thingtwo are sold in the ratio of 4:1, the break-even point is 4565 units using the computer-aided process. This consists of a sales mix of 3652 units of Thingone and 913 units of Thingtwo, representing individual margins of safety of 348 units and 1087 units when compared with the original budget. Launching both products is clearly the most profitable alternative.

It should be noted that the budgeted sales mix is in the ratio of 2:1, and this gives an average contribution per unit of £8 (manual process) and £11.05 (computer-aided process). The break-even point based on this sales mix is 3937 units for both the manual and computer-aided process, consisting of 2625 units of Thingone and 1312 units of Thingtwo. This represents a margin of safety of 1375 units of Thingone (34%) and 688 units of Thingtwo (34%). It is obviously better to sell Thingtwo in preference to Thingone. It is recommended that both products be sold and the computer-aided process be adopted.

(c) For the answer to this question see 'Decision-relevant costs for pricing decisions' and 'Choosing a pricing policy' in Chapter 13. In particular, the answer should stress the need to obtain demand estimates for different selling prices and cost estimates for various demand levels. The optimal *short-run* price is where profits are maximized. However, the final price selected should aim to maximize *long-run* profits and the answer should include a discussion of relevant pricing policies such as price skimming and pricing penetration policies. Competitors' reactions to different selling prices should also be considered.

Before demand estimates are made, market research should be undertaken to find customers' reaction to the new product. In addition, research should be undertaken to see whether a similar product is being developed or sold by other firms. This information might be obtained from trade magazines, market research or the company's sales staff. If a similar product is currently being sold, a decision must be made whether to compete on price or quality. The degree of interdependence of new and existing products must also be considered, and any lost sales from existing products should be included in the analysis. It may be necessary to differentiate the new product from existing products.

Measuring costs and benefits for decision-making

Solutions to Chapter 11 questions

Question summary

Questions 11.16–11.25 are the most difficult, and are more appropriate for a second year course. Questions 11.21 and 11.22 relate to pricing decisions, and can be assigned to Chapter 13. The questions are summarized as follows:

11.1   Make or buy decision.

11.2   Determining minimum short-term acceptable selling price.

11.3–11.4   Comparing relevant costs with a proposed pricing quotation. You may prefer to answer these questions when you have completed Chapter 13.

11.5   Decision on which of two mutually exclusive contracts to accept.

11.6   Decision on whether a project involving sunk and opportunity costs should be continued.

11.7–11.8   These questions involve deleting a segment or product abandonment decisions.

11.9   A recommendation whether to launch a new product.

11.10–11.13   Determining the optimum use of scarce capacity. Question 11.13 also involves a make or buy decision where scarce capacity exists.

11.14   Decision on whether to undertake an advertising campaign.

11.15   Limiting/Key factors and a decision on whether it is profitable to expand output by overtime.

11.16   Identification of limiting factors and allocation of scarce capacity where several production constraints exist.

11.17–11.20   More difficult questions requiring the allocation of scarce capacity to determine the optimum production programme. Questions 11.18 and 11.19 are the most difficult. Question 11.20 includes a discussion of shadow prices. You may prefer to defer this question until Chapter 25 has been completed.

11.21, 11.22   Calculation of relevant costs for pricing decisions. You may prefer to answer these questions after Chapter 13 has been completed.

11.23, 11.24   Deleting a segment. Question 11.23 (part b) requires a knowledge of learning curves.

11.25   Decison on whether to subcontract an appliance repair service or do own maintenance.

Question 11.1 (a)

	(£)
Purchase price of component from supplier	50
Additional cost of manufacturing (variable cost only)	34
Saving if component manufactured	16

The component should be manufactured provided the following assumptions are correct:

(i) Direct labour represents the *additional* labour cost of producing the component.

(ii) The company will not incur any additional fixed overheads if the component is manufactured.

(iii) There are no scarce resources. Therefore the manufacture of the component will not restrict the production of other more profitable products.

(b) (i) Additional fixed costs of £56 000 will be incurred, but there will be a saving in purchasing costs of £16 per unit produced. The break-even point is 3500 units (fixed costs of £56 000/£16 per unit saving). If the quantity of components manufactured per year is less than 3500 units then it will be cheaper to purchase from the outside supplier.

(ii) The contribution per unit sold from the existing product is £40 and each unit produced uses 8 scarce labour hours. The contribution per labour hour is £5. Therefore if the component is manufactured, 4 scarce labour hours will be used, resulting in a lost contribution of £20. Hence the relevant cost of manufacturing the components is £54, consisting of £34 incremental cost plus a lost contribution of £20. The component should be purchased from the supplier.

(c) The book value of the equipment is a sunk cost and is not relevant to the decision whether the company should purchase or continue to manufacture the components. If we cease production now, the written-down value will be written off in a lump sum, whereas if we continue production, the written-down value will be written off over a period of years. Future cash outflows on the equipment will not be affected by the decision to purchase or continue to manufacture the components. For an illustration of the irrelevance of the written down value of assets for decision-making purposes see 'Replacement of equipment' in Chapter 11.

Question 11.4

(a)

Revised cost estimate (opportunity cost approach)

	(£)
Direct materials:	
3000 units of X at NRV	20 000
100 units of Y at replacement cost	13 000
Bought in items at estimated cost	12 000
Direct labour:	
Skilled[a] 2720 hours at 0.8 (£2.50) variable overheads	5 440
Wages of additional worker	1 200
Trainees variable overheads (1), 1250 hours at 0.8 (£1)	1 000
Curing press: rental forgone for one month at £500 per week	2 000
Subcontract work at estimated cost	20 000
Supervisory staff overtime	1 000
Estimating department: sunk cost	0
Administration overhead: apportioned fixed cost that is not a relevant cost	0
Relevant cost	75 640

Note

[a]It is assumed that variable overheads vary with productive hours and that additional variable overheads will be incurred if the contract is undertaken. Note that other labour costs not included in the above estimate will still be paid if the contract is not obtained.

From the information given, the contractor could submit a quotation for £100 000. Total company profits will increase if the quotation is accepted.

(b) (i) See 'Opportunity costs' in Chapter 3 for the answer to this question. The answer should stress that, where a course of action requires the use of scarce resources, it is necessary to incorporate the lost profits which will be forgone from using the scarce resources. If resources have no alternative use, only the *additional* cash outflows resulting from a course of action should be included in the relevant cost calculation.

(ii) See 'Variance analysis and the opportunity cost of scarce resources' in Chapter 20 for the answer to this question.

Question 11.5 (a)

	North East (£)	South coast (£)
Material X from stock (1)	19 440	
Material Y from stock (2)		49 600
Firm orders of material X (3)	27 360	
Material X not yet ordered (4)	60 000	
Material Z not yet ordered (5)		71 200
Labour (6)	86 000	110 000
Site manangement (7)	—	—
Staff accommodation and travel for site management (8)	6 800	5 600
Plant rental received (9)	(6 000)	—
Penalty clause (10)		28 000
	193 600	264 400
Contract price	288 000	352 000
Net benefit	94 400	87 600

(b) (i) If material X is not used on the North East contract the most beneficial use is to use it as a substitute material thus avoiding future purchases of £19 440 (0.9 × 21 600). Therefore by using the stock quantity of material X the company will have to spend £19 440 on the other materials.

(ii) Material Y is in common use and the company should not dispose of it. Using the materials on the South coast contract will mean that they will have to be replaced at a cost of £49 600 (£24 800 × 2). Therefore the future cash flow impact of taking on the contract is £49 600.

(iii) It is assumed that with firm orders for materials it is not possible to cancel the purchase. Therefore the cost will occur whatever future alternative is selected. The materials will be used as a substitute material if they are not used on the contract and therefore, based on the same reasoning as note 1 above, the relevant cost is the purchase price of the substitute material (0.9 × £30 400).

(iv) The material has not been ordered and the cost will only be incurred if the contract is undertaken. Therefore additional cash flows of £60 000 will be incurred if the company takes on the North East contract.

(v) The same principles apply here as were explained in point 4 and additional cash flows of £71 200 will be incurred only if the company takes on the South coast contract.

(vi) It is assumed that labour is an incremental cost and therefore relevant.

(vii) The site management function is performcd by staff at central headquarters. It is assumed that the total company costs in respect of site management will remain unchanged in the short term whatever contracts are taken on. Site management costs are therefore irrelevant.

(viii) The costs would be undertaken only if the contracts are undertaken. Therefore they are relevant costs.

(ix) If the North East contract is undertaken the company will be able to hire out surplus plant and obtain a £6000 cash inflow.

(x) If the South coast contract is undertaken the company will have to withdraw from the North East contract and incur a penalty cost of £28 000.

(xi) The headquarter costs will continue whichever alternative is selected and they are not relevant costs.

(xii) It is assumed that there will be no differential cash flows relating to notional interest. However, if the interest costs associated with the contract differ then they would be relevant and should be included in the analysis.

(xiii) Depreciation is a sunk cost and irrelevant for decision-making.

(a) (i)

	Product I (£000)	Product II (£000)	Product III (£000)	Total (£000)
Sales	2475	3948	1520	7943
Contribution	1170	1692	532	3394
Attributable fixed costs	(275)	(337)	(296)	(908)
General fixed costs^a	(520)	(829)	(319)	(1668)
	(795)	(1166)	(615)	(2576)
Profit	375	526	(83)	818
	= £1.6/unit	= £1.40/unit	= (£0.04/unit)	

Note
^{a}General fixed costs are allocated to products at 21% of total sales revenue (£1668/£7943)

(ii) If Product III is discontinued it is assumed that variable costs and attributable (i.e. specific) fixed costs are avoidable. It is assumed that general fixed costs are common and unavoidable to all products and will remain unchanged if Product III is discontinued. However, it is possible that some general fixed costs may be avoidable in the longer term. The revised profits if Product III is discontinued will be:

	(£000s)
Contribution of Products I and II (£1170 + £1692)	2862
Attributable fixed costs (£275 + £337)	(612)
General fixed costs	(1668)
Profit	582

Profits will decline by £236 000 (£818 − £582) if Product III is discontinued because A Ltd will no longer obtain a contribution of £236 000 (£532 − £296) towards general fixed costs.

(iii) Extra sales of 15 385 units (£80 000 additional fixed costs/£5.20 unit contribution) will be required to cover the additional advertising expenditure. It is assumed that existing fixed costs will remain unchanged.

(iv) The revised unit contribution will be £3.45 (£9.45 − £6).

$$\text{Required sales} = \frac{£1\,692\,000\ (\text{existing total contribution})}{£3.45\ \text{revised unit contribution}}$$

= 490 435 units (an increase of 30.4% over the budgeted sales of 376 000 units)

(b) The following factors will influence cost behaviour in response to changes in activity:

(i) The magnitude of the change in activity (more costs are likely to be affected when there is a large change in activity).

(ii) Type of expense (some expenses are directly variable with volume such as direct materials, whereas others are fixed or semi-fixed).

(iii) Management policy (some expenses are varied at the discretion of management, e.g. advertising).

(iv) The time period (in the long term, all costs can be changed in response to changes in activity whereas in the short term, some costs, e.g. salaries of supervisors, will remain unchanged).

Question 11.8 (a) Company gross profit % = 38% (£3268/£8600 × 100)

Therefore Division 5 gross profit % = 19%
Division 5 sales = £860 000 (10% × £8.6m)
Division 5 gross profit = £163 400 (19% × £860 000)
Division 5 contribution = £479 400 (£316 000 + £163 400)

The situation for the year ahead if the division were not sold would be as follows:

Contribution = £527 340 (£479 400 × 1.1)
Less avoidable fixed costs = £455 700 [£316 000 + (£156 000
− £38 000)] × 1.05
Add contribution from other divisions = £20 000
Expected profit £91 640

If Division 5 were sold, the capital sum would yield a return of £75 400. Therefore the decision on the basis of the above information should be not to sell Division 5.

(b) Other factors that should influence the decision include:
(i) The need to focus on a longer-term time horizon. A decision based solely on the year ahead is too short and ignores the long-term impact from selling Division 5.
(ii) The impact on the morale of the staff working in other divisions arising from the contraction of activities and the potential threat of redundancies.
(iii) Alternative use of the resources currently deployed in Division 5 instead of their current use.

(c) If Division 5 is sold, the capital sum would yield a return of £75 000, but a contribution of £20 000 is lost. Consequently, a profit of £55 000 is required. The required contribution is therefore £510 700 (£55 000 + £455 700) and the percentage increase required is 6.5% (£510 700/£479 400 − 100%).

Question 11.10 (a) (i) Product

	X		Y		Z		
	(£)	(£)	(£)	(£)	(£)	(£)	
Direct materials		50		120		90	
Variable overhead		12		7		16	
Direct labour:							
Department A	70		40		75		
Department B	24		18		30		
Department C	32	126	16	74	60	165	
Variable production cost		188		201		271	
Sales price		210		220		300	

				Total
				£
Unit contribution	22	19	29	
Total contribution	165 000	114 000	174 000	453 000
Fixed costs				300 000
Profit				153 000

(ii) Department B labour hours limitation:
Product X 30 000 hours (7500 × 4 hours)
Y 18 000 hours (6000 × 3 hours)
Z 30 000 (6000 × 5 hours)
78 000 hours

Products	X	Y	Z
Unit contribution	£22	£19	£29
Department B labour hours	4	3	5
Contribution per Department B hour	£5.50	£6.33	£5.80
Ranking	3	1	2

Maximum sales are 9000 units of X (7500 × 1.20), 7500 units of Y (6000 × 1.25) and 8000 of Z (6000 × 1.33). Using the above rankings the optimal product mix is:

Product	Units sold	Department B hours used	Contribution (£)
Y	7500	22 500	142 500
Z	8000	40 000	232 000
X	3875 (15 500/4)	15 500	85 250
		78 000	459 750
Less fixed costs			300 000
Profit			159 750

(iii) Factors to be considered which have not been taken into account in the above analysis include:
  1. The impact on customer goodwill. Some customers may buy all three products and they may choose to buy elsewhere if their supply of Product X is restricted. Also the company may permanently lose Product X customers if the supply is restricted.
  2. Competitors' reactions. If supply of Product X is restricted, competitors may exploit the situation by stressing that they are able to meet demand for Product X and look after their customers and provide a better service.
  3. Some of the fixed costs may be attributable to specific products and avoidable if output is reduced. When avoidable fixed costs are taken into account the product mix specified in (a) (ii) may not be the optimum mix.
(b) Linear programming should be used. This technique enables an objective function to be maximized (e.g. contribution) subject to meeting the requirements of more than one input constraint.

Question 11.11

(a)
The constraints on producing Part A are:

Line S = 6666 units (4000/0.6 hrs)
Line T = 9000 units (4500/0.5 hrs)
Material restriction = 8125 units (13 000/1.6 kg)
Therefore the constraint of Line S limits production to 6666 units

The constraints on producing Part B are:

Line S = 16 000 units (4000/0.25 hrs)
Line T = 8182 units (4500/0.55 hrs)
Material restriction = 8125 units (13 000/1.6 kg)
Maximum production of Part B is 8125 units

Maximum contributions for Parts A and B are:

	Part A (£)		Part B (£)	
Line S machine time	48	(0.6 hrs × £80)	20	(0.25 hrs × £80)
Line T machine time	50	(0.5 hrs × £100)	55	(0.55 hrs × £100)
Materials	20	(1.6 kg × £12.50)	20	(1.6 kg × £12.50)
Variable cost	118		95	
Selling price	145		115	
Unit contribution	27		20	
Maximum output	6666 units		8125 units	
Maximum contribution	£79 982		£162 500	

Therefore Part A should be produced since it yields the largest contribution.

(b) The company will earn a contribution of £179 982 but it cannot meet the maximum call off due to the limitations of Line S.

(c)

	Part A	Part B
Original selling price	145	115
10% reduction in selling price	14.50	11.50
Revised unit contribution	12.50 (£27 − £14.50)	8.50 (£20 − £11.50)
Output	6666 units	8125 units
Total contribution	£83 325	£69 062
Payment for unused machine hours	£70 020	£120 000
Revised contribution	£153 345	£189 062

Note

[a]The payment for unused machine hours is calculated as follows:

	Part A (£)	
Line S at £60 per hour	—	(Fully used)
Line T at £60 per hour	70 020	(4500 − [6666 × 0.5 hrs])
	70 020	

	Part B (£)	
Line S at £60 per hour	118 125	(4000 − [8125 × 0.25 hrs])
Line T at £60 per hour	1875	(4500 − [8125 × 0.55 hrs])
	120 000	

With the alternative pricing arrangement the company should produce Part B.

Question 11.14 (a)

Products	A	B	C	D	Total
Selling price per unit (£)	9.95	11.95	22.95	19.95	
Less variable costs (£)	6.50	7.80	16.50	13.95	
Contribution per unit (£)	3.45	4.15	6.45	6.00	
Machine hours per unit[a]	0.6	0.6	1.0	0.9	
Machine hours required (000 hrs):					
Budget 1	108	168	260	135	671
Budget 2	120	186	285	148.5	739.5
Additional buying in cost per unit (£)	2.40		3.50		
Additional buying in cost per machine hour (£)	4.00		3.50		

Note

[a]Machine hours per unit = variable overheads per unit/variable overhead rate per unit of £1. Existing production capacity is sufficient to meet the requirements of Budget 1, but there is a shortfall of 24 500 hours (739 500 − 715 000) for Budget 2. It is worthwhile buying in product A and product C, because the selling price is in excess of the buying in price and the contribution from the additional sales from Budget 2 is sufficient to cover the additional advertising cost (see workings shown below). It is preferable to meet the shortfall of 24 500 hours by purchasing product C, because the extra cost per machine hour is lower (£3.50 compared with £4 for product A). The extra cost of buying in the 24 500 machine hours is £85 750 (24 500 × £3.50).

The following calculation indicates that it is worthwhile undertaking the advertising campaign and selecting Budget 2:

Products	A	B	C	D	Total
Additional sales volume (000 units)	20	30	25	15	
Unit contribution (£)	3.45	4.15	6.45	6.00	
Additional contribution (£000)	69	124.5	161.25	90	444.75
Less extra buying-in cost (£000)					(85.75)
cost of advertising					(290.00)
Additional profit					69.00

(b) The figures in (a) are based on the following assumptions:
   (i) Fixed costs (other than advertising) will remain unchanged.
   (ii) Variable costs will increase directly in proportion to increases in production.
   (iii) Prices and efficiency will remain unchanged for all levels of output.
   (iv) Production capacity will be restricted to 715 000 hours.
   (v) The estimates of sales volume for each budget are sound estimates and the risk of not achieving these estimates is justified.
   The reasoning behind the advice given is based on the fact that the additional relevant revenues exceed the additional relevant costs and that costs are minimized by buying-in product C.

Question 11.16

(a) Maximum production of each product is as follows:

	Traditional		Modern	
Machine X hour limitation	6800	(1700/0.25)	11 333	(1700/0.15)
Machine Y hour limitation	9600	(1920/0.20)	8533	(1920/0.225)
Timber (m² limitation)	8500	(17 000/2)	8500	(17 000/2)
Maximum sales	7400		10 000	
Maximum possible production	6800		8500	

The contribution per unit of output is:

	Traditional		Modern	
	(£)		(£)	
Variable costs:				
Timber	5.00		5.00	
Machine X	6.25	(0.25 × £25)	3.75	(0.15 × £25)
Machine Y	6.00	(0.20 × £30)	6.75	(0.225 × £30)
	17.25		15.50	
Selling price	45.00		40.00	
Contribution	27.75		24.50	

Assuming that only one of the products can be sold the maximum contribution from the sales of each product is:

Traditional	£188 700 (6800 × £27.75)
Modern	£208 250 (8500 × £24.50)

The company should therefore sell 8500 units of the 'Modern' lampstand.
(b) The spare machine capacity assuming that 6800 units of the 'Traditional' lampstand or 8500 of the 'Modern' lampstand are produced is as follows:

	Machine X (Hours)	Machine Y (Hours)
Production of 6800 of Traditional	Nil [1700 − (6800 × 0.25)]	560 [1920 − (6800 × 0.20)]
Production of 8500 of Modern	425 [1700 − (8500 × 0.15)]	7.5 [1920 − (8500 × 0.225)]

The revised contributions are:

	Traditional (£)	Modern (£)
Original contribution	188 700	208 250
Sales from unused capacity of machine X	Nil	8 500 (425 × £20)
Sales from unused capacity of machine Y	16 800 (560 × £30)	225 (7.5 × £30)
	205 500	216 975

The above figures indicate that the 'Modern' lampstands should still be sold when an alternative sales outlet exists.

(c)

	Traditional		Modern		Total
Units produced and sold	4250		4250		
Timber (metres) used (2 metres per unit)	8500		8500		17 000
Machine X hours used	1062.5	(4250 × 0.25)	637.5	(4250 × 0.15)	1 700
Machine Y hours used	850	(4250 × 0.20)	956.25	(4250 × 0.225)	1 806.25
Contribution	£117 937.50	(4250 × £27.75)	£104,125	(4250 × £24.50)	£222 062.50
Contribution from machine Y spare capacity [(1920 − 1806.25) × £30]					£3 412.50
Total contribution					£225 475

(d) In order to overcome the capacity constraints the following alternative courses of action should be considered:
   (i) Hire addditional machinery to meet short-term demand and evaluate purchase of additional machinery if the shortage of capacity is expected to continue in the long term.
   (ii) Increase output per machine hour by more efficient operating or increasing machine speeds. However, additional costs and lost output might arise from machine breakdowns.
   (iii) Increase machine capacity by introducing additional shifts. This will lead to increased shift and overtime payments and may also result in machine break-downs arising from more intensive use of machinery.
   (iv) Sub-contract production but this will lead to increased costs and possibly lost sales arising from inferior quality products, late delivery etc.
   (v) Seek alternative supplies of timber since this is a limiting factor. Care should be taken to ensure that any additional purchase and delivery costs do not exceed the contribution from increased sales.

Question 11.17 (a) Existing capacity of direct labour:

		(£)
P	4560 kg at £1.96 per kg	8 937.60
Q	6960 kg at £1.30 per kg	9 048.00
R	3480 kg at £0.99 per kg	3 445.20
S	2300 kg at £1.70 per kg	3 910.00
		25 340.80
	5% increase to full capacity	1 267.04
	Direct labour cost at full capacity	26 607.84

If 2000 kg of product Q is purchased from an outside supplier then this will release direct labour by £2600 (2000 kg at £1.30 per kg). Consequently, £3867 capacity is available (£2600 plus extra capacity of £1267) for producing product P. Therefore output of P can be increased by 1973 kg (£3867/£1.96). The impact on profits will be:

	(£)
Additional contribution from P (1973 kg at £6.88)	13 574
Loss of contribution from Q (2000 kg at £3.536[a])	7072
Additional contribution	6502

EF should subcontract 2000 kg of Q and produce an extra 1973 kg of P.

Note
[a]Contribution = selling price (0.9 × £11.64) − variable cost (£6.94) = £3.536

(b)

	P	Q	R	S
	(£)	(£)	(£)	(£)
Proposed subcontract price (90% of selling price)	14.58	10.476	8.928	12.312
Variable cost	9.32	6.94	5.65	7.82
Loss of contribution	5.26	3.536	3.278	4.492

Direct labour released from subcontracting 2000 kg

Additional production (kg) from releasing direct labour

	P	Q	R	S
£3920 from P[a]	—	3015[e]	3959[f]	2305[g]
£2600 from Q[b]	1326[h]	—	2626	1529
£1980 from R[c]	1010	1523	—	1164
£3400 from S[d]	1734	2615	3434	—
Extra 5% of capacity (£1267)	646[i]	974	1280	745

Notes
[a]2000 × £1.96; [b]2000 × £1.30; [c]2000 × £0.99; [d]2000 × £1.70; [e]£3920/£1.30 per kg; [f]3920/£0.99; [g]£3920/£1.70; [h]£2600/£1.96; [i]£1267/£1.96.

	Extra contribution gained (£)			
	P	Q	R	S
Contribution per kg	6.88	4.70	4.27	5.86
2000 kg of P subcontracted	—	8228[a]	11 850[b]	7353[c]
2000 kg of Q subcontracted	6495[d]	—	9 607[e]	6253[f]
2000 kg of R subcontracted	4837[g]	5180[h]	—	4630[i]
2000 kg of S subcontracted	7390[j]	7884[k]	11 144[l]	—

Notes
[a](3015 + 974) × £4.70 − (2000 × £5.26 lost contribution)
[b](3959 + 1280) × £4.27 − (2000 × £5.26 lost contribution)
[c](2305 + 745) × £5.86 − (2000 × £5.26 lost contribution)
[d](1326 + 646) × £6.88 − (2000 × £3.536 lost contribution)
[e](2626 + 1280) × £4.27 − (2000 × £3.536 lost contribution)
[f](1529 + 745) × £5.86 − (2000 × £3.536 lost contribution)
[g](1010 + 646) × £6.88 − (2000 × £3.278 lost contribution)
[h](1523 + 974) × £4.70 − (2000 × £3.278 lost contribution)
[i](1164 + 745) × £5.86 − (2000 × £3.278 lost contribution)
[j](1734 + 646) × £6.88 − (2000 × £4.492 lost contribution)
[k](2615 + 974) × £4.70 − (2000 × £4.492 lost contribution)
[l](3434 + 1280) × £4.27 − (2000 × £4.492 lost contribution)

Recommendations:
The most profitable combination is to subcontract 2000 kg of P and replace this with 5239 kg (3959 + 1280) of R, thus increasing contribution by £11 850.

Question 11.20 (a) The relevant cost of producing the new product is the variable cost plus the lost contribution from selling the processing time to another manufacturer. It is assumed that it is more profitable to spend three days per week producing the established main products. The calculations of the variable overhead rates are:

	Department 4	Department 5
Normal hours (0.9 × 40 hrs × 50 weeks)	1800	1800
Fixed overhead rate per hour (£)	20 (36 000/1800)	28 (50 400/1800)
Total overhead rate per hour (£)	40	40
Variable overhead rate per hour (£)	20	12

The variable costs per hour are:

> Department 4: £60 (£40 power cost + £20 variable overhead)
> Department 5: £72 (£60 power cost + £12 variable overhead)

Note that labour costs are fixed.

If the new product is not developed, Department 4 should sell unused processing time at £70 per hour, but it is not profitable for Department 5 to sell processing time because hourly variable cost is in excess of the selling price. Therefore the relevant costs per processing hour are:

> Department 4: £70 (£60 variable cost + £10 lost contribution)
> Department 5: £72

We can now calculate the relevant cost of producing the new product:

	(£)
Direct material	10.00
Department 4 variable operating cost (0.75hrs × £70)	52.50
Department 5 variable operating cost (0.33 hrs × £72)	24.00
	86.50

The total *additional* contributions for various selling prices and demand levels are:

	(£)	(£)	(£)
Selling price	100	110	120
Unit contribution	13.50	23.50	33.50
Demand	1067[a]	1000	500
Total contribution	14 404	23 500	16 750

Note
[a]Maximum output in Department 4 is 1067 units [(16 weeks × 50 hrs)/0.75 hrs] and 2400 units in Department 5. Output is therefore restricted to 1067 units. Optimum output of the new product is 1000 units at a selling price of £110. An output of 1000 units will require 15 hours per week (20 units per week × 0.75 hrs) in Department 4 and 6.67 hours in Department 5. Department 4 should therefore sell 1 hour per week at £70 per hour, but it is not profitable for Department 5 to sell its spare capacity of 9.33 hours per week.

The weekly *additional* gain from this programme is £470 (20 units × £23.50 contribution). The overall weekly gain is calculated without including the lost contribution of £10 per hour for Department 4. Variable cost is £79 (£86.50 relevant cost less opportunity cost of 0.75 hrs at £10) and contribution is £31 per unit. The total week gain is £630 (20 units at £31 per week plus £10 from the sale of one hour). Without the new product, weekly contribution will be £160 (16 hrs × £10). Therefore there is an additional gain of £470 from introducing the new product.

(b) The shadow prices indicate that if an hour is lost from the existing optimum plan, contribution will decline by £76 for Department 4 and £27 for Department 5. The relevant hourly cost for a scarce resource is:

Variable cost per hour plus lost contribution per hour

Therefore the relevant cost of producing the new product is:

	(£)
Direct material	10
Department 4: 0.75 hrs × (£60 + £76)	102
Department 5: 0.33 hrs × (£72 + £27)	33
	145

The new product will not increase total contribution if the selling price is less than £145.

(c) The shadow price of a scarce resource represents the increase in total contribution that will be obtained if a scarce resource can be increased by 1 unit. Alternatively, the shadow price can be expressed as the loss in total contribution that will occur if the availability of a scarce resource is reduced by 1 unit. The opportunity cost of using a resource is the lost benefit that occurs from using it in the most profitable manner. Shadow prices represent the contribution that would be lost if one unit of a resource were removed from the optimal production programme. In other words, it represents the lost benefit from using it in the most profitable manner. Therefore shadow prices are equivalent to opportunity costs.

(a) <div style="text-align:center">Cost estimate</div> **Question 11.21**

	(£)
Direct materials and components:	
2000 units of A at £20 per unit[a]	40 000
200 units of B at £20 per unit[b]	4 000
Other material components	12 500
	56 500
Direct labour[c]	—
Overhead:	
Department P (200 hours at £30)[d]	6 000
Department Q (400 hours at £8)[e]	3 200
Estimating Department[f]	—
Planning Department[f]	—
	65 700

Notes

[a]It is assumed that using material A on the contract will result in the materials being replaced. Therefore additional (opportunity) costs to the company will be the replacement costs of the materials.

[b]The alternative uses of the materials are to sell them or to use them as substitute materials. The savings are greater when the materials are used as a substitute. Therefore the company will be worse off by £20 per unit of materials used on the contract. Hence the opportunity cost of material B is £20 per unit.

[c]The company appears to have a temporary excess supply of labour. The total labour cost will be the same whether or not the contract is undertaken. Therefore the opportunity cost is zero.

[d]Acceptance of the contract will result in the department losing the opportunity of charging out 200 hours at £30 per hour.

[e]The company will incur £3200 additional costs if the contract is undertaken.

[f]It is assumed that the company will not incur additional costs in the estimating and planning departments if the contract is undertaken. The costs already incurred by the estimating department on the contract are sunk costs. Therefore the opportunity cost is zero for both departments.

(b) The opportunity cost approach is a suitable approach for short-term decision-making. This approach ensures that alternative actions are only charged with the additional costs resulting from the action. Whenever the additional revenues are in excess of the relevant or opportunity costs for a particular course of action, a company will increase its total profits or reduce its total loss. However, in the long term a company must cover all its costs, not just the opportunity costs, if it is to be profitable. In the situation described in the question the opportunity cost approach is appropriate because the company has spare capacity. The opportunity cost of the contract is £65 700, whereas the cost as per the conventional pricing procedure used in the question is £85 500. If the latter cost is used as a basis of a price quotation then there is a danger that the company will lose the contract. As long as the contract price is in excess of the opportunity cost of £65 700, the company will increase its total profits.

The following problems are likely to be encountered:

(i) Fixed costs may be ignored and insufficient contribution may be generated to cover fixed costs (see Chapter 11 for an explanation of this).

(ii) Lack of understanding of opportunity costs and the difficulty in determining opportunity costs. This requires knowledge of alternative uses of resources, and this information might be difficult to obtain in practice.

(c) When a course of action requires the use of scarce resources, it is necessary to incorporate the lost profits which will be forgone from using scarce resources. Only by adopting such an approach can we ensure an optimal allocation of scarce resources. For a more detailed discussion and an illustration of this point see sections on 'Decision-making and the influence of limiting factors' and 'Make or buy decisions' in Chapter 11.

Question 11.23 (a) The question indicates that a choice should be made between the following three alternatives:

(i) Close department K immediately.

(ii) Operate department K for a further year at 10 000 units.

(iii) Operate department K for a further year at 20 000 units.

The *relevant* information is presented in the following schedule:

	Immediate closure (£)	10 000 units (£)	20 000 units (£)
Relevant cost savings and revenues:			
Sales of production	—	90 000	160 000
Material B:			
Saving[b]	18 000	9 000	—
Sale[b]	5 000	—	—
Sale of machine[e]	43 000	35 000	30 000
Total revenue/savings	66 000	134 000	190 000
Relevant costs:			
Labour: Training	—	20 000	20 000
Variable costs	—	30 000	60 000
Material A: Disposal fixed cost[a]	2 000	2 000	2 000
Disposal variable cost[a]	15 000	10 000	5 000
Material B: Purchase cost[b]	—	—	10 000
Variable overhead[f]	—	13 000	26 000
Salary of foreman[d]	2 000	6 000	6 000
Advertising	—	—	15 000
Total relevant costs	19 000	81 000	144 000
Excess of savings and revenues over costs	47 000	53 000	46 000

Notes

[a] Fixed costs of disposing of the materials are common to all alternatives. An alternative presentation is to exclude these fixed costs from the analysis. The disposal variable cost consists of the unused litres of material A for each alternative multiplied by £0.50 per litre.

[b] Immediate closure enables 10 000 units to be used as a substitute material, thus saving £18 000. The remaining 5000 units are sold to yield net revenue of £1 per unit.

Production of 10 000 units will result in 5000 unused units of material B. This results in a saving of substitute materials of £9000 (5000 × £1.80). Production of 20 000 units results in the stock of material B being used. It is also necessary to purchase 5000 additional units at £2 per unit.

[c] Units produced × variable overhead rate of £1.30 per unit.

[d] Immediate closure requires that £2000 be paid to the foreman compared with £6000 if the department is not closed.

[e] Sales value now = £43 000

Sales value in one year = £40 000 − (£0.50 × production level)

On the basis of the above information, Hilton Ltd should operate the department at a level of 10 000 units for the coming year.

(b) (i) The excess of savings and revenues over costs for the immediate closure will be increased by £8000 to £55 000 (£47 000 + £8000). The immediate closure will now be the best action in terms of maximizing short-term profits.

(ii) A 90% learning curve means that each time production doubles the average time taken to produce each unit falls to 90% of the previous average figure (see Chapter 23).

   Average time per unit for 5000 units = 1 hr
   Average time per unit for 10 000 units = 0.9 hrs
   Average time per unit for 20 000 units = 0.81 hrs
   Revised labour cost for 10 000 units = £27 000 (10 000 × 0.9 hrs × £3)
   Revised labour cost for 20 000 units = £48 600 (20 000 × 0.81 hrs × £3)

The analysis in part (a) will be altered as follows:

	10 000 units (£)	20 000 units (£)
Labour costs without learning effect	30 000	60 000
Labour costs with learning effect	27 000	46 600
Reduction in labour costs	3 000	11 400
Revised net saving/revenue	56 000 (53 000 + 3000)	57 400 (46 000 + 11 400)

Hilton Ltd should now operate department K at 20 000 units activity during the coming year.

Question 11.25

(a) In order to evaluate the three alternatives, it is necessary to estimate the annual income receivable from customers if the company undertakes to service the appliances itself. The calculation of income receivable from customers is:

	(£)
Labour: maintenance contract (100/10 × £30 000)	300 000
Labour: ad hoc work (100/15 × £12 000)	80 000
Materials: maintenance contract (137.5[a]/10 × £18 000)	247 500
Materials: ad hoc work (137.5[a]/10 × £6000)	82 500
	710 000

Note

[a] The material price calculation per £100 cost is:

	(£)
Company cost	100
Contractors' price (£100 + 10%)	110
Customers' price (£110 + 25%)	137.5

In other words, it is assumed that for every £137.50 charged to customers the subcontractor obtains £27.50 profit and the remaining £10 represents income received by the company from the sub-contractor.

Option 1

	(£)	(£)
Sales from small items (40% × £710 000)		284 000
Costs: Incremental fixed costs	148 000	
Materials [40% × 100/137.5 × (247 500 + 82 500)]	96 000	244 000
Income from own operations		40 000
Income from subcontractors of large items (60% × £66 000)		39 600
Total net income		79 600

Option 2

	(£)	(£)
Sales from large items (60% × £710 000)		426 000
Costs: Incremental fixed costs	285 000	
Materials [60% × 100/137.5 × (247 500 + 82 500)]	144 000	429 000
Deficit from own operations		(3000)
Income from subcontracting small items (40% × £66 000)		26 400
Total net income		23 400

Option 3

	(£)	(£)
Sales from large and small items		710 000
Costs: Incremental fixed costs	385 000	
Materials [100/137.5 × (247 500 + 82 500)]	240 000	625 000
Income from own operations		85 000

It is assumed that all of the fixed costs relating to own operations represent incremental costs.

Option 3 is recommended since it yields the highest profit and is £19 000 in excess of existing operations. Insufficient information is given to incorporate in the answer the effect of repair work undertaken in the first 6 months of operation for which the subcontractor receives 3.5% of the selling price. It is assumed that this payment is common and unavoidable for all alternatives.

(b) Favourable non-financial features:
  (i) The company will have better control over repairs and maintenance of its products and can ensure that a good customer service is provided.
  (ii) The company's mechanics will specialize only in maintaining the company's own appliances, whereas the subcontractors may service many different manufacturers' appliances. Consequently, the company mechanics may become more experienced in maintaining the appliances.

Adverse non-financial features:
  (i) The new system requires the customers to bring the small appliances to the repair centre. Customers may find this inconvenient compared with the present system.
  (ii) The subcontractors may compete and seek to offer present customers a better service.

Activity-based costing

Solutions to Chapter 12 questions

Question summary

ABC did not emerge until the late 1980s, and therefore very few examination questions have been set on this topic. This chapter contains nine questions.
12.1–12.4 Essay questions.

12.5–12.9 These questions require the computation and comparison of product costs adopting traditional and activity-based costing approaches.

Question 12.2

The answer to the question should describe the two-stage overhead allocation process and indicate that most cost systems use direct labour hours in the second stage. In today's production environment direct labour costs have fallen to about 10% of total costs for many firms and it is argued that direct labour is no longer a suitable base for assigning overheads to products. Using direct labour encourages managers to focus on reducing direct labour costs when they represent only a small percentage of total costs.

Approaches which are being adopted include:
(i) Changing from a direct labour overhead-recovery rate to recovery methods based on machine time. The justification for this is that overheads are caused by machine time rather than direct labour hours and cost.
(ii) Implementing activity-based costing systems that use many different cost drivers in the second stage of the two-stage overhead allocation procedure.

The answer should then go on to describe the benefits of ABC outlined in Chapter 12. Attention should also be drawn to the widespread use of direct labour hours by Japanese companies. According to Hiromoto[1] Japanese companies allocate overhead costs using the direct labour cost/hours to focus design engineers' attention on identifying opportunities to reduce the products' labour content. They use direct labour to encourage designers to make greater use of technology because this frequently improves long-term competitiveness by increasing quality, speed and flexibility of manufacturing.

Question 12.4

(a) Large-scale service organizations have a number of features that have been identified as being necessary to derive significant benefits from the introduction of ABC:
  (i) They operate in a highly competitive environment;
  (ii) They incur a large proportion of indirect costs that cannot be directly assigned to specific cost objects;
  (iii) Products and customers differ significantly in terms of consuming overhead resources;
  (iv) They market many different products and services.

---

[1] Hiromoto, T. (1988) 'Another hidden edge – Japanese management accounting'. *Harvard Business Review*, July/August, pp. 22–6.

Furthermore, many of the constraints imposed on manufacturing organizations, such as also having to meet financial accounting stock valuation requirements, or a reluctance to change or scrap existing systems, do not apply. Many service organizations have only recently implemented cost systems for the first time. This has occurred at the same time as when the weaknesses of existing systems and the benefits of ABC systems were being widely publicized. These conditions have provided a strong incentive for introducing ABC systems.

(b) The following may create problems for the application of ABC:
  (i) Facility sustaining costs (such as property rents etc.) represent a significant proportion of total costs and may only be avoidable if the organization ceases business. It may be impossible to establish appropriate cost drivers;
  (ii) It is often difficult to define products where they are of an intangible nature. Cost objects can therefore be difficult to specify;
  (iii) Many service organizations have not previously had a costing system and much of the information required to set up an ABC system will be non-existent. Therefore introducing ABC is likely to be expensive.

(c) The uses for ABC information for service industries are similar to those for manufacturing organizations:
  (i) It leads to more accurate product costs as a basis for pricing decisions when cost-plus pricing methods are used;
  (ii) It results in more accurate product and customer profitability analysis statements that provide a more appropriate basis for decision-making;
  (iii) ABC attaches costs to activities and identifies the cost drivers that cause the costs. Thus ABC provides a better understanding of what causes costs and highlights ways of performing activities more effectively by reducing cost driver transactions. Costs can therefore be managed more effectively in the long term. Activities can also be analysed into value added and non-value added activities and by highlighting the costs of non-value added activities attention is drawn to areas where there is a potential for cost reduction without reducing the products' service potentials to customers.

(d) The following aspects would be of most interest to a regulator:
  (i) The costing method used (e.g. Marginal, traditional full cost or ABC). This is of particular importance to verify whether or not reasonable prices are being set and that the organization is not taking advantage of its monopolistic situation. Costing information is also necessary to ascertain whether joint costs are fairly allocated so that cross-subsidization from one service to another does not apply;
  (ii) Consistency in costing methods from period to period so that changes in costing methods are not used to distort pricing and profitability analysis;
  (iii) In many situations a regulator may be interested in the ROI of the different services in order to ensure that excessive returns are not being obtained. A regulator will therefore be interested in the methods and depreciation policy used to value assets and how the costs of assets that are common to several services (e.g. corporate headquarters) are allocated. The methods used will influence the ROI of the different services.

Question 12.5 (a) Total machine hours = 120 × 4 hrs) + (100 × 3 hrs) + (80 × 2 hrs) + (120 × 3 hrs)
= 1300 hrs

$$\text{Machine hour overhead rate} = \frac{£10\,430 + £5250 + £3600 + £2100 + £4620}{1300\ \text{hrs}}$$

= £20 per machine hour

Product	A	B	C	D
	(£)	(£)	(£)	(£)
Direct material	40	50	30	60
Direct labour	28	21	14	21

Overheads at £20 per machine hour		80	60	40	60
		148	131	84	114
Units of output		120	100	80	120
Total cost		£17 760	£13 100	£6720	£16 920

(b)

Costs	(£)	Cost driver	Cost driver transactions	Cost per unit (£)
Machine department	10 430	Machine hours	1300 hours	8.02
Set-up costs	5250	Production runs	21	250
Stores receiving	3600	Requisitions raised	80 (4 × 20)	45
Inspection/quality control	2100	Production runs	21	100
Materials handling	4620	Number of orders executed	42	110

Note

Number of production runs = Total output (420 units)/20 units per set-up.
Number of orders executed = Total output (420 units/10 units per order.
The total costs for each product are computed by multiplying the cost driver rate per unit by the quantity of the cost driver consumed by each product.

	A	B	C	D
Prime costs	8 160 (£68 × 120)	7 100	3520	9720
Set ups	1 500 (£250 × 6)	1 250 (£250 × 5)	1000	1 500
Stores/receiving	900 (£45 × 20)	900	900	900
Inspection/quality	600 (£100 × 6)	500	400	600
Handling despatch	1 320 (£110 × 12)	1 100 (£110 × 10)	880	1 320
Machine dept cost[a]	3 851	2 407	1284	2 888
Total costs	16 331	13 257	7984	16 928

Note

[a] A = 120 units × 4 hrs × £8.02: B = 100 units × 3 hrs × £8.02

(c) Cost per unit

Costs from (a)	148.00	131.00	84.00	141.00
Costs from (b)	136.0	132.57	99.80	141.07
Difference	(11.91)	1.57	15.80	0.07

Product A is over-costed with the traditional system. Products B and C are under-costed and similar costs are reported with Product D. It is claimed that ABC more accurately measures resources consumed by products (see 'An illustration of ABC and traditional product costing systems' in Chapter 12. Where cost-plus pricing is used, the transfer to an ABC system will result in different product prices. If activity-based costs are used for stock valuations then stock valuations and reported profits will differ.

Question 12.7

(a) (i) The package material requirements are as follows:

John Ltd	30 000 units (30 000 × 1)
George Ltd	90 000 units (45 000 × 2)
Paul Ltd	75 000 units (25 000 × 3)
	195 000 units

Cost per unit of packaging = £1 950 000/195 000 = £10

Product costs per cubit metre

	John Ltd (£)	George Ltd (£)	Paul Ltd (£)
Packaging material	10 (1 × £10)	20 (2 × £10)	30 (3 × £10)
Labour and overhead[a]	9.40	9.40	9.40
	19.40	29.40	39.40

Note

[a]Labour and overhead average cost per metre = £940 000/100 000 metres
= £9.40.

(ii) The costs are assigned to the following activities:

	Receipt and inspection (£)	Storage (£)	Packing (£)
Labour : Basic	52 500 (15%)	35 000 (10%)	262 500 (75%)
Overtime	15 000 (50%)	4 500 (15%)	10 500 (35%)
Occupancy	100 000 (20%)	300 000 (60%)	100 000 (20%)
Administration and management	24 000 (40%)	6 000 (10%)	30 000 (50%)
	191 500	345 500	403 000

The resource usage for each of the cost drivers is:

	Receipt and inspection hours	Storage (m²)	Packing hours
John Ltd.	2 500 (30 000 × 5 mins.)	9 000 (30 000 × 0.3)	18 000 (30 000 × 36 min)
George Ltd.	6 750 (45 000 × 9 mins.)	13 500 (45 000 × 0.3)	33 750 (45 000 × 45 min)
Paul Ltd.	6 250 (25 000 × 15 mins.)	5 000 (25 000 × 0.2)	25 000 (25 000 × 1 hr)
	15 500	27 500	76 750

The cost driver rates are:

£12.355 per receipt and inspection hour (£191 500/15 500 hours)
£12.564 per m² of material stored (£345 500/27 500 m²)
£5.251 per packing hour (£403 000/76 750 hrs)

Product cost per cubic metre

	John Ltd (£)	George Ltd (£)	Paul Ltd (£)
Packing material	10.00	20.00	30.00
Receipt and inspection[a]	1.03	1.85	3.09
Storage cost[b]	3.77	3.77	2.51
Packing cost[c]	3.15	3.94	5.25
	17.95	29.56	40.85

Notes
[a]£12.355 × 5/60 hrs = £1.03;
£12.355 × 9/60 hrs = £1.85; £12.355 × 15/60 hrs = £3.09.
[b]£12.564 × 0.3 m = £3.77; £12.564 × 0.2 m = £2.51.
[c]£5.25 × 36/60 hrs = £3.15; £5.25 × 45/60 hrs = £3.94, £5.25 × 1 hr.

(b) The company has established cost pools for three major activities (receipt and inspection, storage and packing). The cost driver that causes the receipt and inspection costs to be incurred is the fragility of the different goods (measured by receipt and inspection time). The storage cost is influenced by the average size (measured in square metres) of the incoming product and packing costs are caused by the complexity of packaging and this is measured by the time required to pack the products.

ABC results in the computation of more accurate costs by seeking to measure resources consumed by products. ABC systems assume that activities cause costs and that products create the demand for activities. Costs are assigned to products based on individual products' consumption or demand for each activity. ABC systems simply recognise that businesses must understand the factors that cause each major activity, the cost of activities and how activities relate to products.

ABC has attracted a considerable amount of interest because it provides not only a basis for calculating more accurate product costs but also a mechanism for managing and controlling overhead costs. By collecting and reporting on the significant activities in which a business engages, it is possible to understand and manage costs more effectively. The aim is to manage the forces that cause activities (i.e. the cost drivers), and by reducing cost driver volume, costs can be managed and controlled in the long run.

(a) For the answer to this question see Chapter 12.

Question 12.8

(b) *Machine-related costs*
Machine hours for the period:

$$
\begin{aligned}
A = 500 \times \tfrac{1}{4} &= 125 \\
B = 5000 \times \tfrac{1}{4} &= 1250 \\
C = 600 \times 1 &= 600 \\
D = 7000 \times 1\tfrac{1}{2} &= \underline{10500} \\
&\ \underline{12475}
\end{aligned}
$$

Machine hour rate = £3 per hour (£37 424/12 475 hrs)

Set-up related costs
Cost per set-up = £256.18 (£4355/17)
Set-up cost per unit of output:

$$
\begin{aligned}
\text{Product A } (1 \times £256.18)/500 &= £0.51 \\
B\ (6 \times £256.18)/5000 &= £0.31 \\
C\ (2 \times £256.18)/600 &= £0.85 \\
D\ (8 \times £256.18)/7000 &= £0.29
\end{aligned}
$$

Material ordering related costs
Cost per order = £1920/10 orders = £192 per order
Material ordering cost per unit of output:

$$
\begin{aligned}
\text{Product A } (1 \times £192)/500 &= £0.38 \\
B\ (4 \times £192)/5000 &= £0.15 \\
C\ (1 \times £192)/600 &= £0.32 \\
D\ (4 \times £192)/7000 &= £0.11
\end{aligned}
$$

Material handling related costs
Cost per material handing = £7580/27 = £280.74
Material handling cost per unit of output:

$$
\begin{aligned}
\text{Product A } (2 \times £280.74)/500 &= £1.12 \\
B\ (10 \times £280.74)/5000 &= £0.56 \\
C\ (3 \times £280.74)/600 &= £1.40 \\
D\ (12 \times £280.74)/7000 &= £0.48
\end{aligned}
$$

Spare parts
Cost per part = £8600/12 = £716.67
Administration of spare parts cost per unit of output:

Product A (2 × £716.67)/500 = £2.87
 B (5 × £716.67)/5000 = £0.72
 C (1 × £716.67)/600 = £1.19
 D (4 × £716.67)/7000 = £0.41

Overhead cost per unit of output

Product	A	B	C	D
	(£)	(£)	(£)	(£)
ABC overhead cost:				
Machine overheads	0.75	0.75	3.00	4.50
Set-ups	0.51	0.31	0.85	0.29
Material ordering	0.38	0.15	0.32	0.11
Material handling	1.12	0.56	1.40	0.48
Spare parts	2.87	0.72	1.19	0.41
	5.63	2.49	6.76	5.79
Present system	1.20	1.20	4.80	7.20
Difference	+4.43	+1.29	+1.96	−1.41

The present system is based on the assumption that all overhead expenditure is volume-related, measured in terms of machine hours. However, the overheads for the five support activities listed in the question are unlikely to be related to machine hours. Instead, they are related to the factors that influence the spending on support activities (i.e. the cost drivers). The ABC system traces costs to products based on the quantity (cost drivers) of activities consumed. Product D is the high volume product, and thus the present volume-based system traces a large share of overheads to this product. In contrast, the ABC system recognizes that product D consumes overheads according to activity consumption and traces a lower amount of overhead to this product. The overall effect is that, with the present system, product D is overcosted and the remaining products are undercosted. For a more detailed explanation of the difference in resource consumption between products for an ABC and traditional cost system see 'An illustration of ABC and traditional product costing systems' in Chapter 12.

Accounting information for pricing decisions

Solutions to Chapter 13 questions

Question summary

All the questions in this chapter are applicable to a second-year course.

13.1–13.5 Various discussion questions.

13.6 Cost-plus and relevant cost information for pricing decisions.

13.7 Part (a) requires the allocation of scarce resources using contribution per key factor. Part (b) is based on the principle of comparing marginal revenue with marginal cost to ascertain the optimum output and selling price.

13.8 Selection of optimal selling price based on demand and cost schedules given in the question.

13.9 Impact of a change in selling price on profits based on a given elasticity of demand.

13.10 Calculation of elasticity of demand, optimum selling price and profit.

13.11 Calculation of full cost and relevant cost for a pricing decision and a discussion of cost-plus pricing and relevant cost pricing.

13.12 Recommendation of which market segment a company should enter and a selling price within each market segment.

13.13 Question based on a relevant cost approach requiring the use of demand schedules for pricing decisions.

13.14–13.18 Establishing optimum selling prices from economic cost and revenue functions. Questions 13.17 and 13.18 are difficult, and approximately 2 hours is required for each. Question 13.14 (a) includes the calculation of the optimal output level with one limiting factor.

For additional relevant cost questions requiring the setting of minimum selling prices see 11.21 and 11.22 in Chapter 11. For pricing decisions under conditions of uncertainty see 14.10–14.14 in Chapter 14.

Question 13.1

Several factors should be considered in the determination of pricing policy. The most important is price elasticity of demand, but if price is to be set in order to maximize profits then knowledge of cost structures and cost behaviour will also be of great importance. Knowledge of price–demand relationships and costs at different output levels is necessary to determine the optimum price. This is the price that results in marginal revenue being equal to marginal cost. The emphasis should be placed on providing information on the effect of changes in output on total cost rather than providing average unit cost information.

When cost information is presented using absorption costing, the resulting selling price calculation will be a function of the overhead apportionments and recovery methods used and the assumed volume of production. At best, the calculated selling price will only be appropriate for one level of production, and a different selling price would be produced for different output levels. Single cost figures calculated using absorption costing also fail to supply information on the effect of changes in output on total cost. For other disadvantages that appear when absorption costing is used in the determination of pricing policy see 'Limitations of cost-plus pricing' in Chapter 13.

The advantage claimed from the use of absorption costing in price determination is that all manufacturing costs are included in the cost per unit calculation, so that no major manufacturing cost is overlooked. With variable costing, there is a danger that output will be priced to earn a low contribution that is insufficient to cover total fixed costs. Also, the use of production facilities entails an opportunity cost from the alternative use of capacity forgone. The fixed cost per unit of capacity used can be regarded as an attempt to approximate the opportunity cost from the use of productive capacity. In spite of these claimed advantages, the presentation of relevant costs for pricing decisions (see Chapter 13) is likely to be preferable to information based on absorption cost.

Question 13.2 (a) Short-run profits are maximized at the output level where marginal revenue equals marginal cost. The optimum selling price is that which corresponds to the optimal output level (see Figure 13.3 in Chapter 13). From Figure 13.3 you will see that, with imperfect competition (no pricing decision is necessary with perfect competition), firms are faced with a downward-sloping demand curve. The highest selling price will apply to the first unit sold, but Figure 13.3 indicates that it is unlikely that this will be at the point where marginal revenue equals marginal cost.

(b) The objective is to maximize total contribution not unit contribution. Contribution per unit sold is the difference between marginal revenue and marginal cost. It is unlikely that contribution per unit will remain constant over the entire range of output. In Chapter 10 we noted that variable cost per unit and selling price per unit may change in relation to output. With a downward-sloping demand curve, marginal revenue will decline, thus causing contribution per unit to decline as output is increased. From Figure 13.3 we can see that profit is maximized where MR = MC. This is not at the point where unit contribution (difference between marginal revenue and marginal cost) is the greatest.

(c) Joint costs are allocated on an arbitrary basis, and costs that include arbitrary allocations are inappropriate for product, project or divisional comparisons. Performance should be judged on the basis of comparisons between controllable costs and revenues. With profit centres, measures such as controllable residual income should be used, whereas contribution should be used for comparing products.

(d) This statement presumably refers to the use of cost-plus pricing methods. If prices are set completely on a cost-plus basis then accounting information will determine the selling price. Consequently, the marketing the production people might feel that they have no influence in determining selling prices with pricing dominated by a concern for recovering full costs. If cost-plus pricing is used in a rigid way then marketing and production people may well consider the statement in the question to be correct. Cost information should be used in a flexible manner, and is one of several variables that should be used in determining selling prices. If this approach is adopted then the statement in the question will be incorrect.

(e) Management accounting should not be constrained by the requirements of external reporting. The emphasis should be on assembling financial information so as to help managers make good decisions and to plan and control activities effectively. In Chapter 9 we noted that there are strong arguments for adopting a system of variable costing in preference to absorption costing. If management accounts were consistent with SSAP 9 then the financial information might motivate managers to make wrong decisions.

(f) All costs must be covered in the long run if a firm is to be profitable. Therefore the objective should be to recover R and D expenditure in the long-run. R and D expenditure should be regarded as a pool of fixed costs to which products should generate sufficient contribution. Giant Steps Ltd should not rely on a policy of recovering R and D in relation to expenditure on each individual product. Price/demand relationships for some products might mean that the associated R and D cannot be recovered, while other products might be able to recover more than their fair share. Once a product is launched, only the incremental costs are relevant to the pricing decision. The objective should be to obtain a selling price in excess of relevant short-run costs and to provide a contribution to fixed costs and profit. R and D should be regarded as part of the pool of fixed costs to be recovered.

Question 13.3

(a) See Chapters 11–13 for the answer to this question. In particular, the answer should indicate:
   (i) Information presented to the product manager should be *future* costs, not past costs.
   (ii) *Incremental* cost and revenue information should be presented, and the excess of incremental revenues over incremental costs compared for different selling price and sales quantity levels. Costs that are common to all alternatives are not relevant for decision-making purposes.
   (iii) Decisions involve a choice between alternatives, and this implies that a choice leads to forgoing *opportunities*. Therefore relevant cost information for a pricing decision should include future cash costs and imputed (opportunity) cost.
   (iv) *Sunk costs* are past costs and not relevant to the pricing decision.
   (v) Pricing decisions should be based on estimates of demand schedules and a comparison of marginal revenues and costs.
(b) See 'Reasons for using cost-based pricing formulae' in Chapter 13 for the answer to this question. Note that overhead allocation is an attempt to provide an estimate of the long-run costs of producing a product.
(c) There is no specific answer to this question. The author's views on this question are expressed in Chapter 13.

Question 13.7

(a) The question states that fixed manufacturing costs are absorbed into the unit costs by a charge of 200% of variable cost. Therefore unit variable cost is one third of total unit cost.

Contribution per processing hour

	Product A	Product B	Product C
	(£)	(£)	(£)
Selling price	20	31	39
Variable cost	6	8	10
Production contribution	14	23	29
Contribution per processing hour	14	23	14.50
Ranking	3	1	2

Optimal programme

	Output	Hours used	Contribution
			(£)
Product B	8000	8000	184 000
C	2000	4000	58 000
A	1500	1500	21 000
			263 000

Existing programme

	Output	Hours used	Contribution (£)
Product A	6000	6000	84 000
B	6000	6000	138 000
C	750	1500	21 750
			243 750

Contribution and profits will increase by £19 250 if the optimal production programme is implemented. An additional hour of processing would be used to increase product A by one unit, thus increasing contribution by £14. Therefore the shadow price (or opportunity cost) of one scarce processing hour is £14.

(b)

		Production A			Production B			Production C	
Demand	Price (£)	Total contribution (£000)	Marginal contribution (£000)	Price (£)	Total contribution (£000)	Marginal contribution (£000)	Price (£)	Total contribution (£000)	Marginal contribution (£000)
2 000	24.50	37	37	34	52	52	39.50	59	59
4 000	23.50	70	33	33	100	48	39.00	116	57
6 000	22.50	99	29	32	144	44	38.50	171	55
8 000	21.50	124	25	31	184	40	38.00	224	53
10 000	20.50	145	21	30	220	36	37.50	275	51
12 000	19.50	162	17	29	252	32	37.00	324	49
14 000	18.50	175	13	28	280	28	36.50	371	47

Capacity is limited to 13 500 hours. It is therefore necessary to allocate output on the basis of marginal contribution per hour. Products A and B each require 1 processing hour, whereas product C requires 2 processing hours. To simplify the calculations, hours are allocated in 2000 blocks. Consequently, the allocation of the first 2000 hours will yield a marginal contribution of £37 000 from A, £52 000 from B and £29 500 from C. Note that an output of 2000 units of C will require 4000 processing hours, and will yield a contribution of £59 000. Therefore the contribution from 2000 hours will be £29 500. In other words, the marginal contributions for A and B in the above schedule are expressed in terms of blocks of 2000 hours, whereas the marginal contribution for C is expressed in terms of blocks of 4000 hours. To express the marginal contribution of C in terms of blocks of 2000 hours, it is necessary to divide the final column of the above schedule by 2.

Processing hours are allocated at follows:

	Hours	Marginal contribution (£)
Product B	first 2000	52 000
B	next 2000	48 000
B	2 000	44 000
B	2 000	40 000
A	2 000	37 000
B	2 000	36 000
A	1 500 (balance)	24 250[a]
	13 500	281 250

Note

[a]$3500 \times (£23.50 - £6) - £37\,000 = £24\,250$

The optimum output is £10 000 units of product B at a selling price of £30 and 3500 units of A at a selling price of £23.50, and contribution will be maximized at £281 250. It is assumed that it is company policy to change selling prices only in steps of £1.

(a) Presumably the question is intended to indicate that if competitors increase their prices by 6% and the company maintains its current price then this is equivalent to a price reduction by the company of 6%. An estimated price reduction of 6% and a price elasticity of demand of 1.5 would be expected to increase demand by 9%.

To predict costs for the next period it is necessary to analyse the costs into their fixed and variable elements. The high–low method can be used by comparing the changes in costs between the periods with the changes in activity. However, the current period costs must be deflated by the inflation factor so that they are expressed in the current prices for the previous period.

Current period's costs adjusted to previous period's prices = £1036 (£1077.4/ 1.04. Applying the high–low method:

	Units (000)	Costs (£000)
Current period	106	1036
Previous period	100	1000
	6	36

Variable cost per unit = Increase in costs (£36 000)/Increase in activity (6000 units)
= £6 per unit
Fixed costs = £1 000 000 − (100 000 units × £6) = £400 000

Costs have increased by 4% from the previous to the current period and by a further 6% from the current to the next period:

Variable cost per unit next period = £6 (1.04) (1.06) = £6.6144
Fixed costs next period = £400 000 (1.04) (1.06) = £440 960

Budgeted profit at a selling price of £13

	(£)
Sales (106 000 × 1.09[a] × £13)	1 502 020
Variable costs (106 000 × 1.09[a] × £6.6144)	764 228
Contribution	737 792
Less fixed costs	440 960
Profit	296 832

Note
[a]It is assumed that sales volume and production increase by 9% as a result of the price increase by competitors.

(b) *Budgeted profit assuming that the selling price is increased by 6%*

	£
Sales (106 000 × £13(1.06))	1 460 680
Variable costs (106,000 × £6.6144)	(701 126)
Contribution	759 554
Fixed costs	440 960
	318 594

If the selling price is increased to match that of the competitors it is assumed that demand will remain unchanged.
(c) The report should indicate that on the basis of the information specified in parts (a) and (b) the price should be increased by 6%.
(d) It is assumed that:
(i) Total market volume will remain unchanged and that the sales of the company

will not decline as a result of both the firm and its competitors increasing prices by 6%;

(ii) The estimate of the elasticity of demand is correct;

(iii) All costs are affected by the same rate of inflation;

(iv) All other factors remain constant so that sales will not be influenced by changes in advertising, customer preferences and general economic conditions.

Question 13.11 (a) (i) Contract price for contract A using the normal pricing method.

	(£)
Materials	
Z (100 × £7) + (1000 × £10)	10 700
Y (150 × £40)	6000
X (300 × £35) + (300 × £33)	20 400
W (200 × £20)	4 000
	41 100
Labour: Craftsmen 2 × ($\frac{1}{2}$ × £16 000 + £700)	17 400
Labourers 3 × £4000	12 000
	70 500
Add 100% mark-up	70 500
Contract price	£141 000

(ii) Minimum price based on relevant costs

	(£)
Materials: Z (1100 × £10)	11 000
Y (150 × £44)	6 600
X (300 × £25) + (300 × £33)	17 400
W (200 × £16)	3 200
	38 200
Labour: Craftsmen (£11 800 + 2 × £700)	13 200
Labourers (3 × £4000)	12 000
Equipment: General purpose (£16 400 − £12 600)	3 800
Specialized (£9000 − £5800)	3 200
Administrative expenses	5 000
Contract price	75 400

It is assumed that the specialized equipment would be purchased new for £9000.

(b)

	(£)
Expected sales value (0.7 × £100 000) + (0.3 × £120 000)	106 000
Expected building costs (0.4 × £60 000) + (0.4 × £80 000) + (0.2 × £95 000)	(75 000)
Building plot	(20 000)
Expected profit	11 000

Using expected profit as a measure of the alternative use of the capacity, the minimum price using the relevant cost approach would be £86 400 (£75 400 + £11 000). In other words, Wright would wish to ensure that the contract price is in excess of the profit available from the alternative use of the facilities, and this would depend on his assessment of the 'utility value' of project B. Note that the expected value approach is covered in Chapter 14.

(c) This question requires a discussion of cost-plus pricing and the relevant cost (that is, opportunity cost) approach to pricing. For a discussion of the limitations and merits of cost-plus pricing see 'Limitations of cost-plus pricing' and 'Reasons for using cost-based pricing formulae' in Chapter 13. The advantages of basing selling prices on relevant costs include:

(i) The alternative use of resources are incorporated into the analysis.

(ii) It distinguishes between relevant and irrelevant costs and indicates the incremental cash flows incurred in manufacturing and selling a product.
(iii) It provides the information to enable tenders to be made at more competitive prices.

The limitations include:
(i) It is a cost-based pricing method that ignores demand.
(ii) It may provide an incentive to sell at low prices, resulting in total sales revenue being insufficient to cover total fixed costs.
(iii) There is difficulty in determining the opportunity cost of resources because information on available opportunities may not be known.
(iv) Where special contracts are negotiated that are in excess of relevant (incremental) costs but less than full costs, there is a danger that customers will expect repeat business at this selling price. Care must be taken to ensure that negotiating 'special one-off' contracts does not affect the demand for other products.

Relevant cost pricing is more appropriate for 'one-off' pricing decisions. It is also appropriate in situations where a firm has unutilized capacity or can sell in differentiated markets at different prices. Relevant cost pricing may also be appropriate where the policy is to sell certain products as 'loss leaders'. It is important that cost information be used in a flexible manner and that product costs not be seen as the only factor that should determine the final selling price.

(a) The following represents the quantity of sales that would be required to break even for a range of selling prices within each of the three selling price categories:

Question 13.12

	Selling price (£)	Variable costs[a] (£)	Unit contribution (£)	Break-even point[b] (units)	Break-even % share of market
Category 1					
Low selling price	600	850	0	Not applicable	—
Medium selling price	825	917.50	0	Not applicable	—
High selling price	1050	985	65	8462	38
Category 2					
Low selling price	1450	1105	345	1594	27
Medium selling price	1675	1172.5	502.5	1095	18
High selling price	1900	1240	660	833	14
Category 3					
Low selling price	2500	1420	1080	509	68
Medium selling price	2750	1495	1255	438	58
High selling price	3000	1570	1430	385	51

Notes
[a] (30% × selling price) + £670 variable cost.
[b] (£550 000 fixed costs)/unit contribution.

The average market share per manufacturer in category 1 is 5500 units. AB Ltd would have to sell 8462 units (that is, capture a 38% share of the market) at the maximum price within the range in order to break even. It is likely that there will be a significant demand in the category 1 market for a lower-quality and lower-priced product. It may therefore be unwise to enter the category 1 market.

The average market share per manufacturer in the category 2 market is 1200 units. Given that AB will be able to enter the market with a product of advanced technology and distinctive design, it is likely that it will be able to sell the break-even sales volume of 1594 units (that is, obtain a market share of 27%) at the lowest selling price within the range. At the medium and high selling prices the break-even sales volume is below the average sales volume per manufacturer.

For the category 3 market the average market share per manufacturer is 375 units. This is in excess of the break-even point for the three prices considered in the above analysis. The company would also have to obtain a market share in excess of 50% in order to break even. The technology in this market is also advanced, and consequently competition will be more intensive.

It is therefore suggested that the company market the product within a selling price range of £1450–£1900.

(b) The question does not provide any details of demand information within each price range, and it is therefore questionable whether or not it is possible to recommend a price from the data given. AB's product incorporates some of the most advanced techniques available, together with a very distinctive design, and it is therefore likely that a large market share will be obtained at selling prices at the lower end of the price range. Assuming that a 50% market share could be obtained at a £1500 selling price, 40% at £1700, 30% at £1800 and 20% at £1900, the profits would be as follows:

Selling price	£1 500	£1 700	£1 800	£1 900
3000 units (50%)	£590 000			
2400 units (40%)		£698 000		
1800 units (30%)			£512 000	
1200 units (20%)				£242 000

Note that the above figures have been calculated as follows:

demand × (70% of selling price − £670 variable cost) − £550 000 fixed costs

Assuming that the above estimates of demand were correct, a selling price of £1700 would be recommended.

Question 13.15 (a) (i) If the selling price is £200, demand will be zero. To increase demand by one unit, selling price must be reduced by £1/1000 units or £0.001. Hence the maximum selling price attainable for an output of x units is:

$$P = £200 - 0.001x$$

At an output level of 100 000 units,

$$P = £200 - £0.001 \times 10\ 000$$
$$= £100 \text{ per unit}$$

Total contribution at an output level of 100 000 units

100 000 × (£100 − £50)	5 000 000
Less fixed costs (100 000 × £25)	2 500 000
Profit	2 500 000

(ii) Profit is maximized where MC = MR

MC = £50 per unit variable cost (given)

$$MR = \frac{dTR}{dx}$$

$$TR = x\ (200 - 0.001x)$$
$$= 200x - 0.001x^2$$

$$\frac{dTR}{dx} = 200 - 0.002x$$

Therefore optimum output is where $50 = 200 - 0.002x$ (i.e. where MC = MR). And so

$$150 = 0.002x$$

That is,

$$x = 75\,000 \text{ units}$$

At an output level of 75 000 units, the selling price is £200 − (£0.001 × 75 000) = £125. Therefore profit at 75 000 units:

	(£)
Contribution (75 000 × £75)	5 625 000
Less fixed costs	2 500 000
	3 125 000

(b) (i) Revised fixed costs = £3 000 000.
The optimal output level will not be affected by a change in fixed costs. Therefore the selling price should not be changed. Profit will decline by £500 000.
(ii) Revised marginal cost = £60.
The new optimum is where $60 = 200 - 0.002x$
$$0.002x = 140$$
Therefore $x = 70\,000$ units
At this output level, $P = £200 - £0.001 \times 70\,000$
$$= £130$$

(c) Profit before advertising expenditure:

	(£)
Total contribution [70 000 × (£130 − £60)]	4 900 000
Less fixed costs	3 000 000
Profit	1 900 000

After the introduction of the advertising expenditure:

$$P = 210 - 0.001x$$
$$TR = x(210 - 0.001x)$$
$$= 210x - 0.001x^2$$
Therefore $MR = 210 - 0.002x$

The revised optimum output is where $60 = 210 - 0.002x$
$$0.002x = 150$$
$$x = 75\,000$$

The optimum price at this output level is where $P = £210 - £0.001 \times 75\,000$
$$= £135$$

	(£)
Total contribution [75 000 × (£135 − £60)]	5 625 000
Revised fixed costs	4 000 000
Profit	1 625 000

Therefore profits will decline by £275 000 if the advertising campaign is undertaken.
(d) The original budgeted output of 100 000 units was higher than the optimum output level. The solution to (a) (ii) indicates that the optimum output level is achieved by reducing production to 75 000 units and increasing the selling price to £125. Beyond an output level of 75 000 units, marginal cost per unit is in excess of marginal revenue. This is because selling price is reduced in order to expand output. Consequently, marginal revenue declines and is less than marginal cost. This means that profits decline when output is in excess of 75 000 units. This analysis is based on the following assumptions:

(i) The demand schedule can be predicted accurately.

(ii) Marginal cost per unit is constant at all output levels.

(iii) Fixed costs are constant throughout the entire output range.

The analysis also showed that the change in fixed costs had no effect on the MR and MC function, so that the optimum output level and price did not change. When MC increases, the effect is to decrease output level and increase price.

The effect of the advertising campaign is to shift the demand curve to the right, thus causing sales demand to be higher at each selling price or the selling price to be higher at each demand level. However, the increased advertising costs are in excess of the additional revenue, thus resulting in a reduction in profits.

Question 13.16 (a) Selling prices using the existing policy of full cost + 5%

Cost of 1250 filter elements	(£)
Direct labour	18 750
Materials	43 750
Variable overhead	12 500
Variable cost (£60 per unit)	75 000
Fixed overhead	5 000
Fixed packaging and selling cost	7 000
	87 000

Full cost per filter element $= \dfrac{£87\ 000}{1250} =$ £69.60

Full cost per complete unit = £69.60 + £305 = £374.60

Using full cost + 5%, rounded up to nearest £1:

Selling price tor complete unit = £374.60 × 1.05 = £394.00

Selling price for replacement elements =£69.60 × 1.05 = £74.00

(b) At a selling price of 20% above the market leader for the replacement filter sales of the complete units will not be affected. Therefore the maximum price of £96 (£80 × 1.20) should be charged for replacement filters.

At a selling price of £280 demand is expected to be 800 units (40% × 2000). Each increase in price of £1 causes demand to fall by 5 units. Therefore at a selling price of £440 demand will be zero. To increase demand by one unit the selling price must be reduced by £0.20. Thus the maximum selling price for an output of x units is:

$$SP = £440 - £0.20x$$
Total revenue for an output of x units $= £440x - £0.20x^2$
Marginal revenue $= dTR/dx = £440 - £0.40x$
Total cost $= 305x + 60x + £5000 + £7000$
Marginal cost $= £365$

The sale of one complete unit results in the sale of four replacement filters during its life at a marginal revenue of £96 and a marginal cost of £60 per unit.

Total MC $= £365 + (4 \times £60) = £605$
Total MR $= £440 - 0.4x + (4 \times £96) = £824 - 0.4x$
At the optimal output level where MR = MC:
$£824 - 0.4x = £605$
$x = 548$ units

This gives a selling price of £440 − 0.20(548) = £330.40

(c) *Original selling price*

The profit for each of the years would be constant:

		(£)	(£)
Sales:	complete units 250 @ £394		98 500
	replacement elements 1000 @ £74		74 000
			172 500
Variable costs:	pumps 250 @ £305	76 250	
	other 1250 @ £60	75 000	
			(151 250)
Fixed costs:			21 250
			(12 000)
Profit			9250

Revised selling price

	1992		1993		1994	
	(£)	(£)	(£)	(£)	(£)	(£)
Revenues;						
Complete units						
548 @ £330.40		181 059.20		181 059.20		181.059.20
Replacement						
elements @ £96[a]		96 000.00		124 608.00		153 216.00
		277 059.20		305 667.20		334 275.20
Variable costs:						
Complete units						
548 @ £305	167 140		167 140		167 140	
Replacement						
elements @						
£60[a]	92 880		110 760		128 640	
		(260 020.00)		(277 900.00)		(295 780.00)
		17 039.20		27 767.20		38 495.20
Fixed costs		(12 000.00)		(12 000.00)		(12 000.00)
Profit		5 039.20		15 767.20		26 495.20
Change in profits		(4 210.80)		6 517.20		17 245.20

Note

[a]The number of replacement filters will increase over the next four years because they are replaced at the end of each year (four times during their lifetime). Therefore sales of replacement filters are related to sales in previous periods. The question also states that production of replacement filters must be sufficient to meet annual sales demand plus the production of a filter to be included in the sale of one completed unit. Thus production of filters will exceed sales by 548 filters per year. The sales and production volumes of replacement filters is calculated as follows:

1992	Sales (Based on previous years sales volume)	1000
	Production (1000 + 548)	1548
1993	Sales = $(\frac{3}{4} \times 1000) + (\frac{1}{4} \times [548 \times 4])$	1298
	Production (1298 + 548)	1846
1994	Sales = $(\frac{1}{2} \times 1000) + (\frac{1}{2} \times [548 \times 4])$	1596
	Production (1596 + 548)	2144

(d) The major competitor has set the selling price at £390 and the traditional cost-plus method results in a selling price of £394. The proposed new selling price is £330.40. The major concern with setting the new price is the possible reaction of competitors. Given that the total market is stable, a large decrease in selling price to increase market share is likely to cause competitors to reduce prices. This could result in a price cutting war in which market shares are merely maintained at lower prices. In the long term the company might be worse off.

A further problem is that the lower price may be perceived by customers as indicating an inferior quality product. Customers might therefore be reluctant to switch from their existing suppliers.

To overcome these problems the price reduction should be accompanied with an effective advertising campaign that emphasizes the price and quality aspects of the product.

(e) For the answer to this question see 'Limitations and Cost-plus pricing' and 'Reasons for using cost-plus prices' in Chapter 13.

Decision-making under conditions of uncertainty

Solutions to Chapter 14 questions

Question summary

The questions in this chapter are appropriate for a second-year course. Questions 14.1–14.6 are the easiest.

14.1   Part (a) consists of the use of probabilities for competitive bidding. Part (b) is concerned with subcontracting under conditions of uncertainty.

14.2   The calculation of expected values to determine whether a charity organization should hold a dinner dance.

14.3   Acceptance of a contract at a given price when demand is uncertain.

14.4   Calculation of expected value and the presentation of a probability distribution.

14.5   Cost–volume–profit analysis and uncertainty.

14.6   Expected value calculations and a discussion of its limitations plus a calculation of the margin of safety.

14.7   Choice of alternative types of machines assuming uncertain demand. The question also requires a discussion of managers' different attitudes towards risk and the calculation of the amount payable for perfect information.

14.8   Output decision requiring commitment to an output level

given that demand is uncertain.

14.9   Contracting hotel accommodation based on uncertain demand.

14.10–14.14 Pricing decisions under conditions of uncertainty. Question 14.13 requires the preparation of a decision tree and 14.14 involves a combined pricing and purchasing decision where the purchase price is dependent upon demand.

14.15, 14.16 Both problems are concerned with selecting which machine should be hired given that each machine is capable of producing different output levels. Question 14.15 requires the construction of a decision tree and the application of the maximin criterion.

14.17   Calculation of the expected value of perfect and imperfect information. The calculation of the expected value of information is also required in sections of 14.2, 14.7, 14.8, 14.12, 14.14 and 14.16.

14.18   Calculation of expected net present value and decision whether to abandon a project after one year. For additional questions on expected net present value see 16.20 and 16.21 in Chapter 16.

(a) It is assumed that if XY Ltd and one or more of the other firms bid the lowest **Question 14.1** price, XY Ltd will be awarded the contract. The expected contribution for each bid price is as follows:

Price bid (£)	Total contribution at this bid (£)	Probability that XY Ltd will obtain contract at each bid price	Expected contribution (£)
45	130 000	1.00	130 000
50	180 000	0.95	171 000
55	230 000	0.85	195 500
60	280 000	0.65	182 000
65	330 000	0.40	132 000
70	380 000	0.15	57 000
75	430 000	0.05	21 500

Expected profits will be maximized at a bid price of £55. However, expected value is a long-run decision criterion and may not be appropriate for 'one-off' decisions. Management might prefer to compare the contributions and the associated probabilities for each bid price and make a decision on the basis of their risk/return preference.

(b) *North Area*: No alternative to AB Ltd exists. Therefore servicing in the North will be subcontracted to AB Ltd at £18 000. This cost will be offset by the contribution of £1500 from the sale of necessary spares to AB Ltd.

South Area: There are two alternatives: buy from AB or CD Ltd. Both firms will buy the necessary spares from AB Ltd. Therefore this factor is not relevant to the decision. The relevant information is as follows:

AB Ltd		(£)
Fixed charge of		20 000

CD Ltd		(£)
Fixed charge of		18 000
Expected additional charge:		

(£)	Probability	(£)	
Nil	0.40	—	
900	0.30	270	
2200	0.20	440	
3500	0.10	350	1 060
			19 060

Applying the expected value approach, the work should be subcontracted to CD Ltd. However, an examination of the probability distribution indicates that the charge from CD Ltd could be as high as £21 500 with a probability of 0.10. The probability that the charge will be in excess of £20 200 is 0.3 and the probability that it will be below £20 200 is 0.7. The decision depends on management's attitude towards risk.

Midlands Area: There are two alternatives: AB Ltd, or XY Ltd can use its own organization. The relevant information is as follows:

AB Ltd		(£)
Fixed charge of		11 500

Own organization		
Expected cost of extra staff		

(£)	Probability	(£)
4 500	0.20	900
7 000	0.35	2450
11 000	0.45	4950
		8300

Contribution lost from sales of spares:

2500 units × £0.50   <u>1250</u>
                     <u>9550</u>

If the decision is based on an expected value approach then XY Ltd should use its own organization. However, it should be noted that there is a 0.45 probability that the cost will be £12 250.

Summary of the decisions using the expected value approach
  North: AB Ltd.
  South: CD Ltd.
  MIidlands: Own organization.

(a) Based on past experience, the probability of ticket sales is as follows:

Number of tickets sold	Probability	
250–349	0.2	(4 out of 20)
350–449	0.3	(6 out of 20)
450–549	0.4	(8 out of 20)
550–649	0.1	(2 out of 20)
	1.0	

The average revenue per person from the dinner and dance is £26 (£20 + £5 + £1) and the fixed costs are £4500 (£700 + £2800 + £800 + £200). The expected profit from the dinner and dance is calculated as follows:

(1) Ticket sales (midpoint) taken	(2) Probability	(3) Income (£)	(4) Food (£)	(5) Fixed costs (£)	(6) Profit (loss) (£	(7) Expected value (2 × 6) (£)
300	0.2	7 800	4800	4500	(1500)	(300)
400	0.3	10 400	4800	4500	1100	330
500	0.4	13 000	6000	4500	2500	1000
600	0.1	15 600	7200	4500	3900	390
					Expected profit	1420

Based on past experience, the probability of the number of programme pages sold is:

Programme pages sold	Probability	
24	0.2	(4 out of 20)
32	0.4	(8 out of 20)
40	0.3	(6 out of 20)
48	0.1	(2 out of 20)
	1.0	

The expected profit on programme advertising is calculated as follows:

Programme pages sold	Probability	Income (£)	Costs (£)	Profit/(loss) (£)	Expected value (£)
24	0.2	1680	2120	(440)	(88)

32	0.4	2240	2160	80	32
40	0.3	2800	2200	600	180
48	0.1	3360	2240	1120	112
				Expected profit	236

Total expected profit is £1656 (£1420 + £236).

(b) It is assumed that the policy is not to hold a dinner and dance each year and to accept losses in some years and profits in other years. If this is the policy then there is no point in spending £500 on the market research enquiry.

Spending £500 on market research is justifiable only if it affects action taken. For example, if the expenditure indicated that a loss would be incurred then the function will be cancelled and benefits would be obtained. However, if the expenditure indicated that a profit will be made then no benefits will be obtained. From part (a) it can be seen that a loss will occur only if 300 tickets are sold (if 400 or more tickets are sold a total profit is obtained even if a loss is incurred on programme sales). The expected loss that will be incurred if 300 tickets are sold is calculated as follows:

Loss from sales of 300 tickets (£)	Profit/(loss) on programmes (£)	Total loss (£)	Joint probability	Expected value (£)
(1500)	(440)	1940	$0.2 \times 0.2 = 0.04$	(77.6)
(1500)	80	1420	$0.2 \times 0.4 = 0.08$	(113.6)
(1500)	600	900	$0.2 \times 0.3 = 0.06$	(54.0)
(1500)	1120	380	$0.2 \times 0.1 = 0.02$	(7.6)
			Expected loss	252.8

The expected value of the benefits of market research is £252.8 and the cost of the research is £500. Therefore the expenditure is not justified on an expected value criterion.

Question 14.4 (a) *Profit and Loss Statement for Period Ending 31 May 1992*

	(£)
Revenue (14 400 000 journeys):	
0–3 miles (7 200 000 × £0.20)	1 440 000
4–5 miles (4 320 000 × £0.30)	1 296 000
Over 5 miles (2 880 000 × £0.50)	1 440 000
Juvenile fares (4 800 000 × £0.15)	720 000
Senior citizen fares (4 800 000 × £0.10	480 000
	5 376 000
Advertising revenue	250 000
	5 626 000
Less: Variable costs (20 routes × 4 buses × 150 miles × 330 days × £0.75)	(2 970 000)
Fixed costs	(1 750 000)
Net profit	906 000

(b) Assuming the same passenger mix as 1992 the weighted average fare per passenger for year ending 31 May 1993 is (£5 376 000 × 1.05)/24 000 000 = £0.2352.

The break-even point is where:

Total revenue from fares + Advertising revenue = Total cost

Let x = number of passenger journeys

Break-even point: $0.2352x + £250\,000 = (2\,970\,000 + £1\,750\,000)\,1.1$

$$0.2352x = £4\,942\,000$$

$$x = 21\ 011\ 905$$

Maximum capacity utilization $= 40\ 000\ 000$ passenger journeys $(24\ 000\ 000/0.6)$
Break-even capacity utilization $= 21\ 011\ 905/40\ 000\ 000 = 52.5\%$

(c) (i)

Expected value and probability estimates for 1993

Capacity Utilization		Revenue		Inflation		Costs	Combined probability	Net profit	Expected value
%	(Probability)	Fares (£000)	Adverts (£000)	(%)	(Probability)	(£000)		(£000)	(£000)
70	0.1	6585.6[a]	250	8	0.3	5097.6[b]	0.03	1738.0	52.14
		6585.6	250	10	0.6	5192.0[b]	0.06	1643.6	98.62
		6585.6	250	12	0.1	5286.4[b]	0.01	1549.2	15.49
60	0.5	5644.8[a]	250	8	0.3	5097.6	0.15	797.2	119.58
		5644.8	250	10	0.6	5192.0	0.30	702.8	210.84
		5644.8	250	12	0.1	5286.4	0.05	608.4	30.42
50	0.4	4704.0[a]	250	8	0.3	5097.6	0.12	−143.6	−17.23
		4704.0	250	10	0.6	5192.0	0.24	−238.0	−57.12
		4704.0	250	12	0.1	5286.4	0.04	−332.4	−13.30
							1.00		439.44

Notes
[a]Fare revenues at 60% capacity for 1992 were £5 376 000. Assuming 5% inflation fare revenues for 1993 at 60% capacity will be £5 644 800 (£5 376 000 × 1.05). At 70% and 50% capacity utilization fare revenues will be as follows:

$$70\% = 70/60 \times £5\ 644\ 800 = £6\ 585\ 600$$
$$50\% = 50/60 \times £5\ 644\ 800 = £4\ 704\ 000$$

[b]Variable costs vary with bus miles which are assumed to remain unchanged. Predicted costs at the different inflation levels are as follows:

$$8\% = (£2\ 970\ 000 + £1\ 750\ 000)1.08 = £5\ 097\ 600$$
$$10\% = (£2\ 970\ 000 + £1\ 750\ 000)1.10 = £5\ 192\ 000$$
$$12\% = (£2\ 970\ 000 + £1\ 750\ 000)1.12 = £5\ 286\ 400$$

(c) (ii) The answer to this question requires the preparation of a cumulative probability distribution that measures the cumulative probability of profits/(losses) being greater than specified levels.

Cumulative probability distribution

Losses greater than £300 000   = 0.04 probability
Probability of a loss occurring = 0.40
Profits greater than £600 000   = 0.60
Profits greater than £700 000   = 0.55
Profits greater than £800 000   = 0.10
Profits greater than £1 500 000 = 0.10

(d) The following factors have not been incorporated into the analysis:
   (i) Change in the passenger mix.
   (ii) Changes in the number of routes and the number of days operation per year.
   (iii) Changes in fare structure such as off-peak travel or further concessions for juveniles and senior citizens.
   (iv) Changes in cost levels due to factors other than inflation (e.g. more efficient operating methods).

Question 14.6 (a) For each selling price there are three possible outcomes for sales demand, unit variable cost and fixed costs. Consequently, there are 27 possible outcomes. In order to present probability distributions for the two possible selling prices, it would be necessary to compute profits for 54 outcomes. Clearly, there would be insufficient time to perform these calculations within the examination time that can be allocated to this question. It is therefore assumed that the examiner requires the calculations to be based on an expected value approach.

The expected value calculations are as follows:

(i) *Variable cost*

	(£)
(£10 + 10%) × 10/20 =	5.50
£10 × 6/20 =	3.00
(£10 − 5%) × 4/20 =	1.90
	10.40

(ii) *Fixed costs*

	(£)
£82 000 × 0.3 =	24 600
£85 000 × 0.5 =	42 500
£90 000 × 0.2 =	18 000
	85 100

(iii) *£17 selling price*

	(units)
21 000 units × 0.2 =	4 200
19 000 units × 0.5 =	9 500
16 500 units × 0.3 =	4 950
	18 650

(iv) *£18 selling price*

	(units)
19 000 units × 0.2 =	3 800
17 500 units × 0.5 =	8 750
15 500 units × 0.3 =	4 650
	17 200

Expected contribution

£17 selling price = (£17 − £10.40) × 18 650 = £123 090
£18 selling price = (£18 − £10.40) × 17 200 = £130 720

The existing selling price is £16, and if demand continues at 20 000 units per annum then the total contribution will be £112 000 [(£16 − £10.40) × 20 000 units].

Using the expected value approach, a selling price of £18 is recommended.

(b) Expected profit = £130 720 − £85 100 fixed costs = £45 620
Break-even point = fixed costs (£85 100)/contribution per unit (£7.60)
= 11 197 units
Margin of safety = expected demand (17 200 units) − 11 197 units = 6003 units
% margin of safety = 6003/17 200 = 34.9% of sales
Note that the most pessimistic estimate is above the break-even point.

(c) An expected value approach has been used. The answer should draw attention to the limitations of basing the decision solely on expected values. In particular, it should be stressed that risk is ignored and the range of possible outcomes is not considered. The decision ought to be based on a comparison of the probability distributions for the proposed selling prices. For a more detailed answer see 'Probability distributions and expected value' and 'Measuring the amount of uncertainty' in Chapter 14.

(d) Computer assistance would enable a more complex analysis to be undertaken. In particular, different scenarios could be considered, based on different combinations of assumptions regarding variable cost, fixed cost, selling prices and demand. Using computers would also enable Monte Carlo simulation (see Chapter 16) to be used for more complex decisions.

Question 14.7 (a)

Alternative types of machine hire	Possible outcomes (level of orders)	Probability of outcomes	Payoff (£000)
High	High	0.25	2200 [(0.3 × £15 000) − £2300]
	Medium	0.45	250 [(0.3 × £8500) − £2300]
	Low	0.30	−1100 [(0.3 × £4000) − £2300]

Medium	High	0.25	$\begin{bmatrix} 1700 & (0.3 \times £15\,000) - £1500 \\ & - £1300 \end{bmatrix}$
	Medium	0.45	$1050 \; [(0.3 \times £8500) - £1500]$
	Low	0.30	$-300 \; [(0.3 \times £4000) - £1500]$
Low	High	0.25	$\begin{bmatrix} 1350 & (0.3 \times £15\,000) - £1000 \\ & - £2150 \end{bmatrix}$
	Medium	0.45	$\begin{bmatrix} 700 & (0.3 \times £8500) - £1000 \\ & - £850 \end{bmatrix}$
	Low	0.30	$200 \; [(0.3 \times £4000) - £1000]$

(b) Expected values:

$$\text{High hire level} = (0.25 \times £2200) + (0.45 \times £250) - (0.3 \times £1100)$$
$$= £332\,500$$
$$\text{Medium hire level} = (0.25 \times £1700) + (0.45 \times £1050) - (0.3 \times £300)$$
$$= £807\,500$$
$$\text{Low hire level} = (0.25 \times £1350) + (0.45 \times £700) + (0.3 \times £200)$$
$$= £712\,500$$

Using the expected value decision rule, the medium hire contract should be entered into.

(c) Managers may be risk-averse, risk-neutral or risk-seeking. A risk-averse manager might adopt a maximin approach and focus on the worst possible outcome for each alternative and then select the alternative with the largest payoff. This approach would lead to the selection of the low initial hire level. A risk-seeking manager might adopt a maximax approach and focus on the best possible outcomes. This approach would lead to choosing the high initial hire contract, since this has the largest payoff when only the most optimistic outcomes are considered.

(d) With perfect information, the company would select the advance plant and machinery hire alternative that would maximize the payoff. The probabilities of the consultants predicting high, medium and low demand are respectively 0.25, 0.45 and 0.30. The expected value calculation with the consultant's information would be:

	Advance hire level	Payoff (£000)	Probability	Expected value (£000)
High market	high	2200	0.25	550
Medium market	medium	1050	0.45	472.5
Low market	low	200	0.30	60
				1082.5

	(£)
Expected value with consultant's information	1 082 500
Expected value without consultant's information	807 500
Maximum amount payable to consultant	275 000

(a)

			Question 14.10
Selling price (£)	70	80	90
Maximum demand (£)	75 000	60 000	40 000
Maximum revenue (£)	5 250 000	4 800 000	3 600 000
Total variable cost (£)	3 750 000	3 000 000	2 000 000
Fixed costs (£)	800 000	800 000	800 000
R & D cost (£)	250 000	250 000	250 000
	4 800 000	4 050 000	3 050 000
Estimated profit (£)	450 000	750 000	550 000

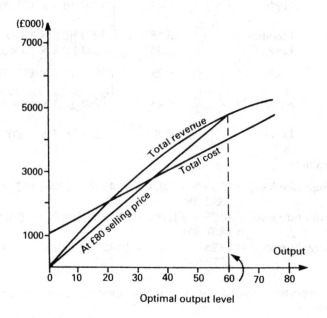

Figure Q14.10

The above analysis is based on the maximum sales demand. On this basis, the analysis indicates that profits are maximized at an output level of 60 000 units when the selling price is £80. It is preferable to use the 'most likely' demand level and to incorporate uncertainty around the 'most likely' demand into the analysis.

(b) Por a selling price of £90 there are three different demand levels, and for each demand level there are three different outcomes for actual unit variable cost. Therefore there are nine possible outcomes. The contribution and probability of each outcome is presented in the following schedule:

(1)	(2)	(3)	(4)	(5)	(6)	(7)	(8)
							Weighted
		Unit			Total	Joint	outcome
Demand		variable		Unit	contribution	probability	(6 × 7)
(000)	Probability	cost	Probability	contribution	(£000)	(2 × 4)	(£000)
		(£)		(£)			
20	0.2	60	0.2	30	600	0.04	24.00
20	0.2	55	0.7	35	700	0.14	98.00
20	0.2	50	0.1	40	800	0.02	16.00
35	0.7	60	0.2	30	1050	0.14	147.00
35	0.7	55	0.7	35	1225	0.49	600.25
35	0.7	50	0.1	40	1400	0.07	98.00
40	0 1	60	0.2	30	1200	0.02	24.00
40	0.1	55	0.7	35	1400	0.07	98.00
40	0.1	50	0.1	40	1600	0.01	16.00
						1.00	1121.25

	(£)
Expected total contribution	1 121 250
Fixed costs	1 050 000
Expected profit	71 250

(c) To compare the three selling prices, it is necessary to summarize the information in part (b) for a £90 selling price in the same way as part (c) of the question.

Note that fixed costs are deducted from the total contribution column in the schedule presented in (b) to produce the following statement:

		Prices under review		
		£70	£80	£90
Probability of a loss				
Greater than or equal to £500 000		0.02	0	0
	£300 000	0.07	0.05	0.18
	£100 000	0.61	0.08	0.20
	0	0.61	0.10	0.34
Probability of a profit				
Greater than or equal to	0	0.39	0.91	0.80
	£100 000	0.33	0.52	0.66
	£300 000	0.03	0.04	0.15
	£500 000	0	0.01	0.01
Expected profit		Loss (£55 750)	£68 500	£71 250

The following items should be included in the memorandum:
(i) The £90 selling price has the largest expected profit, but there is also a 0.34 probability of not making a profit.
(ii) Selling price of £80 may be preferable, because there is only a 0.10 probability of not making a profit. A selling price of £80 is least risky, and the expected value is only slightly lower than the £90 selling price.
(iii) Subjective probability distributions provide details of the uncertainty surrounding the estimates and enable the decision-maker to select the course of action that is related to his personal risk/profit trade-off (see Chapter 14 for an explanation of this).
(iv) Subjective probabilities are subject to all the disadvantages of any subjective estimate (e.g. bias).
(v) Calculations are based on discrete probabilities. For example, this implies that there is a 0.7 probability that demand will be exactly 35 000. A more realistic interpretation is that 35 000 represents the mid-point of demand falling within a certain range. For a discussion of this point see the article by Flower (1971) listed in the references at the end of Chapter 14.

(d) If the increase in fixed costs represents an additional cost resulting from an increase in volume then this incremental cost is relevant to the pricing decision. If the fixed costs represent an apportionment then it is not relevant. Nevertheless, we noted in Chapter 13 that selling prices should be sufficient to cover the common and unavoidable long-run fixed costs.

The research and development expenditure is a sunk cost, and is not a relevant cost as far as the pricing decision is concerned. However, the pricing policy of the company may be to recover the research and development expenditure in the selling price. The amount recovered per unit sold should be a policy decision. Note that the decision to write off research and development in one year instead of three will affect the reported profits.

Question 14.11

(a) The calculations of the product variable costs per unit are:

	Newone (£)	Newtwo (£)
Labour and materials	82	44
Variable overheads	6 (6 hrs × £1)	2 (2 hrs × £1)
Unit variable cost	88	46

Low-price alternative: The contributions per unit are £32 for Newone (£120 − £88) and £14 (£60 − £46) for Newtwo. The probability distributions are as follows:

	Newone			Newtwo	
Demand	Probability	Contribution (£)	Demand	Probability	Contribution (£)
1000	0.2	32 000	3000	0.2	42 000
2000	0.5	32 000[a]	3000	0.5	42 000
3000	0.3	32 000[a]	3000	0.3	42 000

Note
[a]Machine capacity restricts outputs to 1000 units of Newone and 3000 units of Newtwo.

Note that estimates indicate with 100% certainty that Newone will yield a contribution of £32 000 and Newtwo will yield a contribution of £42 000.

Higher price alternative: The contributions per unit are £42 for Newone (£130 − £88) and £24 (£70 − £46) for Newtwo. The probability distributions are as follows:

	Newone			Newtwo	
Demand	Probability	Contribution (£)	Demand	Probability	Contribution (£)
500	0.2	21 000	1500	0.2	36 000
1000	0.5	42 000	2500	0.5	60 000
1500	0.3	42 000[a]	3500	0.3	72 000[a]
	Expected value	37 800		Expected value	58 800

Note
[a]Output is restricted to 1000 units of Newone and 3000 units of Newtwo.

Recommendations
The above probability distributions indicate that Newtwo is preferable to Newone, irrespective of which price is set. At the higher selling price Newtwo yields a higher expected value. There is only a 0.2 probability that a lower contribution will be earned if the higher price is selected in preference to the lower price. The advantage of the lower price is that the outcome is certain, but, given the high probability (0.8) of earning higher profits with the higher-price alternative, a selling price of £70 is recommended. With the higher-price alternative, there is a 0.70 probability that machine hours will not be utilized. Any unused capacity should be used to sell Newone at £130 selling price.

(b) Decision problems require estimates of changes in costs and revenues for choosing alternative courses of action. It is therefore necessary to distinguish between fixed and variable costs. Regression analysis can be used to estimate a cost equation, and tests of reliability can be applied to ascertain how reliable the cost equation is in predicting costs. For a description of regression analysis and tests of reliability you should refer to Chapter 23. A common test of reliability is the coefficient of determination, which can be calculated by squaring the correlation coefficient. The coefficient of determination for the cost equation used in the question is 0.64 (0.8^2). Consequently, 36% of the variation in cost is not explained by the cost equation used in the question. It is possible that activity bases other than machine hours might provide a better explanation of the relationship between costs and activities. Alternatively, changes in costs might be a function of more than one variable. In such circumstances, cost equations based on multiple regression techniques should provide more reliable cost estimates.

Question 14.13 The variable cost per litre is as follows:

	(£)
Direct materials	0.12
Direct wages	0.24
Indirect wages etc. ($16\frac{2}{3}\% \times £0.24$)	0.04
	0.40

and the range of contributions are:

£0.80 for a selling price of £1.20
£0.70 for a selling price of £1.10
£0.60 for a selling price of £1.00

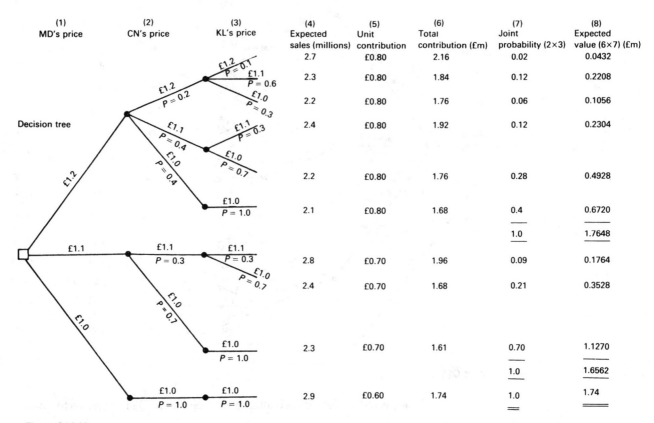

(1) MD's price	(2) CN's price	(3) KL's price	(4) Expected sales (millions)	(5) Unit contribution	(6) Total contribution (£m)	(7) Joint probability (2×3)	(8) Expected value (6×7) (£m)
			2.7	£0.80	2.16	0.02	0.0432
			2.3	£0.80	1.84	0.12	0.2208
			2.2	£0.80	1.76	0.06	0.1056
			2.4	£0.80	1.92	0.12	0.2304
			2.2	£0.80	1.76	0.28	0.4928
			2.1	£0.80	1.68	0.4	0.6720
						1.0	1.7648
			2.8	£0.70	1.96	0.09	0.1764
			2.4	£0.70	1.68	0.21	0.3528
			2.3	£0.70	1.61	0.70	1.1270
						1.0	1.6562
			2.9	£0.60	1.74	1.0	1.74

Figure Q14.13

A decision tree indicating the possible outcomes is presented in Figure 14.13. From this it can be seen that the expected value of the contribution is maximized at a selling price of £1.20. Fixed costs are common and unavoidable to all alternatives, and are therefore not included in the analysis. However, management might prefer the certain contribution of £1.74 million at a selling price of £1.00. From columns 6 and 7 of the decision tree it can be seen that there is a 0.60 probability that contribution will be in excess of £1.74 million when a selling price of £1.20 is implemented. The final decision depends on management's attitude towards risk.

(a) (i) See the decision tree shown in Figure Q14.15.

Question 14.15

(ii) 1. The assumption underlying the maximin technique is that the worst outcome will occur. The decision-maker should select the outcome with the largest possible payoff assuming the worst possible outcome occurs. From the decision tree we can see that the payoffs for the worst possible outcomes are as follows:

	Payoff (£000)
Hire of machine 200	55
Hire of machine 300	45
Hire of machine 600	38.5
Do not franchise	90

The decision is not to franchise using the maximum criterion.

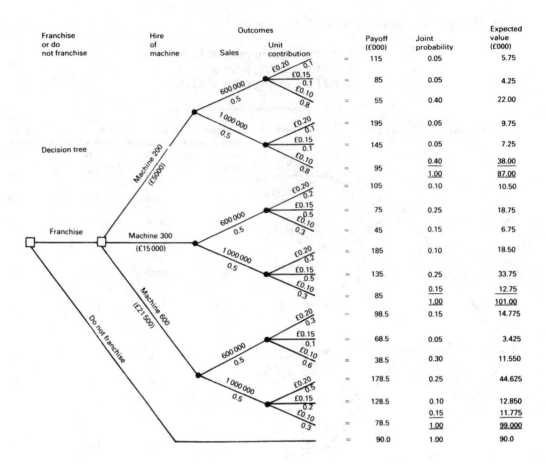

Franchise or do not franchise	Hire of machine	Sales	Unit contribution			Payoff (£000)	Joint probability	Expected value (£000)
			£0.20 0.1	=		115	0.05	5.75
			£0.15 0.1	=		85	0.05	4.25
		600 000 0.5	£0.10 0.8	=		55	0.40	22.00
		1 000 000 0.5	£0.20 0.1	=		195	0.05	9.75
			£0.15 0.1	=		145	0.05	7.25
	Machine 200 (£5000)		£0.10 0.8	=		95	0.40	38.00
							1.00	87.00
			£0.20 0.2	=		105	0.10	10.50
		600 000 0.5	£0.15 0.5	=		75	0.25	18.75
Franchise	Machine 300 (£15 000)		£0.10 0.3	=		45	0.15	6.75
		1 000 000 0.5	£0.20 0.2	=		185	0.10	18.50
			£0.15 0.5	=		135	0.25	33.75
			£0.10 0.3	=		85	0.15	12.75
							1.00	101.00
			£0.20 0.3	=		98.5	0.15	14.775
		600 000 0.5	£0.15 0.1	=		68.5	0.05	3.425
	Machine 600 (£21 500)		£0.10 0.6	=		38.5	0.30	11.550
		1 000 000 0.5	£0.20 0.5	=		178.5	0.25	44.625
			£0.15 0.2	=		128.5	0.10	12.850
Do not franchise			£0.10 0.3	=		78.5	0.15	11.775
							1.00	99.000
				=		90.0	1.00	90.0

Decision tree

Figure Q14.15

2. The expected values for each alternative (see Figure Q14.15) are as follows:

	(£000)
Hire of machine 200	87.0
Hire of machine 300	101.0
Hire of machine 600	99.0
Do not franchise	90.0

The company will maximize the expected value of the contributions if it hires the 300 batch machine.

3. The probability of a contribution of less than £100 000 for each alternative can be found by adding the joint probabilities from payoffs of less than £100 000. The probabilities are as follows:

Hire of machine 200	= 0.85
Hire of machine 300	= 0.55
Hire of machine 600	= 0.65
Do not franchise	= 1.00

The company should hire the 300 machine adopting this decision criterion.

(b) The approaches in part (a) enable uncertainty to be incorporated into the analysis and for decisions to be based on range of outcomes rather than a single outcome. This approach should produce better decisions in the long run. The main problem with this approach is that only a few selected outcomes with related probabilities are chosen as being representative of the entire distribution of possible outcomes. See Flower (1971) for a detailed discussion of this topic. The approach also gives the impression of accuracy, which is not justified. Comments on the specific methods used in (a) are as follows:

Maximin: Enables an approach to be adopted which minimizes risk. The main disadvantage is that such a risk-averse approach will not result in decisions that will maximize long-run profits.

Expected value: For the advantages of this approach see 'Expected value' in Chapter 14. The weaknesses of expected value are as follows:

(i) It ignores risk. Decisions should not be made on expected value alone. It should be used in conjunction with measures of dispersion.

(ii) It is a long-run average payoff. Therefore it is best suited to repetitive decisions.

(iii) Because it is an average, it is unlikely that the expected value will occur.

Probability of earning an annual contribution of less than £100 000: This method enables decision-makers to specify their attitude towards risk and return and choose the alternative that meets the decision-makers risk–return preference. It is unlikely that this approach will be profit-maximizing or result in expected value being maximized.

(a) *Decision tree and expected value calculation for site A*
See Figure Q14.18.

Question 14.18

Year 0 Cash flows	Year 1 Cash flows	Year 2 Cash flows	Joint probability	PV (£)	Expected NPV (£)
		0	0.0625	90 910	5 628
		(0.25)			
	£100 000	£100 000	0.125	173 550	21 694
	(0.25)	(0.50)			
		£200 000	0.0625	256 190	16 012
		(0.25)			
		£100 000	0.125	264 640	33 080
		(0.25)			
Investment	£200 000	£200 000	0.25	347 100	86 775
outlay (£300 000)	(0.50)	(0.50)			
		£300 000	0.125	429 740	53 718
		(0.25)			
		£200 000	0.0625	438 010	27 376
		(0.25)			
	£300 000	£300 000	0.125	520 650	65 081
	(0.25)	(0.50)			
		£350 000	0.0625	561 970	35 123
		(0.25)	1.000		344 487
			Less investment outlay		300 000
			Expected NPV		44 487

Figure Q14.18 *Decision tree and expected value calculation for site A.*

(b) (i) It is assumed that the decision to abandon the project can be taken at the end of year 1. At this point in time, the cash flows for year 2 will be receivable in one year's time, whereas the sale proceeds will be receivable at the point when the decision is taken at the end of year 1. Therefore the decision should be to abandon the project if the PV of the cash flows receivable in one year's time is less than the £150 000 selling price. If the cash inflows in year 1 are £100 000 then the expected PV of the cash flows in year 2 will be:

Cash flows (£)	PV (£)	Probability	Expected PV (£)
100 000	90 910	0.50	45 455
200 000	181 820	0.25	45 455
			90 910

The site should therefore be sold for £150 000. If the cash flow for year 1 is £200 000, the expected PV of the cash inflows in year 2 will be:

Cash flows (£)	PV (£)	Probability	Expected NPV (£)
100 000	90 910	0.25	22 727
200 000	181 820	0.50	90 910
300 000	272 730	0.25	68 182
			181 819

The expected NPV is in excess of the sale proceeds, and therefore the project should not be abandoned.

(ii) If the cash flow in year 1 is £100 000 then the project will be abandoned and sold for £150 000 at the end of year 1. Therefore there is a probability of 0.25 that £250 000 will be received at the end of year 1. Hence the expected NPV will be £56 819. Therefore the entries in the expected value column of the decision tree in (a) for the first three branches (£5628, £21 694 and £16 012, totalling £43 334) will be replaced with an expected value of £56 819. Hence the total expected value will increase by £13 485 to £57 972 (£13 485 + £44 487).

(c) At time zero the financial effect is that the NPV of the project is increased by £13 485.

Capital investment decisions: 1

Solutions to Chapter 15 questions

Question 15.2

(a) The IRR is where:

annual cash inflows × discount factor = investment cost

i.e.   £4000 × discount factor = £14 000

Therefore   discount factor = $\dfrac{£14\ 000}{£4\ 000}$

= 3.5

We now work along the five-row table of the cumulative discount tables to find the discount rate with a discount factor closest to 3.5. This is 13%. Therefore the IRR is 13%.

(b) The annual saving necessary to achieve a 12% internal rate of return is where:

$$\text{annual savings} \times 12\% \text{ discount factor} = \text{investment cost}$$

i.e. annual savings × 3.605 = £14 000
Therefore annual savings = £14 000
                          $\frac{}{3.605}$
                        = £3 883

(c) NPV is calculated as follows:

	(£)
£4000 received annually from years 1–5:	
£4000 × 3.791 discount factor	15 164
Less investment cost	14 000
NPV	1 164

Question 15.4 (a) The answer should stress that NPV is considered superior to the payback method and the accounting rate of return because it takes account of the time value of money. For a description of the time value of money you should refer to 'Compounding and discounting' and 'The concept of net present value' in Chapter 15. The answer should also draw attention to the limitations of the payback method and accounting rate of return described in Chapter 15.

(b) (i) To compute the NPV it is necessary to convert the profits into cash flows by adding back depreciation of £25 000 per annum in respect of the asset purchased at the end of year 3 for £75 000. The NPV calculation is as follows:

Year	Cash flow (£)	Discount factor	NPV
3	(75 000)	0.675	(50 625)
4	35 000	0.592	20 720
5	28 000	0.519	14 532
6	27 000	0.465	12 555
			(2 818)

(ii) The cash flows are based on the assumption that the reinvestment in R is not made at the end of year 3.

Year	Discount factor	Project T cash flows[a] (£)	Project T NPV (£)	Project R cash flows (£)	Project R NPV (£)
1	0.877	27 000	23 679	40 000 (3)[c]	35 080
2	0.769	30 000	23 070	45 000	34 605
3	0.675	32 000	21 600	45 000 (4)[d]	30 375
4	0.592	44 000	26 048		
5	0.519	40 000[b]	20 760		
			115 157		100 060
Investment outlay			70 000		60 000
NPV			45 157		40 060

Payback: T = 2 years + (£70 000 − £57 000)/£32 000 = 2.41 years
          R = 1 year + (£60 000 − £40 000)/45 000 = 1.44 years

The decision should be to invest in Project T because it has the higher NPV.

Notes
[a]Yearly profits plus (£70 000 − £10 000)/5 years depreciation.

^{b}£18.000 profits + £12 000 depreciation + £10 000 sale proceeds.

^{c}Profits plus £60 000/3 years depreciation.

^{d}£75 000 investment outlay − £50 000 = Annual profit (£25 000). Cash flow = £25 000 profit + £20 000 depreciation.

(c) For an explanation of the meaning of the term 'discount rate' see 'The opportunity cost of an investment' in Chapter 15. The discount rate can be derived from observations of the returns shareholders require in financial markets. Where a project is to be financed fully by borrowing, the cost of borrowing could be used as a basis for determining the discount rate.

(a) The PV of the cash outflows is calculated as follows:

Year	Cash outflows (£)	PV at 10%
0	2 000 000	2 000 000
1	100 000	90 910
2	100 000	82 640
3	700 000	525 910
4	100 000	68 300
5	100 000	62 090
		2 829 850

Assuming that the contribution per hour is constant the contribution per hour is £666.67 (£1 600 000/2400 hrs). Over a 5-year period the present value per hour is £2527 (£666.67 × 3.791 discount factor for 5 years at 10%). Thus the annual flying hours to break even are 1120 (£2 829 850/£2527).

If the aircraft is rented the PV of the fixed rental charges is £1 042 500 (£250 000 × [1 + 3.170 discount factor]). The revised net contribution per hour is £305.67 (£666.67 − £361) giving a present value of £1 158.80 (£305.67 × 3.791 discount factor). Thus the annual hours to break even are 900 (£1 042 500/£1158.80).

To determine the indifference point between renting and buying let x = Annual flying hours. The indifference point is where:

$$£2527x − £2 829 850 = £1158.80x − £1 042 500$$
$$1368.2x = £1 787 350$$
$$x = 1306$$

Thus, at an activity level of 1306 flying hours per annum, the two options are equally financially viable. At activity levels of less than 1306 hours renting is preferable, whereas buying is preferable at activity levels in excess of 1306 hours.

(b) Profits are maximized when the aircrafts are operated at full capacity of 2400 hours per year. Thus two aircrafts should be purchased utilizing 4800 hours. A third aircraft will be required for the remaining 950 hours. At this activity level it is more profitable to rent the third aircraft.

(a) The relevant cast flows and their assumed timing are shown below:

	31 December 1983 Delivery ship 1	31 December 1984 Delivery ship 2	31 December 1985 Delivery ship 3
Sales value	250	250	250
Labour costs	(132)	(145)	(160)
Redundancy cost saved (see part b)	132	—	—
Materials	(108)	(117)	—
Variable overhead	(11)	(12)	(13)
	131	(24)	77

The investment cost at time zero is £145 000 consisting of the forgone sales value of the shipyard (£120 000) and materials (£25 000). The present value calculations for each discount rate are as follows:

Cost of capital	12%		16%		20%	
Present value of cash flows (£000)						
Year 1	117	(131 × 0.893)	113	(131 × 0.862)	109	(131 × 0.833)
Year 2	(19)	(24 × 0.797)	(18)	(24 × 0.743)	(17)	(24 × 0.694)
Year 3	55	(77 × 0.712)	49	(77 × 0.641)	45	(77 × 0.579)
	153		144		137	
Less investment cost	145		145		145	
Net present value	8		(1)		(8)	

At a cost of capital of 12% the shipyard should be kept open, but at 16% or 20% it should be closed.

(b) (i) The book value of the equipment is not relevant to the decision, but the £120 000 selling price is relevant since the company will be deprived of this sales revenue if it continues to build ships.

(ii) The question states that redundancy payments are equal to one year's labour cost. It is assumed that the labour cost will be equal to the 1983 labour cost. For the purpose of discounting it is assumed that all labour costs are paid at the end of the year.

(iii) The relevant cost for the first ship is the forgone income from the sale of the stock materials. The relevant material costs for the second and third ships is the replacement price of the materials not in stock, suitably inflated for price rises.

(iv) Depreciation is not a relevant cost, and head office costs will presumably be allocated to other shipyards if this shipyard is closed down.

(v) The cost of capital is assumed to include a premium for inflation. Therefore the cash flows are also adjusted for inflation.

(c) The expected cost of capital is:

$$(12\% \times 0.5) + (16\% \times 0.4) + (20\% \times 0.1) = 14.4\%$$

and the revised NPV calculation is:

$$\frac{131}{1.144} + \frac{(24)}{(1.144)^2} + \frac{77}{(1.144)^3} - 145 = 2.7$$

Therefore the shipyard should be kept open.

An alternative approach is to construct a probability distribution using the calculations in (a):

NPV	Probability	Expected value
8	0.5	4
(1)	0.4	(0.4)
(8)	0.1	(0.8)
		2.8

Applying the expected value approach the project should be undertaken, but management might prefer to examine the probability distribution. The decision will then depend on management's attitude to risk.

(a) *Type A project appraisal*
Cash inflows:
Additional sales revenue from further processing
(2000 × (£12.50 − £2))   21 000
Cash outflows:
Direct costs (2000 × £2.50)   5 000
Fixed costs   10 000
Compensation payment   500   15 500
Annual net cast inflows   5 500
Cumulative discount factor (4 years at 8%)   3.312
PV of net cash inflows   £18 216
Investment outlay   £20 000
Net present value   (£1 784)

It is assumed that the apportioned rental cost of £2500 per annum will still continue if the project is not undertaken.

Type B waste   (£)   (£)
Cash inflows:
Sales income (4000 × £11)   44 000
Savings in contractor's fees (4000 × £14)   56 000
Employee costs   9 000   109 000
Cash outflows:
Direct costs (£13.50 × 4000)   54 000
Fixed costs   20 000   74 000
Net cash inflow   35 000
Discount factor at 15% for 6 years   3.784
Present value of net cash inflows   £132 440
Investment outlay
(£120 000 − sale of containers at £18 000)   £102 000
Net present value   £ 30 440

The project should therefore not be accepted.
The above analysis is based on the assumption that the contract for the sale of the product lasts for 6 years. If the customer does not renew the contract at the end of 4 years, the present value of the net cash inflows will be reduced by £40 898 [£44 000 × (0.4972 + 0.4323)]. This would result in a negative NPV of £10 458 (£30 440 − £40 898) plus any disposal cost of the unwanted product. On the other hand, if the company can sell more than 1023 units of the product [£10 458/(£11 × 0.9295)] in years 5 and 6, the project will have a positive NPV.

The project should be accepted if management are optimistic that the contract will be renewed or are confident that more than 1023 units can be sold in each of years 5 and 6.
(b) The major reservations about the project for Type B waste are as follows:
(i) There could be additional redundancy costs if the existing employee is made redundant. If the employee is not made redundant, there might not be any cash flow savings.
(ii) The technology is new, and operating problems that cannot be foreseen might arise.
(iii) The present system seems to work satisfactorily. Will there be any additional risks, given that the process is hazardous, with the extra processing?

(a) The alternatives being considered should be evaluated using a DCF approach. **Question 15.12**
The analysis should be based on *incremental* cash flows. The share of college overheads represents common and unavoidable fixed costs, which will still

continue even if the unused space is not used to accommodate the kiosk. The interest on capital of 10% will be reflected within the discounting process. Consequently, the interest cost should not be included in the cash flows. It is assumed that salaries represent an incremental cash flow. The annual *relevant* cash flows are:

	(£000)
Sales	100
Less cost of sales	80
Contribution	20
Less salaries	13
Net cash inflow	7

(b)

	(£)
College: PV of cash inflows (£7000 × 3.791)	26 537
Less investment cost	20 000
Net present value	6 537

	(£)
Contractor: PV of cash inflows (£4000 × 3.791)	15 164
Less investment cost	10 000
Net present value	5 164

The college project should therefore be selected. Note that the alternatives are mutually exclusive, and the NPV method should be used in preference to the IRR method. The IRR calculations are shown below:

College: IRR is the discount rate where:
cash inflows (£7000) × discount factor = investment cost (£20 000)
Therefore   discount factor = 2.857 (£20 000/£7000)
             IRR = 22%
Contractor: discount factor = 2.5 (£10 000/£4000)
             IRR = 29%

It can be seen that a conflict in rankings occurs, with the NPV method suggesting the college alternative and the IRR method suggesting the contractor. The NPV method gives the correct ranking (see 'Comparison of net present value and internal rate of return' in Chapter 15 for proof).

(c) The answer should indicate that, based on the quantitative information, the college project should be selected. The answer should explain why the NPV method is superior to the IRR method for evaluating mutually exclusive projects. Other factors to be considered are:

(i) The college alternative is more risky, since cash inflows and outflows are uncertain. Sales might be significantly different from £100 000 per annum. Cash inflows are fixed at £4000 per annum with the contractor alternative. The contractor will bear the risk if trade is less than expected. However, the college will not obtain any additional benefits if trade is better than expected. It might be possible to negotiate with the contractor a clause in the contract for the rental to be increased if sales are in excess of £100 000 per annum.

(ii) The college proposal might result in additional staff time, which is not reflected in the estimates. For example, managerial time might be taken up with staff replacements and general management of the kiosk. Management can avoid these responsibilities if the contractor's proposal is selected.

(a) *Alternative 1*
NPV:

Year	Cash flow (£000)	Discount factor	PV (£000)
0	−100	1.00	−100
1	+255	0.83	+211.65
2	−157.5	0.69	−108.675
		NPV =	2.975

IRR: The cash flow sign changes after year 1, which implies that the project will have two IRRs. Using the interpolation method, the NPV will be zero at a cost of capital of 5% and 50%. Therefore the IRRs are 5% and 50%.

Alternative 2
NPV:

Year	Cash flow (£000)	Discount factor	PV (£000)
0	−50	1.00	−50
1	0	0.83	0
2	+42	0.69	+28.98
3	+42	0.58	+24.36
		NPV =	+ 3.34

IRR: At a 25% discount rate the project has an NPV of −1.616. Using the interpolation formula:

$$IRR = 20 + \frac{3340}{3340 - (-1616)} \times (25 - 20)$$

$$= 23.4\%$$

Summary

	NPV	IRR
Alternative 1	£2975	5% or 50%
Alternative 2	£3340	23.4%

(b) The projects are mutually exclusive and capital rationing does not apply. In these circumstances the NPV decision rule should be applied and alternative 2 should be selected. Because of the reasons described in Chapter 15, the IRR method should not be used for evaluating mutually exclusive projects. Also, note that alternative 1 has two IRRs. Therefore, the IRR method cannot be used to rank the alternatives.

Before a final decision is made, the risk attached to each alternative should be examined. For example, novelty products are generally high-risk investments with short lives. Therefore alternative 1 with a shorter life might be less risky. Other considerations include the possibility of whether the promotion of this novelty product will adversely affect the sales of the other products sold by the company. Also, will the large expenditure on advertising for alternative 1 have a beneficial effect on the sales of the company's other products?

(c) The answer should include a discussion of the payback method, particularly the limitations discussed in Chapter 15. It should be stressed that payback can be a useful method of investment appraisal when liquidity is a problem and the speed of a project's return is particularly important. It is also claimed that payback allows for uncertainty in that it leads to the acceptance of projects with fast paybacks. This approach can be appropriate for companies whose products are subject to uncertain short lives. Therefore there might be an argument for using payback in Khan Ltd.

The second comment by Mr Court concerns the relationship between reported profits and the NPV calculations. Projects ranked by the NPV method can give different rankings to projects that are ranked by their impact on the reported profits of the company. The NPV method results in the maximization of the present value of future cash flows and is the correct decision rule. If investors give priority to reported profits in valuing shares (even if reported profits do not give an indication of the true economic performance of the company) then Mr Court's comments on the importance of a project's impact on reported profits might lead to the acceptance of alternative 1. However, if investors are aware of the deficiencies of published reported profits and are aware of the company's future plans and cash flows then share values will be based on PV of future cash flows. This is consistent with the NPV rule.

Question 15.14 (a)

	Discount factors		Project X		Project Y	
	10%	20%	NPV at 10% (£000)	NPV at 20% (£000)	NPV at 10% (£000)	NPV at 20% (£000)
Year 0	1.000	1.000	(200.00)	(200.00)	(200.00)	(200.00)
1	0.9091	0.8333	31.82	29.16	198.19	181.66
2	0.8264	0.6944	66.11	55.55	8.26	6.94
3	0.7513	0.5787	67.62	52.08	7.51	5.79
4	0.683	0.4823	51.22	36.17	2.73	1.93
5	0.6209	0.4019	12.42	8.04	1.87	1.21
			29.19	(19.00)	18.56	(2.47)

Using the interpolation method, the IRRs are:

$$\text{Project X} = 10\% + [29.19/(29.19 + 19.00)] \times 10\% = 16.05\%$$
$$\text{Project Y} = 10\% + [18.56/(18.56 + \ 2.47)] \times 10\% = 18.83\%$$

(b) The projects are mutually exclusive, and conflicting rankings occur. Where conflicting rankings occur, the NPV method will indicate the correct rankings (see Chapter 15 for an explanation). Therefore project X should be undertaken, since it yields the larger NPV at a discount rate of 10%.

(c) For the answer to this question see 'Comparison of net present value and internal rate of return' in Chapter 15.

(d) The cost of capital at which project Y would be preferred to project X can be ascertained by calculating the IRR on the incremental investment X − Y.

Year	0	1	2	3	4	5
	(£000)	(£000)	(£000)	(£000)	(£000)	(£000)
Project X cash flows	−200	35	80	90	75	20
Project Y cash flows	−200	218	10	10	4	3
Project X − Y	0	−183	+70	+80	+71	+17

The IRR on the incremental investment X − Y is 13%. Therefore if the cost of capital were in excess of 13%, the decision in (b) would be reversed (assuming that one of the projects has a positive NPV). For an explanation of this approach see 'Mutually exclusive projects' in Chapter 15. Alternatively, the discount rate can be found by constructing a graph for the NPVs at different discount rates. You can see from the graph shown in Figure Q15.14 that project Y has a higher NPV for discount rates above 13%.

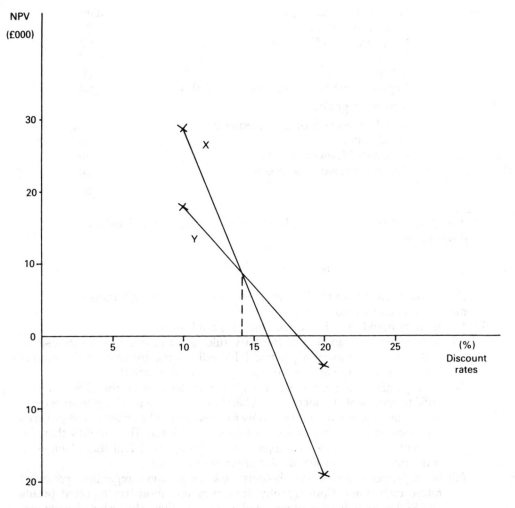

Figure Q15.14

(a) *NPV calculations*

Question 15.16

	Cash flows (£m)	Years	Discount factor	PV (£m)
Initial outlay	(40)	t_0	1.0000	(40.000)
Disposal value	10	t_{10}	0.2472	2.472
Retraining costs[a]	(10)	$t_{0,1}$	1.8696	(18.696)
Annual cost savings	12	t_1-t_{10}	5.019	60.228
Rental income	2	t_{1-10}	5.019	10.038
Software	(4)	t_{1-10}	5.019	(20.076)
Reduction in working capital	5	t_0	1.000	5.000
NPV				(1.034)

It is assumed that taxation should be ignored.

Note
[a]The question implies that retraining costs do not occur at the end of the year. It is therefore assumed that the cash flows occur at the start of years 1 and 2 (that is, t_0 and t_1).

Calculation of accounting rate of return

Year 1 incremental profits:	(£m)
Annual cost savings	12
Retraining costs (20 m/10 years)	(2)
Rental income	2
Software	(4)
Depreciation of equipment (40 − 10)/10 years	(3)
Increase in profits	5

Year 1 incremental capital investment:	
Initial outlay	40
Capitalized retraining costs	20
Reduction in working capital	(5)
	55

It is assumed that ROI is calculated based on the opening written-down value:

$$ROI = 5/55 = 9.1\%$$

The proposed investment fails to meet either of the company's investment criteria and would be rejected.

(b) The answer should include a discussion of the following:

  (i) A theoretical explanation of the NPV rule and a justification for its use. In perfect capital markets a positive NPV reflects the increase in the market value of a company arising from acceptance of the project.

  (ii) An explanation of the impact of market imperfections on the NPV rule. For NPV to represent the increase in shareholders' value resulting from acceptance of an investment, it is necessary for investors to be aware of the project's existence and also the projected future cash flows. This implies that the efficient market hypothesis applies in its strong form and that changes in short-run reported profits do not affect market prices.

  (iii) In imperfect markets shareholders lack information regarding projected future cash flows. Consequently, they may use short-run reported profits and ROI as an indication of potential future cash flows. In such circumstances changes in reported profits will affect share prices. Hence management have reacted to this situation by considering the impact of a project's acceptance on reported ROI.

  (iv) Widespread use of ROI and payback in the UK and USA.

  (v) Shareholders and financial analysts tend to monitor short-run profits and ROI and use these measures as an input that determines their estimates of future share prices. It is therefore not surprising that companies consider the implications of their investment decisions on reported short-run profits and ROI.

(c) The answer should include a discussion of the specific problems that arise in evaluating investments in advanced manufacturing technologies (AMTs) and an explanation of why the financial appraisal might incorrectly reject such investments. In particular, it is claimed that many of the benefits from investing in AMTs are difficult to quantify and tend not to be included in the analysis (e.g. improved product quality). It is also claimed that inflation is incorrectly dealt with and that excessive discount rates are applied which overcompensate for risk.

A further reason that has been cited why companies underinvest in AMTs is that they fail to properly evaluate the relevant alternatives. There is a danger that the investment will be compared incorrectly against an alternative that assumes a continuation of the current market share, selling prices and costs – in other words, the status quo. However, the status quo is unlikely to apply, since competitors are also likely to invest in the new technology. In this situation the investment should be compared with the alternative of not investing, based on assuming a situation of declining cash flow.

The answer should also stress that taxation has not been incorporated into the analysis. In addition, the project has been discounted at the company's normal cost of capital of 15%. This rate is only justified if the risk of the project is equivalent to the average risk of the firm's existing assets.

(a) *Incremental operating costs*

Output (000 units)	Machine X (£000)	Machine Y (£000)
10	53	43
20	80	57
30	96	66
40	122	139

Minimum cost table

	Machine X		Machine Y		Total
Output (000 units)	Output (000 units)	Cost (£000)	Output (000 units)	Cost (£000)	cost (£000)
10	—	—	10	43	43
20	—	—	20	57	57
30	—	—	30	66	66
40	10	53	30	66	119
50	20	80	30	66	146
60	30	96	30	66	162
70	40	122	30	66	188
80	40	122	40	139	261

(b) (i) *Profitability*

Output (000 units)	Sales (£000)	Costs (£000)	Contribution (£000)
10	60	43	17
20	120	57	63
30	180	66	114
40	240	119	121
50	300	146	154
60	360	162	198
70	420	188	232
80	480	261	219

Profits are maximized at an output level of 70 000 units.

(ii) At an output level of 40 000 units machine X has the lowest cost. Machine Y should therefore be offered for sale. It is assumed that if machine Y is not sold, the output from the two machines over the next five years would be 60 000 units (75% × 80 000). The financial effect of selling machine Y would be as follows:

	Two machines (60 000 units) (£)	Machine X only (40 000 units) (£)
Sales	360 000	240 000
Costs	162 000	122 000
Contribution	198 000	118 000
Add annual cost savings		45 000
	198 000	163 000

It is assumed that the company would save £45 000 (£65 000 − £20 000) direct costs in other sections of the company if machine Y were sold. Annual future cash flows would therefore decline by £35 000 (£198 000 − £163 000). The PV of £35 000 annual cash flows for 5 years is £123 095 (£35 000 × 3.517). In addition, there would be a loss of scrap value of £20 000 in year 5. The PV of £20 000 receivable in year 5 is £10 856. Therefore the PV of the lost cash flows if machine Y was sold is £133 951 (£123 095 + £10 856). The minimum selling price is £134 000.

(c) Other factors that should be considered are:
(i) The impact of disruption of supplies if machine X breaks down. With two machines, the company can meet urgent orders if one machine breaks down. With only one machine, there is a distinct possibility that the company will fail to meet delivery dates if machine X breaks down.
(ii) The effect of not being able to meet the annual demand of 60 000 units per annum from LC Ltd. What is the likelihood that LC Ltd will seek another supplier?
(iii) It is assumed that the company will save £45 000 direct expenses elsewhere in the company if machine Y is sold. In practice, such savings might not be made, or may be made gradually. It is important that the company establishes the likely savings over the five-year period prior to negotiating a selling price with LC Ltd.

Question 15.19 (a) The present values of the capital costs are as follows:

Year	Staff (£000)	Expenses	Contingency	Total	Discount factor	Present value (£)
1	20	5	2.5	27.5	0.8772	24 123
2	22	5	2.5	29.5	0.7695	22 700
3	24	5	2.5	31.5	0.675	21 262
4	26	5	2.5	33.5	0.5921	19 835
5	28	5	2.5	35.5	0.5194	18 439
						106 359
Initial outlay						60 000
						166 359

Let x = required net annual income
Therefore the PV of the net annual income over 5 years equates with the PV of the capital costs, where:

$$0.35 \times 0.8772x + 0.65 \times 0.7695x + 0.675x + 0.5921x + 0.5194x = £166\ 359$$
$$2.593x = 166\ 359$$
$$x = £64\ 155$$

If net income is 50% of sales then food sales would need to be £128 310 (£64 155 × 2) in years 3–5. Therefore annual sales required are:

	(£)
Year 1	44 908 (0.35 × £128 310)
2	83 401 (0.65 × £128 310)
3	128 310
4	128 310
5	128 310

(b) Aspects of the proposal that might merit further consideration include:
(i) Is the 14% discount rate equivalent to the opportunity cost of funds allocated by the Management Board?

(ii) Prices, potential demand and product range need to be considered. What is the probability that total income will be sufficient to generate the sales revenue specified in (a)?

(iii) How does the proposed product range, service and price structure compare with other catering facilities available within the locality?

(iv) Is there sufficient expertise and time available for existing staff to operate the new facilities?

(v) What alternative uses are available for the surplus accommodation?

Capital investment decisions: 2

Solutions to Chapter 16 questions

Question summary

These questions are more difficult than those set in Chapter 15.

16.1–16.3   Discussion questions.

16.4–16.6   These focus on the impact of taxation when calculating NPVs and IRRs. Question 16.6 also involves a lease or buy decision and 16.4 requires the calculation of the cost of equity (using the capital asset pricing model) and weighted average cost of capital. Question 16.5 also requires the calculation of the incremental yield.

16.7   NPV calculation and a lease or borrow decision.

16.8   Single-period capital rationing problem. See 25.14–25.18 in Chapter 25 for additional questions on single and multi-period capital rationing.

16.9   Calculation of NPV and the impact on ROI plus a discussion as to whether a project should be accepted which has a positive NPV but a negative impact on ROI.

16.10–16.13   Timing of replacement decisions and the evaluation of projects with unequal lives. Question 16.13 also involves a detailed taxation and NPV calculation

16.14–16.16   Impact of inflation on capital investment decisions. Question 16.15 is time-consuming and complex, and requires a decision on whether to introduce a postal service. Question 16.16 also involves financing costs.

16.17   Calculation of the internal rate of return, requiring the identification of relevant and non-relevant cash flows. Part (b) requires a description of asset betas and part (c) includes sensitivity analysis relating to the potential increase in the corporate tax rate.

16.18, 16.19   NPV and IRR calculations and sensitivity analysis.

16.20, 16.21   Calculation and discussion of expected net present values. Question 16.21 is also concerned with the expected value of additional information.

16.22   Computation of a tender price using cost-plus pricing. This question also involves monthly discounting and the calculation of the sales values at which NPV is zero.

16.23   Calculation of NPV from incomplete data involving taxation, financing costs and identification of relevant cash flows and cost of capital.

Question 16.4 (a)

Revised estimate of the project's net present value
Calculation of tax liability
(£000)

Year	1	2	3	4	5	6
Sales	2950	3820	5200	5400	5600	5800
Direct costs	(1499)	(1940)	(2642)	(2743)	(2845)	(2946)
Incremental overheads	(185)	(240)	(315)	(321)	(328)	(330)

Capital allowances	(140)	(480)	(480)	(480)	(480)	(340)
	1824	2660	3437	3544	3653	3616
Taxable profits	1126	1160	1763	1856	1947	2184
Taxation (40%)	450	464	705	742	779	874

Calculation of NPV

Cash flows

Year	0	1	2	3	4	5	6	7
Land and buildings	(500)	(600)						
Plant and machinery	(700)	(1700)						
Working capital[a]	(230)	(340)	(110)	(20)	(20)	(20)	740	
Operating cash flows[b]		1266	1640	2243	2336	2427	2524	
Taxation[c]			(450)	(464)	(705)	(742)	(779)	(874)
Terminal value							8725	
Tax on terminal value[d]								(3050)
	(1430)	(1374)	1080	1759	1611	1665	11 210	(3924)
Disc. Factor (18%)		0.847	0.718	0.609	0.516	0.437	0.370	0.314
Present values	(1430)	(1164)	775	1071	831	728	4148	(1232)

NPV = £3 727 000

The NPV of the project is estimated to be £3 727 000. On the basis of this information, the project should be accepted.

Interest is not deducted in the calculation of the tax liability, because this is already reflected within the after tax interest rate in the weighted average cost of capital calculation. Also, the interest payments are not included in the cash flows, because this is reflected within the discounting process.

Notes
[a]The cumulative amount of working capital is assumed to be released at the end of year 6.
[b]Operating cash inflows = sales − direct costs − incremental overheads.
[c]Terminal value = Year 6 after tax operating cash inflows (£2524 − £779) × 5 = £8725.
[d]The WDV of plant and machinery for taxation purposes at the end of year 6 is zero. It is assumed that the realizable value of plant and machinery at the end of the planning horizon is 7625 (£8725 − £1100 for land and buildings). This would result in a potential balancing taxation charge of £3050 (£7625 × 0.4).

The risk-adjusted cost of equity capital for this project is derived by applying the beta for a company whose major activity is the manufacture of products that are similar to the proposed projects:

$$\begin{array}{l} \text{cost of} \\ \text{equity} \end{array} = \begin{array}{l} \text{risk-free} \\ \text{rate (12\%)} \end{array} + \left[\begin{array}{l} \text{return on market} \\ \text{portfolio (20\%)} \end{array} - \begin{array}{l} \text{risk-free} \\ \text{rate (12\%)} \end{array} \right] \times \text{beta (1.5)} = 24\%$$

The after-tax cost of debt is 15% × (1 − tax rate) = 9%
The weighted average cost of capital (WACC) is calculated by assuming a capital structure of 60% equity and 40% debt;
WACC = 0.6 (24%) + 0.4 (9%) = 18%
The estimated discount rate is therefore 18%.
The recommended acceptance is subject to the following reservations:

(i) The cash flow estimates do not include any adjustments for estimated price level changes.

(ii) It is extremely difficult to estimate discount rates accurately, and there is a need to ascertain how sensitive the NPV calculation is to higher discount rates.

(iii) The project has not been evaluated over its expected life. An unsophisticated approach has been used to estimate the terminal value. Given that the estimate of the terminal value is critical to the NPV calculation, it is important that the estimate be reviewed before recommending acceptance. Ideally, the project ought to be re-evaluated over its expected life.

(b) The 18% discount rate is an observed nominal discount rate, which will include a premium for inflation. If the cash flows have not been adjusted for inflation, the NPV will have been calculated by discounting real cash flows at a nominal discount rate. This approach is incorrect, and it will be necessary to adjust the cash flows for inflation.

Question 16.6 (a) The annual variable operating cost savings if the company manufactures material Kay are as follows:

Year	Savings per unit	No. of units (£000)	Total savings (£000)
1	5 (£20 − £15)	20	100
2	9 (£24 − £15)	20	180
3	10 (£25 − £15)	20	200
4	13 (£30 − £17)	10	130
5	18 (£35 − £17)	10	180

The cash inflows and outflows are shown in the following schedule.

Cash inflows and outflows (£000)

	Year 0	Year 1	Year 2	Year 3	Year 4	Year 5	Year 6
Variable operating cost savings		100	180	200	130	180	
Handling costs saved		40	40	40	40	40	
Additional rates		(20)	(20)	(20)	(20)	(20)	
Total annual savings		120	200	220	150	200	
Tax on annual savings			(60)	(100)	(110)	(75)	(100)
Purchase of land	(120)					160	
Existing machine and tax	(80)	40				10	(5)
New machine and tax	(400)	200					
Net cash flow	(600)	360	140	120	40	295	(105)
Discount factor at 15%	1.000	0.870	0.756	0.658	0.572	0.497	0.432
Present value	(600)	313.2	105.84	78.96	22.88	146.615	(45.36)

NPV = £22.135

Therefore the project is worthwhile.

(b) The relevant pre-tax discount rates for both methods of financing are 10%. Leasing reduces a firm's debt capacity, and therefore the opportunity cost of capital is considered to be 10% pre-tax. The after-tax cost of capital for both methods of financing is 5%. The present value for each method of financing is calculated as follows:

Purchase

	Year	(£000)	Discount factor at 5%	PV (£000)
Purchase of machine	0	400	1.000	400.00
Tax saving	1	(200)	0.952	(190.40)
			PV of cost	£209.60

Leasing

Year	Rentals (£000)	Tax (£000)	Net cash flow (£000)	Discount factor at 5%	PV (£000)
0	60		60	1.000	60.00
1	100	(30)	70	0.952	66.64
2	100	(50)	50	0.907	45.35
3	100	(50)	50	0.864	43.20
4	100	(50)	50	0.823	41.15
5		(50)	(50)	0.784	(39.20)
				PV of cost	£217.14

Therefore purchase is less expensive than leasing.

(c) Here the tax benefits will not affect cash flows until year 3. Using the same discount rates as before, the PVs of leasing and purchase are as follows:

Purchase

	Year	£000s	PVF at 5%	PV (£000)
Purchase of machine	0	400	1.000	400.00
Tax saving	3	(200)	0.864	(172.80)
			PV of costs	£227.20

Leasing

Year	Rentals (£000)	Tax (£000)	Netcash flow (£000)	Discount factor at 5%	PV (£000)
0	60		60	1.000	60.00
1	100		100	0.952	95.20
2	100		100	0.907	90.70
3	100	(130)	(30)	0.864	(25.92)
4	100	(50)	50	0.823	41.15
5		(50)	(50)	0.784	(39.20)
				PV of costs	£221.93

Because of the impact of the tax delay, leasing proves to be the less expensive alternative *at the discount rates used*.

(d) (i) The merit of Turnbull's policy is that it has established a formal policy for evaluating capital investment decisions. The main danger of its policy is that all projects are appraised initially as if they are to be purchased. If a project fails this test then it is not considered for leasing. However, it is possible that a project that is not worthwhile if purchased will be worthwhile if leased, but with Turnbull's system this will never be determined.

(ii) The tax delay differs between the circumstances in (b) and (c) in the early years of the analysis. In (b) the delay is one year throughout whereas in (c) the delay varies, but after year 2 reverts to one year. The greater the tax delay, the less is the impact of the tax deductability of debt interest, and therefore the higher will be the effective after-tax rate of the debt interest. Therefore, different after-tax discount rates should be used for circumstances (b) and (c).

One solution to the problem is to use the pre-tax rates of 10% and then include the discounted value of cash savings caused by the tax savings from the debt interest. This method is called the Adjusted Present Value Approach. For a discussion of this approach see Brearley and Myers (1990, Ch. 19), listed in References and Further Reading in Chapter 16.

Question 16.8 (a) *Calculations of expected net present value and profitability indices*

Project A
NPV (£70 000 × 3.605) − £246 000 = £6350

Profitablilty index = $\dfrac{\text{present value of cash inflows}}{\text{initial outlay}} = \dfrac{252\,350}{246\,000} = 1.026$

Project B
NPV (£75 000 × 0.893) + (£87 000 × 0.797) + (£64 000 × 0.712) − £180 000
= £1882

Profitability index = $\dfrac{181\,882}{180\,000} = 1.010$

Project C
NPV (£48 000 × 1.69) + (£63 000 × 0.712) + (£73 000 × 0.636) − £175 000
= (£2596)

Profitability index = $\dfrac{172\,404}{175\,000} = 0.985$

Project D
NPV (£62 000 × 3.037) − £180 000 = £8294

Profitability index = $\dfrac{188\,294}{180\,000} = 1.046$

Project E
NPV (£40 000 × 0.893) + (£50 000 × 0.797) + (£60 000 × 0.712) + (£70 000 × 0.636) + (£40 000 × 0.567) − £180 000 = £5490

Profitability index = $\dfrac{185\,490}{180\,000} = 1.031$

Project F
NPV = (£35 000 × 0.893) + (£82 000 × 1.509) − £150 000 = £4993

Profitability index = $\dfrac{154\,993}{150\,000} = 1.033$

Project rankings	NPV	PI
1	D	D
2	A	F
3	E	E
4	F	A
5	B	B
6	C	C

The rankings differ because NPV is an absolute measure whereas the profitability index is a relative measure that takes into account the different investment cost of each project.

(b) The objective is to select a combination of investments that will maximize NPV subject to a total capital outlay of £620 000. Projects A and E are mutually exclusive and project C has a negative NPV. The following are potential combinations of projects:

Projects	Expected NPV (£)	Total expected NPV (£)	Total Outlay (£)
A, B, D	6350 + 1882 + 8294	16 526	606 000
A, B, F	6350 + 1882 + 4993	13 225	576 000
A, D, F	6350 + 8294 + 4993	19 637	576 000
B, D, E	1882 + 8294 + 5490	15 666	540 000
B, D, F	1882 + 8294 + 4993	15 169	510 000
D, E, F	8294 + 5490 + 4993	18 777	510 000

Note that it is not possible to combine four projects within the constraints outlined above and that expected NPV cannot be increased by combining two projects. Accepting projects A, D and F will maximize NPV. This combination will require a total capital outlay of £576 000, and the unused funds will be invested to yield a return of 9%. The risk-adjusted discount rate for the investment will also be 9%. Therefore the NPV of funds invested in the money market will be zero.

(c) Where a company rejects projects with positive NPVs because of capital rationing, the IRR forgone on the most profitable project that has been rejected represents the opportunity cost of capital. For a more detailed explanation of this point see 'Capital rationing' in Chapter 16. Therefore the director is correct in stating that the company's cost of capital might not be appropriate.

(d) *Advantages of mathematical programming:*
   (i) Ability to solve complex problems incorporating the effects of complex inter-actions.
   (ii) Speed in solving the problem using computer facilities.
   (iii) The output from the model can highlight the key constraints to which attention should be directed.
   (iv) Sensitivity analysis can be applied. The effects of changes in the variables can be speedily tested.

   Disadvantages of mathematical programming:
   (i) Divisibility of projects may not be realistic, and integer programming may have to be used.
   (ii) Constraints are unlikely to be completely fixed and precise, as implied in the mathematical models.
   (iii) Not all the relevant information can be quantified.
   (iv) All the information for the model may not be available. For example, it may not be possible to specify the constraints of future periods.
   (v) All the relationships contained within the formulation may not be linear.
   (vi) All the potential investment opportunities may not be identified and included in the analysis.
   (vii) The linear programming formulation assumes that all the project's cash flows are certain, and therefore it cannot incorporate uncertainty. The solution produced can only be considered optimal given this restrictive assumption.

PV of cost of operating new machines

Question 16.10

	(£)
Purchase price (£52 000 × 4)	208 000
PV of annual operating costs for 7 years (£15 000 × 4 × 4.564)	273 840
Salvage value (4× £4000 × 0.4523)	(7 237)
PV of costs over 7-year life	474 603

$$\text{Equivalent annual cost} = \frac{\text{PV of costs}}{\text{annuity factor for } n \text{ years at } R\%} = \frac{£474\ 603}{4.564} = £103\ 988$$

PV of cost of operating old machine

	(£)
Opportunity cost of selling machines (10 × £5000)	50 000
Operating costs (10 × £10 000 × 2.402)	240 200
PV of costs over 3-year life	290 200

Equivalent annual cost (£290 200/2.402) = £120 816

The new machines have the lowest equivalent annual cost. Therefore they should be replaced now. This decision is based on the assumption that no superior or cheaper machines will be available in three years' time. If other opportunities are likely to be available in three years' time then the combination of operating the old machines and replacing with more efficient or cheaper machines should be considered.

The costs of modifying the factory building should be compared with the savings that result from the installation of the new machines. Equivalent annual savings from purchasing the new machines are £16 828 (£120 816 − £103 988) for three years. The PV of these savings is £40 421 (£16 828 × 2.402). It is assumed that if the factory is not modified now, it will have to be modified in three years' time when the current machines reach the end of their life. Assuming the cost of modification will still be £60 000 in three years' time, the relevant cost of the modification is:

	(£)
PV of modification now	60 000
Less PV of modification in 3 years' time (£60 000 × 0.712)	42 720
Relevant cost of modification now	17 280

It is therefore worthwhile to incur a cost of £17 280 now in order to achieve savings with a PV of £40 421.

Question 16.12 (a) *PV of acquiring Exe (12-year life)*

		Discount factor at 10%	Present value
	(£)		(£)
Annual repair costs (years 1–12)	2 000	6.814	13 628
Overhead cost (year 8)	4 000	0.4665	1 866
Purchase price (year 0)	19 000	1.000	19 000
Trade-in value (year 12)	(3 000)	0.3186	(956)
			33 538

PV of acquiring Wye

Annual repair costs (years 1–6)	2 600	4.355	11 323
Overhead cost (year 4)	2 000	0.683	1 366
Purchase price (year 0)	13 000	1.000	13 000
Trade-in value (year 6)	(3 000)	0.5645	(1 694)
			23 995

The machines have unequal lives, and to compensate for this the equivalent annual cost method should be used:
Exe equivalent annual cost = £4922 (£33 538/6.814)
Wye equivalent annual cost = £5510 (£23 995/4.355)
Exe should be purchased, since it has the lowest equivalent annual cost. It is assumed that both machines have the same performance reliability, quality and output and that there is no inflation.

(b) The answer should describe one of the three approaches outlined in Chapter 16. For a description of these approaches see 'A comparison of mutually exclusive investments with unequal lives'.

(c) See 'Life cycle costing' in Chapter 28 for the answer to this question.

(a)

Proposal one

Time	0	1	2	3	4
	(31.12.90)	(31.12.91)	(31.12.92)	(31.12.93)	(31.12.94)
	(£)	(£)	(£)	(£)	(£)
Investment outlay	(62 500)				
Scrap proceeds				5 000	
Net cash inflows		40 000	55 000	70 000	
Tax on net inflows			(20 000)	(27 500)	(35 000)
Writing down allowance[a]		6 250	5 000	4 000	13 500
Working capital[b]	(4 000)	(1 500)	(1 500)	7 000	
Net cash flow	(66 500)	44 750	38 500	58 500	(21 500)
Discount factor[c]	1	0.826	0.696	0.597	0.517
Present values	(66 500)	36 964	26 796	34 925	(11 116)

Net present value = £21 069

Proposal two

Time	0	1	2	3	4
	(31.12.90)	(31.12.91)	(31.12.92)	(31.12.93)	(31.12.94)
	(£)	(£)	(£)	(£)	(£)
Opportunity cost of disposal proceeds foregone[d]		(60 000)			
Balancing charge avoided[d]				30 000	
Net cash inflows[e]		68 000	67 840		
Tax on inflows			(34 000)	(33 920)	
Working capital	(7 000)		7 000		
Net cash flow	(7 000)	8 000	40 840	(3 920)	
Discount factor[c]	1	0826	0696	0597	
Present values	(7 000)	6608	28425	(2340)	

Net present value = £25 693
Proposal two should be chosen because it has the highest NPV.

Notes
[a]The writing down allowances are calculated as follows:

A/c Period ended		(£)		(£)	Time
31.12.90	Investment	62 500			
	WDA at 20%	(12 500)	Tax saved at 50%	6 250	1
		50 000			
31.12.91	WDA at 20%	(10 000)	Tax saved at 50%	5 000	2
		40 000			
31.12.92	WDA at 20%	(8 000)	Tax saved at 50%	4 000	3
		32 000			
31.12.93	Scrap proceeds	(5 000)			
	Balancing allowance	27 000	Tax saved at 50%	13 500	4

^{b}Working capital requirements are 10% of net cash inflows (i.e. £4000 at Time 0, £5500 at Time 1 and £7000 at Time 2). Only incremental changes in working capital are included in the cash flow analysis.

^{c}Because the cash flows have been expressed in nominal terms the discount rates should also be expressed in nominal terms. Nominal discount rate = (1 + Real discount rate) × (1 + Anticipated inflation rate) − 1.

$$1991 = (1.10) \times (1.10) - 1 = 0.21 \quad (21\%)$$
$$1992 = (1.10) \times (1.08) - 1 = 0.188 \ (18.8\%)$$
$$1993 = (1.10) \times (1.06) - 1 = 0.166 \ (16.6\%)$$
$$1994 = (1.10) \times (1.05) - 1 = 0.155 \ (15.5\%)$$

The discount factors are:

$$\text{Time } 1 = 1/1.21 = 0.826$$
$$\text{Time } 2 = 1/1.21 \times 1/1.188 = 0.696$$
$$\text{Time } 3 = 1/1.21 \times 1/1.188 \times 1/1.166 = 0.597$$
$$\text{Time } 4 = 1/1.21 \times 1/1.188 \times 1/1.166 \times 1/1.155 = 0.517$$

The above calculations reflect the fact that different discount rates are used each year. For example, cash flows in Time 4 have to be discounted back to Time 3 at 15.5%, Time 3 back to Time 2 at 16.6%, Time 2 back to Time 1 at 18.8% and Time 1 back to Time 0 at 21%.

^{d}Proposal 2 utilizes existing machinery which would otherwise be sold. Therefore the opportunity cost should be included as a cash flow. If Proposal 2 is not undertaken the company has the choice of either selling the machine at 31 December 1990 for £50 000 or selling it at 1 January 1992 for £60 000.
The PV calculations are:

Sale at 31 December 1990	(£)
Sale at 31 December 1990 (Time 0)	50 000
Balancing charge at 31 December 1991 (Time 1) = £25 000 × 0.826	(20 650)
PV	29 350

Sale at 1 January 1992 (Time 1)	(£)
Sale proceeds (£60 000 × 0.826)	49 560
Balancing charge at 31 December 1993 (Time 3) = £30 000 × 0.597	(17 910)
PV	31 650

Therefore the company should sell the machine at January 1992 if Proposal 2 is not accepted and the latter cash flows therefore represent the relevant cash flows to be included in the analysis.

^{e}The incremental labour cash flows arising from the project are £22 000 for 1991 and £23 760 for 1992, but £20 000 and £21 600 have been included in the operating cash inflows given in the question. Therefore cash inflows must be reduced by £2000 in 1991 and £2160 in 1992.

(b) Reservations relating to the figures used in (a) include:
1. The accuracy of the estimated cash flows, inflation rates and discount rates.
2. It is assumed that all cash flows are received at the year end whereas they are likely to occur throughout the year.
3. The projects may entail different levels of risk but this has been ignored in the analysis.

Question 16.17 (a)

Relevant cash flows

Year	0	1	2	3	4
		(£000)	(£000)	(£000)	(£000)
Sales^a		1320	2021	2183	2355

Cash costs

Direct labour[b]	354	553	608	668
Material Z[c]	102	161	174	188
Components P and Q[d]	250	382	413	445
Other variable costs[e]	25	39	42	45
Management salaries[f]	67	72	77	82
Selling expenses[g]	166	174	183	192
Rental[h]	120	126	132	139
Other fixed overhead[i]	50	53	55	58
	1134	1560	1684	1817
Sales less cash costs	186	461	499	538
Tax[j]	9	(87)	(100)	(114)
Initial investment	(864)			
Residual value				12
	(864)	195	374	399	436

Notes

[a]Sales revenue: year 1 = 12 000 × £110

$\qquad$ 2 = 17 500 × £110 × (1.05)

$\qquad$ 3 = 18 000 × £110 × $(1.05)^2$

$\qquad$ 4 = 18 500 × £110 × $(1.05)^3$

[b]Labour costs: year 1 = 12 000 × £29.50, year 2 = 17 500 × £29.50 × (1.07), year 3 = 18 000 × £29.50 × $(1.07)^2$, year 4 = 18 500 × £29.50 × $(1.07)^3$.

[c]72 000 kg are required in year 1. The relevant cost for the 70 000 kg in stock is £99 000 opportunity cost. The acquisition cost for the remaining 2000 kg is £2920 (2000 × £1.46). For the remaining years the relevant costs are: year 2 = 17 500 × 6 kg × £1.46 × (1.05), year 3 = 18 000 × 6 kg × £1.46 × $(1.05)^2$, year 4 = 18 500 × 6 kg × £1.46 × $(1.05)^3$.

[d]Components P and Q (£20.80 per unit): year 1 = 12 000 × £20.80, year 2 = 17 500 × £20.80 × (1.05), year 3 = 18 000 × £20.80 × $(1.05)^2$, year 4 = 18 500 × £20.80 × $(1.05)^3$.

[e]Year 1 = 12 000 × £2.10, year 2 = 17 500 × £2.10 × (1.05), year 3 = 18 000 × £2.10 × $(1.05)^2$, year 4 = 18 500 × £2.10 × $(1.05)^3$.

[f]Relevant cash outflows for year 1 are (£25 000 × 2) + £17 000 = £67 000, year 2 = £67 000 × (1.07), year 3 = £67 000 × $(1.07)^2$, year 4 = £67 000 × $(1.07)^3$.

[g]Selling expenses £166 000 per annum adjusted at 5% for inflation.

[h]Rental opportunity cost = £120 000 per annum adjusted at 5% for inflation.

[i]Relevant cash flows for other fixed overheads = £70 000 − £20 000 apportioned costs. The cash flows are adjusted at a 5% compound inflation rate for years 2–4.

[j]The tax cash flows are calculated as follows:

Year	1	2	3	4
	(£000)	(£000)	(£000)	(£000)
Sales less cash costs	186	461	499	538
Capital allowances	213	213	213	213
Taxable profits	(27)	248	286	325
Tax at 35%	(9)	87	100	114

It is assumed in year 1 that the company has sufficient taxable profits to set-off the negative table profits from the project.

Apportionment of head office costs are not relevant cash flows.

Interest payments are not included, because the cost of finance is already reflected in the discount rate.

The IRR can be found by using the interpolation method. The objective is to find the discount rate where the sum of the present values for years 1–4 equals

£864 000 initial outlay. At 15% and 25% the NPVs are respectively + £101 000 and − £86 000. Using the interpolation method:

$$IRR = 15\% + \frac{101}{101 - (-86)} \times 10\% = \text{approximately } 20\%$$

(b) An asset beta reflects the beta of the company, assuming all equity financing. In contrast, the equity beta reflects the beta for a particular mixture of debt and equity. Equity betas include the additional financial risk from gearing, and will therefore be higher than asset beta because of the additional risk.

Assuming that Amble plc is all equity-financed, the asset beta can be used to estimate the required rate of return (discount rate for the project):

$$RRR = \frac{\text{risk-free}}{\text{rate (8\%)}} + \left[\frac{\text{market}}{\text{return (15\%)}} - \frac{\text{risk-free}}{\text{rate (8\%)}} \right] \times \text{beta (1.2)}$$
$$= 16.4\%$$

The IRR of 20% is in excess of the required rate of return (16.4%). On a purely financial evaluation the project should be accepted.

(c) Using a discount rate of 17%, the expected NPV is:

Year	Cash flow (£000)	Discount factor	Present value (£000)
0	(864)	1	(864)
1	195	0.855	167
2	374	0.731	273
3	399	0.624	249
4	436	0.534	233
		Net present value	58

The product will not be financially viable when the present value of the additional taxation exceeds £58 000.

The taxable cash flows calculated in (a) are:

Year 1 (£000)	Year 2 (£000)	Year 3 (£000)	.Year 4 (£000)
(27)	248	286	325

Let x = % increase in taxation rate.

Using the discount factors of 0.855, 0.731 etc. for a discount rate of 18%, the increase in the taxation rate can be ascertained from the following formula:

$$-27 \times (0.855x) + 248 \times (0.731x) + 286 \times (0.624x) + 325 \times (0.534x) = 58$$
$$510.1x = 58$$
$$x = 0.11$$

Therefore taxation rates can increase by 11% from 35% to 46% before NPV becomes negative.

Question 16.18 (a) *Calculation of expected NPV (£000)*

Year	0	1	2	3	4	5	6
Investment outlay	(1500)						
Sales at £2 per unit		3000	3000	3000	3000	3000	3000
Variable costs at £1.59 per unit[a]		2385	2385	2385	2385	2385	2385

Taxable cash flows		615	615	615	615	615	615
Tax at 35%		215	215	215	215	215	215
Net cash flow[b]	(1500)	400	400	400	400	400	400

NPV at a discount rate of 8%[c] = (£400 × 4.623) − £1500 = £349 200

Notes

[a] Unit variable cost = Purchase cost (£1.50 × 40%) + copyright fee (20% × £3.95) + £0.20 additional variable cost.

[b] Market research is a sunk cost.

[c] See part (b) of the answer for an explanation of why a discount rate of 8% has been used. Note that the financing costs are incorporated in the discount rate and should not be included in the cash flows as this would lead to double counting.

(b) Assuming that the company wishes to maintain its current capital structure the specific cost of financing the project should not be used as a discount rate. The project has been financed by a bank loan but this will result in less borrowing being used in the future as the company re-balances its finance to achieve the target capital structure. To reflect the company's target capital structure the weighted average cost of capital (WACC) should be used.

The money WACC should be used only if the cash flows are expressed in money/nominal terms (i.e. adjusted for inflation). Current cash flows have been used to calculate NPV. Current cash flows are equivalent to real cash flow when all cash flows increase at the general rate of inflation. This situation occurs in this question and therefore the cash flows are equivalent to real cash flows. Thus the real WACC of capital should be used to discount the cash flows.

The WACC represents the discount rate applicable for the company as a whole and reflects the average risk of all of the company's assets. If the project has a different level of risk from the average risk of the assets of the company as a whole, the existing WACC will not represent the appropriate discount rate. In this situation a separate risk adjusted discount rate should be used.

It is also assumed that all of the cash flows increase at the general rate of inflation. If the cash flows are subject to different rates of inflation it will be incorrect to use current prices. If this situation occurs the cash flows should be adjusted by their specific rates of inflation and a nominal discount rate should be used.

(c) (i) *Initial outlay*

The NPV of the project is £349 200. Therefore the investment outlay could increase by £349 200 before NPV becomes negative. This represents a percentage increase of 23.28% (£349.2/£1500 × 100).

Annual contribution

Let x = annual contribution

With a corporate tax rate of 35% the annual contribution at which NPV will be zero can be calculated from the following formula:

$(1 - 0.35) 4.623x - £1,500 = 0$
$3.005x - 1,500 = 0$
$x = 1,500/3.005 = £499.16$

Therefore annual contribution can decline from the existing figure of £615 000 to £499 160. A percentage decrease of 18.83% (£115.84/£615 × 100). Note that 4.623 and £1500 in the above formula represents the cumulative discount factor and the investment outlay.

The life of the agreement

Let x = Annuity factor at 8%

NPV will be zero where

$400x - £1500 = 0$
$x = 3.75$

From the annuity table shown in Appendix B of the text:
PV of annuity for 4 years at 8% = 3.312
PV of annuity for 5 years at 8% = 3.993
Extrapolating, the PV annuity factor is:

$$4 \text{ years} + \frac{3.75 - 3.312}{3.993 - 3.312} \times 1 \text{ year} = 4.643 \text{ years}$$

This represents a reduction of 22.61% [(6 − 4.643)/6 years × 100]
Discount rate
Let x = PV of annuity for 6 years
NPV will be zero where:

$$400x = 1500$$
$$x = 3.75$$

From the annuity tables (Appendix B) 15% has a PV annuity factor of 3.784 and 16% is 3.685. Thus the discount rate at which NPV will be zero is approximately 15.5%. This represents an increase of 93.75% [(15.5 − 8)/8 × 100).

The above calculations indicate that the annual contribution is the most sensitive variable.
(ii) See 'Sensitivity Analysis' in Chapter 16 for an outline of the limitations of sensitivity analysis.
(d) Possible additional information includes:
  (i) Is the agreement likely to be renewed after 6 years?
  (ii) Are competitors likely to enter the market and what impact would this have on the sales volume and price?
  (iii) How accurate are the estimated cash flows?
  (iv) How reliable is the supplier who supplies microfiche readers? Can the microfiche readers be obtained from any other source or is the company dependent upon the one supplier?

Question 16.21 (a) The present value of the capital costs is:

	(£)
Purchase price	50 000
Costs of making the mine operational (£95 000 × 0.8264)	78 508
Cost of special equipment (£48 000 × 0.8264)	39 667
	168 175

Note that the cash flows of £95 000 and £48 000 arise at t_1.
The life of the project depends on the rock formations:

Rock type A = 10 years (240 tonnes/24 tonnes per year)
Rock type B = 5 years (120 tonnes/24 tonnes per year)
Rock type C = 3 years (72 tonnes/24 tonnes per year)

The net cash flow for the first year of production (received at t_2) is (24 tonnes × £9900) − £187 000 = £50 600. Because of inflation, the cash flows for the remaining years are expected to increase at 10% per annum, so the present value of the net cash flows from t_2 onwards can be calculated as follows:

$$\underset{t_2}{\frac{£50\,600}{(1.21)^2}} + \underset{t_3}{\frac{£50\,600 \times 1.10}{(1.21)^3}} + \underset{t_4}{\frac{£50\,600 \times 1.10}{(1.21)^4}} \cdots$$

For a 3-year life the net cash flows from t_2 to t_4 are discounted, for a 5-year life those from t_2 to t_6 are discounted and for a 10-year life those from t_2 to t_{11} are discounted. It should be noted that the required rate of return of 1.21 can be expressed as 1.10×1.10, and 1.10 also appears in the numerator as the inflation compounding factor. We can therefore take an alternative short-cut approach by initially discounting the cash flows back to t_2 and then discounting the cash flows from t_2 back to t_0. The cash flows can be expressed as follows:

$$50\,600 + \frac{£50\,600 \times 1.10}{£50\,600 \times 1.10 \times 1.10} + \frac{£50\,600 \times (1.10)^2}{(1.10)^2 \times (1.10)^2} + \frac{£50\,600 \times (1.10)^3}{(1.10)^3 \times (1.10)^3} \cdots$$

It can be seen that the above expression is equivalent to discounting £50 600 by 10%. This approach enables the cumulative discount tables to be used.

$$\text{10-year life} = £50\,600 + (£50\,600 \times 5.759) = £342\,005$$
$$\text{5-year life} = £50\,600 + (£50\,600 \times 3.170) = £211\,002$$
$$\text{3-year life} = £50\,600 + (£50\,600 \times 1.736) = £138\,442$$

The above cash flows are expressed in terms of t_2. They are now discounted at 21% back to t_0.

$$\text{10-year life} = £342\,005 \times 0.683 = £233\,589$$
$$\text{5-year life} = £211\,002 \times 0.683 = £144\,114$$
$$\text{3-year life} = £138\,442 \times 0.683 = £94\,556$$

The present values of the machinery sales are:

$$\text{10-year life} = \frac{£48\,000 - (240 \times £200)}{(1.21)^{11}} = 0$$

$$\text{5-year life} = \frac{£48\,000 - (120 \times £200)}{(1.21)^6} = £7647$$

$$\text{3-year life} = \frac{£48\,000 - (72 \times £200)}{(1.21)^4} = £15\,675$$

The NPV can now be calculated by combining the above cash flows:

$$\text{Type A (10-year life)} = £233\,589 + 0 - £168\,175 = £65\,414$$
$$\text{Type B (5-year life)} = £144\,114 + £7647 - £168\,175 = -£16\,414$$
$$\text{Type C (3-year life)} = £94\,556 + £15\,675 - £168\,175 = -£57\,944$$

The expected NPV for the purchase of the mine is:

$$(0.4 \times £65\,414) - (0.4 \times £16\,414) - (0.2 \times £57\,944) = +£8011$$

(b) If the survey is commissioned, the company will avoid the negative NPVs resulting from formation types B and C by cancelling the project. The value of the survey can be found by comparing the expected NPVs with and without the survey:

	(£)
Expected NPV with survey: Rock Type A (£65 414 × 0.4)	26 166
Rock type B (cancel)	0
Rock type C (cancel)	0
	26 166
Expected NPV without survey	8 011
Benefit from survey	18 155
Cost of survey	10 000
Net benefit from survey	8 155

The company should commission the survey based on the expected value decision rule. The major weakness of the expected value approach is that it ignores risk. However, if the range of possible outcomes from the two alternatives is compared, it can be seen that the geological survey substantially reduces the range of outcomes. Without the survey, the outcomes range from −£57 944 to £65 414, whereas with it the range is from −£10 000 (cost of the survey) to £55 414 (£65 414 − £10 000 cost of the survey). This substantial reduction in risk provides a further justification for commissioning the survey.

Question 16.22 (a) Directly attributable costs:

		(£m)
Materials (£715 000 × 15)		10.725
Labour (£380 000 × 15)		5.700
Other direct costs (£50 000 × 15)		0.750
Operating lease (£620 000 × 5)		3.100
Capital costs (£1.8m − £0.9m)		0.900
		21.175
20% mark-up		4.235
Proposed tender price in sterling		25.410

The tender price must be in Zmbland dollars. Using a current exchange rate of Z$46/£ and a predicted rate of Z$57.5/£ (46 × 1.25) in 15 months' time the tender price in Zmbland dollars is:

$$(25.41m \times 0.3 \times 46) + (25.41m \times 0.7 \times 57.5) = Z\$1373.41m$$

(b) The tax liability for the project is based on cash flows. The tax payable is calculated as follows:

	Year 1 (£000)	Year 2 (£000)
Sales	7623 (30% × £25 410)	17 787 (70% × £25 410)
Wages	1140 (3 months)	4560 (12 months)
Materials	2860 (4 months)	7865 (11 months)
Other direct costs	150 (3 months)	600 (12 months)

	Year 1 (£000)	Year 2 (£000)
Leasing payments	620 (1 payment)	2480 (4 payments)
Tax depreciation allowances[a]	450 (25% × £1.8m)	450
Taxable cash flows	2403	1832
Tax payable at 35%	841	641

Note
[a]At the start of year 2 the WDV of the plant is £1.35 million, and the sale proceeds at the end of the year are estimated to be £900 000. Capital allowances for year 2 consist of an annual writing-down allowance plus a balancing allowance, amounting to a total value of £450 000.

NPV calculation

Cash inflows	Month	(£000)	Discount or annuity factor[a]	Present values (£000)
Sales: initial payment	0	7 623	1.000	7 623
final payment	15	17 787	0.861	15 315
Residual value	15	900	0.861	775
				23 713

Cash outflows

Wages	1–15	380	13.87	5 271
Materials[a]	0–14	715	14.00	10 010
Other direct costs	1–15	50	13.87	693
Lease payments	0	620	1.000	620
	3	620	0.971	602
	6	620	0.942	584
	9	620	0.914	567
	12	620	0.887	550
Tax payments	9	841	0.914	769
	21	641	0.811	520
Initial investment[a]	0	1936	1.000	1 936
				22 122
Net present value (23 713 − 22 122)				1591

Notes

[a]The discount factors are obtained from Appendix A of the main text, assuming monthly time periods and a monthly discount rate of 1%. The annuity factors are obtained from Appendix B. Note that the annuity factor for years 0–14 is calculated by adding the annuity factor for years 1–14 (13.000) to the discount factor for time zero (1.000).

[b]Materials are purchased two months in advance, and one month's credit is taken. It is assumed that this implies that cash outflows will consist of 15 monthly payments from time zero to month 14.

[c]If the contract is not undertaken, the plant will be sold for £2m. However, if the plant were sold, tax of £70 000 (0.35 × £200 000) would be payable on a balancing charge of £200 000 (£2m − £1.8m). This payment would be due in month 9. Thus the present value is £63 980 (£70 000 × 0.914), and the net opportunity cost of not selling the plant is £1 936 020 (£2m − £63 980) at time zero.

The minimum tender price would be a price that yields a zero net present value. A change in the tender price would only alter the after-tax sales proceeds. All other cash flows would remain unchanged. The NPV based on the above calculations is £1.591m. Thus if the present value of the after tax cash flows declined by £1.591m, NPV would be zero.

Let x = before-tax decline in the total tender price. Thus we must determine the value of x, where:

$$(0.3x \times 1.000) - (0.35 \times 0.3x \times 0.914) + (0.7x \times 0.861) - (0.35 \times 0.7x \times 0.811)$$
$$= 1.591\text{m}$$
$$x = 2.617\text{m}$$

Note that the first and third terms in the above equation relate to the present value of the change in sale proceeds, and the second and fourth terms to the tax payments on the change in sale proceeds. Thus the tender price can decline to £22.793m (£25.410m − £2.617m) before NPV becomes zero. Therefore the minimum tender price in Zmbland dollars is:

$$(22.793\text{m} \times 0.3 \times 46) + (22.793\text{m} \times 0.7 \times 57.5) = \text{Z\$}1231.96\text{m}$$

The analysis assumes that the cash flow estimates are correct. For example:
(i) The prices of labour, materials and other costs may change.
(ii) The future level of foreign exchange rates may be different from the estimated figures.
(iii) The timing of the cash flows may be different from that predicted resulting in the project not being completed on time.
(iv) The company may be tax-exhausted, thus resulting in the tax cash flows being delayed.

The budgeting process

Solutions to Chapter 17 questions

Question summary

17.1–17.12 Various discussion topics relevant to Chapter 17.

17.13–17.16 Preparation of functional budgets. Question 17.15 also requires the calculation of the break-even sales volume.

17.17 Preparation of materials purchase and usage budget and journal entries for a standard costing system.

17.18–17.23 Preparation of cash budgets. Question 17.23 also requires a decision whether to close down a department and subcontract the work using a decision-relevant approach. This question also requires an adjustment of the cash flows for inflation.

17.24 Calculation of number of budgeted direct labour employees required to meet budgeted production plus the calculation of product direct labour costs.

17.25 Construction of a model in the form of equations for preparation of a cash budget.

Question 17.4 (a) See 'Incremental and zero-base budgeting' in Chapter 17 for the answer to this question. In particular the answer should stress that the first stage should be to explicitly state the objectives that each part of the organization is trying to achieve. The activities for achieving these objectives should be described in a decision package. A decision package should consist of a base package, which would normally represent a minimum level of activity, plus incremental packages for higher levels of activity and costs. The packages are then evaluated and ranked in order of their decreasing benefits. A cut-off point is determined by the budgeted spending level, and packages are allocated according to their ranking until the budgeted spending level is reached.

(b) For the answer to this question see 'Incremental and zero-base budgeting' in Chapter 17.

(c) The problems that might be faced in introducing a zero-base budgeting scheme are:

   (i) Implementation of zero-base budgeting might be resisted by staff. Traditional incremental budgeting tends to protect the empire that a manager has built. Zero-base budgeting challenges this empire, and so there is a strong possibility that managers might resist the introduction of such a system.

   (ii) There is a need to combat a feeling that current operations are efficient.

   (iii) The introduction of zero-base budgeting is time-consuming, and management may lack the necessary expertise.

   (iv) Lack of top-management support.

(d) Beneficial results are likely to be obtained from a company with the following features:

   (i) A large proportion of the expenditure is of a discretionary nature.

   (ii) Management and employees of the company are unlikely to be resistant to change.

(iii) Suitable output measures can be developed.

(iv) A senior manager is employed who has some experience from another organization of implementing zero-base budgeting.

(a) Corporate planning can be defined as 'The systematic study of *long-term* objectives and the strategies required to achieve them'. Budgeting is the preparation of detailed financial and/or quantitative statements that are drawn up and approved prior to a defined period of time (normally one year). For a comparison of the aims and main features of corporate planning and budgeting systems see 'Stages in the planning process' and 'Purposes of budgeting' in Chapter 17. **Question 17.7**

(b) See 'Incremental and zero-base budgeting' in Chapter 17 for the main items that should be included in answering this question.

(a) (i) A three-level budget involves preparing budgets based on the following assumptions about uncertain future events: **Question 17.10**
1. The most likely outcome occurs.
2. The optimistic outcome occurs.
3. The pessimistic outcome occurs.
In its simplest form, a three-level budget might be prepared for sales volume only, but three-level budgets can also be prepared for uncertain cost items such as changes in wage rates or material prices.

(ii) Probabilistic budgets can be prepared using joint probabilities ascertained from decision tree analysis. When more than one variable is uncertain and the value of one variable is dependent on the value of other variables, a decision tree is a useful analytical tool for clarifying the range of alternative courses of action and their possible outcomes. For an illustration of the process see 'Decision tree analysis' and 'Use of cost information for pricing decisions under conditions of uncertainty' in Chapter 14. In the budgeting process a decision tree is a useful tool for calculating the expected values of sales revenues and costs when interdependencies exist. A decision tree is also a useful tool for assisting in constructing probability distributions. Such probability distributions can be used to aid decision-making at the planning stage and assessing the significance of actual deviations from the budget. For example, a probability distribution might indicate that the probability of spending in excess of £100 000 of the expected value is 0.05. If a difference of £100 000 actually occurs then the probability distribution provides a useful indication of the significance of the variance.

(iii) For a discription of how the simulation approach can be applied to the budgeting process see 'Simulation' in Chapter 16.

(b) (i) The three-level budget approach recognizes that more than one outcome is possible, and indicates the range of possible outcomes. Such an approach enables managers to quantify their predictions, and provides more useful information than a single value estimate.

(ii) The probability approach using the decision tree technique is an improvement on method (i) because it enables uncertainly of the range of possible outcomes to be quantified in the form of an expected value calculation. This is preferable to a three-level budget, which merely identifies uncertainty but does not quantify it. When probability distributions are constructed, the budget indicates the probabilities of possible outcomes occurring. It was noted in (a) (ii) that this approach is useful for selecting alternative courses of action at the planning stage and enabling actual outcomes to be interpreted more meaningfully.

Hence, from a decision-making and control point of view, the probability approach is superior to adopting a three-level budget.

(iii) Simulation enables complex inter-relationships to be expressed in terms of probability distributions and expected values. For a description of the advantages of simulation over the decision tree approach see 'Simulation' in Chapter 16. In addition, simulation enables one to test the sensitivity of the outcomes by asking 'What if?' questions for a wide range of eventualities and environmental changes.

Question 17.11 (a) See 'The budgeting process in non-profit organizations' in Chapter 17 for the answer to this question. In particular, the answer should cover the following points:
   (i) Insufficient strategic thinking and long-term planning. The annual budgeting process based on short-term plans was frequently used for policy planning. Allocation of resources should be based on a long-term planning process and not the annual budgeting process.
   (ii) Traditional approaches failed to identify the costs of activities and the programmes to be implemented.
   (iii) Traditional approaches tend to be based on incremental budgeting rather than considering alternative ways of achieving objectives.
   (iv) Emphasis tended to be on separate planning for each department rather than focusing on activities or functions necessary to achieve organizational objectives.

(b) See 'Planning, programming budgeting systems' in Chapter 17 for an illustration of PPBS.

(c) Problems that have made PPBS difficult to introduce include:
   (i) PPBS cuts across departmental activities and focuses on programmes rather than departments. Consequently, the system does not focus on traditional lines of authority and there is a tendency for heads of departments to be resistant to such changes.
   (ii) Difficulty in matching programme structure to the organization's structure for the purpose of cost control (see 'Planning, programming budgeting systems' in Chapter 17 for an explanation of this).
   (iii) Difficulty in defining objectives and stating objectives in quantitative terms. It is extremely difficult to measure the output of *services* and compare actual accomplishments with planned accomplishments. (See 'Control in non-profit organizations' for a discussion of the difficulties in measuring the success in achieving programme objectives.)

Question 17.13 (a) JK Limited production budget

	J	K
Required by sales	10 000	6000
Closing stock	510	680
	10 510	6680
Opening stock	(600)	800)
	9 910	5880

(b) Raw materials purchases budget

	X		Y	
Required by production:				
J	99 100	(9910 × 10)	39 640	(9910 × 4)
K	35 280	(5880 × 6)	47 040	(5880 × 8)
	134 380		86 680	
Closing stock	340		170	
	134 720		86 850	
Opening stock	(400)		(200)	
Purchase quantity	134 320		86 650	
Purchase price	£1.50		£4.00	
Purchase cost	£201 480		£346 600	

(c) Production cost budget

		(£)	(£)
Opening stock of materials (£480 + £600)			1 080
Purchase of materials			548 080
			549 160
Closing stock of materials (£510 + £680)			(1 190)
			547 970

Direct labour:

J	9910 × 6 hrs × £6 =	356 760	
K	5880 × 4 hrs × £6 =	141 120	497 880

Variable overhead:

J	9910 × 6 hrs × £2 =	118 920	
K	5880 × 4 hrs × £2 =	47 040	165 960

Fixed overhead			315 900
			£1 527 710

(d) Budgeted trading account

		(£)	(£)
Sales J (10 000 × £135)		1 350 000	
K (6000 × £145)		870 000	2 220 000
Opening stocks: J		42 000	
K		48 000	
		90 000	
Production costs		1 527 710	
		1 617 710	
Closing stocks: J	51 918[a]		
K	59 976[a]	(111 894)	
			(1 505 816)
Gross profit			714 184)

Notes
[a]Value of finished goods closing stocks:

	J		K	
Material X	15	(10 × £1.50)	9	(6 × £1.50)
Material Y	16	(4 × £4)	32	(8 × £4)
Direct labour	36		24	
Variable overhead	12		8	
Fixed overhead[b]	22.80		15.20	
	£101.80		£88.20	
Closing stock (units)	510		680	
	£51 918		£59 976	

[b]Fixed overhead rate per hour:

$$\frac{£315\ 900 \text{ fixed overheads}}{(9910 \times 6 \text{ hrs}) + (5880 \times 4 \text{ hrs})} = £3.80 \text{ per hour}$$

Question 17.15 (a)

Product		A	B	C	Total
Sales mix weighting		1	2	4	
		(£)	(£)	(£)	(£)
Unit selling price		215	250	300	
Unit costs:					
Frame		20	20	20	
Component D (at £8 per unit)	40		8	24	
E (at £5 per unit)	5		35	25	
F (at £3 per unit)	12	57	15	58	3	52
Labour:					
Skilled (at £6 per hour)	12		9	9	
Unskilled (at £4.50 per hour)	9	21	9	18	13.5	22.5
Variable production overhead		5	4	3.5	
Contribution		112	150	202	
Weighted by sales mix		112	300	808	1220

Required period 1 contribution:

	(£m)
Profit	0.500 (£6.5m/13)
Add fixed costs:	
Production	0.056 (£0.728m/13)
Selling and distribution	0.028 (£0.364m/13)
Administration	0.026 (£0.338m/13)
	0.610

∴ 500 (£610 000/£1220) 'mixes' must be sold each period.

(i) *Sales budget*

	A	B	C
Sales quantities	500	1 000	2 000
Sales value (£)	107 500	250 000	600 000

(ii) *Production budget*

	A	B	C
Sales quantities	500	1 000	2 000
Closing stock	270	630	1 440
	770	1 630	3 440
Opening stock	300	700	1 600
Production	470	930	1 840

(iii) *Material usage budget*

Usage:				Total (units)
Frame	470	930	1 840	3 240
D	2 350	930	5 520	8 800
E	470	6 510	9 200	16 180
F	1 880	4 650	1 840	8 370

(iv) *Purchases budget*

Purchases (units):	Frame	D	E	F
Closing stock	900	3 600	9 000	3 600
Add used in production	3 240	8 800	16 180	8 370
	4 140	12 400	25 180	11 970
Less opening stock	1 000	4 000	10 000	4 000
Purchases (units)	3 140	8 400	15 180	7 970
Cost (£)	62 800	67 200	75 900	23 910

(v) *Manpower budgets*	Machining (hours)	Assembly (hours)
A (units produced × hrs per unit)	940	940
B	1395	1860
C	2760	5520
	5095	8320
Hours available per period (4 × 37.5)	150	150
Number of people required	34	56

(b) The following factors would need to be considered:
   (i) The ability to be able to plan future production requirements, since production might be halted if there was a sudden increase in production. If production is volatile, there is a danger that stockouts might occur.
   (ii) The speed and reliability of the delivery service. If suppliers can deliver at short notice then stockouts are less likely to occur.
   (iii) The extra costs involved arising from more frequent deliveries in terms of ordering costs and quantity discounts.
   (iv) Alternative use of storage space.
   (v) The savings in holding costs arising from the reduction in stocks. Stock reductions in units would be as follows:

	Frames	D	E	F
End of period 1	900	3600	9000	3600
Requirements for 1 week	810 (3240/4)	2200 (8800/4)	4045 (16 180/4)	2092 (8370/4)
Stock reduction	90	1400	4955	1508

(a)

	Product Y (£)	Product Z (£)	**Question 17.16**
Current standards:			
Direct materials:			
A: 30 kg at £5.20 per kg	156.00		
15 kg at £5.20 per kg		78.00	
B: 30 kg at £1.80 per kg	54.00		
40 kg at £1.80 per kg		72.00	
Direct labour:			
Mixing (2.5 hours at £4.50)	11.25	11.25	
Packaging (5 hours at £4)	20.00	20.00	
New standards:			
Direct materials:			
A: 29.333 kg[a] at £5.46 per kg	160.16		
14.667 kg[b] at £5.46 kg		80.08	
B: 30 kg at £1.89 per kg	56.70		
40 kg at £1.89 per kg		75.60	
Direct labour:			
Mixing (2.5 hours at £4.86)	12.15	12.15	
Packaging (5 hours at £4.32)	21.60	21.60	

Notes:
[a]Input for material A excluding loss $=26.667$ kg (30/1.125)
   Revised input for material A $=29.333$ kg (26.667 × 1.10)
[b]Input excluding loss $=13.333$ kg (15/1.125)
   Revised input $=14.667$ kg (13.333 kg × 1.10)

(b) (i) *Production budget*:

	Product Y (units)	Product Z (units)
Sales	1 700 000	950 000
Add closing stock	200 000	125 000
	1 900 000	1 075 000
Less opening stock	190 000	150 000
Production	1 710 000	925 000

(ii) *Material B purchases budget*:

Required for production:		(kg)
Product Y:		
1 710 000 units at 30 kg per hundred		513 000
Product Z:		
925 000 units at 40 kg per hundred		370 000
		883 000
Add closing stock		90 000
		973 000
Less opening stock		95 000
Purchases		878 000

(iii) *Mixing labour budget*:
Total production:

Product Y	1 710 000
Product Z	925 000
	2 635 000 units

at 2.5 hours per hundred
= 65 875 hours

(c) For the answer to this question you should refer to 'Why do we produce budgets' in Chapter 17. In particular, the answer should describe planning, coordinating, communicating, motivating, control and evaluation roles of budgets.

Question 17.19 (a) *Monthly cash budget*

	Month 1 (£000)	Month 2 (£000)	Month 3 (£000)	Month 4 (£000)
Cash inflows:				
Sales (W1)	24.0	93.6	92.6	90.7
Cash outflows:				
Business purchase	315.0	—	—	—
Delivery van	—	15.0	—	—
Raw materials (W2)	—	44.375	29.375	30.625
Direct labour (W2)	27.0	17.25	18.0	18.75
Production overhead (W3)	10.5	10.5	10.5	10.5
Selling and administration overhead (W4)	39.875	14.875	14.875	14.875
	392.375	102.0	72.75	74.75
Surplus/(deficit) for month	(368.375)	(8.4)	19.85	15.95
Opening balance	—	(368.375)	(376.775)	(356.925)
Closing balance	(368.375)	(376.775)	(356.925)	(340.975)

Workings

	Month 1	Month 2	Month 3	Month 4
(W1) Cash inflow from sales	24	24	23	24
Cash inflow from credit sales	—	72	72	69
Less discount	—	(2.4)	(2.4)	(2.3)
		69.6	69.6	66.7
Total cash inflow	24	93.6	92.6	90.7

(W2) Selling price at a mark-up of 60% on production cost is £8 per unit (£5.00 × 1.60).

Sales units = sales revenue/8.

(000 units)	Month 1	Month 2	Month 3	Month 4	Month 5	Month 6
Sales	12	12	11.5	12	12.5	13
+ Closing stock of finished goods	12	11.5	12	12.5	13	
− Opening stock of finished goods	6	12	11.5	12	12.5	
= Production	18	11.5	12	12.5	13	
+ Closing stock of raw materials	5.75	6	6.25	6.5		
− Opening stock of raw materials	6	5.75	6	6.25		
= Purchase of raw materials	17.75	11.75	12.25	12.75		

Raw material cost (£000)	Month 1	Month 2	Month 3	Month 4
= Purchases at £2.50	44.375	29.375	30.265	31.875
Raw material payment (£000)	—	44.375	29.375	30.625
Direct labour cost and payment (£000)				
= Production × £1.50	27	17.25	18	18.75

(W3) Production overhead = £1.00 × 150 000 units
 = £150 000

Less depreciation	£24 000 (£120 000/5)
Annual payment	£126 000
Monthly payment	£10 500

(W4) Selling and administration overhead = £208 000

Less depreciation (year 1)	4 500 (£15 000 × 30%)
	203 500
Less rent and rates	25 000
Year 1 payment	178 500 (excluding rent and rates)
Monthly payment	£14 875 (plus £25 000 in month 1)

(b)

	(£)
Finished goods stock (12 500 units × £5 per unit)	62 500
Raw materials stock (6500 units × £2.50 per unit)	16 250
Debtors	69 600
	148 350
Creditors	31 875

Apart from the purchase of the business, the cash budget suggests that there will be sufficient cash inflows to meet the cash outflows. The current assets and debtors provide sufficient funds to cover the creditors. However, this does not take into account possible funding by bank overdraft to finance the business purchase.

Question 17.20 (a) (i) *Cash budget*

	January (£)	February (£)	March (£)	April (£)
Balance b/d	10 000	9 000	3 890	9 090
Sales (W1)	—	15 200	57 100	80 000
	10 000	24 200	60 990	89 090
Purchases (W3)	—	11 550	24 500	26 950
Wages (W4)	—	4 800	19 800	22 200
Variable overhead (W5)	—	960	4 600	7 080
Fixed overhead (W6)	1 000	3 000	3 000	3 000
	1 000	20 310	51 900	59 230
Balance c/d	9 000	3 890	9 090	29 860

Workings
(W1) Sales

	Amount	20%	Discount 5%	Net	50%	20%	8%	Total cash receipts
January	—	—	—	—	—	—	—	
February	80 000	16 000	800	15 200				15 200
March	90 000	18 000	900	17 100	40 000			57 100
April	100 000	20 000	1000	19 000	45 000	16 000		80 000
May	100 000	20 000	1000	19 000	50 000	18 000	6400	93 400

(W2) Production:

					Total
January	800				800
February	2400	900			3300
March		2700	1000		3700
April			3000	1000	4000
May				3000	
	3200	3600	4000	4000	

(W3) Purchases at £7 per unit:

	Production	Current month	Following month	Total	Value (£)
January	February (3300)		1650	1650	11 550
February	March (3700)	1650	1850	3500	24 500
March	April (4000)	1850	2000	3850	26 950

(W4) Direct wages:

February payment	800 × £6 =	£4 800
March payment	3300 × £6 =	£19 800
April payment	3700 × £6 =	£22 200

(W5) Variable overhead at £2 per unit:

Production	February (£)	March (£)	April (£)	May (£)
January (£1600)	960	640		
February (£6600)		3960	2640	
March (£7400)			4440	2960
	960	4600	7080	2960

(*W6*) Fixed overhead:

	January (£)	February (£)	March (£)	April (£)
January	1000	2000		
February		1000	2000	
March			1000	2000
April				1000
	1000	3000	3000	3000

(ii) It is assumed that the question relates to the amount received from customers in May and not the amount due. The answer is £93 400 (see *W1*).

(b) A software package would eliminate the tedious arithmetical calculations that are necessary to produce cash budgets. Furthermore, it would enable alternative scenarios to be considered, such as what the outcome would be if any of the parameters were changed.

(a) (i) *Cash budget for weeks 1–6*

	Week 1 (£)	Week 2 (£)	Week 3 (£)	Week 4 (£)	Week 5 (£)	Week 6 (£)
Receipts from debtors[a]	24 000	24 000	28 200	25 800	19 800	5 400
Payments:						
To material suppliers[b]	8 000	12 500	6 000	nil	nil	nil
To direct workers[c]	3 200	4 200	2 800	nil	nil	nil
For variable overheads[d]	4 800	3 200	nil	nil	nil	nil
For fixed overhead[e]	8 300	8 300	6 800	6 800	6 800	6 800
Total payments	24 300	28 200	15 600	6 800	6 800	6 800
Net movement	(300)	(4 200)	12 600	19 000	13 000	(1 400)
Opening balance (week 1 given)	1 000	700	(3 500)	9 100	28 100	41 100
Closing balance	700	(3 500)	9 100	28 100	41 100	39 700

Notes
[a]Debtors:

	Week 1	Week 2	Week 3	Week 4	Week 5	Week 6
Units sold*	400	500	400	300	—	—
Sales (£)	24 000	30 000	24 000	18 000	—	—
Cash received (70%)		16 800	21 000	16 800	12 600	
(30%)			7 200	9 000	7 200	5 400
Given	24 000	7 200				
Total receipts (£)	24 000	24 000	28 200	25 800	19 800	5 400

*Sales in week 4 = openings stock (600 units) + production in weeks 1 and 2 (1000 units) less sales in weeks 1–3 (1300 units) = 300 units.

[b]Creditors:

	Week 1 (£)	Week 2 (£)	Week 3 (£)	Week 4	Week 5	Week 6
Materials consumed at £15	9 000	6 000	—	—	—	—
Increase in stocks	3 500	—				
Materials purchased	12 500	6 000				
Payment to suppliers	8 000 (given)	12 500	6 000	nil	nil	nil

[c]Wages:

	Week 1 (£)	Week 2 (£)	Week 3 (£)	Week 4	Week 5	Week 6
Wages consumed at £7	4200	2800	nil	nil	nil	nil
Wages paid	3200 (given)	4200	2800	—	—	—

^{d}Variable overhead payment = budgeted production × budgeted cost per unit.
^{e}Fixed overhead payments for weeks 1–2 = fixed overhead per week (£9000).
less weekly depreciation (£700).
Fixed overhead payments for weeks 3–6 = £8300 normal payment less
£1500 per week.

(ii) *Comments*
   1. Finance will be required to meet the cash deficit in week 2, but a lowering of the budgeted material stocks at the end of week 1 would reduce the amount of cash to be borrowed at the end of week 2.
   2. The surplus cash after the end of week 2 should be invested on a short-term basis.
   3. After week 6, there will be no cash receipts, but cash outflows will be £6800 per week. The closing balance of £39 700 at the end of week 6 will be sufficient to finance outflows for a further 5 or 6 weeks (£39 700/£6800 per week).

(b) The answer should include a discussion of the matching concept, emphasizing that revenues and expenses may not be attributed to the period when the associated cash inflows and outflows occur. Also, some items of expense do not affect cash outflow (e.g. depreciation).

Question 17.25 (a) Let t be the month for which forecast is required, so that:
t_0 = current month
t_1 = next month
t_{-1} = previous month
Let S be the sales for the current month.
The equations for use in the cash budgeting model are as follows:

$$\text{sales} = S(1.01)^t$$

Cost of sales = $0.75S$ (gross profit margin is $33\frac{1}{3}\%$ on cost of sales: therefore cost of sales is 75% of sales)
Cash collections t months from now:

$$0.2S(1.01)^t + 0.8[0.2S(1.01)^{t-1}] + 0.8[0.6S(1.01)^{t-2}] + 0.8[0.2S(1.01)^{t-3}]$$

Purchases t months from now:

$$0.75S(1.01)^{t+2}$$

Payments for purchases t months from now:

$$0.75S(1.01)^{t+1}$$

Payment for expenses t months from now:

$$0.05S(1.01)^{t-1} + 3000 + 10\,000$$

(b) S for June = £100 000

$$t = 3 \text{ (month of September is } t + 3 \text{ months from June)}$$

Collections during September:

$0.2S(1.01)^t + 0.8[0.2S(1.01)^{t-1}] + 0.8[0.6S(1.01)^{t-2}] + 0.8[0.2S(1.01)^{t-3}]$
$= 0.2(100\,000)(1.01)^3 + 0.8(0.2)(100\,000)(1.01)^2 + 0.8(0.6)(100\,000)(1.01)$
$\quad + 0.8(0.2)(100\,000)$
$= £20\,606 + £16\,322 + £48\,480 + £16\,000$
$= £101\,408$

Payments for purchases during September:

$$0.75S(1.01)^{t+1} = 0.75(100\,000)(1.01)^4 = £78\,045$$

Payments for expenses during September:

$$= 0.05S(1.01)^2 + 3000 + 10\ 000$$
$$= £5100 + £3000 + £10\ 000 = £18\ 100$$

The cash flow statement for September is as follows:

	(£)	(£)
Receipts from sales		101 408
Payments; Purchases	78 045	
Payroll	5 100	
Utilities	3 000	
Other costs	10 000	96 145
Increase in cash		5 263

(c) The following procedures can be applied to incorporate uncertainty:
   (i) Sensitivity analysis
   (ii) Expected values
   (iii) Simulation

For an explanation of each of the above items see Chapter 17. The most simple approach for cash budgeting is to apply sensitivity analysis. By asking 'What if?' questions, such as changes in percentages for cash received each month from debtors, or changes in sales growth, the variability of possible outcomes can be ascertained.

Operational control, management control and performance measurement

Solutions to Chapter 18 questions

Question summary

18.1–18.16   Various discussion questions relevant to Chapter 18. Question 18.9 requires some knowledge of standard costing and cost estimation.

18.17   Preparation of functional and flexible budgets. The question also requires the preparation of sales budgets based on limiting factors.

18.18–18.21   Preparation of flexible budgets. Question 18.21 requires that the budgets are flexed on input and output measures and also a discussion of which method of flexing is preferable.

18.22–18.25   Questions on design and review of management control systems. These are questions set at advanced level that test the ability of students to apply the principles outlined in Chapter 18 to practical problems. These questions are also relevant to Chapter 26. Question 18.24 requires comments on an existing performance measurement and bonus system and recommendations for improvement.

Question 18.1   (a) See Chapter 18 for the answer to this question. In particular, your answer should stress:

(i) The need for a system of responsibility accounting based on a clear definition of a manager's authority and responsibility.

(ii) The production of performance reports at frequent intervals comparing actual and budget costs for individual expense items. Variances should be analysed according to whether they are controllable or non-controllable by the manager.

(iii) The managers should participate in the setting of budgets and standards.

(iv) The system should ensure that variances are investigated, causes found and remedial action is taken.

(v) An effective cost control system must not be used as a punitive device, but should be seen as a system that helps managers to control their costs more effectively.

(b) Possible problems include:

(i) Difficulties in setting standards for non-repetitive work.

(ii) Non-acceptance by budgetees if they view the system as a punitive device to judge their performance.

(iii) Isolating variances where interdependencies exist.

Question 18.6   (a) The answer should include the following points:

(i) The system should lead to improved performance measures and cost control.

(ii) Service departments are motivated to provide services efficiently because any excess spending might lead to an investigation as to why it is cheaper to buy from outside the local authority.

(iii) The user departments will have greater independence, since they will be charged the economic price (or lower) for the services they use. The user department is likely to view this as a fairer method than the alternative of a charge based on the costs of the service department only.

(b) Problems that might be encountered include:

  (i) How should cost be determined? Should it include the direct cost of the service department only or should it include indirect costs of the service departments, such as apportionments of central administrative charges?

  (ii) How should the market price be determined if there are several different market prices or the services offered are not identical?

  (iii) Difficulty in monitoring the scheme. The costs might exceed the benefits if the service departments provide a wide variety of services, resulting in many cost and market value comparisons.

  (iv) Acceptance by the service departments. The new system might be seen as a method of imposing punitive controls.

  (v) If the user department charges for its services and its costs include transferred in costs that are below the market price then it may be underpricing its services.

(c) The above problems might be overcome by:

  (i) Market prices could be established by inviting tenders from suppliers and basing the market price on the lowest tender. This is the market price that the user department would have paid if the department were free to obtain the services from outside the organization. However, the minimum market price should represent a long-run price and not a temporary distress price.

  (ii) The scheme should be clearly explained to all interested parties, emphasizing that the aim is to encourage increased efficiency and to help managers control their activities more effectively. It should be emphasized that the objective is not to use the new system as a basis for undertaking punitive post-mortems.

  (iii) Comparisons of market and cost based charges should be on a random basis rather than comparing each transaction.

  (iv) The user department should ensure that margins are added to the service department transferred costs so as to ensure that its services are charged out at a fair market price.

(a) See 'Operational control and performance measurement in service organizations' **Question 18.8** in Chapter 18 for the answer to this question.

(b) Products are often difficult to specify in service organizations. For example, in banks or building societies savers invest funds in savings accounts and these funds are used to provide mortgage loans to customers. Profits can be computed for a combination of both products but to compute profit for each product a transfer price must be established. This transfer price represents revenue for the savings account products and a cost for the mortgage products.

Further problems arise if costs are assigned to the different types of products within each product group. For example, most of the costs incurred in operating savings or mortgage products are joint to all products within each product group. Direct costs at the individual product level within a product group are virtually non-existent.

In service organizations only a very small proportion of total costs are variable. In contrast, variable costs consisting mainly of direct materials, represent a significant proportion of total costs in manufacturing organizations. Thus, marginal/variable costing principles may have little to offer in service organizations.

A further feature relating to service organizations is that they generally do not hold stocks. Thus product costs are not required for stock valuation and service organizations do not therefore have the conflict of producing separate product costs for decision-making and inventory valuation.

(c) In manufacturing organizations quality can be monitored at various stages of the production process and the finished product can be inspected prior to customer delivery. In many service organizations no tangible product is provided and quality can only be measured after the service has been delivered. In contrast, in manufacturing organizations the quality of the product can be judged prior to use.

Fitzgerald *et al*. (See references at the end of Chapter 18) suggest 12 areas of quality in service organizations. They are reliability, responsiveness, aesthetics, cleanliness, comfort, friendliness, communication, courtesy, competence, access, availability and security. For more detailed illustrations of measures of service quality you should refer to the three areas listed in the section in Chapter 18 on operational control and performance measurement in service organizations.

Question 18.9 (a) The desirable attributes of a suitable measure of activity for flexing the budget are as follows:
  (i) The selected measure should exert a major influence on the cost of the activity. The objective is to flex the budget to ascertain the costs that should be incurred for the actual level of activity. Therefore the costs of the activity and the measure selected should be highly correlated.
  (ii) The measure selected should not be affected by factors other than volume. For example, if direct labour cost is selected as the activity measure then an increase in wage rates will cause labour cost to increase even when activity remains constant.
  (iii) The measure should be easily understood. Complicated indexes are unlikely to be satisfactory.
  (iv) The measure should be easily obtainable without too much cost.
  (v) The measure should be based on output rather than input in order to ensure that managers do not obtain larger budget allowances for being inefficient. For an illustration of this point see Example 18.2 in Chapter 18. Standard hours of output should be used rather than actual hours of input.
(b) Because the activities of a service or overhead department tend not to be repetitive, it is unlikely that a system of standard costing can be justified. Output will be fairly diverse, and it may not be possible to find a single output measure that is highly correlated with costs. It might be necessary to flex the budget on inputs rather than outputs. Also, several variables are likely to cause changes in cost rather than a single measure of output, and an accurate flexible budget may require the use of multiple regression techniques. However, because multiple regression measures might not be easily obtainable and understood, a single input measure may be preferable.

It may be necessary to use several measures of activity within a cost centre for the different costs. For example, machine maintenance costs might be flexed according to machine hours, and lighting and heating costs might be flexed according to labour hours of input.
(c) Suitable measures include the following:
  (i) *Standard hours of output*: This measure is suitable when output is sufficiently standardized to enable standard labour times to be established for each activity. It is unsatisfactory where labour efficiency is unlikely to be constant or output is too diverse to enable standard time to be established.
  (ii) *Direct labour hours of input*: This measure is suitable where costs are highly correlated with labour hours of input, output cannot be measured in standard hours and labour efficiency is fairly constant. It is unsatisfactory if these conditions do not hold, because labour hours will be an unsatisfactory guide to output.
  (iii) *Direct labour costs*: This measure is suitable where the same conditions apply as those specified in (ii) and the wage rates are not consistently changing. If these conditions do not apply then it will be unsatisfactory.

(a) Value for money audits are also known as management or performance audits. **Question 18.10**
See 'Management audits' in Chapter 18 for the answer to this question. In particular, the answer should stress that a value for money audit normally consists of an independent appraisal of the economy, efficiency and effectiveness of the activities of a public sector organization (normally a local authority). The basic principles on which value for money audits are conducted are:
  (i) The auditor should ascertain whether or not an appropriate system exists to ensure economy, efficiency and effectiveness.
  (ii) The audit should focus on a number of specific projects and assess how far value for money is being achieved and where appropriate recommendations for improvements should be made.
Examples of methods of analysis that should be employed in practice include:
  (i) Cost comparisons with previous years and other organizations of a similar character. The objective should be to try and keep costs at their most economical level.
  (ii) Management and systems review.
  (iii) Analysis of planning and control processes.
  (iv) Efficiency assessment.
  (v) Effectiveness review.
You will find a detailed explanation of items (i)–(v) in Chapter 18.

(b) The problems experienced with PPBS are:
  (i) PPBS requires that budgeting and planning should be related to specific programme areas that cut across existing functional departmental structures. Consequently, programme structures are unlikely to match the organization's existing structure, and there is a need to change organizational structures and long-term budgeting systems. Staff may be resistant to such changes.
  (ii) PPBS is a long-term planning process, and organizations are reluctant to commit themselves to long-term plans, particularly when top management (in terms of ruling elected political parties in local government) and objectives are likely to change at frequent intervals. The emphasis tends to be on short-term budgets, with frequent changes in policy being preferred, rather than a commitment to long-term plans and policies.
  (iii) PPBS requires that programme objectives be clearly defined. However, the difficulty in clearly specifying objectives and measuring the extent to which they are being achieved has been an important obstacle in implementing PPBS.
The major differences between PPBS and VFM are:
  (i) A value for money audit focuses on an organization's success in achieving economy, efficiency and effectiveness, and such an investigation does not require changes in organizational structures or budget systems.
  (ii) VFM focuses on systems, procedures and comparative statistics, with the emphasis on recommendations for improvements, whereas PPBS focuses on a re-structuring of the organization's long-term planning process. VFM tends to focus on short-term improvements.

(a) (i) For a description of how budgetary control systems can be likened to a system **Question 18.11**
of thermostatic control see 'Control systems' in Chapter 18. This analogy is inappropriate in respect of the following:
    1. Standards cannot always be easily pre-set, and they are unlikely to remain constant over time. Unpredictable changes may have occurred since the plans were made, and thus the current standard may be inappropriate.
    2. Measurement errors may occur in reporting the actual results for the period, and this may distort the control process.
    3. It is not clear what corrective action is required when the process is out of control. The variance may be due to random factors (see Chapter 20), or the pre-determined standard may no longer be appropriate. Alternatively, the process may be out of control and require corrective action. Thus the appropriate response to variances is not easy to specify, and

there is no guarantee that investigation of the variances will ensure that future actions will conform to the existing standard.

4. Human responses are unpredictable and, unlike mechanical control systems, it is possible that responses to 'out of control' situations may not be implemented as intended.

5. With the thermostatic control system the output of the process is continuously monitored, whereas with a budgetary control system the outcomes for a period are measured and reported at discrete periodic intervals. Consequently, there may be a lag between the process going 'out of control' and corrective action being taken, thus allowing matters to get further out of control. Corrective action is also taken on the assumption that conditions that continued in the past will continue in the future. In a dynamic business environment this assumption may not be valid.

(ii) The following items need to be considered when setting a structure for an effective budgetary control system:

1. Clearly defined responsibility centres should be determined so that managers are accountable only for items that are under their control.

2. Appropriate control periods should be established that result in frequent reporting feedback so as to ensure that there is no unnecessary delay in taking corrective action.

3. Budgets and standard should be frequently reviewed, and revised where necessary, in order to ensure that actual results are compared with appropriate standards.

4. Actual results should be compared with ex-post standards (see Chapter 20 for a discussion of ex-post standards).

5. A suitable system for measuring and collecting control information should be established. For a discussion of the factors to be considered see 'Responsibility accounting' in Chapter 18.

(b) The answer to this question should include a discussion of the following points:

(i) Timely reporting and frequent feedback.

(ii) Variances should be suitably analysed in order to help pinpoint where corrective action is necessary.

(iii) For control purposes actual results should be compared against ex-post standards.

(iv) Actual results should be compared with flexed budgets.

(v) Not all variances should be investigated. Clear rules should be established as to the criteria that should be used to establish whether a variance investigation is justified (see Chapter 20).

(vi) The behavioural considerations specified in Chapter 21 should be taken into account when operating a system of budgetary control.

Question 18.12 (a) The cybernetic system referred to in the question is illustrated in Fig. 18.1 in Chapter 18. The main limitations are:

(i) The human dimension is ignored. Individual behaviour varies and they do not react to deviations from objectives in a single prescribed manner as predicted by the model.

(ii) The time dimension is not incorporated into the model. If feedback response and action is too rapid then this may be counterproductive, whereas inefficiencies will be allowed to continue if feedback is too slow.

(iii) The model is based on feedback controls whereas it is more appropriate for organizations to focus on feedforward controls.

(iv) The model assumes that control operates only on the inputs to the system, whereas control may entail changing the goals, expected outputs or the measurement system.

(b) (i) The main pre-requisites are:
1. A single clearly specified objective (or multiple objectives if they are all consistent).
2. A clear input–output relation so that the impact that changing the inputs has on outputs can be predicted.
3. Outputs can be easily and accurately measured.
4. Clearly specified control responses where actual outcomes differ from predicted outcomes.

If the above conditions exist then it is likely that the system will work in a similar manner to that predicted by the mechanical control system.

(ii) For an explanation of the difficulties of applying control in NPOs see 'Control in non-profit organizations' in Chapter 18. In particular, the answer should draw attention to the fact that there is no single unifying objective such as profit. Instead, they are likely to have several objectives some of which may conflict. Consequently, it is difficult to specify clear aims for the system. Furthermore, management perceptives of what are the major objectives may differ. This is likely to result in conflict and raise political issues.

Because of the multiple objectives and the absence of an over-riding profit motive it is difficult to measure the outputs. Hence, there is a greater emphasis on subjective rather than objective measurement. Control is therefore difficult to implement because it is difficult to predict the impact that changes in inputs will have on outputs. As a result, there tends to be an overemphasis on measuring inputs rather than outputs.

Question 18.14

(a) The factors influencing the preferred costing system are different for every firm. The benefits from implementing ABC are likely to be influenced by the level of competition, the number of products sold, the diversity of the product range and the proportion of overheads and direct costs in the cost structure. Companies operating in a more competitive environment have a greater need for more accurate cost information, since competitors are more likely to take advantage of any errors arising from the use of distorted cost information generated by a traditional costing system. Where a company markets a small number of products special studies can be undertaken using the decision-relevant approach. Problems do not arise in determining which product or product combinations should be selected for undertaking special studies. Increased product diversity arising from the manufacture and sale of low-volume and high-volume products favours the use of ABC systems. As the level of diversity increases so does the level of distortion reported by traditional costing systems. Finally, organizations with a large proportion of overheads and a low proportion of direct costs are likely to benefit from ABC, because traditional costing systems can be relied upon only to report accurately direct product costs. Distorted product costs are likely to be reported where a large proportion of overheads are related to product variety rather than volume.

(b) For a more detailed answer to this question you should refer to 'Activity-based management' in Chapter 18. In particular, the answer should draw attention to the fact that ABM attaches costs to activities and identifies the cost drivers that cause the costs. Thus ABM provides a better understanding of what causes costs, and highlights ways of performing activities more efficiently by reducing cost driver transactions.

Costs can therefore be managed more effectively in the long run. Activities can be analysed into value added and non-value added activities and by highlighting the costs of non-value added activities attention is drawn to areas where there is an opportunity for cost reduction, without reducing the products' service potentials to customers.

Finally, the cost of unused activity capacity is reported for each activity, thus drawing attention to where capacity can be reduced or utilized more effectively to expand future profitability.

(c) See 'Target Costing' in Chapter 13 for the answer to this question.

Question 18.16 (a) (i) Efficiency measures focus on the relationship between outputs and inputs. Optimum efficiency levels are achieved by maximizing the output from a given input or minimizing the resources used in order to achieve a particular output. Measures of effectiveness attempt to measure the extent to which the outputs of an organization achieve the latter's goals. An organization can be efficient but not effective. For example, it can use resources efficiently but fail to achieve its goals.

In organizations with a profit motive, effectiveness can be measured by return on investment. Inputs and outputs can be measured. Outputs represent the quality and amount of service offered. In profit-orientated organizations output can be measured in terms of sales revenues. This provides a useful proxy measure of the quality and amount of services offered. In non-profit-making organizations outputs cannot be easily measured in monetary terms. Consequently, it is difficult to state the objectives in quantitative terms and thus measure the extent to which objectives are being achieved.

If it is not possible to produce a statement of a particular objective in measurable terms, the objectives should be stated with sufficient clarity that there is some way of judging whether or not they have been achieved. However, the focus will tend to be on subjective judgements rather than quantitative measures of effectiveness. Because of the difficulty in measuring outputs, efficiency measures tend to focus entirely on input measures such as the amount of spending on services or the cost per unit of input. For a discussion of these measures see 'Control in non-profit organizations' in Chapter 18.

(ii) Similar problems to those of measuring effectiveness and efficiency in non-profit-making organizations arise in measuring the performance of non-manufacturing activities in profit-orientated organizations. This is because it is extremely difficult to measure the output of non-manufacturing activities. For a discussion of the problems that arise when measuring the performance of non-manufacturing activities see 'Control of non-manufacturing costs' in Chapter 18.

(b) (i) *Adherence to appointment times*
1. Percentage meeting appointment times.
2. Percentage within 15 minutes of appointment time.
3. Percentage more than 15 minutes late.
4. Average delay in meeting appointments.
Ability to contact and make appointments
It is not possible to obtain data on all those patients who have had difficulty in contacting the clinic to make appointments. However, an indication of the difficulties can be obtained by asking a sample of patients at periodic intervals to indicate on a scale (from no difficulty to considerable difficulty) the difficulty they experienced when making appointments. The number of complaints received and the average time taken to establish telephone contact with the clinic could also provide an indication of the difficulty patients experience when making appointments.
Monitoring programme
1. Comparisons with programmes of other clinics located in different regions.
2. Questionnaires asking respondents to indicate the extent to which they are aware of monitoring facilities currently offered.
3. Responses on level of satisfaction from patients registered on the programme.
4. Percentage of population undertaking the programme.

(ii) Combining the measures into a 'quality of care' measure requires that weights be attached to each selected performance measure. The sum of the performance measures multiplied by the weights would represent an overall performance measure. The problems with this approach are that the weights are set subjectively, and there is a danger that staff will focus on those performance measures with the higher weighting and pay little attention to those with the lower weighting.

(a) See 'Determining the factor that restricts performance' and 'Preparation of the sales budget' in Chapter 17 for the answer to this question. In particular, the answer should stress that the principal budget factor is the factor that determines the level of activity. This will normally be the level of sales, but it could also be any resource in the business that restricts the volume of sales (e.g. machine capacity, labour or shortage of materials). The principal budget factor is therefore important, because it determines the level of activity on which all budgets will be based.

(b) A fixed budget is a budget that remains unchanged irrespective of the volume of activity whereas a flexible budget is adjusted to the level of activity which is actually attained. See 'Flexible budgeting' in Chapter 18.

Flexed budgets should be used for control purposes; costs should be controlled by comparing actual costs with the actual level of activity and not some level of activity that was assumed when the budget was prepared. Fixed budgets are appropriate for planning purposes for determining the planned level of activity, but for control purposes actual expenses should be compared with an adjusted budget based on the actual level of activity.

(c) (i) The direct labour hours required for the first sales forecast are:

	Product A	Product B	Product C	Total
First sales forecast (£)	44 000	60 000	6 000	110 000
Second sales forecast (£)	60 000	75 000	7 000	142 000

The principal budget factors are:

First sales forecast = sales
Second sales forecast = direct labour

(ii) *Sales limitation (first forecast)*

	A	B	C	Total
Sales volume	22 000	40 000	6 000	
Contribution per unit (£)	4	2	2	
Total contribution (£)	88 000	80 000	12 000	180 000
			Less fixed costs (£)	150 000
			Profit (£)	30 000

Direct labour limiting factor (second sales forecast)

	A	B	C
1. Contribution per unit (£)	3	1.70	1.60
2. Contribution per £1 of labour (£)	1.50 (3/2)	1.13 (1.70/1.50)	1.60 (1.60/1)
3. Ranking	2	3	1
4. Sales allocation[a]	30 000	45 333	7 000
5. Contribution [(1) × (4)] (£)	90 000	77 066	11 200

	(£)
Total contribution	178 266
Fixed costs	150 000
Profit	28 266

Note

[a]The sales allocation is calculated as follows:

	Sales volume		Direct labour cost (£)	Balance of direct labour cost available (£)
Product C	7 000		7 000	128 000
Product A	30 000		60 000	68 000
Product B	45 333	(£68 000/£1.50)	68 000	0

Question 18.18 (a) A fixed budget refers to a budget that is designed to remain unchanged irrespective of the level of activity, whereas a flexible budget is a budget that adjusts the expense items for different levels of activity. See 'Flexible budgeting' Chapter 18 for an explanation of the objectives of flexible budgeting.

(b) (i)

Direct labour (£)	180 000	202 500	225 000
Direct labour hours	48 000	54 000	60 000

Flexible budget (overhead expenditure)

Activity levels	80%	90%	100%
Direct labour hours	48 000	54 000	60 000
Variable costs:	(£)	(£)	(£)
Indirect labour at £0.75 per direct labour hour	36 000	40 500	45 000
Consumable supplies at £0.375 per direct labour hour	18 000	20 250	22 500
Canteen and other welfare services at 6% of direct plus indirect wages	12 960	14 580	16 200
Semi-variable: variable (*W1*)	9 600	10 800	12 000
	76 560	86 130	95 700
Semi-variable: fixed (*W1*)	8 000	8 000	8 000
Fixed costs:			
Depreciation	18 000	18 000	18 000
Maintenance	10 000	10 000	10 000
Insurance	4 000	4 000	4 000
Rates	15 000	15 000	15 000
Management salaries	25 000	25 000	25 000
	156 560	166 130	175 700

Working

(*W1*) Obtained by using high and low points method:

			(£)
High	64 000	Direct labour hours	20 800
Low	40 000	Direct labour hours	16 000
	24 000		4 800

$$\frac{4800}{24\,000} = \text{£0.20 per direct labour hour}$$

$$64\,000 \times \text{£0.20} = \text{£12 800 variable costs}$$

Total cost £20 800

Therefore fixed costs = £8 000

(ii)

	(£)
Variable cost	90 915 [(57 000/60 000) × £95 700]
Fixed costs	80 000
Budgeted cost allowance	170 915

Flexible budget at 85% activity

	(£)	(£)
Variable cost		
Direct materials[a]	1 386 056	
Direct wages[b]	2 356 949	
Variable production overhead[c]	489 584	
Variable selling and distribution overhead[d]	69 940	
		4 302 529
Fixed costs		
Fixed production overhead[c]	330 115	
Fixed selling and distribution overhead[d]	161 266	
Administration overhead	132 000	623 381
Total cost		4 925 910
Sales[e]		5 911 092
Profit		985 182

Notes

[a] Costs increase by £153 800 for each of the changes in activity. Thus at 85% capacity level costs will be (£1 153 800 + £153 800) 1.04 after taking account of the predicted price change of 4%.

[b] Costs have increased by increments of £269 150. At 85% capacity level predicted costs are (£2 019 150 + £269 150) 1.03.

[c] Costs have increased by increments of £53 830. However, the question indicates that there is a fixed and variable element. Therefore at 85% capacity variable costs are predicted to be 8.5 (10% increments) × £53 830 per 10% increment = £457 555 × 1.07 price increase = £489 584. The fixed cost element before the price increase is £703 830 total costs at 75% capacity less variable costs of 7.5 (10% increments) × £53 830 = £300 105. The predicted fixed costs after the price increase are £300 105 (1.10) = £330 115.

[d] Costs have increased in increments of £7690. Using the same principles as those outlined in [c] variable costs at 85% capacity are predicted to be 8.5 × £7690(1.07 inflation factor) = £69 940. Fixed cost element = £207 690 total cost at 75% capacity less 7.5 (£7690) = £150 015 before the price increase. After the price increase the estimated fixed costs will be £150 015(1.075) = £161 266.

[e] Total cost (£4 925 910) × 100/83.333.

(b) Problems that can arise from a change in capacity level include:
1. Step increase in fixed costs to enable output to be expanded (See 'Changes in fixed costs and selling prices' in Chapter 10).
2. Inability to sell the increased output resulting in an increase in stocks.
3. Working the plant more intensively might result in bottlenecks and machine breakdowns and this may result in an increase in unit variable costs because of diminishing returns to scale (See 'Economist's model' in Chapter 10).

(c) The budget committee should consist of high level executives who represent the major segments of the business. For example, the committee might consist of the chief executive (or his or her deputy), the production manager, the marketing manager, the management accountant and the human resource manager. Its major task is to communicate the long-term objectives of the organization, ensure that the budgets are realistically established and that they are coordinated satisfactorily.

Question 18.23 (a) Recommendations are as follows:

    (i) For cost control and managerial performance evaluation, expenses should be separated into their controllable and non-controllable categories. Two separate profit calculations should be presented: controllable profit, which is appropriate for measuring managerial performance, and a 'bottom-line' net profit, which measures the economic performance of each store rather than the manager.

    (ii) The report should be based on an ex-post basis. In other words, if the environment is different from that when the original budget was set, actual performance should be compared with a budget that reflects any changed conditions. For example, the budget should be adjusted to reflect the effect of the roadworks.

    (iii) Actual expenses should be compared with flexed budgets and not the original budget.

    (iv) Each store consists of three departments. The report should therefore analyse gross profits by departments. Selling prices and the cost of goods sold are beyond the control of the stores' managers, but each departmental manager can influence sales volume. An analysis of gross profits by departments and a comparison with previous periods should provide useful feedback on sales performance and help in deciding how much space should be allocated to each activity.

    (v) Stock losses should be minimized. Such losses are controllable by departmental managers. The cost of stock losses should therefore be monitored and separately reported.

    (vi) The budget should include cumulative figures to give an indication of trends, performance to date and the potential annual bonus.

    (vii) Any imputed interest charges should be based on economic values of assets and not historic costs (see 'Valuation of controllable investments' in Chapter 26 for a discussion of this point).

(b) The report should include a discussion of the following:

    (i) *Review of delegation policies*: Head office purchases the goods for sale, fixes selling prices, appoints permanent staff and sets pay levels. Stores managers are responsible for stores' running expenses, employment of temporary staff and control of stocks.

        Purchasing is centralized, thus enabling the benefits of specialized buying and bulk purchasing to be obtained. Purchasing policies are coordinated with expected sales by consultation between head office buyers and stores and departmental managers. It is wise to make stores managers responsible for controlling stocks because they are in the best position to assess current and future demand.

        Managers are responsible for sales volume but they cannot fix selling prices. There are strong arguments for allowing stores to set selling prices, and offer special discounts on certain goods. Central management may wish to retain some overall control by requiring proposed price changes beyond certain limits referred to them for approval. There are also strong arguments for allowing the stores managers to appoint permanent staff. The stores managers are likely to be in a better position to be able to assess the abilities necessary to be a successful member of their own team.

    (ii) *Strengths of the management control system*:

        1. Sales targets are set after consultation between head office and the departmental managers.

        2. The budgets are prepared well in advance of the start of the budget year, thus giving adequate time for consultation.

        3. Performance reports are available one week after the end of the period.

        4. Budgets are adjusted for seasonal factors.

        5. Significant variations in performance are investigated and appropriate action is taken.

(iii) *Weaknesses of the management control system*:
1. There is no consultation in the setting of expense budgets.
2. Actual costs are compared with a fixed budget and not a flexible budget.
3. Costs are not separated into controllable and non-controllable categories.
4. Budgets are set on an incremental basis with budgets set by taking last year's base and adjusting for inflation.
5. Budgets are not revised for control purposes. Targets set for the original budget before the start of the year may be inappropriate for comparison with actual expenses incurred towards the end of the budget year.
6. Using a budget that does not include ex-post results and that is not linked to controllable profit is likely to be demotivating, and results in managers having little confidence in the budget system.

(iv) *Recommendations*:
1. Compare actual costs with a flexed budget.
2. The performance report should separate costs into controllable and uncontrollable categories, and controllable profit should be highlighted. Any bonus payments should be related to controllable profit and not 'bottom-line' profits.
3. Introduce monthly or quarterly rolling budgets.
4. Ensure that the stores managers participate in setting the budget and accept the target against which they will be judged.
5. Set targets using a zero-base approach.
6. Consider extending the bonus scheme to departmental managers.

Standard costing and variance analysis: 1

Solutions to Chapter 19 questions

Question summary

19.1	Discussion question relating to variance analysis.
19.2, 19.3	These questions require the calculation of labour and material variances, and are appropriate as an introduction to variance analysis.
19.4	Calculation of labour and material variances from incomplete information.
19.5	Calculation of budgeted inputs and overhead variances.
19.6–19.9	Calculation of overhead variances. Question 19.8 also requires the calculation of labour and material variances.
19.10–19.12	Reconciliation of standard and actual cost.
19.13–19.16	Calculation of actual inputs working backwards from reported variances given in the question and the calculation of variances from incomplete information.
19.17–19.19	Calculation of production ratios.

Question 19.17 also requires the calculation of labour and material variances.

19.20	Preparation of an operating control statement and calculation of labour, material and overhead variances.
19.21–19.24	Reconciliation of budgeted and actual profit incorporating materials, labour, overhead and sales variances. These questions are appropriate for a second-year course.
19.25	The application of variance analysis to a taxi firm in order to explain the difference between budgeted and actual profit.
19.26	Comparison of variable and absorption standard costing.
19.27	Calculation of sales variances on a variable and absorption costing basis and reconciliation of actual with budgeted margin.

Question 19.1 (a) Standard prices are often set on an annual basis, with the target representing the average price for the year. Price changes will occur throughout the year, and it is unlikely that the actual price paid will equal the average for the year as a whole – even if actual prices are identical with the prices used to set the average standard price. Consequently, actual prices will be less than the average early in the year (showing favourable variances) and above the average standard later in the year (showing adverse variances).

The problem can be overcome by setting different standards for different periods throughout the year.

(b) This variance is due to unavoidable normal losses. Standards for usage should be set that include an allowance for normal losses. If variances are due to unavoidable losses, this indicates that either a normal loss has not been incorporated in the standard or that an insufficient allowance is included in the present standard.

The problem can be overcome by incorporating in the standard a fair allowance for unavoidable losses. Ideally, this allowance should be based on input/output relationships based on engineering studies.

(c) The causes are likely to be the same as those described for the direct material price variance; that is, price increases over the year and the standard reflecting the average for the year. With labour, the timing of price increases will be easier to ascertain because they are likely to occur at given times of the year and normally once per year.

This problem can be overcome by setting standards before and after the normal specified date for changes in wage rates. Sometimes wage rate variances occur because the wrong grade of labour has been used to perform particular tasks. This variance can be highlighted by comparing the specified grade of labour used to set the standard with the actual grade of labour used to perform an operation.

(a) The calculation of the standard purchase price for each item of materials is as **Question 19.3** follows:

Powder: £1.50 per tube. Each tube requires 2 lb of powder, and so price per lb = £0.75

Chemicals: £0.60 per tube. Each tube requires $\frac{1}{4}$ litre of chemical, and so price per litre = £2.40

Tube: £0.30 per tube

The standard wage rate is £4.50 per hour and the standard cost of producing one tube is £1.80. Therefore the standard time is 0.4 hours (£1.80/£4.50).

Material price variances = (standard price − actual price) × actual purchases

		(£)	(£)	(£)
Powder	(£0.75 − £0.70) × 10 000		500F	
Chemicals	(£2.40 − £2.30) × 600	£60F		
	(£2.40 − £2.50) × 600	£60A	nil	
Tubes	(£0.30 − £0.40) × 200	£20A		
	(£0.30 − £0.30) × 5000	nil	20A	480F

Material usage variances = (standard quantity − actual issues) × standard price

Powder	[(4500 × 2 = 9000) − 9800] × £0.75	600A	
Chemicals	[(4500 × $\frac{1}{4}$ = 1125) − 1050] × £2.40	180F	
Tubes	[(4500 × 1 = 4500) − 4520] × £0.30	6A	426A

Wage rate = (standard rate − actual rate) × actual hours
= [£4.50 − (£8910/2050)] × 2050   315F

Labour efficiency = (standard hours − actual hours) × standard rate
[(4500 × 0.4 hrs = 1800 hrs) − 2050] × £4.50   1125A   810A

(b) See Chapter 19 for a discussion of the possible causes of material and labour variances. Causes that might be specifically related to this question include:
  (i) Favourable price variance and adverse usage variance for powder. This may be due to the purchase of inferior quality materials, resulting in excessive usage and an adverse labour efficiency variance.
  (ii) The adverse usage variance for powder may also be due to inefficient handling or split bags.

(a) (i) An increase in output of 4000 tonnes results in total overhead costs increasing **Question 19.5** by £36 000. It is assumed that fixed costs will remain unchanged within this level of activity. Therefore the variable overhead rate per unit of output will be £9 (36 000/4000 tonnes).

(ii) At 3000 tonnes budgeted output the costs are as follows:

	(£)
Total budgeted overhead	72 000
Variable element (3000 × £9)	27 000
Fixed element (balance)	45 000

(iii) £45 000/(£18 − £9) = 5000 units
(iv) (5500 tonnes × £9 for variable overheads) + £45 000 fixed overheads = £94 500
(v) 5500 units × £18 = £99 000
(vi) No information is given in the question about hours of input. It is therefore assumed that variable overheads vary with output. Most textbooks assume that variable overheads vary with direct labour or machine hours of input.

Variable overhead expenditure variance		(£)
Budget flexed on output (5500 units × £9)	=	49 500
Actual variable overheads incurred	=	52 000
Variance		2 500A

(vii) Fixed overhead expenditure variance:
(Budgeted fixed overheads − Actual fixed overheads)
(£45 000 − £53 750) = £8750A
(viii) Fixed overhead volume variance:
(Actual production − Budgeted production) × Fixed overhead rate
(5500 tonnes − 5000 tonnes) × £9 = £4500F

(b) See 'Flexible budgeting' in Chapter 18 for an explanation of why it is advantageous to use flexible budgets for the control of production overhead expenses.
(c) (i) Power for the operation of machinery.
(ii) Indirect materials.
(d) See 'Types of cost standards' in Chapter 19 for the answer to this question.

Question 19.6

(a) *Workings*:
Budgeted output = 9600 normal capacity/2 hrs = 4800 units
Budgeted fixed overhead rate per unit of output = £120 000/4800 units = £25
Budgeted fixed overhead rate per standard hour = £25/2 hrs = £12.50
 (i) *Variable overhead expenditure variance*
(Actual hours × variable overhead rate) − Actual cost
(9300 × £3) = £27 900 − £28 900 = £1000A
 (ii) *Variable production overhead efficiency variance*
(Standard hrs − Actual hrs) × Variable overhead rate
(5000 × 2 hrs = 10 000 − 9300) × £3 = £2100F
 (iii) *Fixed production overhead expenditure variance*
Budgeted cost − Actual cost
£120 000 − £118 000 = £2000F
 (iv) *Fixed production overhead volume variance*
(Actual production − Budgeted production) × Standard rate
(5000 units − 4800 units) × £25 = £5000F
Alternatively, output can be measured in standard hours:
(10 000 Standard hrs − 9600 Budgeted hrs) × £12.50 = £5000F
(b) The volume variance can be subdivided into a volume efficiency variance and a volume capacity variance:

Volume efficiency variance
(Standard hours − Actual hours) × Fixed overhead rate
(10 000 −9300) × £12.50 = £8750F

Volume capacity variance
(Actual hours − Budgeted hours) × Fixed overhead rate
(9300 − 9600) × £12.50 = £3750A

For an explanation of the meaning of the above variances see 'Volume efficiency and capacity variances' in Chapter 19.

Question 19.8

(a) *Calculation of standard unit cost* (£)
Materials (336 000 kg/240 000 units = 1.40 kg at £4.10 per kg)   5.74
Direct labour (216 000 hrs/240 000 units = 0.9 hrs at £4.50 per hour   4.05
Variable overhead (0.9 hrs at £475 200/216 000 hrs = £2.20 per hour)   1.98
Fixed overhead (£1 521 600/240 000 units)   6.34
   18.11

Variance calculations

Material price: (Standard price − Actual price) × Actual quantity
(£4.10 − £1 245 980/313 060 kg)313 060 kg   £37 566F

Material usage: (Standard quantity − Actual quantity) × Standard price
(220 000 units × 1.40 kg = 308 000 kg − 313 060 kg)
× £4.10   £20 746A

Wage rate: (Standard rate − Actual rate) × Actual hours
(£4.50 − £886 886/194 920 hrs)194 920 hrs   £9 746A

Labour efficiency: (Standard hours − Actual hours) × Standard rate
(220 000 units × 0.9 hrs)
= 198 000 hours − 194 920 hrs × £4.50   £13 860F

Variable overhead efficiency: (Standard hours − Actual hours)
× Standard rate
(198 000 − 194 920) × £2.20   £6 776F

Variable overhead expenditure: (Actual hours × Standard rate) −
Actual cost
(194 920 × £2.20 = £428 824) −
£433 700   £4 876A

Fixed overhead expenditure: (Budgeted cost − Actual cost)
(£1 521 600 − £1 501 240)   £20 360F

Fixed overhead volume: (Actual output − Budget output) ×
Standard rate
(220 000 − 240 000) × £6.34   £126 800A
Total variances   £831 606A

(b) The favourable labour efficiency variance may be due to:
  (i) Efficient production in less than standard time due to efficiency of the labour force.
  (ii) Easily attainable standard.
  (iii) Lack of production delays.
  The variable overheads are absorbed on the basis of direct labour hours and therefore the variable overhead efficiency variance will be a direct result of the labour efficiency variance.
  The fixed overhead volume variance is due to actual production being less than budgeted production. This may be due to reduced sales or reduction in stock levels. However, because the fixed overhead is a sunk cost changes in volume will not result in a change in fixed overheads incurred and the variance is of a dubious value for cost control purposes.

Question 19.10 (a) *Standard cost of output produced (18 000 units)*

	(£)
Direct materials	864 000
Direct labour	630 000
Variable production overhead	180 000
Fixed production overhead	900 000
	2 574 000

(b)

	Standard cost of output (£)	Variances (£)	Actual cost (£)
Direct materials	864 000		
Price variance[a]		76 000 (F)	
Usage variance[b]		48 000 (A)	
Actual cost			836 000
Direct labour	630 000		
Rate variance[c]		16 800 (A)	
Efficiency variance[d]		42 000 (F)	
Actual cost			604 800
Variable production overhead	180 000		
Expenditure variance[e]		4 000 (A)	
Efficiency variance[f]		12 000 (F)	
Actual cost			172 000
Fixed production overhead	900 000		
Expenditure variance[g]		30 000 (A)	
Volume variance[h]		100 000 (A)	
Actual cost			1 030 000
	2 574 000	68 800 (A)	2 642 800

Notes

[a] (Standard price − Actual price) × Actual quantity
(£12 − £836 000/76 000) × 76 000 = £76 000 (F)

[b] (Standard quantity − Actual quantity) × Standard price
(18 000 × 4 kg = 72 000 − 76 000) × £12 = £48 000 (A)

[c] (Standard rate − Actual rate) × Actual hours
(£7 − £604 800/84 000) × 84 000 = £16 800 (A)

[d] (Standard hours − Actual hours) × Standard rate
(18 000 × 5 hrs = 90 000 − 84 000) × £7 = £42 000 (F)

[e] (Actual hours × Standard rate) − Actual cost
(84 000 × £2 = £168 000 − £172 000 = £4000 (A)

[f] (Standard hours − Actual hours) × Standard rate
(18 000 × 5 hrs = 90 000 − 84 000) × £2 = £12 000 (F)

[g] Budgeted fixed overheads − Actual fixed overheads
(20 000 × £50 = £1 000 000 − £1 030 000) = £30 000 (A)

[h] (Actual output − Budgeted output) × Standard rate
(18 000 − 20 000) × £50 = £100 000 (A)

(c) The statement in (b) can be used to provide a detailed explanation as to why actual cost exceeded standard cost by £68 800 for the output achieved. The statement provides attention-directing information by highlighting those areas that require further investigation. Thus management can concentrate their scarce time on focusing on those areas that are not proceeding according to plan. By investigating variances, management can pinpoint inefficiencies and take steps to avoid them re-occurring. Alternatively, the investigation may indicate that the current standards are inappropriate and need changing to take account of the changed circumstances. This may result in an alteration in the plans or more up-to-date information for decision-making.

(a) (i) Material price variance $= (SP - AP)AQ = (SP \times AQ) - (AQ \times AP)$
$= (£1.20 \times 142\,000) - £171\,820$
$= £1420A$

(ii) Material usage variance $= (SQ - AQ)SP$
$= (1790 \times 9 = 16\,110 - 16\,270) \times £1.20$
$= £192A$

(iii) Actual price per kg in period 1 $= £1.21$ ($£171\,820/142\,000$ kg)
The actual price per kg for period 2 is not glven and must be calculated from the data given in the question.

Standard price $= £1.20 \times 1.06 = £1.272$
$(SP \times AQ)$ $= £1.272 \times 147\,400$ (AQ) $= £187\,492.80$
Price variance ($£1031.80F$) $= (SP \times AQ) - (AQ \times AP)$
$£1031.30F$ $= £187\,492.80 - (147\,400 \times AP)$
$$AP = \frac{£187\,492.80 - £1031.80}{147\,400}$$
$= £1.265$ per kg
Cost inflation $= (£1.265/£1.21 - 1) \times 100\% = 4.5\%$

(iv) Actual usage per unit in period 1 $= 16\,270$ kg$/1790$ units $= 9.0894$ kg
Actual usage in period 2 $= 0.995 \times 9$ kg Standard usage $= 8.995$ kg
Change in usage $(9.0894 - 8.995)/9.0894 \times 100\% = 1.5\%$ improvement.

(b) See 'Types of cost standards' in Chapter 19 for the answer to this question.

(a) Wage rate variance $= (SP - AP)AH = (SP \times AH) - (AP \times AH)$
$= (£5 \times 53$ workers $\times 13$ weeks $\times 40$ hrs$) - £138\,500$
$= £700A$
Labour efficiency $= (SH - AH)SP$
SH (Standard hours) $= (35\,000 \times 0.4$ hrs$) + (25\,000 \times 0.56$ hrs$)$
$= 28\,000$
AH (Actual hours) $= 53$ workers $\times 13$ weeks $\times 40$ hrs $= 27\,560$
Variance $= (28\,000 - 27\,560) \times £5 = £2200A$

(b) Material price variance $= (SP - AP)AQ$
$= (AQ \times SP) - (AQ \times AP)$
$£430F$ (given) $= 47\,000$ SP $- £85\,110$
$$SP \text{ (Standard price)} = \frac{£430 + 85\,110}{47\,000}$$
$= £1.82$

Material usage variance $= (SQ - AQ)SP$
$= (SQ \times SP) - (AQ \times SP)$
$£320.32A$ (given) $= £1.82$ SQ $- (33\,426 \times £1.82)$
$-£320.32A$ $= £1.82SQ - £60\,835.32$
$£1.82$ SQ $= £60\,515$
SQ $= £60\,515/£1.82 = 33\,250$
Note that SQ $=$ Actual productlon ($35\,000$ units) $\times$ Standard usage
Therefore $35\,000 \times$ Standard usage $= 33\,250$
Standard usage $= 33\,250/35\,000$
$= 0.95$ kg per unit of component X

(c) For the answer to this question you should refer to the detailed illustration of the budget process shown in Chapter 17. In particular, the answer should indicate that if sales are the limiting factor the production budget should be linked to the sales budget. Once the production budget has been established for the two components, the production quantity of each component multiplied by the standard usage of material A per unit of component output determines the required quantity of material to meet the production requirements. The budgeted purchase quantity of material A consists of the quantity to meet the production usage requirements plus or minus an adjustment to take account of any planned change in the level of raw material stock.

Question 19.17 (a) Material price variances:

$$\text{(standard price } - \text{ actual price)} \times \text{quantity purchased}$$
$$A = (\text{£}3.25 - \text{£}158\,750/50\,000) \times 50\,000 = \text{£}3750F$$
$$B = (\text{£}4 - \text{£}105\,000/25\,000) \times 25\,000 = \text{£}5000A$$

Usage variances:

$$\text{(standard quantity } - \text{ actual quantity)} \times \text{standard price}$$
$$A = (400 \times 10\,\text{kg} = 4000\,\text{kg} - 4800\,\text{kg}) \times \text{£}3.25 = \text{£}2600A$$
$$B = (400 \times 5\,\text{kg} = 2000\,\text{kg} - 1800\,\text{kg}) \times \text{£}4 = \text{£}800F$$

(b) Labour rate variances:

$$\text{(standard rate } - \text{ actual rate)} \times \text{actual hours}$$
$$\text{Dept 1} = (\text{£}4 - \text{£}11\,800/3000) \times 3000 = \text{£}200F$$
$$\text{Dept 2} = (\text{£}5 - \text{£}13\,250/2400) \times 2400 = \text{£}1250A$$

Labour efficiency variances:

$$\text{(standard hours } - \text{ actual hours)} \times \text{standard rate}$$
$$\text{Dept 1} = (400 \times 8\,\text{hrs} = 3200 - 3000) \times \text{£}4 = \text{£}800F$$
$$\text{Dept 2} = (400 \times 5\,\text{hrs} = 2000 - 2400) \times \text{£}5 = \text{£}2000A$$

(c) Material A price: purchase of inferior quality materials
Material B price: general increase in market prices
Material A usage: inefficient usage of materials
Material B usage: better training of workers, resulting in less wastage
Dept 1 wage rate: use of a lower grade of labour
  2 wage rate: general increase in wage rates
  1 labour efficiency: introduction of more efficient working practices, resulting in a saving in labour hours
  2 labour efficiency: failure to maintain machinery in proper condition, resulting in additional labour hours to complete the operations

(d) (i) Production volume ratio:

$$\frac{\text{standard hours of actual output}}{\text{budgeted hours of output}} \times 100$$

$$\text{Department 1:} \frac{400 \times 8\,\text{hrs}}{3400\,\text{hrs}} \times 100 = 94.12\%$$

$$\text{Department 2:} \frac{400 \times 5\,\text{hrs}}{2600\,\text{hrs}} \times 100 = 76.92\%$$

(ii) Efficiency ratio:

$$\frac{\text{standard hours of actual output}}{\text{actual hours worked}} \times 100$$

$$\text{Department 1:} \frac{400 \times 8\,\text{hrs}}{3000} \times 100 = 106.67\%$$

$$\text{Department 2: } \frac{400 \times 5\text{ hrs}}{2400} \times 100 = 83.33\%$$

(e) In Chapter 19 it was argued that the material price variance should be extracted at the time of purchase. The only justification for extracting the material price variance at the time of usage is for profit measurement purposes. Where the material price variance is calculated on purchases, the variance is charged as an expense to the periods in which the materials are purchased. On the other hand, when the variance is calculated on issues, the variance is allocated to the periods when the materials are issued. For profit measurement purposes it could be argued that material variances should be recognized as an expense in the period when the materials are used and not in the period when the materials are purchased.

Question 19.18

(a) (i)

$$\text{Production volume ratio} = \frac{\text{Standard hours of actual output}}{\text{Budgeted hours of output}} \times 100$$

$$= \frac{(400 \times 5) + (300 \times 2.5) + (140 \times 1)}{(400 \times 5) + (400 \times 2.5) + (100 \times 1)} \times 100 = 93.2\%$$

$$\text{Production efficiency ratio} = \frac{\text{Standard hours of output}}{\text{Actual hours worked}} \times 100$$

$$= \frac{(400 \times 5) + (300 \times 2.5) + (140 \times 1)}{2800\text{ hrs}} \times 100 = 103.2\%$$

(ii) The production volume ratio shows the relationship between the actual output and budgeted output (both measured in standard hours). Therefore the ratio shows the extent to which the budgeted output was met. The fixed overhead volume variance represents the monetary measure equivalent of the production volume ratio.

The production efficiency ratio represents a labour efficiency measure. During the period 2890 hours of output were produced but only 2800 hours were used thus resulting in an efficiency level in excess of 100%. The monetary equivalent variances of this ratio are the labour efficiency, volume efficiency and variable overhead efficiency variances.

(b) Practical capacity is the level of capacity at which a department can normally be expected to operate. It includes an allowance for unavoidable losses in capacity arising from such factors as planned machine maintenance and set-ups.

Budgeted capacity represents the capacity level which is planned to meet the budgeted output for the period. It is based on the budgeted level of efficiency for the period.

Full capacity represents the level of output that could be achieved without any losses or inefficiencies occurring.

Question 19.20

(a)

| | Month ended 31 October 1989 | | | |
	Original budget	Flexible budget	Actual results	Variance against flexible budget
Units	5000	4500	4500	—
	(£)	(£)	(£)	(£)
Sales	600 000	540 000	550 000	10 000 (F)
Less variable costs:				
Direct materials	150 000	135 000	130 000	5 000 (F)
Direct labour	200 000	180 000	189 000	9 000 (A)

Variable production overhead	50 000	45 000	46 000	1 000	(A)
Variable selling overhead	75 000	67 500	72 000	4 500	(A)
Total variable cost	475 000	427 500	437 000	9 500	(A)
Contribution	125 000	112 500	113 000	500	(F)
Less fixed production overhead	25 000	25 000	29 000	4 000	(A)
Fixed selling overhead	50 000	50 000	46 000	4 000	(F)
Profit	50 000	37 500	38 000	500	(F)

Volume variance against original budget (37 500 − 50 000)	12 500	(A)
Variances, actual against flexible budget	500	(F)
Total variances per original statement	12 000	(A)

(b) The variances have been calculated using a variable costing approach.
Sales margin volume:
(actual sales volume − budgeted sales volume)
$\quad$ × standard contribution margin
(4500 − 5000) × £25 (W1) $\qquad$ = £12 500A
Sales margin price:
(actual price − budgeted price) × actual sales volume
(£550 000/4500 − £120) × 4500 $\qquad$ = £10 000F
Direct material cost:
(as per statement in (a)) $\qquad$ = £5 000F
Wage rate:
(SR − AR) × actual hours
(£4 − £189 000/47 500) × 47 500 $\qquad$ = £1 000F
Labour efficiency:
(Standard hours − actual hours) × standard rate
[(90% × 50 000 = 45 000) − 47 500] × £4 $\qquad$ = £10 000A
Variable overhead efficiency:
(SH − AH) × variable overhead rate
(45 000 − 47 500) × £1 $\qquad$ = £2 500A
Variable overhead expenditure:
DLH's flexed budget − actual cost
(47 500 × £1 − £46 000) $\qquad$ = £1 500F
Variable selling overhead:
flexed budget (£67 500 − £72 000) $\qquad$ = £4 500A
Fixed overhead expenditure variances (budgeted cost − actual cost):
Production overhead (£25 000 − £29 000) $\qquad$ = £4 000A
Fixed selling overhead (£50 000 − £46 000) $\qquad$ = £4 000F
Total variances $\qquad$ £12 000A

Working
(W1) Standard contribution per unit
$\qquad$ = budgeted contribution (£125 000)/budgeted volume (5000 units)
(c) The report is based on a variable costing approach and shows the lost contribution arising from a decline in sales volume. With a variable costing system, fixed overheads are not allocated to products, and therefore the volume variance is not applicable. The report compares actual costs with a flexible budget in order to derive the cost variances. (For a description of flexible budgets see 'Flexible budgeting' in Chapter 18). In addition, the original budget is compared with the flexible budget in order to highlight the decline in profits arising from a failure to achieve the budgeted sales volume.

The report for this period shows that the total cost variances were £500 favourable, but the major problem relates to the decline in sales volume, which accounted for a reduction in profits of £12 500.

(a) The following variances can be calculated.

Question 19.23

$(£)$

(i) Wage rate: (standard wage rate − actual wage rate) × actual hours

$[£2 − (£14\,000/6500)] × 6500$ .... = 1 000A

(ii) Labour efficiency: (standard hours − actual hours) × standard rate

$[(500 × 14 = 7000) − 6500] × £2$ .... = 1 000F

(iii) Price variance: (standard price − actual price) × actual quantity

(Output of Dept A) $[£9 − (£21\,000/1400)] × 1400$ .... = 8 400A

(iv) Usage variance: (standard quantity − actual quantity) × standard rate

(Output of Dept A) $[(500 × 3 = 1500) − 1400] × £9$ .... = 900F

(v) Price variance: (standard price − actual price) × actual quantity

(Material X) $[£5 − (£11\,500/1900)] × 1900$ .... = 2 000A

(vi) Usage variance: (standard quantity − actual quantity) × standard rate

(Material X) $[(500 × 4 = 2000) − 1900] × £5$ .... = 500F

(vii) Variable overhead: (flexed budget − actual variable overheads)

Expenditure $(6500 × £1 = £6500) − £8000$ .... = 1 500A

(viii) Variable overhead: (standard hours − actual hours) × variable overhead rate

Efficiency $(7000 − 6500) × £1$ .... = 500F

(ix) Fixed overhead expenditure: (budgeted fixed overheads × actual fixed overheads)

Department B	$(400 × £3 = £1200) − £1600$	=	400A
Allocated	$(400 × £8 = £3200) − £2900$	=	300F

(x) Volume variance: (actual production − budgeted production) × fixed overhead rate

Department B	$(500 − 400) × £3$	=	300F
Allocated	$(500 − 400) × £8$	=	800F

Departmental standard cost for actual production (500 × £100)	= 50 000
Actual cost	= 59 000
Total departmental variance	9 000A

Variances 1–10 add to £9000 adverse. However, not all of the variances are within the control of department B. From the information given in the question, it is not possible to specify which variances are controllable and non-controllable by department B. The following are assumed to be non-controllable:

Wage rate: assumed wage rates are set by the personnel department and that the correct grade of labour has been used.

Material price: Assumed that a central purchasing department exists and that the purchasing officer is responsible for the price variance of material X. The manager of department A is responsible for the price variance for the output of department A.

Allocated fixed overhead expenditure variance: This expenditure is controllable at the point where it is incurred. The actual spending on allocated fixed overheads is not determined by department B.

The following variances might be controllable by the manager of department B:

> Labour efficiency
> Material usage
> Variable overhead efficiency
> Fixed overhead volume
> Fixed overhead expenditure

Fixed overhead volume might be due to a failure to achieve budgeted sales, or machine breakdowns may have occurred that are beyond the control of department B. Any meaningful analysis of the overhead expenditure variance requires a comparison of actual and budgeted expenditure for each individual item. Only by comparing individual items of expenditure and ascertaining the reasons for the variance can one determine whether the variances are controllable or non-controllable. The foregoing analysis assumes the volume variance and overhead expenditure variances to be controllable by the manager of department B. The performance report should analyse variances into their controllable and non-controllable elements:

Department B performance report: Month 7

	(£)	(£)	(£)
Standard cost for actual production			50 000
Controllable variances			
Labour efficiency		1 000F	
Material usage: Department A	900F		
Material X	500F	1 400F	
Overhead expenditure: Fixed	400A		
Variable	1500A	1 900A	
Variable overhead efficiency		500F	
Volume variance: Department B	300F		
Allocated	800F	1 100F	2 100F
Non-controllable variances			
Wage rate		1 000A	
Material price: Department A	8400A		
Material X	2000A	10 400A	
Fixed overhead expenditure (allocated)		300F	11 100A
Actual cost			59 000

(b) The standard costing system is not being operated effectively at present. The variances attributed to department B are not analysed into their controllable and non-controllable elements. In addition, the production manager appears to be using the system in an incorrect manner. He or she appears to be using the system in a punitive manner that might lead to some of the behavioural problems discussed in Chapter 21. Performance reports should be used to help managers control their activities and not as a recriminatory device.

Question 19.24 (a)   (i) *Direct material price variance (cost centre 2)*
(standard price − actual price) × actual quantity

	(£)
102(£15 − £15) × 1120	= 0
103(£4 − £4.20) × 4160	= 832A
	832A

(ii) *Direct material usage (cost centre 2)*
(standard quantity − actual quantity) × standard price

102[(4 × 300 = 1200) − 1120] × £15	= 1200F
103[(6 × 600 = 3600) − 4160] × £4	= 2240A
	1040A

(iii) *Direct labour efficiency (cost centre 1)*
(standard hours − actual hours) × standard rate

A[(10 × 300 = 3000) − 2880] × £3.40	= 408F
B[(6 × 300) + (14 × 6000) − 11 000] × £2.40	= 1920A
	1512A

(iv) *Direct labour rate (cost centre 1)*
(standard rate − actual rate) × actual hours
$$A(£3.40 − £3.70) × 2880 \qquad\qquad 864A$$
$$B(£2.40 − £2.20) × 11\,000 \qquad\qquad = \underline{2200F}$$
$$\underline{1336F}$$

(v) *Production overhead efficiency (cost centre 1)*
Note that CIMA Management Accounting Official Terminology
defines this variance in terms of the *total* overhead rate:
(standard hours − actual hours) × standard total overhead rate
$$[(10 × 300) + (6 × 300) + (14 × 600) − (11\,000 + 2880)]$$
$$× £2.60\ (W1) \qquad\qquad = £1768A$$

(vi) *Production overhead expenditure (cost centre 2)*
budgeted overhead cost − actual overhead cost
$$\text{Fixed } (£18\,180 − £17\,000) \qquad\qquad = 1180F$$
$$\text{Variable } [(£12\,720 × £0.50 = £6360) − £7360] \qquad = \underline{1000A}$$
$$\underline{180F}$$

(vii) *Production overhead volume (cost centre 1)*
This variance is not the fixed overhead volume variance as
illustrated in Chapter 19. The CIMA Official Terminology (1984)
provides a confusing definition of this variance. You will find
that this definition is equivalent to the capacity variance which
was described in Chapter 19. The variance is calculated as
follows:
(actual hours − budgeted hours) × fixed overhead absorption rate
$$(13\,880 − 13\,260)(W1) × £2 \qquad\qquad = 1240F$$

Working

(W1)	Cost centre 1		Cost centre 2	
Budgeted fixed overhead	£26 520		£18 180	
Budgeted direct labour hours	13 260	$\begin{bmatrix} \text{K: } 330 × 16 \\ \text{P: } 570 × 14 \end{bmatrix}$	12 120	$\begin{bmatrix} \text{K: } 330 × 16 \\ \text{P: } 570 × 12 \end{bmatrix}$
Fixed overhead rate	£2.00		£1.50	
Variable overhead rate (given)	£0.60		£0.50	
Total overhead rate	£2.60		£2.00	

(b) *Profit and loss reconciliation statement*
The question asks for a profit and loss statement. To reconcile budget and actual
profit, it is necessary to calculate sales margin variances. The calculations are as
follows:

Sales volume: (actual volume − budgeted volume) × standard margin

$$K\ (340 − 320) × £44.20\ (W1) = £\ 884F$$
$$P\ (560 − 620) × £50.40\ (W1) = \underline{£3024A}$$
$$\underline{£2140A}$$

Sales margin price: (actual margin − standard margin) × actual volume

$$K \begin{bmatrix} (£315 − £270.80\ (W1)) − (£315 − £270.80) × 290 \\ (£360 − £270.80) − (£315 − 270.80) × 50 \end{bmatrix} = 2250F$$

$$P \begin{bmatrix} (£270 − £219.60\ (W1)) − (£270 − £219.60) × 500 \\ (£255 − £219.60) − (£270 − £219.60) × 60 \end{bmatrix} = 900A$$

Working

	K (£)		P (£)
(W1) Standard selling price	315.00		270.00
Standard cost:			

	(£)		(£)	
Per question	214.80		173.60	
Fixed overhead				
CC1 (16 × £2)	32.00		28.00 (14 × £2)	
CC2 (16 × £1.50)	24.00	270.80	18.00 (12 × £1.50)	219.60
Standard profit margin		44.20		50.40

Profit and loss statement period 10[a]

	(£)	(£)	(£)
Budget profit product K (320 at £44.20 each)		14 144	
P (620 at £50.40 each)		31 248	45 392
Sales variances:			
Product K			
Volume	884		
Price	2 250	3 134	
Product P			
Volume	(3 024)		
Price	(900)	(3 924)	(790)
Standard operating gross profit			44 602
Production variances:			
Cost centre 1			
Direct material price	6 240		
Direct material usage	(12 000)		
Direct labour efficiency	(1 512)		
Direct labour rate	1 336		
Production overhead efficiency	(1 768)		
Production overhead expenditure	(1 032)		
Production overhead volume	1 240	(7 496)	
Cost centre 2			
Direct material price	(832)		
Direct material usage	(1 040)		
Direct labour efficiency	(1 296)		
Direct labour rate	—		
Production overhead efficiency	(1 440)		
Production overhead expenditure	180		
Production overhead volume	900	(3 528)	(11 024)
Actual operating gross profit			33 578
Less marketing and administration costs			18 000
Actual net profit			£15 578

Note
[a] Adverse variances are indicated by parentheses.

(c) Actual costs for cost centre 1 exceeded standard cost by £7496, whereas costs for cost centre 2 exceeded standard by £3528. However, it is likely that the price/spending variances are not controllable at departmental level. The following variances are likely to be controllable at departmental level.

	Cost centre 1	Cost centre 2
	(£)	(£)
Material usage	12 000A	1040A
Labour efficiency	1 512A	1296A
Overhead efficiency	1 768A	1440A
	15 280A	3776A

It would appear that both departments failed to meet the standard cost for actual production and that the performance of cost centre 2 was more acceptable than cost centre 1. However, it is difficult to draw conclusions without additional information. For example, the adverse material usage variance for cost centre 1 may have been due to purchase of inferior materials by the purchasing officer.

Question 19.26

(a)

			(£)
Standard cost for actual production (*W1*)			31 638
Material variances:	Favourable	Adverse	
	(£)	(£)	
Price (*W2*)	85		
Usage (*W3*)	196		
Labour variances:			
Rate (*W4*)		154	
Overtime (*W4*)		100	
Efficiency (*W5*)		250	
Variable overhead efficiency (*W6*)		30	
Overhead expenditure variance		288	
	281	822	541A
Actual cost			32 179

Workings

(*W1*) Variable cost per unit:	(£)
Direct materials	49
Direct labour	25
Variable overhead	3
	77

Standard cost for actual production:	
Variable cost	22 638 (294 × £77)
Fixed cost	9 000
	31 638

Note that the above calculation is based on a variable costing basis, with fixed costs treated as a period cost.

(*W2*) Material price variance: [£7 − (£14 125/2030)] × 2030 = £85F

(*W3*) Material usage variance: [(294 × 7 = 2058) − 2030] × £7 = £196F

(*W4*) Wage rate variance: [£5 − (£7854/1520)] × 1520 = £254A

£100 of the variance is due to overtime (40 hrs at £2.50)

(*W5*) Labour efficiency: [(294 × 5 = 1470) − 1520] × £5 = £250A

(*W6*) Variable overhead efficiency: [(294 × 5 = 1470) − 1520] × £0.60 = £30A

(*W7*) Overhead expenditure: [£9000 + (1520 × £0.60)] − £10 200 = £288A

(b) A variable costing approach has been adopted in (a). Therefore the fixed overheads are not unitized and included in the product costs. Consequently, a fixed overhead volume variance does not arise. With a variable costing system, the fixed overhead volume variance is not considered to be of economic significance, since fixed overheads are a sunk cost. The fixed overhead expenditure variance should be calculated, because actual expenditure may be different from budget, and is therefore of economic significance. It is not possible to separate the expenditure variance into the fixed and variable elements from the information given in the question. In practice, the variances should be separated, since this will provide more useful control information. Note that the variable overhead efficiency variance is included with the labour variances, since this is due to labour efficiency.

An alternative presentation would have been to calculate the variances based on an absorption costing system. This approach would result in the following additional variances:

$$\text{Volume capacity } [1520 - (300(W1) \times 5)] \times £6 \quad = £120F$$
$$\text{Volume efficiency } [(294 \times 5 = 1470) - 1520] \times £6 = \underline{£300A}$$
$$\text{Volume variance} \qquad\qquad\qquad\qquad\qquad\qquad \underline{180A}$$

The revised report is as follows:

	Favourable	Adverse	(£)
Standard cost for actual production (294 × £107)			31 458
Variances calculated in (a)		541	
Volume capacity	120		
Volume efficiency		300	
Actual cost	$\underline{120}$	$\underline{841}$	$\underline{721A}$
			$\underline{\underline{32\ 179}}$

Note that fixed overheads are now unitized and charged to production at £30 per unit. This approach is necessary for external reporting, but is questionable for cost control. The amounts attached to the volume capacity and efficiency variances have no economic significance because the fixed overheads are a sunk cost. (For a more detailed discussion see 'A relevant cost approach to variance analysis' in Chapter 20.)

Working
(W1) Budgeted fixed overheads are £9000 and the budgeted rate per unit is £30. Therefore budgeted production is 300 units (9000/30).
(c) For a description of the approaches see 'Establishing cost standards' in Chapter 19 and 'Engineering methods' Chapter 23. Note that the approaches outlined in Chapter 19 also refer to engineering methods. If the product has been produced in the past the standard quantity can be estimated from historical records. The limitation of this approach is that standard quantities might be set that incorporate existing inefficiencies. Any adjustments from the historical standard are likely to be resisted unless inducements are offered. The advantage of using historical records is that it avoids the intensive and expensive studies of operations (e.g. time and motion studies) which are associated with engineering methods. Operatives may also be hostile to a standard costing system if time and motion studies are employed to set standard times.

The advantage of engineering methods is that the most efficient methods of operating are established and rigorous scientific methods are used to set standards. This might result in tight standards that are not internalized by the budgetees. It is therefore important that production staff participate in setting the standards.

It is normally possible to set reliable quantity standards, but this is unlikely to be the case with price standards. Price changes are normally due to external factors that are beyond the control of the purchasing officer (for materials) or the personnel officer (for wages rates). It is likely that price variances are due to incorrect forecasts rather than purchasing performance. Nevertheless, feedback information should be produced indicating the ability of the purchasing officer to predict future prices. This feedback might help to improve the accuracy of future forecasts of material prices.

A major problem in setting standards is that future changes might occur that were not envisaged when the standard was set. It is therefore important that standards be reviewed frequently and changes made. Wherever possible, variances should be split into planning and operational variances.

Standard costing: 2 Further aspects

Solutions to Chapter 20 questions

Question summary

20.1–20.5	Various discussion questions relevant to Chapter 20.
20.6–20.9	Accounting entries for a standard costing system. Question 20.6 requires the preparation of the stores ledger account when the price variance is extracted at the time of issue and also at the time of purchase. Question 20.8 assumes that a variable costing system is in operation.
20.10	Calculation of optimal output using calculus plus the preparation of process accounts for a standard costing system.
20.11–20.13	Computation of mix and yield variances. Question 20.13 involves the computation of labour mix and yield variances.
20.14	Calculation of sales, labour, material and overhead variances. This question is similar to the questions set in Chapter 19, but it also includes the calculation of sales mix, material mix and yield variances.
20.15	Comparison of the performance of two sales territories using variance analysis.
20.16	Accounting disposition of variances.
20.17–20.22	Ex-post variance analysis and the segregation of planning and operating variances. Question 20.17 involves mix and yield variances.
20.23	A relevant cost approach to variance analysis.
20.24	Variable costing reconciliation of budgeted and actual contribution and a discussion of the role of standard costing in a modern manufacturing environment.
20.25	Evaluation of performance using variance analysis. This is a difficult question and requires a good conceptual understanding of variance analysis rather than a rote-learning approach.
20.26–20.28	Investigation of variances.

Question 20.2 (a) For the answer to this question see 'Investigation of variances' in Chapter 20. In particular the answer should explain that variances may be due to several causes, and not all are worthy of investigation. In addition the answer should stress the possible approaches to investigating variances:

   (i) *Use of rule of thumb percentages:* For example, all variances in excess of 10% of standard cost might be investigated. This approach ignores the costs and benefits of investigation.

   (ii) *Use of statistical quality control charts*: Control limits are set using an analysis of historical results to indicate suitable confidence intervals. This method utilizes a statistical probability approach of not investigating a variance unless there is a high probability that the process is out of control.

   (iii) *Use of a statistical decision theory approach*: This approach is described in Chapter 20.

It is unlikely that statistical decision theory can be applied in practice, because of the difficulty in estimating costs and benefits of investigation. Nevertheless, the approach provides a suitable model that gives a manager an insight into the important factors that should be considered when deciding whether or not to investigate a variance. Experience and an understanding of the model is likely to be the best way of establishing whether or not investigation is worthwhile.

(b) See Chapter 21 for the answer to this question.

    (i) The level of budget difficulty is likely to have a motivational influence on a manager's actions to eliminate variances. If a manager believes a target to be unattainable, he or she is unlikely to strive to eliminate variances. (See 'The use of budgets as targets' in Chapter 21.)

    (ii) Managers may manipulate information in order to avoid adverse variances. This is most likely to occur if a budget-constrained style of performance evaluation is used Genuine performance improvements are most likely to occur if a profit-conscious style of evaluation is used. For a detailed discussion of styles of evaluation see 'Managerial use of accounting information in performance evaluation' in Chapter 21.

    (iii) Managers are most likely to strive to eliminate variances if they accept the budget and this becomes a motivational target. Budget acceptance is more likely to be achieved by participation and not by imposed budgets. See 'Participation in the budgeting and standard setting process' in Chapter 21 for a more detailed discussion of the influence of participation on acceptance of budgets.

    (iv) The extent to which performance appraisal, future promotion and cash bonuses are tied to meeting the budget will provide a major motivation stimulus to meeting the budget. However, if too much stress is placed on meeting the budget, there is a danger that over-generous budgets will be sought or information will be distorted so as to avoid adverse variances.

    (v) Performance reports comparing actual with budget should be provided soon after the end of the budget period (weekly or monthly). A manager is more likely to be motivated to eliminate variances if feedback reports are timely and understandable. A climate of failure and punishment should be avoided, and the emphasis should be on *helping* managers to eliminate adverse variances.

Question 20.4

(a) The management accountant should consider the following factors when deciding whether or not to investigate variances:

    (i) *The size of the variances*: This may be expressed in terms of percentage variation from standard or budget. Alternatively, statistical techniques can be used to determine the probability of the variance occurring when it is under control. The size of the variance indicates the likelihood that the variance is due to an assignable cause.

    (ii) *Costs and benefits of investigation*: The management accountant should assess whether the costs of investigation are less than the benefits that are expected to result from the investigation.

    (iii) *Nature of the standard*: Are expected or ideal standards used? If ideal standards are used then investigation of the variances is unlikely to result in the variances being eliminated.

    (iv) *Cumulative variances*: A variance showing an increase in size over time may justify an investigation even when the variance for the particular period is not significant. Alternatively, a variance that is significant for a particular period but that is decreasing over time may be under control.

    (v) *Validity of standard or budget*: The validity of the standard will help the accountant to gauge the significance of the variance. A price variance in times of rapidly rising prices is unlikely to be due to an assignable cause.

(b) The management accountant can take the following action to improve the chances of achieving positive results from investigating variances:

    (i) *Speedy identification and reporting of variances*: Significant delays between the occurrence of a variance and its notification to managers will limit the degree of control that managers can achieve. The sooner a variance is identified, the sooner it can be investigated and acted upon.

   (ii) *Analysis of variances*: The accountant should provide clues as to the possible reasons for the variances by pinpointing where the variances have arisen. For example, the accountant might identify the reason for a direct material variance as being due to excessive usage of a certain material in a particular process. This should assist the responsibility manager in quickly identifying the cause of the excessive usage.

   (iii) *Statistical procedures*: Statistical procedures and quality control charts should be used so as to determine the probability that variances are due to an assignable cause. If managers are frequently required to investigate variances that are due to random variations then it is unlikely that they will give detailed attention to the investigation process. However, if the majority of variances reported are significant then managers will attach greater importance to the investigation process.

   (iv) *Develop a team effort approach*: The accountant should be seen by managers as supportive within the control process. If a team effort approach is developed then it is likely that managers will be more actively involved in the investigation process.

Question 20.5 (a) The following problems might occur during periods of rapid inflation:

   (i) The standards will presumably include some assumptions about inflation. If this assumption is not clearly stated then it is difficult to determine how much of a price variance is due to inflation and how much is due to buying efficiency.

   (ii) Price indices tend to reflect average price changes. Consequently, it is difficult for a company to predict future costs and interpret variances if the specific rate of inflation for its inputs is considerably different from the general rate of inflation.

   (iii) Inflation may result in relative changes in the prices of inputs. Therefore standard mixes requiring different inputs may no longer be the most efficient mix.

   (iv) If standard prices are not adjusted then the efficiency variances will be understated.

   (v) The impact of inflation will have an immediate effect on cash flows, but some delay will occur before the full extent of the variances is ascertained. Therefore management may not respond quickly enough to pricing, output and sourcing decisions in order to effectively control cash flows.

   (vi) Sharp rises in prices will raise questions as to whether unadjusted standards can be used in the decision-making process (e.g. pricing decisions).

   (vii) Administrative work in maintaining up-to-date standards when prices are constantly changing.

   (b) (i) When establishing standards, the inflation factor that has been assumed should be clearly stated so that variances can be analysed by price and efficiency changes.

   (ii) Internal indices of price changes could be maintained for cost items that do not move in line with the general rate of inflation.

   (iii) Variances should be analysed by their forecasting and operational elements as indicated in Chapter 20.

   (iv) Standard mixes should be established for a range of prices for the material inputs, and management should be prepared to implement changes in the mix immediately price changes dictate that a change is necessary.

Question 20.6 (a) *Workings*

   (i) *Material price variance identified on purchase of material*
   Variance = (SP − AP) × quantity purchased
   4 November (£1.04 − £10 530/10 000) × 10 000 = £130A
   23 November: (£1.04 − £8480/8000) × 8000   = £160A

Material Z stock account

	(£)		(£)
Opening balance		2/11 WIP (2000 × £1.04)	2 080
(9000 kg at £1.04)	9 360	7/11 WIP (4500 × £1.04)	4 680
4/11 Purchases			
(10 000 × £1.04)	10 400	20/11 WIP (4000 × £1.04)	4 160
23/11 Purchases			
(8000 × £1.04)	8 320	27/11 WIP (6000 × £1.04)	6 240
		Closing balance	
		(10 500 × £1.04)	10 920
	28 080		28 080

Creditors account

			(£)
		4/11 Material Z stock	
		account	10 400
		4/11 Material price	
		variance account	130
		23/11 Material Z stock	
		account	8 320
		23/11 Material price	
		variance account	160

Material price variance account

4/11 Creditors account	130	30/11 Profit and Loss	
23/11 Creditors account	160	account	290

(ii) *Material price variance identified at time of issue of material*

Using the weighted average basis, the actual issue prices are calculated as follows:

	(£)
Opening balance (9000 × £1.07)	9 630
2 November issue (2000 × £1.07)	(2 140)
Balance 7000 at £1.07 (£7490/7000)	7 490
4 November purchase (10 000 kg)	10 530
Balance (17 000 kg at £1.06)	18 020
7 November issue (4500 × £1.06)	(4 770)
20 November issue (4000 × £1.06)	(4 240)
Balance (8500 × £1.06)	9 010
23 November purchase (8000 kg)	8 480
Balance (16 500 kg at £1.06)	17 490
27 November issue (6000 kg × £1.06)	6 360

Variance = (SP − AP) × actual issues
2 November: (£1.04 − £1.07) × 2000 = £60A
7 November: (£1.04 − £1.06) × 4500 = £90A
20 November: (£1.04 − £1.06) × 4000 = £80A
27 November: (£1.04 − £1.06) × 6000 = £120A

Note that the entries in the stock account in (a)(i) are based on the approach described in Chapter 20 whereby the stock account is debited at the standard cost and the variances are extracted at the time of purchase. Where variances are extracted at the time of issue, it is preferable to use an alternative approach when preparing the stock account. With this approach, the stock account is debited at actual cost, and issues are recorded at standard cost and the price variances are recorded within the stock account.

(iii)

Material Z

	(kg)	(£/unit)	(£)		(kg)	(£/unit)	(£)
1/11 Opening balance	9 000	1.07	9 630	2/11 Work-in-process	2 000	1.04	2 080
4/11 Purchases	10 000	1.053	10 530	2/11 Materials price			
23/11 Purchases	8 000	1.06	8 480	variance			60
				7/11 Work-in-process	4 500	1.04	4 680
				7/11 Materials price			
				variance			90
				20/11 Work-in-process	4 000	1.04	4 160
				20/11 Materials price			
				variance			80
				27/11 Work-in-process	6 000	1.04	6 240
				27/11 Materials price			
				variance			120
				30/11 Closing balance	10 500	1.06	11 130
	27 000		28 640		27 000		28 640

Material price variance

	(£)		(£)
2/11 Material Z	60	30/11 profit and loss	350
7/11 Material Z	90		
20/11 Material Z	80		
27/11 Material Z	120		
	350		350

(b) The method by which variances are extracted at the time of purchase is preferred because variances are reported at the earliest opportunity. In addition, the stock recording system is simplified.

(c) *Workings*:

Equivalent units

	Materials	Labour and overhead
Completed production	9 970	9 970
Add closing WIP	8 000	6 000
	17 970	15 970
Less opening WIP	6 000	3 000
Equivalent production	11 970	12 970

Material usage variance
(actual usage − standard usage) × standard price
[6000 kg − (11 970 units × 0.5)] × £1.04
£15.60A

Labour efficiency variance
(actual hours − standard hours) × standard rate
[1340 hrs − (12 970 units × 0.1)] × £4.80
£206.40A

Overhead variance
actual cost − standard cost
6680 − (12 970 units × 0.1 × £5.00)
£195A

Standard cost per unit: product X
Materials   0.5 kg × £1 .04/kg   =£0.52
Direct labour 0.1 hrs × £4.80/hr   =£0.48

Overhead   0.1 hrs × £5.00/hr   = £0.50

£1.50

Process 1

	(£)		(£)
Opening balance:		Finished goods:	
Materials:		9970 units × £1.50	14 955
6000 units × £0.52		Closing balance:	
Direct labour and overhead:		Materials:	
3000 units × £0.98	6 060	8000 units × £0.52	
Materials:		Direct labour and overhead:	
6000 kilos × £1.04	6 240	6000 units × £0.98	10 040
Direct labour:		Material usage variance	15.6
1340 hours × £4.80	6 432	Labour efficiency variance	206.4
Overheads	6 680	Overhead variance	195
	25 412		25 412

(a) *Variance analysis*

Question 20.7

Material price = (standard price − actual price) × actual purchases

X $\quad$ = (£20 − £20.50) × 9000

$\quad$ = £4500A

Y $\quad$ = (£6 − £5.50) × 5000

$\quad$ = £2500F

Material usage = (standard usage − actual usage) × standard price

X $\quad$ = (800 × 10 kg − 7800 kg) × £20

$\quad$ = £4000F

Y $\quad$ = (800 × 5 litres − 4300 litres) × £6

$\quad$ = £1800A

Wage rate = [standard rate (£6) − actual rate (£24 150/4200)]

$\quad\quad\quad$ × actual hours (4200)

$\quad$ = £1050F

Labour efficiency = [standard hours (800 × 5 hrs) − actual hours (4200)]

$\quad\quad\quad\quad\quad$ × standard rate (£6)

$\quad\quad\quad$ = £1200A

Fixed overhead expenditure = budgeted cost (10 800/12 × £50)

$\quad\quad\quad\quad\quad\quad\quad$ − actual cost (£47 000)

$\quad\quad\quad\quad\quad$ = £2000A

Volume efficiency = [standard hours (800 × 5 hrs) − actual hours (4200)]

$\quad\quad\quad\quad\quad$ = × (£50/5 hours)

$\quad\quad\quad\quad\quad$ = £2000A

Volume capacity[a] = [actual hours (4200) − budgeted hours[b] (4500)]

$\quad\quad\quad\quad\quad$ × FOAR (£50/5 hours)

$\quad\quad\quad\quad\quad$ = £3000A

Notes

[a]Note that the CIMA Terminology (1984) describes the volume variance as being equivalent to the volume capacity variance.

[b]Budgeted hours = monthly budgeted output (10 800/12) × 5 hrs

(b)

Stores control

	(£)		(£)
K Ltd: X (AQ × SP)	180 000	WIP: (SQ × SP)	160 000
C Ltd: Y (AQ × SP)	30 000	WIP: (SQ × SP)	24 000
Material usage variance (X)	4 000	Material usage variance (Y)	1 800
		Balance	28 200
	£214 000		£214 000

Wages control account

	(£)		(£)
Cash	20 150	Wages owing b/fwd	6 000
PAYE and NI	5 000	Labour efficiency	1 200
Accrued wages	5 000	WIP (SQ × SP)	24 000
Wage rate variance	1 050		
	£31 200		£31 200

WIP control account

	(£)		(£)
Stores control: X	160 000	Finished goods control a/c	248 000
Y	24 000		
Wages control	24 000		
Fixed overhead	40 000		
	£248 000		£248 000

Fixed overhead control

	(£)		(£)
Expense creditors	33 000	WIP (SQ × SP)	40 000
Depreciation provision	14 000	Expenditure variance	2 000
		Efficiency variance	2 000
		Capacity variance	3 000
	£47 000		£47 000

Finished goods control

	(£)		(£)
WIP control	£248 000	Cost of sales	£248 000

Cost of sales

	(£)		(£)
Finished goods control	£248 000	Profit and loss (P/L)	£248 000

Material price variance

	(£)		(£)
K Ltd: X	4500	C Ltd: Y	2500
		P/L	2000
	£4500		£4500

Material usage variance

	(£)		(£)
Stores control: Y	1800	Stores control: X	4000
P/L	2200		
	£4000		£4000

Labour rate variance

	(£)		(£)
P/L	£1050	Wages control	£1050

Labour efficiency variance

	(£)		(£)
Wages control	1200	P/L	1200

Fixed overhead expenditure variance

	(£)		(£)
Overhead control	2000	P/L	2000

Fixed overhead efficiency variance

	(£)		(£)
Overhead control	2000	P/L	2000

Fixed overhead capacity variance

	(£)		(£)
Overhead control	£3000	P/L	£3000

Sales

	(£)		(£)
P/L	320 000	Debtors	320 000

K Limited

			(£)
		Stores control	180 000
		Price variance account	4 500

C plc

	(£)		(£)
Price variance account	2500	Stores control	30 000

Expense creditors

			(£)
		Fixed overhead control	33 000

Provision for depreciation

	(£)		(£)
		Fixed overhead control	14 000

Profit and loss account

	(£)	(£)	(£)
Sales			320 000
Cost of sales			248 000
			72 000
Variances	(F)	(A)	
Material price	—	2 000	
usage	2 200	—	
Labour rate	1 050	—	
efficiency	—	1 200	
Overhead expenditure	—	2 000	
efficiency	—	2 000	
volume	—	3 000	
	3 250	10 200	6 950
Gross profit			65 050

(c) The difference of £250 in the accounts is due to the fact that the material price variance has been calculated on purchases (instead of usage) and written off as a period cost. In the question the raw material stocks are recorded at actual cost, and therefore the £250 is included in the stock valuation and will be recorded as an expense next period.

Question 20.12 (a) *Preliminary workings*

		Standard cost of 1 mix (£)	Standard cost per kg of output (£)
Material X	60 kg at £2	= 120	
Material Y	40 kg at £1	= 40	
Material Z	100 kg at £1.40	= 140	
	200	= 300	
Normal loss	20	—	
	180	= 300	1.667 (£300/180 kg)
Wages (180 kg/40 kg) × £4 × 10 employees[a]		= 180	1.000 (£180/180 kg)
Fixed production overhead [(£270 000/90 000) × 180]		= 540	3.000 (£540/180 kg)
		1020	5.667

Note
[a] Output is 40 kg per hour from 10 employees.

	(1) Standard quantity in standard proportions at standard prices (W1)		(2) Actual input in standard proportions at standard prices		(3) Actual input in actual proportions at standard prices		(4) Actual input in actual proportions at actual prices	
Materials		(£)		(£)		(£)		(£)
X	11 mixes × 60 kg × £2	= 1320	2260 × 0.3 × £2	= 1356	700 × £2	= 1400	700 × £1.80	= 1260
Y	11 mixes × 40 kg × £1	= 440	2260 × 0.2 × £1	= 452	440 × £1	= 440	440 × £1.10	= 484
Z	11 mixes × 100 kg × 1.40	= 1540	2260 × 0.5 × £1.40	= 1582	1120 × £1.40	= 1568	1120 × £1.30	= 1456
		3300		3390		3408		3200

Usage variance (1) − (3)		Mix variance (2) − (3)	
	(£)		(£)
Material X	80A	Material X	44A
Y	0	Y	12F
Z	28A	Z	14F
	108A		18A

Price variance (3) − (4)		Direct material total variance (1) − (4)	
	(£)		(£)
Material X	140F	Material X	60F
Y	44A	Y	44A
Z	112F	Z	84F
	208F		100F

Working

(W1) For an output of 1980 kg, 11 mixes are required (1980 kg/180 kg) standard output per mix).

(b) *Direct material yield variance*

An input of 2260 kg should yield an output of 2034 kg [(2260/220) × 180].
(actual yield − standard yield from actual input) × standard cost per unit of output
(1980 kg − 2034) × £1.667 = £90A

Direct labour efficiency variance
(standard hours − actual hours) × standard rate
[(1980/40) × 10 employees = 495) − (10 × 45 hrs)] × £4 = £180F

Overhead volume variance
(actual production − budgeted production) × fixed overhead rate
[1980 − (90 000 kg/50 weeks)] × £3 = £540F

(c)

Direct materials control account

Creditors (AQ × SP)	3408	WIP a/c (SQ × SP)	3300
		Material usage variance	108
	3408		3408

WIP control account

Materials control account		Finished goods stock	
(SQ × SP)	3 300	(1980 units at £5.667	
Direct wages (SQ × SP)	1 980	standard cost per unit)	11 220
Fixed overhead (SQ × SP)	5 940		
	11 220		11 220

Variance account

Materials control account	108	Creditors	208
		Labour efficiency variance	180
		Volume variance	540

Creditors account

Variance account	208	Material control	3408

The standard composition of a work team is as follows:

Question 20.13

	Proportions
2 supervisors	0.083
10 fitters	0.417

6 electricians	0.25
2 electronic engineers	0.083
4 labourers	0.167
24	1.000

The standard cost for an output of 90 standard hours is:

		(£)
8.3 hours (supervisors) at £8 per hour	=	66.40
41.7 hours (fitters) at £6 per hour	=	250.20
25 hours (electricians) at £6 per hour	=	150.00
8.3 hours (electronic engineers) at £7 per hour	=	58.10
16.7 hours (labourers) at £4 per hour	=	66.80
		591.50

Standard cost per standard hour of output = £6.572 (£591.50/90 hours).

(a) *Wage rate variance*
Actual hours at standard rate:

		(£)
Supervisors (170 × £8)	=	1 360
Fitters (820 × £6)	=	4 920
Electricians (420 × £6)	=	2 520
Electronic engineers (230 × £7)	=	1 610
Labourers (280 × £4)	=	1 120
		11 530
Actual wages cost		£11 721
Wage rate variance (£11 530 − £11 721)		£191A

(b) (i) *Team composition variance*
(Actual hours at standard mix − actual hours at actual mix) × standard rate
(1920 × 0.083 = 159.36 − 170) × £8 = −£85.12
(1920 × 0.417 = 800.64 − 820) × £6 = −£116.16
(1920 × 0.25 = 480 − 420) × £6 = £360.00
(1920 × 0.083 = 159.36 − 230) × £7 = −£494.48
(1920 × 0.167 = 320.64 − 280) × £4 = £162.56
£173.20A

(ii) *Team productivity variance*
(actual output − standard output) × standard cost per unit of output
[1650 standard hours − (0.9 × 1920 standard hours)]
× £6.5722 per standard hour = £512.62A

(iii) *Labour efficiency variance*
(actual output × standard cost per unit of output)
− (actual hours × standard rate)
(1650 standard hours × £6.5722 = £10 844.16) − £11 530 = £685.82
Alternatively, the labour efficiency variance can be computed by adding the
productivity and composition variances (£512.62 + £173.20 = £685.82)

(c) The team composition and the team productivity variances are similar to the
material mix and yield variances. For a discussion of the meaning of these
variances and their limitations see 'Mix and yield variances' in Chapter 20.

Question 20.14 (a) *Cost variance calculations*
Material price:

	(£)	(£)
(SP − AP) × AQ		
A(£0.30 − £0.20) × 8000		800F
B(0.70 − £0.80) × 5000		500A

Material mix:
(actual wage in standard proportions − actual wage in actual proportions)
× SP

A (6500 − 8000) × £0.30	450A	
B (6500 − 5000) × £0.70	1050F	600F

Material yield: [a]
(actual yield − standard yield)
× SC per unit of output

(12000 − 13000) × £0.50		500A

Wage rate:
(SR − AR) × AH

Skilled (£3 − £2.95) × 6000		300F
Semi-skilled (£2.50 − £2.60) × 3150		315A

Labour mix: [b]
(AQ in standard and proportions
− AQ in actual proportions) × SR

Skilled (5799 − 6000) × £3	603A	
Semi-skilled (3351 − 3150) × £2.50	503F	100A

Labour productivity: [c]
(SQ in standard and proportions
− AQ in standard proportions) × SR

Skilled (5400 − 5799) × £3	1197A	
Semi-skilled (3120 − 3351) × £2.50	578A	1775A

Fixed overhead spending:
BC − AC

£10 000 − £9010		990F

Variable overhead spending:
flexed budgeted − AC

12 000 × £0.50 = 6000 − £7500		1500A

Fixed overhead volume:
(actual production − budgeted production) × FOAR

(12 000 − 10 000) × £1		2000F
Total cost variances		Nil

Sales margin variance calculations
Sales volume variance: (£)
(actual sales volume − budgeted volume)
× standard margin

(11 000 − 10 000) × £1		1000F

Sales margin price variance:
(actual selling price − budgeted selling price)
× actual sales volume

(£5 − £5) × 7000 = 0		
(£4.75 − £5) × 4000 = 1000A		1000A
Total sales variances		nil

The question requires the calculation of the material usage variance and the labour efficiency variance. These variances are calculated as follows:

$$\text{direct material usage variance} = \text{mix variance} + \text{yield variance}$$
$$= £600F + £500A = £100F$$

$$\text{labour efficiency variance} = \text{mix variance} + \text{productivity variance}$$

	(£)
Skilled = £603A + £11 97A =	1800A
Unskilled = £503F + £578A =	75A
	1875A

Reconciliation of actual and budgeted profit
The total of the cost variances and the sales variances are zero. Therefore actual profit equals budgeted profit.

Notes
[a]Budgeted usage is 1 kg of materials for 1 unit of output. The standard yield for an input of 13 000 kg is therefore 13 000 units.
The standard material cost per unit of output is:

	(£)
A (0.5 × £0.30) =	0.15
B (0.5 × £0.70) =	0.35
	0.50

[b]
$$\text{Skilled} = 9150 \text{ hrs} \times 4500/7100 = 5799 \text{ hrs}$$
$$\text{Semi-skilled} = 9150 \text{ hrs} \times 2600/7100 = 3351 \text{ hrs}$$

[c]The standard labour quantity is 0.45 skilled hours and 0.26 unskilled hours for each unit of output. For an output of 12 000 units the standard labour hours are:

$$\text{skilled} = 5400 \ (12 \ 000 \times 0.45 \text{ hrs})$$
$$\text{semi-skilled} = 3120 \ (12 \ 000 \times 0.26 \text{ hrs})$$

(b) The sales volume variance shows the effect on profit from sales volume being in excess of budget (assuming standard costs remain unchanged). The adverse sales price variance of £1000 indicates the lost profits from selling below the standard price. However, the reduction in the selling price will be partly accounted for by the increase in sales volume. An ex-post budget comparison should be used. For example, a revised target for sales that could have been obtained at the actual selling prices should be used to calculate the volume variance.

The price paid for material A is less than standard and the price paid for B is above standard. This might explain why the company has substituted material A for B during the period. The usage variance is £100 favourable, but £600 of this is due to the change in the materials mix. The difference of £500 represents the excess wage when the mix variance is not taken into account. The analysis does not indicate whether the excess usage is due to using a non-standard mix or to inefficient usage.

The wage rate variances arise because the skilled rate is below standard but the semi-skilled rate is above the standard. There is a significant adverse labour efficiency variance, which should be investigated. The mix and productivity variances are unlikely to provide any helpful clues in explaining the adverse efficiency variance.

The fixed overhead volume variance arises because output is in excess of budget but this variance is not particularly useful (see 'Volume variance' in Chapter 19 for an explanation). The variable overhead expenditure variance is partly a spending variance and a usage variance, and on its own is not very meaningful. Any meaningful analysis of this variance requires a comparison of the actual expenditure with budget for each variable cost item.

(a) (i) *Actual absorption costing*
Inventory is 20% of the output for the period, and there are no opening stocks. Therefore value of inventory = 20% × £4 080 000 = £816 000

(ii) *Standard absorption costing with variances written off*
Standard cost of production for period = 50 000 × £75
$$= £3\ 750\ 000$$
Therefore closing stock = 20% × £3 750 000
$$= £750\ 000$$
The variances are written off as a period cost and not included in the stock valuation.

(iii) *Standard absorption costing with variances pro-rated between cost of sales and inventory*
Variances for the period = £330 000A (4 080 000 − £3 750 000 standard cost)
Variances pro-rated to inventory = £66 000 (£330 000 × 20%)
Inventory valuation = standard cost of inventory (£750 000) + pro-rated variances (£66 000) = £816 000

(iv) *Actual direct costing*
Value of inventory = 20% × actual variable costs (£3 700 000)
$$= £740\ 000$$

(v) *Standard direct costing with variances written off*
Standard variable cost of production = £3 250 000 (50 000 × £65 variable standard unit cost)
Inventory valuation = £650 000 (20% × £3 250 000)

(vi) *Standard direct costing with variances pro-rated between cost of sales and inventory*
Standard variable cost of production = £3 250 000
Standard variable cost of production = £3 700 000
Variance = £450 000A
Inventory valuation = standard variable cost of inventory (£650 000) + pro-rated variances (20% × £450 000) = £740 000

(b) Inventory valuations based on absorption costing treats fixed production overheads as product costs. This will cause the stock valuation to be influenced by the level of activity that is used to determine the fixed overhead rate per unit. In addition, profits will be influenced by the production and stock-holding policy.

Variable absorption costing methods treat fixed production overheads as period costs, resulting in lower stock valuations compared with absorption costing. Profits are a function of sales volume only.

When actual costing methods are used, inefficiencies are included in stock valuation. In theory, they should be written off in the period when they are incurred. Where a standard costing system is used and variances are pro-rated between cost of sales and inventory, the stock valuations are identical with the valuations based on actual cost systems. Therefore the same criticism regarding the inefficiencies being included in the stock valuation apply.

When a standard costing system is used and all variances are written off, inefficiencies are not included in the stock valuation. However, not all variances represent inefficiencies. Some may be due to permanent changes in standard (e.g. price variances). Variances that do not reflect inefficiencies should be pro-rated between cost of sales and inventories, whereas variances that represent inefficiencies should be written off as a period cost.

(c) (i) *Discussion of the relevance of overhead cost absorption procedures for pricing*
The answer should include the following:
1. Disadvantages of arbitrary apportionment of joint costs to products.
2. Influence of activity level in calculating predetermined overhead rates. Overhead will only be recovered in sales revenue if demand is equivalent to the activity level that was used to calculate the overhead rate.
3. Limitations that apply when common costs are apportioned to products and an example of how this can lead to incorrect decisions.
4. Limitations of cost-plus pricing.
5. Arguments in support of cost-plus pricing.
6. An indication that full costs including overhead apportionments might provide an indication of the long-run production cost.
Most of the above points are included in Chapters 11–13.
(ii) *Overhead cost absorption cost procedures for control of costs*
The answer should state that costs should be analysed into controllable and non-controllable elements. Apportioned costs should be separately shown in a section headed 'Uncontrollable costs' in the performance report. The answer should stress accountability and responsibility when costs are attributed to individuals for control purposes. Overhead absorption should be used for product costing purposes, but not for cost control purposes.

Question 20.17 (a)

	Original standard		Revised standard		Actual	
		(£)		(£)		(£)
Fruit	400 × 0.16	64	400 × 0.19	76	428 × 0.18	77.04
Glucose	700 × 0.10	70	700 × 0.12	84	742 × 0.12	89.04
Pectin	99 × 0.332	32.868	99 × 0.332	32.868	125 × 0.328	41.00
Citric acid	1 × 2.00	2	1 × 2.00	2	1 × 0.95	0.95
	1200	168.868	1200	194.868	1296	208.03
Labour		58.500		58.500	—	60.00
	1200	227.368	1200	253.368	1296	268.03
Loss	36	—	36	—	132	—
	1164	227.368	1164	253.368	1164	268.03

Planning variances:	(£)
Fruit extract (£64 − £76)	12A
Glucose syrup (£70 − £84)	14A
Total	26

(b) Ingredients operating variances:

Total (£194.868 − £208.03)	£13.162A
Price variances: (SP − AP) × AQ	
Fruit extract (£0.19 − £0.18) × 428	£4.28F
Glucose syrup	Nil
Pectin (£0.332 − £0.328) × 125	£0.50F
Citric acid (£2 − £0.95) × 1	£1.05F
	£5.83F

Usage variances: (SQ for output of one batch − AQ) × SP

	(£)
Fruit extract (400 − 428) × £0.19	5.32A
Glucose syrup (700 − 742) × £0.12	5.04A
Pectin (99 − 125) × £0.332	8.632A
Citric acid	nil
	18.992A

(c) The advantages of distinguishing between planning and operation variances are:
   (i) Comparisons are made against targets that take into account the changing conditions from when the targets were originally set. The revised ex-post standard thus compares actual results with an adjusted standard that reflects these changed conditions.
   (ii) Variances reflect only factors under control of managers, and managers will be more highly motivated if their performance is compared against more realistic targets.
   (iii) Planning variances provide useful feedback information on the accuracy of predicting standards and budgets.
   The disadvantages are:
   (i) Difficulty in establishing revised standards.
   (ii) Managers accountable for variances might try and influence the allocation of the variances to the planning/uncontrollable category.

(d) *Mixture variance*

actual usage in standard mix	−	actual usage in actual mix	×	standard price		
				(£)		(£)
432	−	428	×	0.19	=	0.76F
756	−	742	×	0.12	=	1.68F
106.92	−	125	×	0.332	=	6.003A
1.08	−	1	×	2.00	=	0.16F
1296		1296				3.403A

Yield variance: (actual yield − standard yield from actual input) × standard cost per unit of output
$$[1164 − (0.97 × 1296)] × £194.868/1164$$
$$= £15.589A$$
Usage variance (£18.992) = mix variance (£3.403) + yield variance (£15.589)

(e) Total variance = £227.368 − £268.03 = £40.662A
The total variance is analysed as follows:

	(£)
Ingredients planning variances	26.00A
Ingredients operating variances	13.162A
Labour operating variance (£58.50 − £60)	1.50A
	40.662

Question 20.21

(a) The traditional variance analysis is as follows:

	(£)
Sales margin volume variance:	nil
(actual sales volume = budgeted sales volume)	
Sales margin price variance:	
(actual unit margin − standard unit margin)	
× actual sales volume	
(£84 − £26) × 1000	58 000F
	58 000F

	(£)
Material price:	
(standard price − actual price) × actual quantity	
(£5 − £9) × 10 800	43 200A

Material usage:
  (standard quantity − actual quantity) × standard price
  (10 000 − 10 800) × £5   4 000A   47 200A

Wage rate:
  (standard rate − actual rate) × actual hours
  [£4 − (£34 800/5800)] × 5800   11 600A
Labour efficiency:
  (standard hours − actual hours) × standard rate
  [(1000 × 6 = 6000) − 5800] × £4   800F   10 800A

                                                Total variances   nil

Reconciliation:
  Budgeted contribution (1000 × £26)   26 000
  Add adverse cost variances   58 000
  Less favourable sales variances   (58 000)

                                                Actual contribution   26 000

(b)

	(A) *Original plan*	(B) *Revised ex-post plan*	(C) *Actual results*
	(£)	(£)	(£)
Sales (1000 × £100) = 100 000	(1000 × £165) = 165 000	(100 × £158) = 158 000
Labour (6000 × £4) = 24 000	(6000 × £6.25) = 37 500	(5800 × £6) = 34 800
Materials:			
Aye (10 000 × £5) = 50 000	(10 000 × £8.50) = 85 000	(10 800 × £9) = 97 200
Bee	(10 000 × £7) = 70 000	

Uncontrollable planning variances (A − B)	(£)	
Sales price	65 000F	
Wage rate	13 500A	
Material price[a] (50 000 − 70 000)	20 000A	
Substitution of materials variance[a] (85 000 − 70 000)	15 000A	16 500F

Operational variances		
Sales price (B − C)	7 000A	
Wage rate (5800 × £0.25)	1 450F	
Labour efficiency (200 hrs at £6.25)	1 250F	
Material price (10 800 × £0.50)	5 400A	
Material usage (800 × £8.50)	6 800A	16 500A
Total variances		nil

Note
[a] If the purchasing officer is committed to buying Aye and it is not possible to change to Bee in the short term then the £15 000 substitution variances is an uncontrollable price variance, and the total planning variance will be £35 000 for materials. However, if the purchasing officer can respond to changes in the relative prices then the £15 000 should be added to the operational price variance.

Comment on operational variances
The operational variances are calculated on the basis of the revised ex-post plan. The ex-post plan represents what the target would have been, given the benefit of hindsight. This represents a more realistic target than the original plan. For example, given the conditions for the period, the target sales should have been £165 000. Actual sales were £158 000. Therefore the operational sales variance is £7000 adverse. An explanation of planning and operational variances is presented in 'Criticisms of standard costing variance analysis' in Chapter 20.

(c) *Advantages*

    (i) The traditional price variance includes unavoidable/uncontrollable elements due to change in environment of £20 000 or £35 000. The revised analysis is more indicative of current purchasing efficiency.

    (ii) Traditional approach incorrectly values deviations from budgeted efficiency in calculating usage or efficiency variances. A better indication is provided by attributing the current standard cost per unit to the deviations (a variance of £6800 is a better indication of the excess usage of the materials than the £4000 under the traditional method).

Disadvantages

    (i) Classification into planning (uncontrollable) and avoidable may be difficult (e.g. substitution variance) and arbitrary.

    (ii) Any error in producing ex-post standards will cause a corresponding error in the classification of the variances (for example, we could have used a £9 ex-post standard for materials, thus affecting both the planning and operational variance).

    (iii) Excessive costs compared with benefits derived.

    (iv) Who sets the ex-post standard? If the purchasing officer sets the standard then there is a danger that the standard may be biased to avoid unfavourable operational variances.

(a) It is assumed that the actual selling price for the period was the same as the budgeted selling price.

Question 20.22

Sale volume variance = (Actual sales volume − Budgeted sales volume)
          × Standard contribution
          = (2850 − 2500) × £78
          = £27 300F

Material price variance = (Standard price − Actual price) Actual quantity
          = (£20 − £18) × 12 450
          = £24 900F

Material usage variance = (Standard quantity − Actual quantity) Standard price
          = (2850 × 4 kg = 11 400 − 12 450) × £20
          = £21 000A

Wage rate variance = (Standard rate − Actual rate) Actual hours
          = (£7 − £8) × 18 800
          = £18 800A

Labour efficiency variance = (Standard hour − Actual hours) Standard rate
          = (2,850 × 6 hrs = 17 100 hrs − 18 800 hrs) × £7
          = £11 900A

Reconciliation Statement

	(£)	(£)
Budget contribution		195 000
Sales volume variance	27 300F	
Sales price variance	−	
		27 300F
Material usage variance	21 000A	
Material price variance	24 900F	
		3 900F
Wage rate variance	18 800A	
Labour efficiency variance	11 900A	
		30 700A
Actual contribution		195 500

(b) (i) *Original Standard*

		(£)
Materials	2500 × 4 kg × £20	= 200 000
Labour	2500 × 6 hrs × £7	= 105 000
		305 000
Sales	2500 × £200	= 500 000
Contribution		195 000

(ii) *Revised ex-post standard*

		(£)
Materials	2500 × 4.5 kg × £16.50	= 185 625
Labour	2500 × 6 hrs × £6.50	= 97 500
		283 125
Sales	2500 × £200	= 500 000
Contribution		216 875

(iii) *Actual*

		(£)
Materials	12 450 kg × £18	= 224 100
Labour	18 800 hrs × £8	= 150 400
		374 500
Sales	2850 × £200	= 570 000
Contribution		195 500

The total variances consist of a favourable planning variance of £21 875 (£216 875 − £195 000) and an adverse operational variance of £21 375 (£216 875 − £195 500). The analysis of these variances is shown below.

Planning variances (1 − 2)	(£)	(£)
Material usage[a] (2500 × 0.5 kg × £20)	25 000A	
Material price[a] (£20 − £16.50) × (2500 × 4 kg)	35 000F	
Joint price/quantity variance		
(2500 × 0.50 kg) × (£20 − £16.50)	4 375F	
		14 375F
Wage rate (2500 × 6 hrs × £0.50)		7 500F
		21 875F

Operational variances		
Material usage		
(2850 × 4.5 kg = 12 825 kg − 12 450) £16.50	6 187.50F	
Material price (£16.50 − £18) × 12 450 kg	18 675.00A	
		12 487.50A
Labour efficiency		
(2850 × 6 hrs = 17 100 hrs − 18 800) × £6.50	11 050.00A	
Wage rate (£6.50 − £8) × 18 800 hrs	28 200.00A	
		39 250.00A
Sales volume (350 units at £86.75 revised unit contribution[b])		30 362.50F
		21 375.00A

Notes

[a]It is questionable whether it is meaningful to analyse the materials planning variance into its price and quantity elements because of the joint price/ quantity variance. An alternative answer would be to present only the total materials planning variance of £14 375 (£200 000 − £185 625).

^{b}Operational variances should be valued at the ex-post standard. The ex-post unit contribution is £200 selling price − (6 hrs × £6.50 labour) − 4.5 kg × £16.50 materials) = £86.75.

Reconciliation Statement

	(£)	(£)
Budgeted contribution		195 000
Planning variances:		
Materials	14 375F	
Wage rate	7 500F	
		21 875.00F
Operational variances		
Materials usage	6 187.50F	
Materials price	18 675.00A	
		12 487.50A
Labour efficiency	11 050A	
Wage rate	28 200A	
		39 250.00A
Sales volume		30 362.50F
Actual contribution		195 500.00

(c) The answer to this question should explain the meaning of planning and operational variances and why it is preferable to analyse the variances into their planning and operational elements. In particular, the answer should explain why the conventional approach reports an adverse material usage variance and a favourable price variance whereas the ex-post approach highlights a favourable usage and an adverse price variance.

(a) *Variance calculations*

Question 20.24

Sales volume: (Actual sales volume − Budgeted sales volume) × Standard unit contribution (450 − 500) × £79	3950A
Sales price: (Actual price − Budgeted price) Actual sales volume (83 250/450 − £175) × 450	4500F
Material price: (Standard price − Actual price) Actual quantity (£2 − £7650/3690) × 3690	270A
Material usage: (Standard quantity − Actual quantity) × Standard price (450 × 8 kg = 3600 kg − 3690) × £2	£180A
Wage rate: (Standard rate − Actual rate) Actual hours (£5 − £8100/1840 hrs) × 1840 hrs	1100F
Labour efficiency: (Standard hours − Actual hours) × Standard rate (450 × 4 hrs = 1800 hrs − 1840 hrs) × £5	200A
Variable overhead efficiency: (Standard hours − Actual hours) × Standard rate (450 × 4 hrs = 1800 hrs − 1840 hrs) × £15	600A
Variable overhead expenditure: (Actual hours × Standard rate − Actual cost) (1840 × £15 = £27 600) − £28 350	750A
Fixed overhead expenditure: (Budgeted Cost − Actual cost) (£25 000 − £24 650)	350F

Reconciliation statement

	(£)	(£)
Budgeted sales revenue	87 500	
Budgeted standard variable cost	48 000	
Budgeted contribution		39 500

Sales contribution variances

volume	(3 950)	
price	4 500	550
		40 050

Variable cost variances

Materials		
usage	(180)	
price	(270)	(450)
Labour		
efficiency	(200)	
rate	1 100	900
Variable overhead		
efficiency	(600)	
expenditure	(750)	(1 350)
Actual contribution		39 150
Fixed costs		
budgeted	(25 000)	
expenditure variance	350	24 650
Actual profit		14 500

(b) The revised presentation differs from the original because it takes into account changes in the production volume by flexing the budget. The original presentation adopts a fixed budgeting approach and compares the budgeted costs for the original budget of 500 units with the actual costs for an actual output of 450 units. Thus, like is not being compared with like and favourable variances are likely to be incorrectly recorded for variable costs whenever actual production is less than the original fixed budget.

Variance reporting should be based on flexing the budget, as shown in the revised presentation. The revised presentation supports the comments of the managers because it shows adverse production variances, and that sales have been made at above standard prices, but volume is down on budget.

(c) A number of writers have questioned the usefulness of standard costing in a modern manufacturing environment. They question whether variance analysis is meaningful in those situations where costs are not variable in the short run. Where costs are fixed and sunk within the performance reporting operating period the reported variances may be of little use for short-term operational cost control. In a modern manufacturing environment a large proportion of costs may be unrelated to short-term changes in production volume and efficiencies/inefficiencies.

The value of reporting of traditional material price variances has been questioned in those firms that have adopted JIT purchasing techniques. If purchasing price variances are used to evaluate the performance of purchasing management, it is likely that the purchasing manager will be motivated to focus entirely on obtaining materials at the lowest possible price even if this results in:

(i) The use of many suppliers (all of them selected on the basis of price);
(ii) Large quantity purchases thus resulting in higher inventories;
(iii) Delivery of lower quality goods;
(iv) Indifference to attaining on-time delivery.

JIT companies will want to focus on performance measures which emphasize quality and reliability, rather than material price variances, which draw attention away from the key factors.

It is also claimed that the setting of standards is not consistent with today's climate of continuous improvement. When standards are set, a climate is created whereby they represent a target to be achieved and maintained, rather than a philosophy of continuous improvement.

Standard costing systems have also been criticized because they emphasize cost control rather than reporting on areas such as quality, reliability, lead times, flexibility in responding to customer requirements and customer satisfaction. These variables represent the critical areas where firms must be successful to compete in today's competitive environment.

Nevertheless, despite these criticisms, standard costing systems continue to be widely used because they provide cost data for many different purposes. For example, they provide data for setting budgets, simplifying the task of inventory valuation, predicting future costs for use in decision-making, and providing data for cost control and performance appraisal. Standard costs and variance analysis would still be required for other purposes even if variance analysis were abandoned for cost control and performance appraisal.

(a) (i)   (£) **Question 20.27**

Material price variance:
(standard price − actual price) × actual quantity
[£0.05 − (£45/1000)] × 105 000   525F

Material usage variance:
(standard quantity − actual quantity) × standard price
(100 000 − 105 000) × £0.05   250A

Total variance   275F

(ii)

	Dr (£)	Cr (£)
Dr Stores ledger control account (AQ × SP)	5250	
Cr Creditors control account (AQ × AP)		4725
Cr Material price variance account		525
Dr Work in progress (SQ × SP)	5000	
Dr Material usage variance account	250	
Cr Stores ledger control account (AQ × SP)		5250

(iii) On the basis of the above calculations, the buyer would receive a bonus of £52.50 (10% × £525) and the production manager would not receive any bonus. It could be argued that the joint price/usage variance should be separated if the variances are to be used as the basis for calculating bonuses. (For a discussion of joint price/usage variances see Chapter 19.) The revised analysis would be as follows:

                                                          (£)

Pure price variance:
(standard price − actual price) × standard quantity
(£0.05 − £0.045) × 100 000   500F

Joint price/usage variance:
(standard price − actual price) × excess usage
(£0.05 − £0.045) × 5000   25F

Buyer's viewpoint
At the purchasing stage the buyer can influence both quality and price. Consequently, the buyer can obtain favourable price variances by purchasing inferior quality materials at less than standard price. The adverse effects in terms of excess usage, because of the purchase of inferior quality of materials, are passed on to the production manager and the buyer gains from the price reduction. Indeed, if the joint price/usage is not isolated (see above), the buyer gains if production uses materials in excess of standard. Therefore the bonus system might encourage the buyer to purchase inferior quality materials, which results

in an overall adverse *total* material cost variance and inferior product quality. In summary, the bonus system appears to be biased in favour of the buyer at the expense of the production manager.

Production manager's viewpoint

The isolation of the joint price/usage variance might encourage the buyer not to purchase inferior quality materials, and this will be to the production manager's advantage. Nevertheless, the problem of the control of material quality still exists. The production manager would need to ensure that the quality of material purchased is in line with the quality built into the standard. Therefore some monitoring device is necessary. If variations do occur, the quantity standard should be adjusted for the purpose of performance reporting and bonus assessment.

Company's viewpoint

The objective of the bonus system is to encourage goal congruence and increase motivation. Interdependencies exist between the two responsibility centres, and it is doubtful that the bonus system encourages goal congruence or improves motivation. If the quality of materials that can be purchased from the various suppliers does not vary then the adverse effects of the bonus system will be reduced. Nevertheless, interdependencies will still exist between the responsibility centres. One solution might be to base the bonuses of both managers on the *total* material cost variance. In addition, standards should be regularly reviewed and participation by both managers in setting the standards encouraged.

(b) (i) The minimum present value of expected savings that would have to be made in future months in order to justify making an investigation is where

$$\text{IC} + (P \times \text{CC}) = Px$$

where IC = investigation costs, P = probability that process is out of control, CC = correction cost, x = present value of expected savings if process is out of control

Therefore £50 + (0.5 × £100) = 0.5x

$$0.5x = £100$$
$$x = £200$$

Therefore the minimum present value of expected savings that would have to be made is £200.

(ii) The standard cost will probably represent the mean value, and random variations around the mean value can be expected to occur even when the process is under control. Therefore it is unlikely that the £500 variance will be eliminated completely, because a proportion of the variance simply reflects the randomness of the variables affecting the standard. If the process is found to be out of control, the corrective action will only confine variances to the normal acceptable range of standard outcomes. If the £500 is an extreme deviation from the standard then it is likely that the potential savings from investigation will be insignificant.

(iii) Applying the notation used in (i), the firm will be indifferent about whether to conduct an investigation when the expected savings resulting from correction are equal to the expected cost of correction. That is, where

$$\text{IC} + (P \times \text{CC}) = Px$$

if x = £600 then

$$50 + P \times 100 = P \times 600$$
$$500P = 50$$
$$P = 10\%$$

if $x = 250$ then

$$50 + P \times 100 = P \times 250$$
$$150P = 50$$
$$P = 33\tfrac{1}{3}\%$$

(a) (i) *Decision tree if an investigation is carried out*

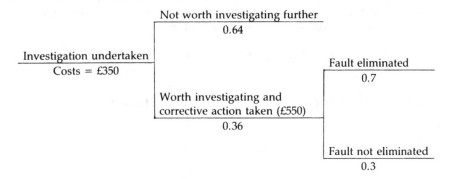

It is assumed that the £550 correction cost applies to all variances that the initial investigation indicates are worthy of further investigation. The expected cost if the investigation is carried out is:

$$£350 + 0.36 \times £550 \text{ (corrective action)}$$
$$+ \ 0.36 \times 0.3 \times £2476^a \text{ (continuing variance)} = \underline{\underline{£815}}$$

Note
[a] £2476 represents the PV of £525 for 5 months at 2% (£525 × 4.7135) for variances that are not eliminated.

(ii) *Decision tree if an investigation is not carried out*

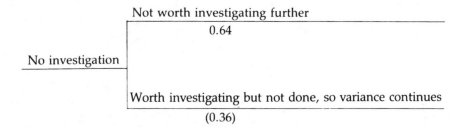

The expected cost if no investigation is undertaken is:

$$0.36 \times £525 \times 4.7135 = £891$$

(b) Applying the expected value decision rule, the company should follow a policy of investigating variances as a matter of routine. The expected cost of investigation is £815, compared with an expected cost if no investigation is undertaken of £891. On average, the benefits from investigation are £75 per variance.

(c) Examples of category 1 variances include:
   (i) The variance is due to random uncontrollable factors and is under control. (See 'Random uncontrollable factors' in Chapter 20 for an explanation.)
   (ii) Where the cause is obvious (e.g. a machine fault) and future action has been taken to remedy the situation.

Examples of category 2 variances include:
- (i) Excessive usage of materials and labour due possibly to wrong working practices on a repetitive operation which is likely to continue if not corrected.
- (ii) Where the variance is significant and exceeds a specified percentage of standard usage.

(d) The above analysis assumes that the average variance is £525 and additional costs of £525 in excess of standard continue for five months. Presumably, working practices are changed every five months. Costs of investigation and corrective action are £350 and £550 irrespective of the amount of the variance. It would therefore be appropriate to determine the value of variances which justify investigation. Let x = savings per month. The expected cost of investigation is equal to the expected cost of no investigation where:

$$£350 + (0.36 \times £550) + (0.36 \times 0.3 \times 4.7135x) = 0.36 \times 4.7135x$$
$$x = £461$$

Only variances in excess of £461 should be investigated.

Behavioural aspects of accounting control systems

Solutions to Chapter 21 questions

Question summary

The questions set in this chapter consist of a range of discussion questions on various behavioural aspects of accounting control systems. Questions 21.12–21.15 are discussion questions that do not require specific answers. They are intended to test independent thought and initiative in relating the behavioural literature to the questions asked. Therefore answers are not provided to these questions. Question 21.20 requires comments on the behavioural implications of a performance report and a discussion of the way in which a budget system is being used. Question 21.21 requires a discussion on the impact of aggregating budget estimates on the probability of budgets being achieved, and 21.22 relates to commenting on the budgeting and performance measurement system of a company that operates in the financial services sector.

Question 21.3

(a) See 'Planning', 'Motivation' and 'Performance evaluation' in Chapter 17 for the answer to this question. The answer should emphasize that the role of motivation is to encourage goal congruence between the company and the employees.

(b) See 'Conflicting roles of budgets' in Chapter 21 for an explanation of how the planning and motivation roles can conflict. Prior to the commencement of the budget period, management should prepare budgets that represent targets to be achieved based upon anticipated environmental variables. It is possible that at the end of the budget period the *actual* environmental variables will be different from those envisaged when the budget was prepared. Therefore actual performance will be determined by the actual environmental variables, but the plans reflected in the budget may be based on different environmental variables. It is inappropriate to compare actual performance based on one set of environmental variables with budgeted performance based on another set of environmental variables. Consequently, a budget that is used for planning purposes will be in conflict with one that is used for performance evaluation.

The conflict between motivation and evaluation is described by Barrett and Fraser (1977) (see 'References and further reading' in Chapter 21) as follows:

> In many situations the budget that is most effective in the evaluation role might be called an ex-post facto budget. It is one that considers the impact of uncontrollable or unforeseeable events, and it is constructed or adjusted after the fact.
>
> The potential role conflict between the motivation and evaluation roles involves the impact on motivation of using an ex-post facto standard in the evaluation process. Managers are unlikely to be totally committed to achieving the budget's objectives if they know that the performance standards by which they are to be judged may change.

In other words, for evaluation purposes the budget might be adjusted to reflect changes in environmental variables. If a manager expects that the budget will be changed for evaluation purposes, there is a danger that he or she will not be as highly motivated to achieve the original budget.

(c) (i) The planning and motivation conflict might be resolved by setting two budgets. A budget based on most likely outcomes could be set for planning purposes and a separate, more demanding budget could be used for motivation purposes.

(ii) The planning and evaluation role conflict can be resolved by comparing actual performance with an ex-post budget. See 'Criticisms of standard costing variance analysis' in Chapter 20 for an illustration of how this conflict can be resolved.

(iii) Barrett and Fraser (1977) suggest the following approach for resolving the motivation and evaluation conflict:

> The conflict between the motivation and evaluation roles can also be reduced by using 'adjustable budgets.' These are operational budgets whose objectives can be modified under predetermined sets of circumstances. Thus revision is possible during the operating period and the performance standard can be changed.
>
> In one company that uses such a budgeting system, managers commit themselves to a budget with the understanding that, if there are substantial changes in any of five key economic or environmental variables, top management will revise the budget and new performance criteria will be set. This company automatically makes budget revisions whenever there are significant changes in any of these five variables. Naturally, the threshold that triggers a new budget will depend on the relative importance of each variable. With this system, managers know they are expected to meet their budgets. The budget retains its motivating characteristics because it represents objectives that are possible to achieve. Uncontrollable events are not allowed to affect budgeted objectives in such a way that they stand little chance of being met. Yet revisions that are made do not have to adversely affect commitment, since revisions are agreed to in advance and procedures for making them are structured into the overall budgeting system.

A more detailed answer to this question can be found in Barrett and Fraser (1977).

Question 21.4 (a) The answer should include a discussion of the following points:

(i) Constant pressure from top management for greater production may result in the creation of anti-management work groups and reduced efficiency, so that budgetees can protect themselves against what they consider to be increasingly stringent targets.

(ii) Non-acceptance of budgets if the budgetees have not been allowed to participate in setting the budgets.

(iii) Negative attitudes if the budget is considered to be a punitive control device instead of a system to help managers do a better job. The negative attitudes might take the form of reducing cooperation between departments and also with the accounting department. Steps might be taken to ensure that costs do not fall below budget, so that the budget will not be reduced next year. There is a danger that data will be falsified, and more effort will be directed to finding excuses for failing to achieve the budget than trying to control or reduce costs.

(iv) Managers might try and achieve the budget at all costs even if this results in actions that are not in the best interests of the organization, e.g. delaying maintenance costs.

(v) Organizational atmosphere may become one of competition and conflict rather than one of cooperation and conciliation.

(vi) Suspicion and mistrust of top management, resulting in the whole budgeting process being undermined.

(vii) Belief that the system of evaluation is unjust and widespread worry and tension by the budgetees. Tension might be relieved by falsifying information, blaming others or absenteeism.

(b) For the answer to this question see 'Conclusion' in Chapter 21.

Question 21.5

The answer should include a discussion of the following:
(i) The impact of targets on performance.
(ii) The use of accounting control techniques for performance evaluation.
(iii) Participation in the budgeting and standard setting process.
(iv) Bias in the budget process.
(v) Management use of budgets and the role of the accountant in the education process.
See Chapter 21 for a discussion of each of the above items.

Question 21.6

(a) See Chapter 21 for the answer to this question.
(b) See the conclusion to Chapter 21 for the answer to this question.
(c) Figure 18.2 in Chapter 18 illustrates the importance of feedback (information comparing planned and actual outcomes in the control process). Feedback takes the form of control reports issued by the accountant to the managers responsible for controlling inputs. Effective control requires that corrective action be taken so that actual outputs conform to planned outputs in the future. In order to assist managers in controlling activities, the performance reports should highlight those areas that do not conform to plan. The performance reports should also provide clues as to why the actual outputs differ from the planned outputs. Feedback information is necessary to provoke corrective managerial action.

It should be noted that accounting reports of performance also have a direct effect on motivation by giving the department manager knowledge of performance. Knowledge of results has been shown in various psychological experiments to lead to improved performance. This is partly because it conveys information that can be used for acting more effectively on the next trial; but also partly because knowledge of results motivates through satisfying the achievement need. Stok (1959) investigated the effect of control systems using visual presentation of quality on workers quality performance. He found that visual presentation of quality had both an information and a motivation effect and both were instrumental in improving performance. It appears that communicating knowledge of results acts as a reward or punishment. It can serve either to reinforce or extinguish previous employee behaviours.

(d) The purpose of goal congruence is to encourage an individual manager's goals to be in agreement with the organization's goals. For a description of this process see 'The use of accounting control techniques for performance evaluation' in Chapter 21.

Reference
Stok, T.L. (1959) *De Arbeider en de Zichbaarmaking van de Kwaliteit*, Leiden, Stenfert Kruese.

Question 21.7

Managers may be reluctant to participate in setting budgets for the following reasons:
(i) Managers may consider that they do not engage in true participation if they cannot influence the budget. They may consider the process to be one of the senior managers securing formal acceptance of previously determined target levels.

(ii) Personality of budgetees may result in authoritarian managers having authoritarian expectations of their superiors. Consequently, authoritarian budgetees may be reluctant to participate in the budget process.

(iii) The degree to which individuals have control over their own destiny (see Brownell's (1981) research in Chapter 21) appears to influence the desire for participation. Managers may believe that they cannot significantly influence results and thus consider participation to be inappropriate.

(iv) Bad management/superior relationships.

(v) Lack of understanding of the budget process or a belief by the budgetees that they will be engaging in a process that will be used in a recriminatory manner by their superiors.

The unwanted side-effects that might arise from the imposition of budgets by senior management include the following:

(i) Non-acceptance of budgets.

(ii) The budgetees might consider the method of performance evaluation to be unjust.

(iii) Creation of anti-management cohesive work groups.

(iv) Reduced efficiency by work groups so as to protect themselves against what they consider to be increasingly stringent targets.

(v) The budget system will be undermined. The real problem is the way management use the system rather than inadequacies of the budget system itself.

(vi) An increase in suspicion and mistrust, so undermining the whole budgeting process.

(vii) Encouraging budgetees to falsify and manipulate information presented to management.

(viii) Organizational atmosphere may become one of competition and conflict rather than one of cooperation and conciliation.

(ix) Managers might try to achieve the budget at all costs even if this results in actions that are not in the best interests of the organization.

Question 21.8 (a) See 'The use of budgets as targets' in Chapter 21 for the answer to this question.

(b) See 'Participation in the budgeting and standard setting process' in Chapter 21 for the answer to this question.

(c) Management by exception is based on the principle that accounting reports should highlight those activities that do not conform to plans, so that managers can devote their scarce time to focusing on these items. Effective control requires that corrective action be taken so that actual outcomes conform to planned outcomes. These principles are based on the following assumptions:

(i) Valid targets and budgets can be set.

(ii) Suitable performance measures exist that enable divergencies from plans to be correctly measured.

(iii) Plans and divergencies from plan are communicated to the individuals who are responsible for implementing the plan.

(iv) Performance reports correctly distinguish those items that are controllable by a manager from those that are non-controllable.

(v) Feedback information is translated into corrective action.

(vi) Management intervention is not required where no adverse variances exist.

(vii) Divergencies from plan can only be remedied by corrective action.

Management by exception as an effective system of routine reporting will depend on the extent to which the above conditions hold. The system will have to be supplemented by informal controls to the extent that the above conditions do not hold. Management by exception can only be a very effective means of control if behavioural factors are taken into account when interpreting the divergencies from plan. Otherwise there is a danger that other systems of control will have a greater influence on future performance.

(d) The answer should include the following:

(i) An explanation of why it is considered necessary to distinguish between controllable and uncontrollable costs at the responsibility level.

(ii) Difficulty in assigning variances to responsibility centres when dual responsibilities apply or interdependencies exist.

(iii) Possible dysfunctional consequences that might occur when a manager's performance is measured by his or her success in controlling only those items that have been designated as controllable by him or her.

(iv) Arguments for including those uncontrollable items that a manager might be able to influence in a separate section of the performance report.

The above items are discussed in 'Responsibility accounting' in Chapter 18.

(e) Budget statements should not be expressed only in monetary terms. This is because all aspects of performance relating to a firm's goals cannot be expressed in monetary terms. Therefore budgetary statements should be supplemented by non-monetary measures. Monetary gains can be made at the expense of items that cannot easily be measured in monetary terms but that may be critical to an organization's long-term profitability. For example, monetary gains can be made by hierarchical pressure to cut costs, but such gains might be at the expense of adverse motivational changes, increased labour turnover and reduced product quality. The long-term costs of these items might be far in excess of the cost-cutting benefits.

A range of non-monetary measures is presented in the section on 'Non-financial performance measures' in Chapter 18. Some qualitative variables (e.g. measurement of attitudes) are difficult to measure, but judgements based on interviews can be made. The inclusion of behavioural and qualitative factors in budget statements more accurately reflects the complexity of managerial performance in relation to a number of objectives rather than a single monetary objective. The difficulty with incorporating qualitative variables into budget statements is not sufficient grounds for expressing budget statements only in monetary terms.

Question 21.9

See 'The use of budgets as targets' in Chapter 21 and 'Establishing cost standards' in Chapter 19 for the answer to this question.

Question 21.10

(a) For the answer to this question see 'The use of budgets as targets' in Chapter 21. In particular, the answer should stress that a tight budget is preferable for motivation purposes, whereas for planning and control purposes an expected target should be set that management believes will be achieved. Consequently, a conflict occurs between the motivational and management reporting objectives.

(b) The levels of efficiency that may be incorporated in the standards used in budgetary control and/or standard costing include the following:

(i) *Perfection*: Standards based on perfection are termed 'ideal standards'. Case 6 illustrated in Figure 21.1 in Chapter 21 is typical of a standard based on perfection. Ideal standards have no motivational advantages and are unsatisfactory for planning and control purposes.

(ii) *Tight standards*: These standards represent targets that are set at a level of performance that is difficult, but not impossible, for budgetees to achieve. Cases 3–5 illustrated in Figure 21.1 represent tight standards. It can be seen from the figure that tight standards should increase aspiration levels and actual performance. Because tight standards may not be achieved, they are unsatisfactory for planning and control purposes.

(iii) *Expected performance*: Expected performance standards are based on the level of efficiency expected to be attained (i.e. Case 2 in Figure 21.1). One advantage of expected standards is that variances indicate deviations from management's expectations. A further advantage is that expected standards can be used for planning purposes. Expected standards are likely to be unsatisfactory for motivational purposes, since they may not provide a challenging target.

(iv) *Loose standards*: With loose standards, the level of efficiency implied by the standard is less than expected. Case 1 illustrated in Figure 21.1 represents a loose standard. Loose standards are poor motivators and are unsatisfactory for planning and control purposes.

(c) See 'Participation in the budgeting and standard setting process' in Chapter 21 for the answer to this question.

Question 21.11 (a) (i) Budgets are used for a variety of purposes, one of which is to evaluate the performance of budgetees. When budgets form the basis for future performance evaluation, there is a possibility that budgetees will introduce bias into the process for personal gain and self-protection. Factors that are likely to cause managers to submit budget estimates that do not represent their best estimates include:

1. *The reward system*: If managers believe that rewards depend upon budget attainment then they might be encouraged to underestimate sales budgets and overestimate cost budgets.
2. *Past performance*: If recent performance has been poor, managers may submit favourable plans so as to obtain approval from their supervisors. Such an approach represents a trade-off advantage of short-run security and approval against the risk of not being able to meet the more optimistic plans.
3. *Incremental budgeting*: Incremental budgeting involves adding increments to past budgets to reflect expected future changes. Consequently, the current budget will include bias that has been built into previous budgets.
4. *External influences*: If managers believe that their performance is subject to random external influences then, from a self-protection point of view, they might submit budgets that can easily be attained.
5. *Style of performance evaluation*: A budget-constrained style of evaluation might encourage the budgetee to meet the budget at all costs. Consequently, budgetees will be motivated to bias their budget estimates.

(ii) The following procedures should be introduced to minimize the likelihood of biased estimates:

1. Encourage managers to adopt a profit-conscious style of evaluation.
2. Adopt a system of zero-base budgeting.
3. Key figures in the budget process (e.g. sales estimates) should be checked by using information from different sources.
4. Planning and operating variances (see 'Criticisms of standard costing variance analysis' in Chapter 20 for a discussion of planning and operating variances) should be segregated. Managers might be motivated to submit more genuine estimates if they are aware that an ex-post budget will be used as a basis for performance appraisal.
5. Participation by the budgetees in the budget process should be encouraged so as to secure a greater commitment to the budget process and improve communication between budgetees, their superior and the budget accountants.

Question 21.17 (a) For a discussion of feedback and feedforward controls see Chapter 18. The remaining terms are discussed in Chapter 21.
(b) See the conclusion and summary to Chapter 21 for the answer to this question.

Question 21.18 (a) See 'Standard costing in an advanced manufacturing environment' in Chapter 20 and 'Role of standard costing' in Chapter 28 for the answer to this question.
(b) The creation of budget centres at the lowest defined management level would enable managers to participate in the budget setting process. Lower level managers would therefore be involved in the budget negotiation process, and this should improve communication with their superiors and create a greater awareness of the need for the activities of the budget centres to be in congruence with the goals of the organization. By participating in the process, it is claimed that managers will be more committed and strive to achieve their budgets. The creation of budget centres should also improve a manager's attitude towards the budget system. In particular, the potential for improved communication and the acceptance of budgets as relevant standards to achieve should lead to improved motivation.

Creating budget centres at lower levels will place greater administrative demands on operating the system and lengthen the budget preparation period.

In addition, the cost of reporting will be increased. Whether or not the additional benefits exceed the additional costs is likely to depend on the circumstances of the company. For example, in an environment where an organization faces considerable uncertainty or where an organization undertakes a diverse range of activities, decentralization and the creation of budget centres at lower levels might be preferable. However, where the activities of an organization can be programmed in detail and close coordination and swift reaction is necessary it might be preferable not to create budget centres at lower levels. In particular, if the activities of budget centres are heavily dependent on the activities of other centres, there is a greater likelihood that the benefits from increased motivation will not outweigh the administrative and coordination difficulties.

Question 21.21

(a) The number of standard deviations by which each regional manager's estimate deviates from the mean of the distribution assumed by the sales director is:

$$\text{Northern } Z = \frac{5.7 - 5.0}{1.0} = 0.7$$

$$\text{Southern } Z = \frac{10.9 - 10.0}{1.0} = 0.9$$

$$\text{Eastern } Z = \frac{7.9 - 8.0}{1.0} = -0.1$$

$$\text{Western } Z = \frac{7.5 - 7.0}{1.0} = 0.5$$

The likelihood of sales being equal or greater than the estimate is obtained by ascertaining the probabilities for the Z scores from a normal distribution table. The probabilities are:

$$\text{Northern} = 0.242$$
$$\text{Southern} = 0.1841$$
$$\text{Eastern} = 1 - 0.4602 = 0.5398$$
$$\text{Western} = 0.3085$$

Note that the negative Z score calculation for the Eastern territory indicates that the probability of sales being less than £7900 is 0.4602. Therefore the probability of sales being £7900 or more is 0.5398.

The standard deviation for the total sales is calculated from the sum of the four variances:

$$\text{Standard deviation} = \sqrt{[4 \times (1 \text{ m})^2]} = \text{£2 m}$$

$$Z = \frac{32 - 30}{2} = 1.00 = 0.1587 \text{ probability}$$

Therefore the probability that the total sales will be equal to or greater than £32m is 0.1587.

Otley and Berry (1979) have illustrated the consequences of submitting non-mean (most likely) estimates rather than the expected value of the estimates when they are aggregated at successive levels in the organizational hierarchy. They have demonstrated that estimates that are only slightly optimistic at the unit level (30% probability of achievement) become highly optimistic when nine such units are aggregated at the next level in the hierarchy (16% probability of achievement). This process applies in this question. The aggregation of the budgets results in the overall budget having a relatively low chance of being achieved.

(b) See 'Bias in the budget process' in Chapter 21 for the answer to this question. In particular, the answer should stress that managers tend to overestimate costs and underestimate sales in order to obtain slack budgets which can be achieved. In some situations the reverse may apply where managers seek to enhance their position in the short term by submitting optimistic budgets. However, such budgets carry the risk of failure if the budget is not met. Managers may be tempted to overstate budgeted costs in order to preserve previous budget allocations. They will then spend to this limit in order to ensure that future budget allocations are maintained. A superior's budget may also differ from the budget submitted by the manager because they do not have detailed knowledge of the budgetees' activities. Consequently, the superior's budget is unlikely to represent an accurate estimate of future outcomes.

Recommendations for overcoming the above problems include:

(i) Ensure that more emphasis is given to the negotiation and participation process so that differences can be resolved and differing expectations and assumptions clarified.

(ii) Adjusting budgets to the differing aspirations and capabilities of the budgetees (see 'The effect of budget levels on performance' in Chapter 21).

(iii) Require managers to produce appropriate evidence to justify their budgets.

(iv) Use two sets of budgets – one for planning purposes and a more demanding budget for motivational purposes (see 'Conflicting roles of budgets' in Chapter 21).

(v) Avoid a budget constrained style of evaluation. This approach is likely to encourage substantial bias in the budget process.

(c) The proposed bonus system will encourage budgetees to submit pessimistic budgets so that bonuses can be obtained. Managers will engage in defensive behaviour and put too much effort into trying to justify pessimistic budgets. The process of negotiating budgets will be undermined, and relationships between superior and budgetee may deteriorate. The process might lead to defensive behaviour by the budgetee, and the sales director will find it extremely difficult to negotiate a more demanding budget.

The proposed system will encourage managers merely to achieve the target but not to achieve a performance in excess of standard. Consequently, lost sales orders might result. Where managers are having difficulty in achieving the target, there is a danger that they may seek to stimulate sales by taking on customers with high credit risk. Alternatively, they might be motivated to sell goods with a high probability of subsequently being returned.

Placing too much emphasis on meeting the budget target can undermine the whole budget process, and there are strong arguments for not implementing the proposed system. Possible amendments to the system would be:

(i) Relate the bonuses to a comparison of the growth in market shares for each territory and pay the bonuses according to a 'league table' of market shares.

(ii) Abandon the present bonus system and pay higher wages to competent staff. Bonuses could be paid only for performance significantly in excess of budget.

(iii) Set a series of percentage bonus scales, with the percentage related to a number of ranges in excess of budget. The higher the range achieved, the higher the percentage bonus.

References

Berry, A.J. and Otley, D.T. (1975) The aggregation of estimates in hierarchical organizations, *Journal of Management Studies*, May, 175–93.

See also Otley, D.T. and Berry, A.J. (1979) Risk distribution in the budgetary process, *Accounting and Business Research*, 5, 231–46.

Mathematical approaches to cost estimation

Solutions to Chapter 23 questions

(a) The first stage is to convert all costs to a 1981 basis. The calculations are as follows: **Question 23.6**

	1977 (£000)	1978 (£000)	1979 (£000)	1980 (£000)
Raw materials ⎫ Skilled labour ⎬ Unskilled labour ⎭	$242(1.2)^4$	$344(1.2)^3$	$461(1.2)^2$	$477(1.2)$
Factory overheads	$168(1.15)^3(1.2)$	$206(1.15)^2(1.2)$	$246(1.15)(1.2)$	$265(1.2)$
Power	$25(1.1)(1.25)^3$	$33(1.25)^3$	$47(1.25)^2$	$44(1.25)$
Raw materials ⎫ Skilled labour ⎬ Unskilled labour ⎭	500.94	595.12	663.84	572.4
Factory overheads	306.432	326.304	339.48	318
Power	53.625	64.35	73.32	55
Total (1981 prices)	861 000	986 000	1 077 000	945 000
Output (units)	160 000	190 000	220 000	180 000

The equation $Y = a + bx$ is calculated from the above schedule of total production costs (1981 prices) and output. The calculations are as follows:

Output in units (000)	Total cost (£000)		
x	y	x^2	xy
160	861	25 600	137 760
190	986	36 100	187 340

	220	1077	48 400	236 940
	180	945	32 400	170 100
	$\Sigma x = 750$	$\Sigma y = 3869$	$\Sigma x^2 = 142\,500$	$\Sigma xy = 732\,140$

We now solve the following simultaneous equations:

$$\Sigma y = Na + b\Sigma x$$
$$\Sigma xy = \Sigma xa + b\Sigma x^2$$

Therefore

$$3869 = 4a + 750b \tag{1}$$

$$732\,140 = 750a + 142\,500b \tag{2}$$

Multiply equation (1) by 190 (142 500/750) and equation (2) by 1. Then equation (1) becomes

$$735\,110 = 760a + 142\,500b \tag{3}$$

Subtract equation (2) from equation (3):

$$2970 = 10a$$
$$a = 297$$

Substitute for a in equation (1):

$$3869 = 4 \times 297 + 750b$$
$$2681 = 750b$$
$$b = 3.57$$

The relationship between total production costs and volume for 1981 is:

$$y = £297\,000 + 3.57x$$

where y = total production costs (at 1981 price) and x = output level.

(b) See Chapter 23 for the answer to this question, particularly 'Requirements for using mathematical techniques' and 'Problems when applying mathematical cost equations'.

(c) General company overheads will still continue whether or not product LT is produced. Therefore the output of LT will not affect general production overheads. Consequently, the regression equation should not be calculated from cost data that includes general company overheads. General company overheads will not increase with increments in output of product LT. Hence short-term decisions and cost control should focus on those costs that are relevant to production of LTs. Common and unavoidable general fixed costs are not relevant to the production of LT, and should not be included in the regression equation.

Question 23.7 (a)

x	y	x^2	xy
150	162	22 500	24 300
180	184	32 400	33 120
200	184	40 000	36 800
230	248	52 900	57 040
760	778	147 800	151 260

The regression equation can be found from the following equations:

$$\Sigma y = Na + b\Sigma x$$
$$\Sigma xy = a\Sigma x + b\Sigma x^2$$

Therefore

$$778 = 4a + 760b \tag{1}$$

$$151\,260 = 760a + 147\,800b \tag{2}$$

To solve for b, multiply equation (1) by 190 to give:

$$147\,820 = 760a + 144\,400b \tag{3}$$

Subtracting equation (3) from equation (2) gives

$$3400b = 3440$$
$$b = 1.012$$

Substituting for b in equation (1):

$$778 = 4a + 760 \times 1.012$$
$$a = 2.22$$

At the planned output level of 260 000 units the contribution is:
$$2.22 + 1.012 \times 260 = 265.34 = £265\,340$$

(b) The 95% confidence limit is

$$265.34 \pm 4.303 \times 14.5 = 265.34 \pm 62.39$$

Upper limit	£327 730
Lower limit	£202 950

These are the limits within which we can be 95% certain the actual value of the contribution will be, given the assumptions made.

(c) The advantages of using linear regression are:
 (i) It takes into account all available observations and yields more accurate results
 than the high–low method.
 (ii) It determines the line of best fit mathematically, and is more accurate than visually determining the line of best fit using graphical or scattergraph method.
 (iii) It is a statistically valid method, and is preferable to subjective methods based on guesswork from past observations.

For a discussion of the limitations of the technique see 'Requirements for using mathematical techniques' and 'Problems that may arise when using mathematical cost equations' in Chapter 23.

(a) An estimate of the *normal* fixed and variable costs of production is required. The figures shown below therefore exclude the winter heating costs of £10 000 in January and February.

Question 23.9

	Output x (000)	Total cost y (£000)	xy (000)	x^2 (000)
January	9	105.2[a]	946.8	81
February	14	172.0	2408.0	196
March	11	125.4	1379.4	121
April	8	96.0	768.0	64
May	6	78.0	468.0	36
June	12	140.4	1684.8	144
	60	717.0	7655.0	642

Note
[a] (9000 X £12.80) − £10 000

The regression equation can be derived from the following two equations (see formulae (23.1) and (23.2) in Chapter 23) and solving for a and b:

$$\Sigma y = Na + b\Sigma x$$
$$\Sigma xy = a\Sigma x + b\Sigma x^2$$

Inserting the above computations into the formulae:

$$717 = 6a + 60b \tag{1}$$
$$7655 = 60a + 642b \tag{2}$$

Multiplying equation (1) by 10:

$$7170 = 60a + 600b \tag{3}$$

Subtracting equation (3) from equation (2):

$$485 = 42b$$
$$b = 11.5476$$

Substituting the value for b in one of the above equations gives a value of 4.024 for a.

Alternatively, the formula outlined in the question can be used:

$$b = \frac{n\Sigma xy - \Sigma x\Sigma y}{n\Sigma x^2 - (\Sigma x)^2}$$

$$b = \frac{6 \times 7655 - 60 \times 717}{6 \times 642 - (60)^2} = 11.5476$$

$$\bar{y} = a + b\bar{x}$$
$$a = \bar{y} - b\bar{x} = (717/6) - 11.5476 \times (60/6) = 4.024$$

(b) The question implies that unit variable cost changes at a particular output level. Figure Q23.9 suggests that the change takes place at approximately 11 000 units of output.

The linear cost relationships for the two sections of the graph can be estimated using the high–low method, regression analysis or reading directly from the graph. Using the high–low method, the cost equations are:

$$\text{variable cost per unit below 11 000 units} = \frac{£125\ 400 - £78\ 000}{11\ 000\ \text{units} - 6000\ \text{units}} = £9.48$$

$$\text{monthly fixed costs} = £78\ 000 - (6000 \times £9.48) = £21\ 120$$

$$\text{variable cost per unit (11 000 units or more)} = \frac{£172\ 000 - £125\ 400}{14\ 000 - 11\ 000} = £15.53$$

$$\text{monthly fixed cost} = £125\ 400 - (11\ 000 \times £15.53) = -£45\ 467$$

The cost function for activity in excess of 11 000 units implies that fixed costs are negative. An examination of the graph suggests that fixed costs are approximately £21 000 and unit variable costs increase at 11 000 units. Assuming estimated fixed costs of £21 120 for output levels in excess of 11 000 units, the estimated unit variable cost (VC) at an output level of 12 000 units can be derived from the following equation:

$$\text{total cost (£140 400)} = \text{fixed costs (£21 120)} + (11\ 000 \times £9.48) + 1000\text{VC}$$
$$\text{VC} = £15$$

In other words, the cost equation is:

$$y = 21\,120 + £9.48x_1 + £15x_2$$

where x_1 = output levels up to 11 000 units
x_2 = output levels over 11 000 units $- x_1$

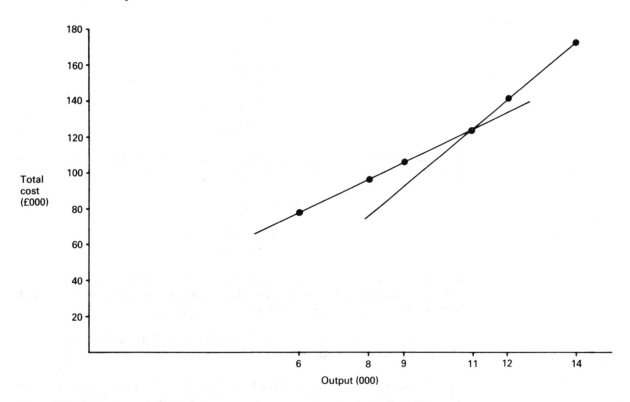

Figure Q23.9

(c)

	Output (000)	Observed costs (£000)	costs[a] (£000)	Estimated Difference (£000)
January	9	105.2	106.44	(1.24)
February	14	172.0	170.40	1.6
March	11	125.4	125.40	0
April	8	96.0	96.96	(0.96)
May	6	78.0	78.00	0
June	12	140.4	140.40	0

Note
[a]Based on cost equation $21\,120 + 9.48x_1 + 15x_2$

(d) For the answer to this question see 'Problems that may arise when using mathematical cost equations' and 'Requirements for using mathematical techniques' in Chapter 23.

(a)
$$5000 = 10 \times 5000^{-0.3}$$
$$= 10 \times 0.07768$$
$$= 0.7768$$

Question 23.12

The average time taken to produce 1 unit is 0.7768 hours. Therefore 3884 hours (5000 × 0.7768) will be required to produce 5000 units. It is assumed that 3884 hours per annum will be available for years 2 and 3. Hence the cumulative hours for years 1 and 2 will be 7768 (3884 × 2). It is therefore necessary to determine the number of units of output that will require 7768 hours.

Let y_t = total number of hours. Then the average time (y) required to produce 1 unit of output is y_t/x, where x represents the number of units of output. Applying the learning-curve formula

$$y = ax^b$$
$$y_t/x = ax^b$$
$$y_t = ax^{b+1}$$
$$7768 = 10x^{0.7}$$
$$x^{0.7} = 776.8$$
$$x = 776.8^{1/0.7}$$
$$= 776.8^{1.428\ 57}$$
$$= 13\ 460$$

Thus the output for year 2 will be 8460 units (13 460 − 5000). For years 1–3 there are 11 652 hours (3884 × 3) available. Applying the above approach:

$$11\ 652 = 10x^{0.7}$$
$$x^{0.7} = 1165.2$$
$$x = 1165.2^{1.428\ 57}$$
$$= 24\ 020$$

Thus the output for year 3 will be 10 560 units (24 020 − 13 460).

Instead of applying the above method, we can use a trial-and-error approach to determine the output for years 2 and 3. For year 2:

$$13\ 000 \text{ units} = 10 \times 13\ 000^{-0.3} = 0.5832 \times 13\ 000 = 7581 \text{ hrs}$$
$$14\ 000 \text{ units} = 10 \times 14\ 000^{-0.3} = 0.5704 \times 14\ 000 = 7986 \text{ hrs}$$

By trial and error, the learning-curve formula is applied to output levels between 13 000 and 14 000 units until the time required is equal to 7768 hours.

NPV calculations

Years	1	2	3
Output	5000	8460	10 560
	(£)	(£)	(£)
Sales (×£42)	210 000	355 320	443 520
Less costs:			
Labour (3884 × £6)	23 304	23 304	23 304
Material (×£30)	150 000	253 800	316 800
Overheads	25 000	25 000	25 000
Total costs	198 304	302 104	365 104
Net cash flows	+11 696	+53 216	+78 416
Discount factor	0.8696	0.7561	0.6575
Present values	10 171	40 237	51 559

NPV = £101 967 − £50 000 = £51 967

The contract should be undertaken on the basis of the NPV decision rule

(b) The answer should include a discussion of the following points:
  (i) A discussion of the assumptions relating to the learning curve. The learning rate based on past experience may not apply to this product. The learning effect may not continue over the whole range of the curve, and the 'steady state' may occur at a different point from that implied by the learning-curve formula.

(ii) The impact of inflation has been ignored.

(iii) The company cost of capital has been used. This rate is appropriate only if this project has the same risk as the average risk of the firm's existing assets.

(iv) Presumably all of the skilled labour capacity is used to meet the requirements of a single customer. It may be unwise to be committed to a single customer. The financial position of the customer should be investigated before acceptance of the order.

(v) The alternative use of the scarce labour should be explored and the present values from the alternative uses compared with the NPV calculated in (a).

(vi) The impact on customer goodwill if the demand from existing customers cannot be met.

(a) (i) The learning curve is expressed as:

Question 23.13

$$yx = ax^b$$

The exponent b is defined as the ratio of the logarithm of the learning curve improvement rate divided by the logarithm of 2. For an 80% learning curve:

$$b = \log 0.8/\log 2 = -0.322$$

For an output of 14 units:

$y_{14} = 40 \times 14^{-0.322} = 17.1$ hours per unit
Time taken for 14 units $= 14 \times 17.1 = 239.4$ hrs
Actual hours $= 240$

It would therefore appear that an 80% learning effect is a reasonable assumption.

(ii) For an output of 50 units:

$$y_{50} = 40 \times 50^{-0.322} = 11.35 \text{ hours per unit}$$

Hours required for 50 units: $= 50 \times 11.35 = 567.5$ hrs
For an output of 30 units:

$$y_{30} = 40 \times 30^{-0.322} = 13.38 \text{ hours per unit}$$

Hours required for 30 units $= 30 \times 13.38 = 401.4$ hours
The time required for the additional 20 units $= 166.1$ hours ($567.5 - 401.4$)

(iii) *Estimated cost for an order of 30 units*

	(£)
Direct materials (30 × £30)	900.00
Direct labour (401.4 hrs × £6)	2408.40
Variable overhead (401.4 hrs × £0.50)	200.70
Fixed overhead (401.4 × £5)[a]	2007.00
	5516.10

The above product cost has been calculated on an absorption costing basis in accordance with the current standard absorption costing system.

Note
[a]Fixed overhead for the period $= £6000$

Direct labour hours for the period = 1200 (75% × 40 hrs × 10 employees
× 4 weeks)

Fixed overhead hourly rate = £5 (£6000/1200)

Where the learning effect is present, unit product costs and labour hours will not be constant per unit of output. Significant variations in product costs and labour hours per unit of output are likely to occur at lower output levels. It is therefore necessary to estimate the extent of the learning effect for standard settings, budgeting and selling price quotations. Failure to take into account the presence of the learning effect can result in significant errors in cost estimates and planned labour requirements. If standards are not adjusted, they will cease to represent meaningful targets and lead to the reporting of erroneous favourable variances.

(b) The statement refers to the fact that, with modern technology, there is a dramatic decrease in the direct labour content of most goods and services. Recent studies suggest that direct labour represents less than 10% of manufacturing cost and that overheads are more closely related to machine hours than direct labour hours. With modern technology, output tends to be determined by machine speeds rather than changes in labour efficiency. Consequently, the presence of the learning effect as workers become more familiar with new operating procedures is of considerably less importance.

The question implies that the learning curve is being replaced by an experience curve. The experience curve relates to the fact that output and efficiency are determined by manufacturing technologists such as engineers and production planners. As these groups of individuals gain experience from a range of applications of the new technology, efficiency improves and costs are minimized. It is therefore claimed that the experience curve has replaced the learning curve. However, the experience curve is extremely difficult to determine, and its impact is likely to take place over a much longer time period. It is therefore extremely difficult to capture the 'experience effect' within short-term standard setting, budgeting and cost estimation activities.

Question 23.15 (a) Variation 1 requires the production of a 200 unit initial batch. Labour hours per unit are given in the question and it is assumed that they represent the average labour hours per unit for the 200 batch. If production is doubled from 1 batch to 2 batches (i.e. 400 units) then it is assumed that the average time per unit for 400 units will be 80% of the time taken per unit for the first 200 unit batch. The learning curve principle is applied to batches of production (with each batch consisting of 200 units).

Variation 1

	(£)	(£)	(£)
Direct materials cost			120.00
Conversion cost:			
Direct labour:			
AR (8 hrs at £3.00 per hour)	24		
AS (100 hrs at £3.60 per hour)	360		
AT (30 hours at £2.40 per hour)	72	456	
Variable overhead 25% of £456		114	
Fixed overhead:			
AR (8 hrs at £5 per hour)	40		
AS (100 hrs at £3 per hour)	300		
AT (30 hrs at £2 per hour)	60	400	970.00
			1090.00
Profit (3% on direct materials of £120)			3.60
(10% on conversion cost of £970)			97.00
Selling price per unit			£1190.60

Variation 2

Production is being expanded from one batch of 200 units to cumulative production of three batches of 200 units, making 600 units in total. When two batches are produced, cumulative production is two batches, and the x axis will be two batches divided by one batch, resulting in an x-axis reading of 2.0. Hence the y axis (the cumulative average time taken) will be 80% of the average hours of the previous cumulative production (i.e. the hours taken for the first batch). If three batches are produced (i.e. 600 units in total) then the x axis will be three batches divided by one, giving a reading of 3. Hence the average time per unit of cumulative production will be 70.7% (as per table given in the question) of the average time for producing the first batch. Therefore the average time per unit will be 70.7 hours for Department AS (70.7% × 100 hours) and 21.21 hours (70.7% × 30 hours) for Department AT. Note that the learning curve does not apply to Department AR. An alternative approach is to use the formula $y_x = ax^b$:

$$y_3 = 100 \times 3^{-0.322} = 70.2 \text{ hours for Department AS}$$

Note that cumulative production is measured in batches. The selling price per unit for variation 2 is calculated as follows:

	(£)	(£)	(£)
Direct materials cost			120.00
Conversion cost:			
Direct labour:			
AR (8 hrs at £3.00 per hour)	24		
AS (100 hrs at 70.7% = 70.7 at £3.60 per hour)	254.52		
AT (30 hrs at 70.7% = 21.21 at £2.40 per hour)	50.904	329.424	
Variable overhead 25% of 329.424		82.356	
Fixed overhead:			
AR (8 hrs at £5 per hour)	40		
AS (70.70 hrs at £3 per hour)	212.10		
AT (21.21 hrs at £2 per hour)	42.42	294.52	706.30
			826.30
Profit (3% on direct materials of £120)			3.60
(10% on conversion cost of £706.30)			70.63
Selling price per unit			£900.53

Variation 3

Order no. 1: Unit selling price = £1190.60 per unit (the same as variation 1).

Order no. 2 Cumulative 300 units (W1)		Order no. 3 Cumulative 400 (W2)		Order no. 4 Cumulative 480 (W3)	
Conversion costs	(£)		(£)		(£)
Direct labour AR at £3	24.00		24.00		24.00
(87.6 hrs) AS at £3.60	315.36	(80 hrs)	288.00	(76 hrs)	273.60
(26.28 hrs) AT at £2.40	63.072	(24 hrs)	57.60	(22.8 hrs)	54.72
	402.432		369.60		352.32
Variable overhead 25%					
(of £402.432)	100.608	(£369.60)	92.40	(£352.32)	88.08
Fixed overhead					
AR at £5	40.00		40.00		40.00
AS at £3	262.80		240.00		228.00
AT at £2	52.56		48.00		45.60
	858.40		790.00		754.00
Direct materials cost	120.00		120.00		120.00

	Profit	3% on £120	3.60			3.60			3.60
		10% on £858.40	85.84	(on £790)		79.00	(on £754)		75.40
			1067.84			992.60			953.00

Workings

(W1) 300 units/200 units = 1.5 *x*-axis, and labour hours are 87.6% of hours for 200 units.

(W2) 400 units/200 units = 2.0 *x*-axis, and labour hours are 80% of hours for 200 units.

(W3) 480 units/200 units = 2.4 *x*-axis, and labour hours are 76% of hours for 200 units.

Order no. 2		(£)
Cumulative orders	300 at £1067.84	320 352
Previous orders	200 at £1190.60	238 120
Incremental order	100 at a cost of	82 232

Unit selling price £822.32

Order no. 3		(£)
Cumulative orders	400 at £992.60	397 040
Previous orders	300 at £1067.84	320 352
Incremental order	100 at a cost of	76 688

Unit selling price £766.88

Order no. 4		(£)
Cumulative orders	480 at £953.00	457 440
Previous orders	400 at £992.60	397 040
Incremental order	80 at a cost of	60 400

Unit selling price £755.00

(b) Factors that might influence the learning curve not to be considered when setting standards are.

   (i) The budgetees view the standard as too difficult, and this causes their aspiration level and productivity to decline. This situation may arise when the budgetees have had no prior experience of the learning curve and view a standard time for future output which is lower than the time presently taken to be unacceptable.

   (ii) Previous experience from similar operations has indicated that the learning curve is inappropriate.

   (iii) Where the learning rate is very low (say a 95% learning curve).

   (iv) A budget-constrained style of evaluation is used, resulting in budgetees seeing increased targets as a threat instead of a more realistic target.

Question 23.16 (a)

Cumulative production (boats)	Completion time (days)	Cumulative time (days)	Average time (days)
1	10.0	10.0	10.0
2	8.1	18.1	9.05 (18.1/2)
3	7.4	25.5	8.50 (25.5/3)
4	7.1	32.6	8.15 (32.6/4)

As production doubles from one to two boats, average time falls to 90.5% of the time for producing the first boat. As production doubles from two to four boats, average time falls to 90.06% (8.15/9.05) of the previous average. The objective is to calculate the *average* learning rate. You should now refer to Exhibit 23.5 in Chapter 23. You can see that the average time for producing four units is 0.64 of the time for producing the first unit (1280/2000). The average learning rate is $\sqrt{(0.64)} = 0.8$ or 80%. The average time for producing eight units is 0.512 of the time for producing the first unit (1024/2000). The average learning rate is $^3\sqrt{(0.512)} = 0.8$. Similarly, the average time for producing 16 units is 0.4095 of the time for producing the first unit (819/2000). The average learning rate is $^4\sqrt{(0.4095)} = 0.80$. In Exhibit 23.5 the learning rate remained constant at 80% throughout, and it was therefore unnecessary to calculate the average learning rate.

Applying the approach outlined above, the average time for four boats is 0.815 of the time for the first boat, thus indicating an average learning rate of $\sqrt{(0.815)} = 0.903$ or 90.3%

An alternative approach is to use the learning curve equation:

$$y_x = ax^b$$

where y_x is defined as the cumulative average time required to produce x units, a is the time required to produce the first unit of output and x is the number of units of output under consideration. The exponent b is defined as the ratio of the logarithm of the learning curve improvement rate to the logarithm of 2. Therefore

$$y^4 = 10 \times 4^b$$
$$8.15 = 10 \times 4^b$$
$$4^b = 0.815$$

Our objective is to calculate the exponent function that, when multiplied by 4, equals 0.815. A trial-and-error approach is now adopted:

exponent function for 80% learning curve = -0.322 (see Chapter 23)
exponent function for 90% learning curve = -0.152 (log 0.9/log 2)
exponent function for 91% learning curve = -0.136 (log 0.91/log 2)

$$4^{-0.322} = 0.64$$
$$4^{-0.152} = 0.810$$
$$4^{-0.136} = 0.828$$

The average learning rate is between 90% and 91%.
(b) The following points should be discussed:
  (i) Only four observations have been used, and this might be insufficient to establish an average learning rate for the production of 15 boats.
  (ii) It is assumed that working methods, equipment and staff will remain constant. Improvements in working procedures, staff changes or absenteeism might affect the learning rate.
  (iii) Uncertainty as to when the learning process will stop. If the learning process stops before the steady-state phase is reached then the assumption that the learning rate will continue might result in inaccurate estimates.
  (iv) The learning rate may not be constant throughout the process, and the use of an average learning rate might result in inaccurate estimates for different output levels.
(c) Materials, other direct expenses and overheads will remain unchanged irrespective of whether the boats are completed in normal time (possibly involving penalties) or working weekends. Overheads appear to be fixed since they are allocated on the basis of *normal* working days. The total times required, assuming a 90% learning rate, are as follows:

Average time for 15 boats = $y_{15} = 10 \times 15^{-0.152}$ = 6.6257 days
Total time for 15 boats = 15×6.6257 = 99.4 days
Total time for 14 boats = $14 \times 10 \times 14^{-0.152}$ = 93.7 days
Total time for 13 boats = $13 \times 10 \times 13^{-0.152}$ = 88.0 days

The contract is for 4 months (therefore 92 working days are available without overtime or 120 days with overtime) and penalties are charged at £10 000 per boat late. Thirteen boats can be delivered within the contract period. To complete 15 boats within the contract period, it will be necessary to work 7.4 days (99.4 days − 92 days) overtime. If overtime is not worked, two boats will incur a penalty. Without overtime, the total labour cost plus penalties will be:

$$(99.4 \text{ days} \times £2500 = £248\,500) + (2 \times £10\,000) = £268\,500$$

With overtime, the total labour cost will be:

$$(92 \text{ days} \times £2500 = £230\,000) + (7.4 \text{ days} \times 5000) = £267\,000$$

It is assumed that payments can be made for part days only. It is slightly cheaper to work overtime and avoid the penalty cost. Another possibility is to complete 14 boats using overtime and deliver 1 boat late:

Cost for 14 boats = (92 days × £2500) + (1.7 days × £5000) = £238 500
Cost for 15th boat = (5.7 days × £2500) + (1 × £10 000)   = £ 24 250
                                                              £262 750

The most profitable alternative is to deliver one boat late. Other factors to be considered include:
  (i) the four factors outlined in part (b);
 (ii) the possibility of bad weather affecting production times;
(iii) the effect on customer goodwill and the possibility of not obtaining future orders if the contract is not completed on time;
(iv) the promise of overtime work might induce the workforce to slow down in order to obtain overtime work.

Quantitative models for the planning and control of stocks

Solutions to Chapter 24 questions

Question summary

Questions 24.1–24.5 should be regarded as general introductory questions on the EOQ model. Questions 24.11–24.21 are the most difficult.

24.1–24.5 General introductory questions on the EOQ model.

24.6 An evaluation of quantity discounts.

24.7 Make or buy decisions incorporating ordering and holding costs.

24.8 Calculation of minimum purchase cost when the purchasing cost per unit is not constant.

24.9 Calculation of EOQ and evaluation of quantity discounts.

24.10, 24.11 Decision-making problems using the EOQ model.

24.12 Calculation of reduction in storage costs from the implementation of JIT production and purchasing.

24.13 Calculation of EOQ and cash payments to creditors. This question also requires a discussion of the limitations of the EOQ approach and a description of JIT production and purchasing.

24.14–24.21 Questions requiring a discussion and calculation of safety stocks when demand is uncertain. Questions 24.16 and 24.19 also require the calculation of stockholding costs and a discussion of a JIT inventory policy. Question 24.20 involves the calculation of the EOQ, an estimate of the level of safety stocks, an evaluation of quantity discounts and the expected costs for different levels of safety stocks.

Question 24.1

(a) (i) Continuous stocktaking refers to a situation where a sample of stores items are counted regularly on, say, a daily basis. Sufficient items should be checked each day so that during a year all items are checked at least once. The alternative system of stocktaking is a complete physical stockcount where all the stock items are counted at one point in time. Continuous stocktaking is preferable because production is not disrupted and any discrepancies and losses are revealed earlier.

(ii) A perpetual inventory system is a stock recording system whereby the balance is shown for a stock item after each receipt or issue. In a non-computerized system the records are maintained on bin cards or stores ledger cards. A separate record is maintained for each item of materials in stores. Therefore the stock balance for each stores item is available at any point in time.

(iii) For an explanation of ABC inventory analysis see 'Control of stocks through classification' in Chapter 24.

(b) For the answer to this question you should refer to Chapter 24 ('Relevant costs for quantitative models under conditions of certainty' and 'Determining the economic order quantity').

(c) Normal control levels are the reorder level, minimum level, and maximum level.

$$\text{Reorder level} = \text{maximum usage} \times \text{maximum lead time}$$
$$= 800 \text{ kg} \times 14 \text{ days}$$
$$= \underline{11\,200} \text{ kg}$$

$$\text{Minimum level} = \text{re-order level} - \text{average usage in average lead time}$$
$$= 11\,200 \text{ kg} - (600 \text{ kg} \times 12 \text{ days})$$
$$= \underline{4000 \text{ kg}}$$

$$\text{Maximum level} = \text{re-order level} + \text{EOQ} - \text{minimum usage in minimum lead time}$$
$$= 11\,200 \text{ kg} + 12\,000 \text{ kg} - (400 \text{ kg} \times 10 \text{ days})$$
$$= \underline{19\,200 \text{ kg}}$$

Question 24.2 (a) *Item A32: storage and ordering cost schedule*

No. of orders per year	4	5	6	7	8	9	10	11	12
Order size (boxes)	1250	1000	833	714	625	556	500	455	417
Average stock (boxes)	625	500	417	357	313	278	250	228	208
	(£)	(£)	(£)	(£)	(£)	(£)	(£)	(£)	(£)
Storage costs (average stock × 25% of £2)	312.5	250.0	208.5	178.5	156.5	139.0	125.0	114.0	104.0
Orderring costs (£12.5 per order)	50.0	62.5	75.0	87.5	100.0	112.5	125.0	137.5	150.0
Total cost	£362.5	£312.5	£283.5	£266.0	£256.5	£251.5	£250.0	£251.5	£254.0

(b) The number of orders which should be placed in a year to minimize costs is 10.

(c)
$$\text{EOQ} = \sqrt{\left(\frac{2DO}{H}\right)}$$

where D = total demand for period, O = ordering cost per order, H = holding cost per unit.

(d)
$$\text{EOQ} = \sqrt{\left(\frac{2 \times 5000 \times 12.5}{0.5}\right)}$$
$$= 500 \text{ units}$$

(e) The maximum saving that could be made if the authority process four orders per year would be
$$\frac{£362.50 - £250}{£362.50} = 31\%$$

(f) (i) Reducing the number of stock items by eliminating slow moving and obsolete stocks.
(ii) Standardization of stock items thus reducing the total number of items in stock.

Question 24.3 (a) (i)
$$\text{EOQ} = \sqrt{\left(\frac{2DO}{H}\right)}$$

where D = annual demand, O = ordering cost per order, H = holding cost per unit. Therefore
$$\text{EOQ} = \sqrt{\left(\frac{2 \times 48\,000 \times £0.60}{10\% \times £10}\right)}$$
$$= 240$$

(ii) Number of orders required per year is:

$$\frac{\text{annual requirements}}{\text{EOQ}} = \frac{48\,000}{240} = 200 \text{ orders per year}$$

(iii) Total cost = holding costing + ordering cost

$$= \frac{240\,(£1)}{2} + \frac{48\,000\,(£0.60)}{240}$$

$$= £240$$

(b) Usage per day = 133.33 (48 000/360 days)
Number of days' usage in closing stock = 3 (400/133.33)
Lead time = 3 days
Therefore the next order should be placed immediately.

(c) Some problems when attempting to apply the EOQ formula are:
   (i) Inventory is not always used at a constant rate, and the constant usage assumption is implicit in the EOQ formula.
   (ii) The EOQ formula requires estimates of (a) annual sales, (b) ordering costs, (c) purchase price per unit and (d) cost of carrying inventories. These items may be extremely difficult to estimate in practice.

Question 24.6

(a)
$$\text{EOQ} = \sqrt{\left(\frac{2DO}{H}\right)}$$

$$= \sqrt{\left(\frac{2 \times 50\,000 \times 100}{0.40}\right)}$$

$$= 5000$$

(b)

	(£)
Savings in purchase price (50 000 × £0.02)	= 1000
Saving in ordering cost[a]	

$$\frac{DO}{Q_d} - \frac{DO}{Q} = \frac{50\,000 \times 100}{10\,000} - \frac{50\,000 \times 100}{5000} = 500$$

| | Total savings | 1500 |

Note
[a]Q_d represents quantity ordered to obtain discount and Q represents EOQ.
The additional holding cost if the larger quantity is purchased is calculated as follows:

$$\frac{(Q_d - Q)H}{2} = \frac{(10\,000 - 5000) \times 0.40}{2} = £1000$$

As the total savings exceed the total cost increase, the company should take advantage of the quantity discount.

Question 24.11

(a) The question requires the calculation of the optimum number of units to be manufactured in each production run in order to secure the lowest annual cost. In Chapter 24 we noted that the formula for the optimum number of units to be manufactured (Q) is as follows:

$$Q = \sqrt{\left(\frac{2DS}{H}\right)}$$

where D = total demand for period, S = set-up costs, H = holding cost per unit. The set-up costs and holding cost per unit to be used in the formula are relevant or incremental costs. Those costs that will not change as a result of changes in the number of units manufactured in each batch should not be included in the analysis. These costs include:

(i) Skilled labour costs. (Skilled labour is being paid idle time. Its total cost will not alter as a result of the current decision.)

(ii) Fixed overheads. (These costs are independent of the batch size.)

Therefore the relevant cost of producing product Exe is as follows:

		(£)
Raw materials − external suppliers		13
− Dee standard cost: Raw materials	8	
Unskilled labour	4	
Variable overheads	3	15
Unskilled labour		7
Variable overheads		5
Incremental cost of production		40

The relevant decision variables for the formula are as follows:

Annual demand of Exe (D)	= 4000 units
Set-up costs (S)	= £70 (skilled labour of £66 is not an incremental cost)
Annual holding costs	= £14 [cost of storage (£8) plus cost of capital tied up in stocks (£6)]

Storage cost per unit (0.40 m² × £20) = £8

Incremental interest tied up in each unit of Exe stock
  (15% × £40 incremental cost of Exe) = £6

Applying the above figures to the formula, we have:

$$Q = \sqrt{\left(\frac{2 \times 4000 \times £70}{£14}\right)}$$

$$= 200 \text{ units}$$

Cost of current policy

	(£)
Set-up costs (4 production runs at £70)	280
Holding costs (average stocks × unit holding cost)	
$\dfrac{1000}{2} \times £14$	7000
Total cost	7280

Cost of optimum policy

Set-up costs [(4000/200) production runs at £70]	1400
Holding costs (average stocks × unit holding cost)	
$\dfrac{200}{2} \times £14$	1400
Total cost	2800
Annual savings (£7280 − £2800)	£4480

(b)

$$Q = \sqrt{\left(\frac{DO}{H}\right)}$$

where D = annual demand, O = incremental ordering cost per order, H = holding cost per unit. For producing Wye:

$$Q = \sqrt{\left(\frac{2 \times 10\,000 \times £100}{£8}\right)} = 500 \text{ units}$$

Buying in larger quantities in order to take advantage of bulk discounts results in the following savings:
  (i) a saving in purchase price for the period consisting of the total amount of the discount for the period;
  (ii) a reduction in total ordering cost because of fewer orders being placed to take advantage of bulk discounts.
The above cost savings must be compared with the increased holding costs resulting from higher stock levels.

We now compare the cost savings with the increased holding costs from increasing the quantity purchased from the EOQ of 500 units to the lowest purchase quantity at which Wye can be purchased at £19.80 per unit (i.e. 1000 units):

	(£)
Savings in purchase price (10 000 annual purchases at £0.20)	2000

Saving in ordering cost[a]

$$\frac{DO}{Q_d} - \frac{DO}{Q} = \frac{10\,000 \times 100}{1000} - \frac{10\,000 \times 100}{500} \qquad 1000$$

Total savings	3000

Note
[a] Q_d represents quantity ordered to obtain discount and Q represents EOQ.
The additional holding cost if the larger quantity is purchased is calculated as follows

$$\frac{(Q_d - Q)H}{2} = \frac{(1000 - 500) \times £8}{2} = £2000$$

Therefore a saving of £1000 is made if the firm purchases in quantities of 1000 units at a price of £19.80 per unit.

We now follow the same procedure in order to determine whether it would be better to purchase in quantities of 2000 units:

	(£)
Savings in purchase price (10 000 annual purchases at £0.40)	4000

Saving in ordering cost

$$\frac{DO}{Q_d} - \frac{DO}{Q} = \frac{10\,000 \times 100}{2000} - \frac{10\,000 \times 100}{500} \qquad 1500$$

Total savings	5500

The additional holding cost if we purchase in 2000-unit quantities instead of 500-unit quantities is as follows:

$$\frac{(Q_d - Q)H}{2} = \frac{(2000 - 500) \times £8}{2} = £6000$$

Therefore an additional £500 will be incurred if the firm purchases in 2000-unit batches compared with purchasing in 500-unit batches.

The above analysis indicates that Pink should purchase in batches of 1000 units at a price of £19.80 per unit.
(c) Limitations include the following:
  (i) It is very difficult to obtain relevant data. Incremental holding, ordering and set-up costs are very difficult to estimate in practice. In addition, many of the fixed costs that were excluded in the analysis may not be fixed over the whole range of output. Some fixed costs may increase in steps as the quantity purchased is increased.
  (ii) Model assumes certainty. A more sophisticated approach is required where the demand and the cost structure are uncertain.

(iii) Model assumes that demand is constant throughout the year. In practice, there may be seasonal variations in demand throughout the year.

Question 24.12 (a) Annual material costs are £9m (30% × £30m) and conversion costs are £7.5m (25% × £30m).

Current stock levels are:		(£)
Raw materials (10% × £9 m)		900 000
Work in progress:		
Materials element	£1 350 000 (15% × £9m)	
Conversion cost	675 000 (15% × £7.5 m × 60%)	2 025 000
Finished goods:		
Materials element	£1 080 000 (12% × £900 000)	
Conversion cost	900 000 (12% × £7.5m)	1 980 000

The stockholding costs for each category of stocks are are follows:

	Existing	Revised
Raw material stock:	(£)	(£)
Fixed holding and acquisition costs	100 000	20 000
Variable holding and acquisition costs	90 000 (10%)	12 600 (20% × £900 000 × 7p)
Financial charges	180 000 (20%)	36 000 [20% × (20% × £900 000)]
	370 000	68 600
Work in progress:		
Fixed movement and control costs	140 000	56 000 (40% × £140 000)
Variable movement and control costs	67 500 (5% × £1.35 m)	8 100 [£0.03 × (20% × £1.35m)]
Financial charges	405 000 (20% × £2.025 m)	81 000 [20% × (20% × £2.025m)]
	612 500	145 100
Finished goods:		
Fixed holding and control costs	180 000	72 000 (40% × £180 000)
Variable holding and control costs	39 600 (2% × £1.98m)	4 950 [0.01 × (25% × £1.98m)]
Financial charges	396 000 (20% × £1.98m)	99 000 [20% × (25% × £1.98m)]
	615 600	175 950

Summary of cost savings

	Existing situation (£)	Revised situation (£)	Savings (£)
Raw material stock	370 000	68 600	301 400
Work in progress	612 500	145 100	467 400
Finished goods	615 600	175 950	439 650
	1 598 100	389 650	1 208 450

(b) Possible reasons for the reduction in costs for each item of stock are as follows:
Raw material stock
(i) Reduction in insurance and clerical costs
(ii) Reduction in number of staff required
(iii) Savings arising from reduction in warehouse space
(iv) Reduction in materials handling cost
(v) Reduced financing costs

Work in progress
   (i) Reduction in losses arising from moving WIP from one department to another
   (ii) Reduction in materials handling equipment and staff
   (iii) Savings or additional cash flows arising from reduced storage space
   (iv) Reduced financing costs
Finished goods stock
   (i) Reduction in insurance costs
   (ii) Savings arising from reduction in warehouse space and staff
   (iii) Reduction in finished goods handling costs
   (iv) Reduced financing costs

(c) For just-in-time purchasing it is essential that reliable suppliers can be found who will deliver to match the company's production demands. Any later deliveries may result in stockout costs. Suppliers may increase purchase costs to compensate for synchronizing their delivery and production schedules to the JIT production requirements of Prodco. Alternatively, savings might arise from negotiating large long-term contracts with fewer suppliers. Dealing with fewer suppliers should result in a significant reduction in administrative costs. The reduction in stocks should create excess storage space which might be used to increase production capacity. Alternatively, it may be posisble to sub-let the space.

The move to a cell layout should enable the company to respond quickly to changes in sales demand or to meet special orders. Thus additional sales might be generated. Additional training costs will be necessary to train the workers to operate different types of machines and carry out routine maintenance. Set-up costs may increase as the company moves from producing large batches using batch production techniques to producing small or single unit batches using flow production techniques.

JIT manufacturing should reduce finished goods stocks since the aim is to produce the required quantities at the precise time they are required. This should result in improved customer goodwill if production is more sensitive to meeting customer delivery requirements. The reduction in finished goods stock requirements will create additional storage space which might generate additional rental income from sub-letting.

(a) *EOQ* **Question 24.13**

$EOQ = \sqrt{(2DO/H)}$
where D = demand for period (43 200 units)
   O = ordering cost per unit (£900 + £750)
   H = holding cost per unit (15% × £30 + 2 × £3.25) = £11

Note that, assuming constant demand, the average stock level is one-half of the EOQ. In this question the holding costs applicable to storage space will depend upon maximum (rather than average) stock levels. It is therefore necessary to double the holding cost per unit given in the question.

$$EOQ = \sqrt{[(2 \times 43\ 200 \times £1650)/£11]} = 3600 \text{ units}$$

The EOQ is equivalent to one month's sales. Safety stocks equivalent to one month's sales are maintained. Consequently, stock levels will vary between 3600 and 7200 units.

Cash payments to trade creditors
The budgeted stock level of 21 600 units could be reduced to 7200 units. This represents stock reduction of 14 400 units, which is equivalent to 4 months' stocks. In other words, for the next four months, sales demand can be met from stocks. From month 5, purchases would be 3600 units per month.

Budgeted monthly cost of sales = £108 000 (1296/12)

Trade creditors are therefore equivalent to 2 months' cost of sales. The schedule of payments to trade creditors would be as follows:

July and August 1989	£108 000 per month
September to December 1989	No payments made
January and February 1990	£108 000 per month

(b) (i) *Cash operating cycle at 20 June 1989*

	Months
Stock holding period (£21 600/3600)	6
Debtors average credit period [198/(2376/12)]	1
Creditors average payment period (per (a))	(2)
	5

(ii) *Cash operating cycle at 30 June 1990*

	Months
Stockholding period (7200 units)	2
Debtors (no change)	1
Creditors (no change)	(1)
	1

(c) The answer should include a discussion of the EOQ assumptions and the extent which these may be appropriate in a practical situation. The following points should be included in the answer:
   (i) The formula assumes that demand can be accurately estimated and that usage is constant throughout the period. In practice, demand may be uncertain and subject to seasonal variations. Most firms hold safety stocks as a protection against variations in demand.
   (ii) The ordering costs are assumed to be constant per order placed. In practice, most of the ordering costs are fixed or subject to step functions. It is therefore difficult to estimate the incremental cost per order.
   (iii) Holding costs per unit are assumed to be constant. The financing charge for the investment in stocks is based on the average investment multiplied by the cost of capital. This will result in a reasonable estimate, provided that demand can be accurately estimated and that usage and the purchase price are constant throughout the period. Many holding costs are fixed throughout the period and are not relevant to the model, but other costs (e.g. store-keepers' salaries) are step fixed costs. Opportunity costs of the warehouse space and labour are other relevant holding costs that are included in the model. However, identifying lost opportunities from holding stocks is difficult to determine. Consequently, it is extremely difficult to accurately predict the holding cost for a unit in stock for one year.
   (iv) Purchasing cost per unit is assumed to be constant for all purchase quantities. In practice, quantity discounts can result in purchasing economies of scale.
   (v) Despite the fact that much of the data in the model represent rough approximations, the EOQ formula is likely to provide a reasonable guide of the EOQ because it is very insensitive to errors in predictions (see 'Effect of approximations' in Chapter 24). The EOQ model can also be adapted to incorporate quantity discounts. For a discussion of other issues relevant to this answer see 'Assumptions of the EOQ formula' in Chapter 24.
(d) The advantages of adopting a JIT approach include:
   (i) Substantial savings in stockholding costs.

(ii) Elimination of waste.
(iii) Savings in factory and warehouse space, which can be used for other profitable activities.
(iv) Reduction in obsolete stocks.
 (v) Considerable reduction in paperwork arising from a reduction in purchasing, stock and accounting transactions.
The disadvantages include:
 (i) Additional investment costs in new machinery, changes in plant layout and goods inwards facilities.
(ii) Difficulty in predicting daily or weekly demand, which is a key feature of the JIT philosophy.
(iii) Increased risk due to the greater probability of stockout costs arising from strikes, or other unforeseen circumstances, that restrict production or supplies.

Question 24.14

(a)

Safety stock	Stockout	Stockout cost at £10 (£)	Probability	Expected cost (£)	Total (£)
500	0	0	0	0	0
400	100	1000	0.04	40	40
300	200	2000	0.04	80	
	100	1000	0.07	70	150
200	300	3000	0.04	120	
	200	2000	0.07	140	
	100	1000	0.10	100	360
100	400	4000	0.04	160	
	300	3000	0.07	210	
	200	2000	0.10	200	
	100	1000	0.13	130	700
0	500	5000	0.04	200	
	400	4000	0.07	280	
	300	3000	0.10	300	
	200	2000	0.13	260	
	100	1000	0.16	160	1200

Safety stock	Stockout cost (£)	Holding cost (£)	Total cost (£)
0	1200	0	1200
100	700	100	800
200	360	200	560
300	150	300	450
400	40	400	440
500	0	500	500

The optimal safety stock is 400 units.
(b) The probability of being out of stock at an optimal safety stock of 400 units is 0.04.

Question 24.17

(a) The re-order point based on the expected usage and lead time is calculated as follows:

Total demand during lead time	Joint probability	Expected value (usage)
75 000 (15 × 5000)	0.1	7 500
105 000 (15 × 7000)	0.1	10 500
100 000 (20 × 5000)	0.25	25 000
140 000 (20 × 7000)	0.25	35 000

$$
\begin{array}{lll}
125\,000\ (25 \times 5000) & 0.15 & 18\,750 \\
175\,000\ (25 \times 7000) & \underline{0.15} & \underline{26\,250} \\
& \underline{1.00} & \underline{123\,000}
\end{array}
$$

With a re-order level of 150 000 units, the safety stock (buffer stock) is 27 000 units (150 000 − 123 000).

(b) The probability of a stockout (i.e. demand in excess of 150 000 units) is 0.15.

(c)
$$
\text{EOQ} = \sqrt{\left[\frac{2 \times (6000 \times 240) \times 1000}{0.15}\right]} = 138\,564 \text{ units}
$$

Note that the expected daily demand of 6000 units is calculated as follows:

$$(0.5 \times 5000) + (0.5 \times 7000)$$

The average number of orders per annum is:

$$\frac{6000 \times 240}{138\,564} = 10.39$$

The expected annual stockouts in units per annum is:

$$0.15 \times (175\,000 - 150\,000) \times 10.39 = 38\,962 \text{ units}$$

(d) The additional annual holding cost if the re-order level is increased to 175 000 units is £3750 (25000 × £0.15).

At a re-order level of 150 000 units, the expected value of the stockouts per annum is 38 962 units.

Therefore the increase in stock is justified where the stockout cost per unit is greater than 9.6 pence (£3750/38 962 units).

(e) Many companies are now giving increasing attention to reducing stocks to a minimum by adopting just-in-time (JIT) purchasing and production techniques. For a description of JIT techniques you should refer to Chapters 2 and 24. The main disadvantage of JIT purchasing is that a successful JIT philosophy depends on finding suppliers who can provide a reliable delivery service at frequent intervals. With the absence of stocks, the system is dependent on a reliable service being maintained with no delay in deliveries. JIT companies therefore become very dependent upon the reliability of the supplier, and any failure by the latter to meet delivery schedules could have a serious impact on a whole production process.

Question 24.18 (a) Order costs consist of variable purchasing costs (£300) plus transportation costs (£750 or £650). Note that the timing of the payments for 4200 units will be the same irrespective of the order size. Consequently, the cost of capital is omitted from the stockholding costs because it will be the same for all order quantities.

$$
\text{EOQ with transportation costs of £750} = \sqrt{\left(\frac{2 \times 1050 \times 4200}{4}\right)}
$$

$$= 1485 \text{ units}$$

At this level the company qualifies for the lower transport costs. Therefore the EOQ should be based on ordering costs of £950:

$$
\text{EOQ} = \sqrt{\left(\frac{2 \times 950 \times 4200}{4}\right)} = 1412 \text{ units}
$$

The company should therefore place orders for 1412 units.

Improvement in profit

		(£)
Gross profit (unchanged)		64 000
Purchasing department costs:		
Variable (4200/1412) × £300	(892)	
Fixed	(8400)	(9 292)
Transportation costs:		
(4200/1412) × £650		(1 933)
Insurance costs on average stockholding:		
[200 safety stock + (1412/2)] × £4		(3 624)
Warehouse fixed costs		(43 000)
Revised profit		6 151
Original profit		3 250
Improvement		2 901

(b) The re-order level should be based on the expected usage during the period plus a safety stock to provide a cushion in the event of demand being in excess of the expected usage.

$$\text{Expected usage} = (500 \times 0.15) + (600 \times 0.20) + (700 \times 0.30) + (800 \times 0.20)$$
$$+ (900 \times 0.15) = 700$$

Thus it is necessary to consider safety stocks of 0, 100 or 200 units.

Expected usage (units)	Safety stock (units)	Re-order point (units)	Stockout (units)	Annual stockout cost[a] (£18 per unit)	Probability	Annual expected stockout cost (£)	Holding cost[b] (£)	Total expected cost (£)
700	0	700	200	21 600	0.15	3240		
			100	10 800	0.20	2160		
						5400	0	5400
700	100	800	100	10 800	0.15	1620	1800	3420
700	200	900	0	0		0	3600	3600

Notes

[a] Note that expected costs are calculated on an *annual* basis by multiplying 200 units × £18 × 6 (that is, 6 two-monthly periods).

[b] In the answer to part (a) the interest on the value of the stock was not included, because the timing of the payments for stocks was not affected by the order quantity. Consequently, the interest charge was not relevant in calculating the EOQ. The holding cost in the above calculation consists of £14 interest cost (20% of £70 purchase cost) plus £4 insurance cost. It is assumed that the safety stock represents an investment over and above the annual order quantity of 4200 units. In other words, safety stocks represent an incremental investment, and interest on safety stocks is therefore relevant to the safety stock decision.

Recommendation

Expected costs are minimized at a re-order point of 800 units (this includes a safety stock of 100 units).

(c) The answer to this question should include a discussion of the assumptions of the EOQ model (see 'Assumptions of the EOQ formula' in Chapter 24). The answer should stress that because demand is uncertain and not uniform and lead time is not constant, it is necessary to adjust the EOQ model to take account of these facts. The safety stock model applied in (b) is subject to a number of practical difficulties – for example, the difficulty of producing probability distributions for demand and lead time. In addition, stockout costs are extremely difficult to determine in practice. A further problem is that discrete distributions as estimated in (b) are unlikely to be a representation of reality because they are based on a limited number of outcomes. The answer produced represents the *expected value* of the stockholding costs, and as such represents a long-run average outcome. An alternative is to use continuous distributions, but this requires that the distribution conform to one that can easily be described mathematically (e.g. a normal distribution).

In practice, it is likely that stockout costs will be the most significant cost, and the problem is one of determining the minimum level of stock that is consistent with always satisfying demand. Most small companies are likely to concentrate on frequently reviewing stock levels and use their previous experience to subjectively determine order levels.

Question 24.20 (a) Expected annual demand = 10 000 units × 52 weeks = 520 000 units
Holding cost per unit   = 18% of purchase price (£4.50) = £0.81

$$\text{EOQ} = \sqrt{\left(\frac{2 \times 520\,000 \times £311.54}{0.81}\right)}$$
$$= 20\,000 \text{ units}$$

(b) The average usage during the two week lead time is 20 000 units. If sales were always 10 000 units per week, the re-order point would be 20 000 units and stocks would be replenished when the stock level had fallen to zero. No safety stocks would be required. However, if demand is in excess of 20 000 units, stockouts will occur if no safety stocks are maintained. Consideration should therefore be given to holding safety stocks.

Maintaining safety stocks reduces the probability of running out of stock and incurring stockout costs, but this policy also results in additional holding costs. The annual holding cost per unit is £0.81. Over a two-week period, the holding cost per unit is £0.031 15 (£0.81/26 weeks). Stockout costs consist of the costs associated with losing orders. The cost of losing an order is the contribution per unit of £1.50 [£6.30 − (£4.50 + £0.30)]. The lost contribution applies to 25% of the orders in any two-week period. The expected stockout cost is therefore £0.375 (0.25 × £1.50) per unit.

The expected costs for various levels of safety stocks are as follows:

Safety stock (units)	Re-order point (units)	Stockout (units)	Probability of stockout	Expected stockout cost (£)	Holding cost (£)	Total Expected cost (£)
8000	28 000	0	0	0	249[a]	249
4000	24 000	4000	0.05	75[b]	125[a]	200
0	20 000	4000	0.20	300[b]		
		8000	0.05	150[b]	0	450

Expected costs are minimized when safety stocks are 4000 units. Therefore the recommended level of safety stocks is 4000 units.

Notes
[a] Safety stocks of 8000 units = holding cost of 8000 × £0.031 15 = £249
Safety stocks of 4000 units = holding cost of 4000 × £0.031 15 = £125.
[b] Safety stocks of 4000 units: stockout of 4000 units × £0.375 × 0.05 probability = £75

Safety stocks of zero: if demand is 24 000 units (probability = 0.20), there will be a 4000 units stockout, with an expected cost of 4000 × £0.375 × 0.2 = £300. If demand is 28 000 units (probability = 0.05), there will be a stockout of 8000 units, with an expected cost of 8000 × £0.375 × 0.05 = £150.

(c) If 30 000 units are ordered instead of 20 000 units, there will be an annual purchase cost saving of £23 400 (1% × 520 000 units × £4.50) resulting from the quantity discount. The annual savings in order costs will be as follows:

$$(520\ 000/30\ 000 \times £311.54) - (520\ 000/20\ 000 \times £311.54) = £2700$$

Total annual savings are therefore £26 100 (£23 400 + £2700). The annual holding costs are as follows:

30 000 units = 18% × £4.455 revised purchase price × 15 000 units average
                stock = £12 028
20 000 units = 18% × £4.50 purchase price × 10 000 units average stock = £8100

Therefore the additional holding cost is £3928 (£12 028 − £8100) and the overall net saving is £22 172 (£26 100 − £3928). It would therefore be beneficial to take advantage of the quantity discount.

(d) Total relevant costs would be as follows:

50% higher (30 000 units)	= £0.81 × (30 000/2) + £311.54 × (520 000/30 000)
	= £17 550
50% lower (10 000 units)	= £0.81 × (10 000/2) + £311.54 × (520 000/10 000)
	= £20 250
Original EOQ (20 000 units)	= £0.81 × (20 000/2) + £311.54 × (520 000/20 000)
	= £16 200

It is assumed that this part of the question refers to the original data given and that the quantity discount is not available. Total annual costs are 8.3% higher than the original EOQ at the 30 000-units order level and 25% higher at the 10 000-units order level. Therefore stock management costs are relatively insensitive to substantial changes in the EOQ.

(e) It would be necessary to establish seasonal periods where sales are fairly constant throughout each period. A separate EOQ would then be established for each distinct season throughout the year.

(f) The EOQ model is a model that enables the costs of stock management to be minimized. The model is based on the following assumptions.

  (i) Constant purchase price per unit irrespective of the order quantity.
 (ii) Ordering costs are constant for each order placed.
(iii) Constant lead times.
(iv) Constant holding costs per unit.

More sophisticated versions of the above model have been developed that are not dependent on the above assumptions. However, the EOQ is fairly insensitive to changes in the variables used in the model.

    Recently, some companies have adopted just-in-time (JIT) purchasing techniques whereby they have been able to negotiate reliable and frequent deliveries. This has been accompanied by the issue of blanket long-term purchase orders and a substantial reduction in ordering costs. The overall effect of applying the EOQ formula in this situation ties in with the JIT philosophy: that is, more frequent purchases of smaller quantities.

(a)

Question 24.21

$$EOQ = \sqrt{\frac{2DO}{H}} = \sqrt{\frac{2 \times 10\ 000 \times 25}{(45 + 5)}} = 100 \text{ units}$$

(b) Without any discount prices the EOQ = $\sqrt{\dfrac{2 \times 10\,000 \times 25}{(45 + 5.01)}}$ = 99.99 units

Thus it is preferable to purchase 100 units at £50 rather than pay £50.10 for purchasing 99 units. To ascertain whether it is worthwhile increasing the purchase quantity from 100 to 200 units we must compare the total costs at each of these quantities:

	(£)
Total costs with a reorder quantity of 100 units	
Annual holding cost (100/2 × £50)	2 500
Annual ordering costs (10 000/100 × £25)	2 500
	5 000
Purchasing manager's bonus (10% × £5000)	500
Annual purchase cost (10 000 × £50)	500 000
Total annual costs	505 500
Total costs with a reorder quantity of 200 units	
Annual holding costs (200/2 × £49.99)	4 999
Annual ordering costs (10 000/200 × £25)	1 250
	6 249
Purchasing manager's bonus (10% × (£10 000 − £6249))	375
Annual purchase cost (10 000 × £49.90)	499 000
Total annual costs	505 624

The optimal order quantity is still 100 units.
(c) The probability distribution of demand over the three day lead time is as follows:

Demand lead time	Frequency	Probability	Expected value
106	4	0.04	4.24
104	10	0.10	10.40
102	16	0.16	16.32
100	40	0.40	40.00
98	14	0.14	13.72
96	14	0.14	13.44
94	2	0.02	1.88
	100	1.00	100.00

It is assumed that the reorder point will be set at 100 units (expected value). The expected costs for various levels of safety stock are as follows:

Safety stock (units)	Reorder point (units)	Stockout per order (units)	Stockout per year[a] (units)	Probability of stockout	Expected stockout cost[b] (£)	Holding cost[c] (£)	Total expected cost[d] (£)
6	106	0	0	0	0	270	270
4	104	2	200	0.04	80	180	260
2	102	2	200	0.10	200		
		4	400	0.04	160	90	450
0	100	2	200	0.16	320		
		4	400	0.10	400		
		6	600	0.04	240	0	960

Notes
[a]During the year 100 orders will be made (10 000 units annual demand/EOQ of 100 units). Stockout per year in units is calculated by multiplying the stockouts per order by 100 orders;
[b]Expected stockout costs = Annual stockout in units × probability of

^{c}Holding cost = Safety stock × (Holding cost of £50 − saving of 10% on
purchasing manager's bonus)

^{d}It is assumed that stockout costs are equal to the lost contribution on the lost sales.

Conclusion

Costs are minimized if a safety stock of 4 units is maintained.

(d) The following items should be included in the report:
  (i) The disadvantages of ordering from only one supplier (e.g. vulnerability of disruption of supplies due to strikes/production difficulties or bankruptcy);
  (ii) Failure to seek out cheap or alternative sources of supply;
  (iii) It is assumed no large price increases are anticipated that will justify holding additional stocks or that the stocks are not subject to deterioration or obsolescence;
  (iv) It is assumed that lead time will remain unchanged. However, investigations should be made as to whether this, or other suppliers, can guarantee a shorter lead time;
  (v) The need to ascertain the impact on customer goodwill if a stockout occurs. The answer to (c) assumes that the company will merely lose the contribution on the sales and long-term sales will not be affected if a stockout occurs.

The application of linear programming to management accounting

Solutions to Chapter 25 questions

Question 25.2 (a)

	W (£)	B (£)
Materials	24.00 (8 kg at £3)	42.75 (14.25 kg at £3)
Labour	69.76 (21.8 hrs at £3.20)	24.00 (7.5 hrs at £3.20)
	93.76	66.75
Selling price	128.00	95.00
Contribution	34.24	28.25

Let W = number of units of Product W produced
B = number of units of Product B produced
The linear programming model is as follows:

$$\text{Maximise } 34.24W + 28.25B \text{ subject to:}$$
$$4W + 3B \le 1200 \text{ kg processing hours}$$
$$8W + 14.25B \le 4000 \text{ kg (materials)}$$
$$21.8W + 7.5B \le 6000 \text{ labour hours}$$

The above constraints are plotted on the graph shown in Figure Q25.2 as follows:

Processing hours: Line from $W = 300$, $B = 0$ to $B = 400$, $W = 0$
Materials: Line from $W = 500$, $B = 0$ to $B = 281$, $W = 0$
Labour hours: Line from $W = 275$, $B = 0$ to $B = 800$, $W = 0$

The feasible region is area ABCD. The objective function line drawn on the graph is based on an arbitrary selected contribution of £6848 (the contribution if only 200 units of Product W is produced). This contribution can also be obtained if just 242 units (£6848/£28.25 per unit) of Product B are produced.

If the contribution line is extended outwards the optimum point is B on the graph. At this point the output is 155 units of Product W and 194 units of Product B. The optimum point can be determined mathematically by solving the simultaneous equations for the constraints that intersect at point B:

$$8W + 14.25B = 4000$$
$$4W + 3B = 1200$$

The values of W and B when the above equations are solved are 155 for W and 194 for B. This will yield a total contribution of £10 788.

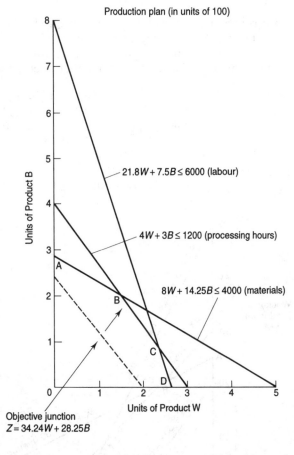

Production plan (in units of 100)

Units of Product B

21.8W + 7.5B ≤ 6000 (labour)

4W + 3B ≤ 1200 (processing hours)

8W + 14.25B ≤ 4000 (materials)

Units of Product W

Objective junction
$Z = 34.24W + 28.25B$

Figure Q25.2

(b) For the answer to this question you should refer to 'Practical problems in applying linear programming' in Chapter 25. In addition, the answer should also include the following points:
  (i) Few production resources are entirely fixed in the short term apart from machine capacity. Steps can often be taken to remove the constraints, such as obtaining materials from alternative sources or increasing machine capacity by working longer hours;
  (ii) A narrow focus has been adopted. Consideration should be given to increasing selling prices to the point where demand is equal to maximum output arising from the current production considerations;

(iii) The approach ignores marketing considerations. Long-term profits might be maximized by concentrating production on one of the products to capture a large market share so that market dominance can be established and more substantial profits obtained;

(iv) Linear programming tends to focus on the short term whereas the emphasis should be on maximizing long-run profits.

Question 25.5 (a) Let X = number of units of XL produced each week
Y = number of units of YM produced each week
Z = total contribution

The linear programming model is:
Maximize $Z = 40X + 30Y$ (product contributions) subject to

$$4X + 4Y \leqslant 120 \text{ (materials constraint)}$$
$$4X + 2Y \leqslant 100 \text{ (labour constraint)}$$
$$X + 2Y \leqslant 50 \text{ (plating constraint)}$$
$$X, Y \geqslant 0$$

The above constraints are plotted on Figure Q25.5. The optimum output is at point C on the graph, indicating that 20 units of XL and 10 units of YM should be produced. The optimum output can be determined exactly by solving the simultaneous equations for the constraints that intersect at point C:

$$4X + 4Y = 120$$
$$4X + 2Y = 100$$

Subtracting
$$2Y = 20$$
$$Y = 10$$

Substituting for Y:

$$4X + 40 = 120$$
$$X = 20$$

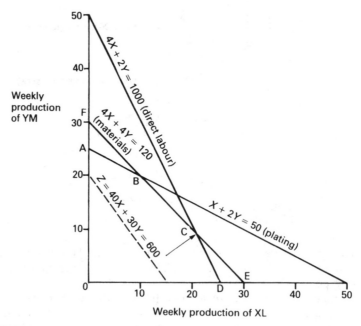

Figure Q25.5

The maximum weekly profit is:

$$(20 \times £40) + (10 \times £30) - £700 \text{ fixed costs} = £400$$

(b) The present objective function is $40X + 30Y$ and the gradient of this line is $-40/30$. If the selling price of YM were increased, the contribution of YM would increase and the gradient of the line ($-40/30$) would decrease. The current optimal point is C because the gradient of the objective function line is greater than the gradient of the line for the constraint of materials (the line on which the optimal point C falls). If the gradient of the objective function line were equal to the gradient of the line for the materials constraint, the optimal solution would be any point on FC. The gradient for the materials constraint line is -1. If the gradient for the objective function line were less than -1, the optimal solution would change from point C to point B. The gradient of the line for the current objective function of $40X + 30Y$ will be greater than -1 as long as the contribution from YM is less than £40. If the contribution from YM is £40 or more, the optimum solution will change. Therefore the maximum selling price for YM is £190 (£150 variable cost + £40 contribution).

(c) If plating time can be sold for £16 per hour then any hour devoted to XLs and YMs loses £16 sales revenue. The relevant cost per plating hour is now £16 opportunity cost. The contributions used in the objective function should be changed to reflect this opportunity cost. The contribution should be reduced by £4 (1 hour at £16 − £12) for XL and by £8 (2 hours at £16 − £12) for YL. The revised objective function is:

$$Z = 36X + 22Y$$

(d) The scarce resources are materials and labour. This is because these two constraints intersect at the optimal point C. Plating is not a scarce resource, and the shadow price is zero.

If we obtain an additional unit of materials the revised constraints will be:

$$4X + 4Y = 121 \text{ (materials)}$$
$$4X + 2Y = 100 \text{ (labour)}$$

The values of X and Y when the above equations are solved at 10.5 for Y and 19.75 for X. Therefore YM is increased by 0.5 units and XL is reduced by 0.25 units and the change in contribution will be as follows:

	(£)
Increase in contribution of YM (0.5 × £30)	15
Decrease in contribution of XL (0.25 × £40)	10
Increase in contribution (shadow price)	5

If we obtain one additional labour hour, the revised constraints will be:

$$4X + 4Y = 120 \text{ (materials)}$$
$$4X + 2Y = 101 \text{ (labour)}$$

The values of X and Y when the above equations are solved are 9.5 for Y and 20.5 for X. Therefore XL is increased by 0.5 units and YM is reduced by 0.5 units, and the change in contribution will be as follows:

	(£)
Increase in contribution from XL (0.5 × £40)	20
Decrease in contribution from YM (0.5 × £30)	15
Increase in contribution (shadow price)	5

The relevant cost of resources used in producing ZN consists of the acquisition cost plus the shadow price (opportunity cost). The relevant cost calculation is:

	(£)
Material A [5 kg at (£10 + £5)]	75
Labour [5 hours at (£8 + £5)]	65
Plating (1 hour at £12)	12
Other variable costs	90
	242

The selling price is less than the relevant cost. Therefore product ZN is not a profitable addition to the product range.

(e) The shadow price of labour is £5 per hour. Therefore the company should be prepared to pay up to £5 in excess of the current rate of £8 in order to remove the constraint. An overtime payment involves an extra £4 per hour, and therefore overtime working is worthwhile.

Increasing direct labour hours will result in the labour constraint shifting to the right. However, when the labour constraint line reaches point E, further increases in labour will not enable output to be expanded (this is because other constraints will be binding). The new optimal product mix will be at point E, with an output of 30 units of XL and zero of YM. This product mix requires 120 hours (30 × 4 hrs). Therefore 120 labour hours will be worked each week. Note that profit will increase by £20 [20 × (£5 − £4)].

(f) The limitations are as follows:

(i) It is assumed that the objective function and the constraints are linear functions of the two variables. In practice, stepped fixed costs might exist or resources might not be used at a constant rate throughout the entire output range. Selling prices might have to be reduced to increase sales volume.

(ii) Constraints are unlikely to be completely fixed and as precise as implied in the mathematical model. Some constraints can be removed at an additional cost.

(iii) The output of the model is dependent on the accuracy of the estimates used. In practice, it is difficult to segregate costs accurately into their fixed and variable elements.

(iv) Divisibility of output is not realistic in practice (fractions of products cannot be produced). This problem can be overcome by the use of integer programming.

(v) The graphical approach requires that only two variables (products) be considered. If several products compete for scarce resources, it will be necessary to use the Simplex method.

(vi) Qualitative factors are not considered. For example, if overtime is paid, the optimum solution is to produce zero of product YM. This will result in the demand from regular customers for YM (who might also buy XM) not being met. This harmful effect on customer goodwill is not reflected in the model.

Question 25.6 (a) The calculations of the product contributions are:

	Private (£)	Commercial (£)
Selling price	2400	3200
Material[a]	(200)	(250)
Direct labour	(90)	(108)
Variable production costs	(250)	(312)
Contribution	1860	2530

Note
[a]The contribution should reflect the additional cash flow contribution from selling an extra roll. The material costs given in the question represent sunk costs and are not relevant costs to be included in the contribution calculation. The relevant

cost of materials is the lost sales value of £1 per lb of wool or nylon (that is, 200 lb at £1 for private use and 250 × £1 for commercial use).

Let X = number of rolls of private use
Let Y = number of rolls of commercial use

Then the linear programming formulation is:

Maximize $1860X + 2530Y$ subject to
$$40X + 200Y \leqslant 24\ 000 \text{ (wool constraint)}$$
$$160X + 50Y \leqslant 25\ 000 \text{ (nylon constraint)}$$
$$30X + 36Y \leqslant 6\ 600 \text{ (machine time constraint)}$$
$$X \geqslant 0$$
$$Y \geqslant 0$$

The above constraints are plotted on the graph in Figure Q25.6 as follows:

Wool constraint: line from $X = 600$, $Y = 0$ to $Y = 120$, $X = 0$
Nylon constraint: line from $X = 156.25$, $Y = 0$ to $Y = 500$, $X = 0$
Capacity constraint: line from $X = 220$, $Y = 0$ to $Y = 183.33$, $X = 0$

At the optimum point (B in the graph) the output mix is 100 rolls for private use and 100 rolls for business use. The optimum point can be determined mathematically by solving the simultaneous equations for the constraints that intersect at point B:

$$30X + 36Y = 6\ 600$$
$$40X + 200Y = 24\ 000$$

The values of X and Y when the above equations are solved are 100 for X and 100 for Y. The optimum output requires 24 000 lb of wool to be used but only 21 000 lb of nylon. Therefore 4000 lb of nylon will be sold off at £1 per lb. The total contribution for the quarter is:

	(£)
Rolls for private use (100 × £1600)	160 000
Rolls for commercial use (100 × £1980)	198 000
Loss on sale of nylon [4000 × (£2 − £1)]	(4 000)
	354 000

The above calculation reflects the contribution that would be shown in the accounting statements using accrual accounting. Alternatively, the contribution can be calculated using the relevant cost approach. This alternative contribution calculation reflects the additional contribution over and above that which would be obtained from the alternative use of materials.

(b) If the variable costs increase then the contribution will decline by £110 for private sales and £40 for commercial sales. The revised contribution will be:

$$Z = 1750X + 2490Y$$

You will find that the gradient of the revised objective function line is such that the optimal point remains unchanged, and therefore the optimal output remains the same.

(c) The scarce resources are machine hours and wool. This is because these two constraints intersect at the optimum point B. If an additional machine hour were obtained, the binding constraints would become:

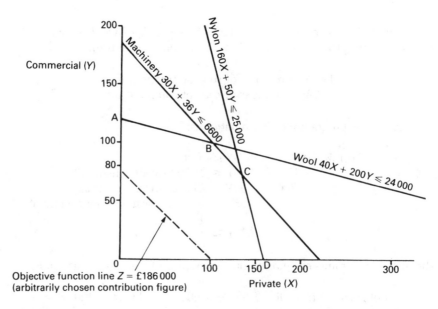

Objective function line Z = £186 000
(arbitrarily chosen contribution figure)

Figure Q25.6

Wool	$40X + 200Y = 24\ 000$
Machine capacity	$30X + 36Y = 6\ 601$

The value of X and Y when the above equations are solved are 100.04 for X and 99.99 for Y. Therefore X increases by 0.04 rolls and Y decreases by 0.01 rolls, and the change in contribution will be as follows:

	(£)
Increase in contribution of X (0.04 × £1860)	74.40
Decrease in contribution of Y (0.01 × £2530)	25.30
Increase in contribution	49.10

If an additional lb of wool were obtained, the optimal solution would change such that X should be decreased by 0.01 rolls and Y increased by 0.01 rolls. Contribution would increase by £6.70.

(d) The answer should stress the advantages of valuing variances at opportunity cost (i.e. relevant cost) rather than acquisition cost. For a detailed explanation of the opportunity cost approach see 'A relevant cost approach to variance analysis' in Chapter 20. The answer should also include a discussion of the limitation placed on opportunity costs because of the limitations of linear programming. The limitations include:
 (i) Linearity is assumed. In practice, stepped fixed costs might exist or resources might not be used at a constant rate throughout the entire output range. Selling prices might have to be reduced to increase volume.
 (ii) The output of the model is dependent on the accuracy of the estimates used. In practice, it is difficult to segregate costs into their fixed and variable elements.
 (iii) The objective function must be quantifiable and not of a qualitative nature.
 (iv) Constraints are unlikely to be as completely fixed and precise as implied in the mathematical model. Some constraints can be removed at an additional cost.

Question 25.8 (a) It is assumed that sales demand for Alpha is restricted to 200 units.

$$\text{Maximize } 400x_1 + 200x_2 + 300x_3$$
$$\text{Subject to: } 2x_1 + 3x_2 + 2.5x_3 \leqslant 1920 \text{ (Process 1)}$$

$$3x_1 + 2x_2 + 2x_3 \leqslant 2200 \text{ (Process 2)}$$
$$x_1 \leqslant 200 \text{ (Alpha sales)}$$
$$x_1, x_2, x_3 \geqslant 0 \text{ (Minimum sales constraint)}$$

(b)

	x_1	x_2	x_3
$x_4 = 1920$	-2	-3	-2.5
$x_5 = 2200$	-3	-2	-2
$x_6 = 200$	-1	0	0
$Z = 0$	$+400$	$+200$	$+300$

Slack variables represent unused resources and unused sales potential.

(c) There are several ways of formulating the tableau for a linear programming model. The tableau given in the question can be reproduced as follows:

		x_3	x_4	x_6
x_2	506.7	-0.83	-0.33	0.67
x_5	586.7	-0.33	0.67	1.67
x_1	200	0	0	-1
Z	181 333.3	-66.67	-66.67	266.7

In Chapter 25 the approach adopted was to formulate the first tableau with positive contribution signs and negative signs for the slack variable equations. The optimal solution occurs when the signs in the contribution row are all negative. The opposite procedure has been applied with the tableau presented in the question. Therefore the signs have been reversed in the above tableau in order to ensure that it is in the same format as that presented in Chapter 25. Note that an entry of 1 in the tableau presented in the question signifies the product or slack variable that is to be entered in each row of the above tableau.

The total contribution is £181 333.3, consisting of 200 units of Alpha and 506.7 units of Beta. Process 1 (x_4) is fully utilized, but 586.7 hours (x_5) of Process 2 are unused. There is no unused sales demand for Alpha. The Z row (contribution row) indicates the shadow prices. The shadow price of £66.67 for Gamma (x_3) indicates that contribution will decline by £66.67 for each unit of Gamma produced. The shadow price of £66.67 for Process 1 (x_4) indicates that for each additional hour of Process 1 contribution would increase by £66.67. This would be achieved by increasing output of Beta by 0.33 units, and the effect of this would be to reduce Process 2 capacity by 0.67 hrs. The shadow price of £266.7 for Alpha (i.e. the slack variable) implies that for every Alpha sale above 200 units contribution would increase by £266.7. In order to produce one unit of Alpha, output of Beta will be reduced by 0.67 units, thus releasing the 2 hrs (0.67×3 hrs) required for Alpha in Process 1. This substitution process will result in a decline of 1.67 hrs in Process 2.

(d) The optimal responses are indicated in the final tableau:

   (i) Increase output of Beta by 6.66 units (20×0.33) at a contribution of £200 per unit. Therefore total contribution will increase by £1332 to £182 665.7. Alternatively, the change in contribution can be obtained by multiplying the 20 additional hours by the shadow price of £66.67.

   (ii) This will increase total contribution by £2667 (10 units × £266.7 shadow price). In order to produce an additional unit of Alpha, the output of Beta must be reduced by 6.7 units (10×0.67). This will release 20 hours (6.7 units × 3 hrs for Beta) in Process 1, which are required to produce the 10 units of Alpha (10×2 hrs). This substitution process requires 16.7 Process 2 hours, and results in a £2667 increase in total contribution (10 units of Alpha at £400 per unit less 6.7 units of Beta at £200 per unit).

   (iii) Total contribution will be reduced by £666.7 (10 units × £66.7 shadow price). In order to obtain the hours required to produce Gamma in Process 1, the output of Beta must be reduced by 8.3 units (0.83 × 10 units required for Gamma). This will release 25 hrs (8.3 × 3 hrs) in Process 1, which is required to produce 10 units (10 × 2.5 hrs) of Gamma. This substitution process will reduce Process 2 unused capacity by 3.3 hrs and reduce total contribution by £666.7 (10 units of Gamma at £100 per unit less 8.3 units of Beta at £200 per unit).

Question 25.9 (a)

	Product 1	Product 2	Product 3	Total
Maximum sales value (£)	57 500	96 000	125 000	
Unit selling price (£)	23	32	25	
Maximum demand (units)	2 500	3 000	5 000	
Hours required on type A machine	2 500 (2500 × 1)	6 000 (3000 × 2)	15 000 (5000 × 3)	23 500
Hours required on type B machine	3 750 (2500 × 1½)	9 000 (3000 × 3)	5 000 (5000 × 1)	17 750

We now compare the machine capacity available with the machine hours required to meet the maximum sales so as to determine whether or not production is a limiting factor.

	Machine type A	Machine type B
Hours required (see above)	23 500	17 750
Hours available	9 800	21 000

Because hours required are in excess of hours available for machine type A, but not for machine type B, it follows that machine type A is the limiting factor. Following the approach illustrated in Example 11.4 in Chapter 11, we calculate the contribution per limiting factor. The calculations are as follows:

	Product 1	Product 2	Product 3
Unit contribution (£)	5	7	8
Contribution per hour of type A machine time (£)	5 (5/1)	3.50 (7/2)	2.67 (8/3)
Ranking	1	2	3

The optimal allocation of type A machine hours based on the above ranking is as follows:

Production	Machine hours used	Balance of machine hours available
2500 units of product 1	2500	7300 (9800–2500)
3000 units of product 2	6000	1300 (7300–6000)
433 units of product 3	1300	—

The 433 units of product 3 are obtained by dividing the 1300 unused machine hours by the 3 machine hours required for each unit of product 3. The proposed production programme results in the following calculation of total profit:

	(£)
2500 units of product 1 at £5 per unit contribution	12 500
3000 units of product 2 at £7 per unit contribution	21 000
433 units of product 3 at £8 per unit contribution	3 464
Total contribution	36 964
Less fixed overheads	21 000
Profit	15 964

(b) There are several ways of formulating the tableau for a linear programming model. The tableau from the computer package can be reproduced as follows:

	Quantity	S1	S4	S5
S2	1150	−0.5	−0.143	0.429
X2	1850	0.5	0.143	−0.429
S3	3800		0.429	−0.286
X3	1200		−0.429	0.286
X1	2500	−1	0	0
C	35 050	−1.5	−2.429	−0.714

In Chapter 25 the approach adopted was to formulate the first tableau with positive contribution signs and negative signs for the slack variable equations. The optimal solution occurs when the signs in the contribution row are all negative. The opposite procedure has been applied with the tableau presented in the question. Therefore the signs have been reversed in the above tableau to ensure that it is in the same format as that presented in Chapter 25. Note that an entry of 1 in the tableau presented in the question signifies the product or slack variable that is to be entered in each row of the above tableau.

The total contribution is £35 050, consisting of:

2500 units of product 1 at a contribution of £5 per unit
1850 units of product 2 at a contribution of £7 per unit
1200 units of product 3 at a contribution of £8 per unit

The revised fixed overheads are £18 000, resulting in a total profit of £17 050. This is higher than the profit before the fire (£15 964) because the fixed overheads saved by the fire exceed the lost contribution.

The shadow prices (or opportunity costs) for S4 indicate that if an additional type A machine hour can be acquired then profits will increase by £2.429 by increasing production of product 3 by 0.429 units and reducing production of product 2 by 0.143 units. Similarly, if an additional Type B machine hour can be acquired, then profits will increase by £0.714 by increasing production of product 2 by 0.429 units and reducing production of product 3 by 0.286 units. An extra unit of demand for product 1 will yield a contribution of £5, but, in order to obtain the resources, it is necessary to sacrifice half a unit of product 2. This will result in a loss of contribution of £3.50 ($\frac{1}{2}$ × £7). Therefore the net gain is £1.50.

The shadow prices indicate the premium over and above the present acquisition costs that the company should be willing to pay in order to obtain extra hours of machine time. The shadow price for product 1 indicates the upper limit to advertising or promotional expenses that should be incurred in order to stimulate demand by one further unit.

(c) In part A there was only one limiting factor. In Chapter 25 we noted that the optimal solution can be derived by using the contribution per key factor approach whenever there is only one production constraint. Where more than one limiting factor exists then it is necessary to use linear programming to determine the optimal production programme.

Question 25.11

(a) The calculation of the contributions for each product is:

	X1	X2	X3
	(£)	(£)	(£)
Selling price	83	81	81
Materials[a]	(51)	(45)	(54)
Manufacturing costs[b]	(11)	(11)	(11)
Contribution	21	25	16

Notes
[a]The material cost per tonne for each product is:

$$X1 = (0.1 \times £150) + (0.1 \times £60) + (0.2 \times £120) + (0.6 \times £10) = £51$$
$$X2 = (0.1 \times £150) + (0.2 \times £60) + (0.1 \times £120) + (0.6 \times £10) = £45$$
$$X3 = (0.2 \times £150) + (0.1 \times £60) + (0.1 \times £120) + (0.6 \times £10) = £54$$

[b]It is assumed that manufacturing costs do not include any fixed costs. The initial linear programming model is as follows:

Maximize $Z = 21X1 + 25X2 + 16X3$
subject to $0.1X1 + 0.1X2 + 0.2X3 \leqslant 1200$ (nitrate)
$0.1X1 + 0.2X2 + 0.1X3 \leqslant 2000$ (phosphate)
$0.2X1 + 0.1X2 + 0.1X3 \leqslant 2200$ (potash)
$X1, X2, X3 \geqslant 0$

(b) The slack variables are introduced to represent the amount of each of the scarce resources unused at the point of optimality. This enables the constraints to be expressed in equalities. The initial Simplex tableau is:

	X1	X2	X3
X4 (nitrate) = 1200	−0.1	−0.1	−0.2
X5 (phosphate) = 2000	−0.1	−0.2	−0.1
X6 (potash) = 2200	−0.2	−0.1	−0.1
Z (contribution)= 0	21	25	16

(c) The starting point for the first iteration is to select the product with the highest contribution (that is, X2), but production of X2 is limited because of the input constraints. Nitrate (X4) limits us to a maximum production of 12 000 tonnes (1200/0.1), X5 to a maximum production of 10 000 tonnes (2000/0.2) and X6 to a maximum production of 22 000 tonnes (2200/0.1). We are therefore restricted to a maximum production of 10 000 tonnes of product X2 because of the X5 constraint. The procedure which we should follow is to rearrange the equation that results in the constraint (that is, X5) in terms of the product we have chosen to make (that is, X2). Therefore the X5 equation is re-expressed in terms of X2, and X5 will be replaced in the second iteration by X2. (Refer to 'Choosing the product' in Chapter 25 if you are unsure of this procedure.) Thus X2 is the entering variable and X5 is the leaving variable.

(d) Following the procedure outlined in Chapter 25, the final tableau given in the question can be reproduced as follow:

	Quantity	X3	X4	X5
X1	4000	−3	−20	+10
X2	8000	+1	+10	−10
X6	600	+0.4	+3	−1
Z	284 000	−22	−170	−40

In Chapter 25 the approach adopted was to formulate the first tableau with positive contribution signs and negative signs for the slack variable equations. The optimal solution occurs when the signs in the contribution row are all negative. The opposite procedure has been applied with the tableau presented in the question. Therefore the signs have been reversed in the above tableau to ensure it is in the same format as that presented in Chapter 25. Note that when an entry of 1 is shown in a row or column for a particular product or slack variable then the entry does not appear in the above tableau. For example, X1 has an entry of 1 for the X1 row and X1 column. These cancel out and the entry is not made in the above tableau. Similarly, an entry of 1 is omitted in respect of X2 and X6.

The optimum solution is to produce 4000 tonnes of X1, 8000 tonnes of X2 and zero X3 each month. This gives a monthly contribution of £284 000, uses all the nitrate (X4) and phosphate (X5), but leaves 600 tonnes of potash (X6) unused.

The opportunity costs of the scarce resources are:

$$\text{Nitrate } (X4) \qquad £170 \text{ per tonne}$$
$$\text{Phosphate } (X5) \qquad £40 \text{ per tonne}$$

If we can obtain an additional tonne of nitrate then output of $X1$ should be increased by 20 tonnes and output of $X2$ should be reduced by 10 tonnes.

Note that we reverse the signs when additional resources are obtained. The effect of this substitution process on each of the resources and contribution is follows:

	Nitrate $(X4)$ (tonnes)	Phosphate $(X5)$ (tonnes)	Potash $(X6)$ (tonnes)	Contribution $(£)$
Increase $X1$ by 20 tonnes	$-2(20 \times 0.1)$	-2	-4	$+420$
Reduce $X2$ by 10 tonnes	$+1(10 \times 0.1)$	$+2$	$+1$	-250
Net effect	-1	0	-3	$+170$

The net effect agrees with the $X4$ column in the final tableau. That is, the substitution process will use up exactly the one additional tonne of nitrate, 3 tonnes of unused resources of potash and increase contribution by £170.

To sell one unit of $X3$, we obtain the resources by reducing the output of $X1$ by 3 tonnes and increasing the output of $X2$ by 1 tonne. (Note the signs are not reversed, because we are not obtaining additional scarce resources.) The effect of this substitution process is to reduce contribution by £22 for each tonne of $X3$ produced. The calculation is as follows:

$$\text{Increase } X3 \text{ by 1 tonne} = +£16 \text{ contribution}$$
$$\text{Increase } X2 \text{ by 1 tonne} = +£25 \text{ contribution}$$

$$\text{Reduce } X1 \text{ by 3 tonnes} = -£63$$
$$\text{Loss of contribution} \quad = -£22$$

(e) (i) Using the substitution process outlined in (d), the new values if 100 extra tonnes of nitrate are obtained will be:

$$X1 \ 4000 + (20 \times 100) = 6000$$
$$X2 \ 8000 - (10 \times 100) = 7000$$
$$X6 \ 600 - (3 \times 100) = 300$$
$$\text{Contribution } 284\,000 + (£170 \times 100) = £301\,000$$

Hence the new optimal solution is to make 6000 tonnes of $X1$ and 7000 tonnes of $X2$ per month, and this output will yield a contribution of £301 000.

(ii) Using the substitution process outlined in (d), the new values if 200 tonnes per month of $X3$ are supplied will be:

$$X1 \ 4000 - (3 \times 200) \quad = 3400$$
$$X2 \ 8000 + (1 \times 200) \quad = 8200$$
$$X6 \ 600 + (0.4 \times 200) = 680$$
$$X3 \quad 0 + (1 \times 200) \quad = 200$$
$$\text{Contribution } £284\,000 - (£22 \times 200) = 279\,600$$

Hence the new optimal solution is to produce 3400 tonnes of $X1$, 8200 tonnes of $X2$ and 200 tonnes of $X3$, and this output will yield a contribution of £279 600. (Note that the signs in the final tableau are only reversed when *additional* scarce *resources* are obtained.)

(a)   Let a = proportion of project A undertaken
       b = proportion of project B undertaken

Question 25.14

$$c = \text{proportion of project C undertaken}$$
$$d = \text{proportion of project D undertaken}$$
$$e = \text{proportion of project E undertaken}$$
$$f = \text{proportion of project F undertaken}$$
$$s_0 = \text{Amount invested in rival company at time 0}$$
$$s_1 = \text{Amount invested in rival company at time 1}$$

The linear programming model is as follows:

Maximize $0.36a + 0.34b + 0.31c + 0.34d + 0.39e + 0.56f$
Subject to $2a + 0.5b + 2.2c + 4d + 1.4e + s_0 \leqslant 5$ (Time 0 cash constraint)
$3.2b + 0.8c + 3f + s_1 \leqslant 2.5 + 1.15s_0 + 0.8a + 0.5c + 1.1d$
(Time 1 cash constraint)
$3000a + 4000e \leqslant 5000$ (Special component constraint)
$a, b, c, d, e, f \leqslant 1$ (Maximum investment constraint)
$a, b, c, d, e, f, s_0, s_1 \geqslant 0$ (Non-negativity constraint)

Note that the NPV from a cash investment in a rival company can be ignored since the cost of capital is equal to the return on investment. Thus cash investments will yield a zero NPV.

(b) The linear programming process will provide information on:
1. The project mix that will maximize NPV subject to the constraints.
2. Which constraints are limiting and which are not limiting.
3. The opportunity costs of scarce funds.
For an explanation of how the information can be used see 'The uses of linear programming in capital budgeting' in Chapter 25.

Question 25.15 (a) Let a, b, c, d, e, f and g represent the proportion of projects A, B, C, D, E, F and G accepted and X represent the amount of money placed on deposit in 1989 in £000. The NPV of £1000 placed on deposit is:

$$\frac{£1000(1.08)}{1.10} - £1000 = -£18 = £-0.018 \text{ (in £000)}$$

Maximize $Z = 39a + 35b + 5c + 15d + 14e + 32f + 24g - 0.018X$
subject to $80a + 70b + 55c + 60d + X + \text{DIV0} \leqslant 250$ (1989 constraint in £000)
$30a + 140e + 80f + 100g + \text{DIV1} \leqslant 150 + 20b + 40c + 30d + 1.08X$
(1990 constraint in £000)
$\text{DIV0} \geqslant 100$
$\text{DIV1} \geqslant 1.05 \text{ DIV0}$
$a, b, c, d, e, f, g \geqslant 0$
$a, b, c, d, e, f, g \leqslant 1$

Note that surplus funds are placed on deposit only for 1989. After 1991, capital is available without limit. Consequently, it is assumed at 1990 that it is unnecessary to maintain funds for future periods by placing funds on deposit to yield a negative NPV. It is assumed that capital constraints can be eased by project generated cash flows.

(b) The dual or shadow prices indicate the opportunity costs of the budget constraints for 1989 and 1990. The dual values indicate the NPV that can be gained from obtaining an additional £1 cash for investment in 1989 and 1990. The zero dual value for 1990 indicates that the availability of cash is not a binding constraint in 1990, whereas in 1989 the dual value indicates that £1 additional cash for investment in 1989 will yield an increase in total NPV of £0.25.

The dual values also indicate how much it is worth paying over and above the existing cost of funds. In this question it is worth paying up to £0.25 over and above the existing cost of capital for each £1 invested in 1989. In other words, the company should be prepared to pay up to 35% (10% acquisition cost + 25% opportunity cost) to raise additional finance in 1989.

Dual values can also be used to appraise any investments that might be suggested as substitutes for projects A to G. If the company identifies another project with a life of one year and a cash outflow of £130 000 at t_0 and an inflow of £150 000 at t_1, the NPV would be £3364 at a cost of capital of 10%. However, acceptance of the project would result in a reduction in NPVs from diverting funds from other projects of £32 500 (£130 000 × £0.25). The project should therefore be rejected.

Dual values are not constant for an infinite range of resources. They apply only over a certain range. The question indicates that the values apply over a range between £120 000 and £180 000. Outside this range, it will be necessary to develop a revised model to ascertain the dual values that would be applicable. If resources continued to be increased, a point would be reached at which all potential projects with positive NPVs would have been accepted. Beyond this point, there would be no binding constraints and capital rationing would cease to exist.

(c) Capital rationing can be defined as a situation where there are insufficient funds available to undertake all those projects that yield a positive NPV. The literature distinguishes between hard and soft capital rationing. Hard capital rationing refers to those situations where firms do not have access to investment funds and are therefore unable to raise any additional finance at any price. It is most unlikely that firms will be subject to hard capital rationing.

Soft capital rationing refers to those situations where capital rationing is internally imposed. For various reasons, top management may pursue a policy of limiting the amount of funds available for investment in any one period. Such policies may apply to firms that restrict their financing of new investments to internal funds. Alternatively, in a large divisionalized company, top management may limit the funds available to divisional managers for investment. Such restrictions on available funds may be for various reasons. For example, a company may impose its own restrictions on borrowing limits or avoid new equity issues because of a fear of outsiders gaining control of the business.

Where capital rationing exists, the NPV rule of accepting *all* positive NPV projects must be modified. Where capital is rationed for a single period, the approach outlined in Chapter 16 (see 'Capital rationing') should be applied. Where capital is rationed for more than one period, the optimal investment plan requires the use of mathematical programming (see Chapter 25). The application of the latter is based on a number of underlying assumptions that are unlikely to hold in the real world. For a discussion of these assumptions see 'Practical problems in applying linear programming' in Chapter 25.

(a) Let x_1 = proportion of project A undertaken

Question 25.16

x_2 = proportion of project B undertaken
x_3 = proportion of project C undertaken
x_4 = proportion of project D undertaken
x_5 = proportion of project E undertaken
x_6 = cash unused at time 1 and carried forward to time 2
x_7 = cash unused at time 2 and carried forward to time 3

The linear programming model is as follows:

Maximize $x_1 + 0.8x_2 - 0.6x_3 + 3x_4 + 0.7x_5$
subject to

$7x_1 + 6x_2 + 2x_3$	≤ 12 (time 0 cash available)
$-1.5x_1 - 2x_2 - 4x_3 + 8x_4 \quad + x_6$	≤ 2 (time 1 cash available)[a]
$-2x_1 - x_2 + 0.5x_3 + 2x_4 + 3x_5 \quad + x_7$	$\leq 1.08x_6$ (time 2 cash available)[b]
$-2x_1 - x_2 + 2x_3 + x_4 - x_5$	$\leq 1.08x_7$ (time 3 cash available)[c]
$0.6x_1 + 0.8x_2 - 0.1x_3$	$+ 10 \geq 11$ (year 1 profit constraint)[d]
$0.6x_1 + 0.3x_2 - 0.2x_3 - 0.3x_4$	$+ 12 \geq (0.6x_1 + 0.8x_2 - 0.1x_3 + 10)$

$$1.4x1 + 0.8x_2 - 0.3x_3 - 0.2x_4 + 1.5x_5 \quad +11 \geqslant (0.6x_1 + 0.3x_2 - 0.2x_3 - 0.3x_4 + 12) \times 1.1$$

× 1.1 (year 2 profit constraint: year 1 profit plus 10%)

(year 3 profit constraint: year 2 profit + 10%)

$x_1, x_2, x_3, x_4, x_5, x_6, 7 \geqslant 0$ (non-negativity constraint)

$x_1, x_2, x_3, x_4, x_5 \leqslant 1$ (maximum investment constraint)

An alternative presentation is to transfer the negative items that are listed to the left of the ≤ sign to the right of the sign. These variables will now be entered as positive items.

Notes		(£m)
[a]Time 1 cash available = New equity		7.5
	Less loan repayment	5.5
		2.0

[b]Time 2 cash available = unused cash at time 1 plus interest.
[c]Time 3 cash available = unused cash at time 2 plus interest.
[d]Minimum profit target = £10m + 10% = £11m.

(b) It may be rational in the following circumstances to undertake a project with a negative NPV:
  (i) Where the qualitative factors outweigh the negative NPV. For example, the building of a works canteen or the provision of recreational facilities for employees.
  (ii) A project with a negative NPV that provides large cash inflows in the early years, thus enabling an additional project to be accepted with an NPV in excess of the negative NPV of the first project.

(c) *Merits of mathematical programming*
  (i) Ability to solve complex problems incorporating the effects of complex interactions.
  (ii) Speed in solving the problem using computer facilities.
  (iii) The output from the model can highlight the key constraints to which attention should be directed.
  (iv) Sensitivity analysis can be applied. The effects of changes in the variables can be speedily tested.

Limitations of mathematical programming
  (i) Divisibility of projects may not be realistic and integer programming may have to be used.
  (ii) Constraints are unlikely to be completely fixed and as precise as implied in the mathematical models.
  (iii) Not all the relevant information can be quantified.
  (iv) All the information for the model may not be available. For example, it may not be possible precisely to specify the constraints of future periods.
  (v) All the relationships contained within the formulation may not be linear.
  (vi) All the potential investment opportunities may not be identified and included in the analysis.
  (vii) The linear programming formulation assumes that all the project's cash flows are certain and therefore it cannot incorporate uncertainty. The solution produced can only be considered optimal given this restrictive assumption.

Measuring divisional profitability

Solutions to Chapter 26 questions

Question summary

26.1–26.12 Various discussion questions relating to topics covered in Chapter 26.

26.13–26.15 Calculation of divisional ROCE/RI for various transactions and a discussion as to whether the divisional ROCE/RI measures will encourage goal congruence. These questions require NPV calculations and a comparison with RI and ROCE performance measures. Question 26.15 also requires a discussion of how the conflict between the capital investment decision model and the performance evaluation model can be resolved.

26.16 Merits and problems associated with three proposed divisional performance measures.

26.17 Inter-service department allocations adopting the approaches outlined in Chapter 5, discussion of appropriate activity measures for allocating service department costs, and a discussion of the arguments for and against the allocation of costs for evaluating profit centre managerial and economic performance.

26.18 Calculation of ROI and RI and a discussion of the conflict between decision-making and performance evaluation.

26.19 Discussion of the role of RI and ROCE in evaluating divisional performance and also how to deal with head office costs when measuring divisional performance.

26.20 Calculation of the performance-related salaries of divisional managers and the recommendation of an alternative improved system.

26.21 Discussion of suitable measures of performance for each of the stated goals of an organization that has multiple goals.

26.22 Performance reporting and a discussion of the key measurement issues in a recently incorporated power company.

26.23 Discussion on the impact on performance measures arising from a change from historical cost to current cost asset valuation.

26.24–26.26 Calculation and comparison of RI and ROCE based on conventional depreciation methods and the annuity method and a comparison with the NPV decision rule.

26.27 Discussion question on a range of topics relating to divisional performance evaluation.

Questions 18.22–18.25 in Chapter 18 are also relevant to this chapter.

Question 26.1

(a) If divisional budgets are set by a central planning department and imposed on divisional managers then it is true that divisional independence is pseudo-independence. However, if budget guidelines and goals are set by the central planning department and divisional managers are given a large degree of freedom in the setting of budgets and conduct of operations then it is incorrect to claim that pseudo-independence exists.

    One of the reasons for creating a divisionalized organization structure is to improve motivation by the delegation of responsibility to divisional managers, thus giving them greater freedom over the control of their activities. Nevertheless, complete independence cannot be granted, since this would destroy the very idea that divisions are an integral part of a single business. The granting of freedom to divisions in conducting their operations can be allowed only if certain limits are applied within which that freedom can be exercised. This normally takes the form of the presentation of budgets by divisions to corporate management for approval. By adopting this approach, divisions pay a modest price for the extensive powers of decentralized decision-making.

As long as budgets are not imposed by the central planning department, and divisions are allowed to determine their own budgets within the guidelines set, then divisional managers will have greater independence than the managers of centralized organizations.

(b) The answer should consist of a discussion of divisional profit, return on capital employed and residual income. A discussion of each of these items is presented in Chapter 26.

Question 26.4 (a) Examples of the types of decisions that should be transferred to the new divisional managers include:
- (i) Product decisions such as product mix, promotion and pricing.
- (ii) Employment decisions, except perhaps for the appointment of senior managers.
- (iii) Short-term operating decisions of all kinds. Examples include production scheduling, subcontracting and direction of marketing effort.
- (iv) Capital expenditure and disinvestment decisions (with some constraints).
- (v) Short-term financing decisions (with some constraints).

(b) The following decisions might be retained at company head office:
- (i) Strategic investment decisions that are critical to the survival of the company as a whole.
- (ii) Certain financing decisions that require that an overall view be taken. For example, borrowing commitments and the level of financial gearing should be determined for the group as a whole.
- (iii) Appointment of top management.
- (iv) Sourcing decisions such as bulk buying of raw materials if corporate interests are best served by centralized buying.
- (v) Capital expenditure decisions above certain limits.
- (vi) Common services that are required by all profit centres. Corporate interests might best be served by operating centralized service departments such as an industrial relations department. Possible benefits include reduced costs and the extra benefits of specialization.
- (vii) Arbitration decisions on transfer pricing disputes.
- (viii) Decisions on items which benefit the company rather than an individual division, e.g. taxation and computer applications.

(c) The answer to this question should focus on the importance of designing performance reports which encourage goal congruence. For a discussion of this topic see Chapter 26.

Question 26.10 (a) The following factors should be considered:
- (i) *Definition of profit*: The question states that the measure should be used for performance measurement. It is therefore necessary to define 'controllable profit' for the companies. Clearly, apportionment of group headquarters expenditure should be excluded from the calculation of controllable profit. If investment decisions are made by the companies then depreciation should be included as a controllable expense. Otherwise, companies can increase controllable profit by substituting capital equipment for direct labour when this is not in the best interest of the group as a whole.
- (ii) *Definition of capital employed*: There are many different definitions of capital

employed, and it is important that the same basis of measurement be used for comparing the performance of the different companies. Capital employed might be defined as total assets or net assets. All assets that are controlled by the companies should be included in the valuation. If debtors are controlled by the companies but not included in the capital employed then there is a danger that managers rnight lengthen the credit period to increase sales even when this is not in the best interests of the group. The benefits from the increased credit period accrue to the companies, but the increased investment is not reflected in the capital employed.

(iii) *Valuation of capital employed*: Capital employed can be valued on an historical cost basis, or an alternative method such as replacement cost might be used. If historical cost is used then assets might be valued at written-down value or gross value. Both approaches can result in misleading comparisons. If written-down value is used then an asset that yields a constant profit will show an annual increase in ROCE because the written-down value will decline over the asset's life. Therefore those companies with old assets and low written-down values might incorrectly show higher ROCE calculations. For a more detailed discussion of this topic see 'Valuation of controllable investment' in Chapter 26.

(iv) *Alternative accounting methods*: For comparisons, it is important that the same accounting methods be applied to all companies within the group. For example, one company may capitalize major expense items such as advertising, lease rentals, and research and development expenditure, whereas another company might not capitalize these items. For example, if company A capitalizes lease payments and company B does not then the accounting treatment will result in the capital employed of company B being understated and consequently ROCE overstated.

(b) A single ROCE might not be an adequate measure because:

(i) Companies operate in different industries and a single ROCE measure might not give an adequate measure of performance. For example, if companies A and B have ROCEs of 20% and 10%, respectively, one might conclude that company A has produced the better performance. However, the industry ROCEs might be 25% for the industry in which A operates and 5% for the industry in which B operates. Relative to industry performance, company B has performed better than company A. The ROCE should therefore be compared with other companies and supplemented by other measures such as percentage market shares

(ii) Companies with a high existing ROCE might reject projects whose returns are in excess of the cost of capital but less than existing ROCE. Such companies might be reluctant to expand and be content with a high ROCE and low absolute profits. The ROCE should be supplemented with a measure of absolute profits (e.g. residual income) and details of investment in new projects. This would indicate whether or not the companies were restricting growth in order to preserve their existing high ROCE.

(iii) Concentration on short-run ROCE at the expense of long-run profitability. For an illustration of points that could be considered here see 'Use of non-accounting measures' in Chapter 26.

(a) For cost control and performance measurement purposes it is necessary to measure performance at frequent intervals. Managers tend to be evaluated on short-term (monthly, quarterly or even yearly) performance measures such as residual income (RI) or return on investment (ROI). Such short-term performance measures focus only on the performance for the particular control period. lf a great deal of stress is placed on managers meeting short-term performance measure targets, there is a danger that they will take action that will improve short-term performance but that will not maximize long-term profits. For example, by skimping on expenditure on advertising, customer services, maintenance, and training and staff development costs, it is possible to improve

Question 26.11

short-term performance. However, such actions may not maximize long-term profits.

Ideally, performance measures ought to be based on future results that can be expected from a manager's actions during a period. This would involve a comparison of the present value of future cash flows at the start and end of the period, and a manager's performance would be based on the increase in present value during the period. Such a system is not feasible, given the difficulty in predicting and measuring outcomes from current actions.

ROI and RI represent single summary measures of performance. It is virtually impossible to capture in summary financial measures all the variables that measure the success of a manager. It is therefore important that accountants broaden their reporting systems to include additional non-financial measures of performance that give clues to future outcomes from present actions.

It is probably impossible to design performance measures which will ensure that maximizing the short-run performance measure will also maximize long-term performance. Some steps, however, can be taken to improve the short-term performance measures so that they minimize the potential conflict. For example, during times of rising prices, short-term performance measures can be distorted if no attempt is made to adjust for the changing price levels. ROI has a number of deficiencies. In particular, it encourages managers to accept only those investments that are in excess of the current ROI, and this can lead to the rejection of profitable projects. Such actions can be reduced by replacing ROI with RI as the performance measure. However, merely changing from ROI to RI will not eliminate the short-run versus long-run conflicts.

(b) One suggestion that has been made to overcome the conflict between short-term and long-term measures is for accountants to broaden their reporting systems and include non-financial performance measures in the performance reports. For example, obtaining feedback from customers regarding the quality of service encourages managers not to skimp on reducing the quality of service in order to save costs in the short term. For a discussion of the potential contribution from including non-financial measures in the reporting system see 'Use of non-accounting measures' in Chapter 26.

Other suggestions have focused on refining the financial measures so that they will reduce the potential for conflict between actions that improve short-term performance at the expense of long-term performance. For a description of these suggestions see 'The impact of depreciation' and 'The effect of performance measurement on capital investment decisions' in Chapter 26.

Question 26.12 (a) For the answer to this question see 'Return on investment' and 'Residual income' and 'The effect of performance measurement on capital investment decisions' in Chapter 26. Note that discounted future earnings are the equivalent to discounted future profits described in Chapter 26.

(b) The existing ROCE is 20% and the estimated ROCE on the additional investment is 15% (£9000/£60 000). The divisional manager will therefore reject the additional investment, since adding this to the existing investments will result in a decline in the existing ROCE of 20%.

The residual income on the additional investment is £600 (£9000 average profit for the year less an imputed interest charge of 14% × £6000 = £8400). The manager will accept the additional investment, since it results in an increase in residual income.

If the discounted future earnings method is used, the investment would be accepted, since it will yield a positive figure for the year (that is, £9000 × 3.889 discount factor).

Note that the annual future cash flows are £19 000 (£9000 net profit plus £10 000 depreciation provision). The project has a 6-year life. The annual cash inflow must be in excess of £15 428 (£60 000/3.889 annuity factor − 6 years at 14%) if the investment is to yield a positive NPV. If annual cash flows are £19 000 each year for the next 6 years, the project should be accepted.

The residual income and discounted future earnings methods of evaluation will induce the manager to accept the investment. These methods are consistent with the correct economic evaluation using the NPV method. If ROCE is used to evaluate performance, the manager will incorrectly reject the investment. This is because the manager will only accept projects that yield a return in excess of the current ROCE of 20%.

Note that the above analysis assumes that the cash flows/profits are constant from year to year.

right**Question 26.13**

(a) Current budgeted ROCE = 330/(1500 − 720) + 375 = 330/1155 = 28.57%

    (A) Profit − 8

        Current assets − 30

        Revised ROCE = 322/1125   = 28.62%

    (B) Profit + 15

        Current assets + 40

        Revised ROCE = 345/1195   = 28.87%

    (C) Loss on sale (60 WDV − 35 sale proceeds) = (25)

        Loss of profits   = (45)

        Reduced depreciation   = 60

        Net impact on profits   (10)

Note that the above calculation assumes that the £45 000 profit contribution relates to profits before deduction of £60 000 depreciation. If the £45 000 profit is after deduction of depreciation, the £60 000 reduction in depreciation should not be included in the above calculation. It is assumed that capital employed will decline by £60 000 arising from the deletion of the £60 000 WDV of the asset. However, sale proceeds are £35 000, and it could be argued that this will increase capital employed. It is assumed that the £35 000 is remitted to group headquarters, and thus the overall impact of the transaction increases capital employed by £60 000. The revised ROCE is (330 − 10)/(1155 − 60) = 29.22%

    (D) Profit (+52.5 − 36 depreciation)   = +16.5

        Fixed assets (+ 4/5 × 180)   = +144

        Revised ROCE = 346.5/1299   = 26.67%

An alternative assumption is that capital employed would be reduced by a further £180 000 to reflect the cash payment for the asset. It is assumed in the above calculations that group headquarters provides the cash for acquiring the asset.

If divisional managers are evaluated on ROCE, the divisional manager would accept transactions A, B and C since they would result in an increase in ROCE. Transaction D would be rejected because it would result in a lower ROCE.

(b) (i) The evaluation should be based on NPV calculations in order to determine whether or not the non-routine transactions are in the best interests of the group as a whole. The NPV calculations are as follows:

Transaction	Year	Cash inflows (£000)	Cash outflows (£000)	Net cash flow (£000)	Discount factor (15%)	NPV (£000)
A	1	30	(8)	22	0.8696	19.131
	2–4		(8)	(8)	1.9854	(15.883)
						+3.248
B	1	15	(40)	(25)	0.8696	(21.74)
	2–4	15		15	1.9854	29.781
						+8.041

		C		0	35		35	1.000	35.000
				1		(45)	(45)	0.8696	39.132
									−(4.132)
		D		0		(180)	(180)	1.000	(180.000)
				1–5	52.5		52.5	3.352	175.980
									−(4.020)

Transactions A and B yield positive NPVs and should be undertaken, while transactions C and D should be rejected.

There is goal congruence between G Ltd and GAP Group plc in respect of transactions A, B and D, but there is no goal congruence for transaction C.

(ii) The answer should not support the proposal to substitute a ROCE investment criterion in place of DCF techniques for appraising capital projects. In particular, the answer should stress that ROCE ignores the time value of money and the opportunity cost of capital. For a discussion of the limitations of ROCE of an investment appraisal technique see 'Accounting rate of return' in Chapter 15.

Question 26.17 (a) (i) *Direct method of cost allocation*: With the direct method, inter-service department allocations are ignored; service department costs are reapportioned to production departments only:

	Air (£000)	Marine (£000)	Administration (£000)	Maintenance (£000)	Transport (£000)	Total (£000)
Service department costs			390	195	390	975
Administration	274 (94/134)	116 (40/134)	(390)			
Maintenance	124 (7/11)	71 (4/11)		(195)		
Transport	226 (234/404)	164 (170/404)			(390)	
	624	351				975

(ii) *Step-down-method*: This method is the specified order of closing described in Appendix 5.1. The percentages of work provided for other service departments are:

$$\text{Administration} \quad 23.4\% \quad [(15 + 26)/175]$$
$$\text{Maintenance} \quad 21.4\% \quad [(2 + 1)/14]$$
$$\text{Transport} \quad 23.0\% \quad [(90 + 31)/525]$$

Adopting this approach, the order for allocating service department costs is administration, maintenance, transport.

	Air (£000)	Marine (£000)	Administration (£000)	Maintenance (£000)	Trasport (£000)	Total (£000)
Service department costs			390	195	390	975
Administration						
(94 : 40 : 15 : 26)	210	89	(390)	33	58	
Transport						
(234 : 170 : 31)	241	175		32	(448)	
Maintenance						
(7 : 4)	166	94		(260)		
	617	358				975

(b) The direct method is simple to use and provides a reasonable approximation to more accurate methods where service department costs are a small proportion of total costs. Given the arbitrary method of many cost allocations, the method could be viewed as being sufficiently accurate for cost allocation purposes. However, it fails to recognize the reciprocal service arrangements. This method is unsuitable where variable costs represent a significant proportion of service department costs.

The step-down method gives partial recognition to inter-service department transfers and provides a more accurate approach than the first method. It may not provide a satisfactory approximation of inter-service department allocations where variable costs represent a significant proportion of service department costs. The most accurate method would be to adopt the repeated distribution method.

The service department reallocation process should distinguish between fixed and variable service department costs. Variable costs should be charged to user departments. Fixed overheads can be allocated using one of the approaches outlined above. Recently, activity-based costing (ABC) has been advocated as the method that ought to be adopted for tracing service department overheads to products. With ABC, service department costs are not reallocated to production departments. Instead, service department costs are charged directly to products according to service department activities consumed. For a description of ABC you should refer to Chapter 12.

The activity measures that are chosen to allocate service department costs to production departments should be related to the benefits that the production departments derive from the service rendered. Administration costs tend to be mainly fixed, and it is questionable whether an obvious cause and effect relationship can be identified. Activity measures based on labour hours are frequently recommended. It is assumed that the greater the number of hours worked, the greater the administration costs in the long run. Alternative activity measures include number of employees and total wages cost. However, it is doubtful whether these measures would be an improvement on the existing method.

The existing method of allocating maintenance department costs on the basis of hours of maintenance work would seem to be appropriate. An alternative measure would be to use machine hours as the activity measure, based on the assumption that maintenance department costs are related to the number of machine hours.

Miles of vehicle usage is an appropriate basis for allocating transport costs. An alternative basis would be the number of hours' transport usage or an analysis of usage according to types of vehicles used.

(c) The question refers to the performance of profit centres and their managers. The former refers to a measure of the economic performance of the profit centre in which the focus is on how successful the centre is as an economic entity. The latter refers to how successful the manager is in controlling the activities of the centre.

Arbitrary cost allocations should be avoided for the purpose of measuring managerial performance. Only costs that are controllable by managers should be allocated to profit centres. It is sometimes argued that non-controllable costs should be allocated to managers in order to make them aware of the cost of supporting their activities. Allocation is advocated because it is considered to make managers more cost-conscious, which will lead to more pressure on overhead cost control and therefore influence service department costs. For a more detailed discussion of cost allocations for managerial performance measurement see 'Guidelines for reporting' in Chapter 18 and 'Alternative divisional profit measures' in Chapter 26.

Cost allocations are advocated for economic performance measurement in order to ensure that all costs are covered when assessing profit centre profitability. Allocations provide an approximate indication of the overhead costs consumed by profit centres in the long run. For short-run profit measurement it is advocated that profit should be measured before arbitrary allocations of common fixed costs. The long-run performance measure should be interpreted with care. Where poor profit performance is reported, the measure should be used to trigger off a detailed investigation of the viability of a centre's activities. In a recent empirical study of the rationale for cost allocations, Ramadan (1989) reported the following as being the most important reasons for cost allocations:

1. Profit centres would incur such costs if they were independent units or if the services were not provided centrally;
2. To make managers aware that central costs exist.

It is likely that research and development (R & D) expenditure is totally outside the control of department managers. Charging R & D costs to departments is likely to demotivate the managers. Furthermore, any charges are likely to be arbitrary and have no economic significance. It is therefore recommended that R & D expenses be borne by central headquarters and not recharged to profit centres.

Reference
Ramadan, S., The rationale for cost allocations: a study of UK divisionalised companies, *Accounting and Business Research*, Winter 1989, 31–7.

Question 26.18 (a) The annual ROI and residual income calculations for each plant are as follows:

Aromatic	19×2	19×3	19×4	19×5	Total
(1) Net cash flow (£m)	2.4	2.4	2.4	2.4	9.6
(2) Depreciation	1.6	1.6	1.6	1.6	
(3) Profit	0.8	0.8	0.8	0.8	3.2
(4) Cost of capital (16% of 6)	(1.02)	(0.77)	(0.51)	(0.26)	
(5) Residual income	(0.22)	0.03	0.29	0.54	
(6) Opening WDV of asset	6.4	4.8	3.2	1.6	
(7) ROI (Row 3/Row 6)	12.5%	16.67%	25%	50%	

Zoman					
(1) Net cash flow	2.6	2.2	1.5	1.0	7.3
(2) Depreciation	1.3	1.3	1.3	1.3	
(3) Profit	1.3	0.9	0.2	(0.3)	2.1
(4) Cost of capital (16%)	(0.83)	(0.62)	(0.42)	(0.21)	
(5) Residual income	0.47	0.28	(0.22)	(0.51)	
(6) Opening WDV of asset	5.2	3.9	2.6	1.3	
(7) ROI	25%	23%	7.7%	(23%)	

The answer should indicate:
  (i) Over the whole life of the project both ROI and residual income (RI) favour the Aromatic plant. The average ROI and RI figures are 25% and £0.16m (£0.64m/4) for the Aromatic plant and 20% and £0.005m (£0.02m/4) for the Zoman plant. The ROI calculations are based on expressing the average profits as a percentage of the average investment (defined as one half of the initial capital investment).
  (ii) An explanation that Mr Elton will favour the Zoman plant because it yields a higher ROI and RI over the first two years. Mr Elton will probably focus on a two-year time horizon because of his personal circumstances, since choosing the Aromatic plant is likely to result in him losing his bonus. Therefore he will choose the plant with the lower NPV and there will be a lack of goal congruence.
  (iii) Suggestions as to how alternative accounting techniques can assist in reconciling the conflict between accounting performance measures and DCF techniques:
    1. Avoiding short-term evaluations and evaluating performance at the end of the project's life. Thus bonuses would be awarded with hindsight;

2. Use alternative asset valuations other than historic cost (e.g. replacement cost);
3. Choose alternative depreciation methods that are most consistent with NPV calculations (e.g. annuity depreciation);
4. Incorporate a range of variables (both financial and non-financial when evaluating managerial performance) that give a better indication of future results that can be expected from current actions.

(b) Managers may use pre-tax profits to evaluate divisional performance because it is assumed that taxation is non-controllable. Taxation payable is based on total group profits and present and past capital expenditure rather than individual divisional profitability. After tax cash flows are used to appraise capital investments because the focus is on decision-making and accepting those projects that earn a return in excess of the investors' opportunity cost of capital. To do this IRRs and NPVs should be based on after-tax cash flows.

The following potential problems can arise:
  (i) Managers may ignore the taxation impact at the decision-making stage because it is not considered when evaluating their performance;
  (ii) Confusion and demotivation can occur when different criteria are used for decision-making and performance evaluation.

Possible solutions include evaluating divisional profitability after taxes or evaluating performance based on a comparison of budgeted and actual cash flows. Adopting the latter approach is an attempt to ensure that the same criteria is used for decision-making and performance evaluation.

(c) Steps that can be taken to avoid dysfunctional behaviour include:
  (i) Not placing too much emphasis on short-term performance measures and placing greater emphasis on the long term by adopting a profit-conscious style of evaluation.
  (ii) Focusing on controllable residual income combined with asset valuations derived from depreciation models that are consistent with NPV calculations (see Appendix to Chapter 26). Alternatively, performance evaluation might be based on a comparison of budgeted and actual cash flows. The budgeted cash flows should be based on cash flows that are used to appraise capital investments.
  (iii) Supplementing financial performance measures with non-financial measures when evaluating performance (see 'Use of non-accounting measures' in Chapter 26).
  (iv) For additional points you should refer to the conclusion to Chapter 21.

(a) *Region 3 manager's remuneration* **Question 26.20**

	1990 (£)		1991 (£)
Basic salary	18 000		19 000
Sales bonus			
$(£2.4m - £2.25m) \times 0.75\%$	1 125	$(£2.75m - £2.7m) \times 0.75\%$	375
ROCE bonus:			
$(£123/£1850 = 6.65\%)$		$(147/2260 = 6.5\%)$	
$2\% \times £1.85m \times 6.65\%$	2 460	$(3\% \times £2\,260\,000 \times 6.5\%)$	4 407
	21 585		23 782

Increase in remuneration = £2197

Region 7 manager's remuneration

Basic salary	22 000		22 000
Sales bonus			
$(£3.7m - £3.4m) \times 0.75\%$	2 250	$(£3.6m - £3.6m)$	—

ROCE bonus:
 (£166/£2800 = 5.93%)   (£241/£2900 = 8.31%)
 3% × £2 800 000 × 5.93% 4 981 (3% × £2 900 000 × 8.31%) 7 230
             29 231   29 230

Decrease in remuneration = £1.

(b) The following comparisons of 1991 with 1990 should be taken into account in assessing the performance of the two divisions:

	Region 3	Region 7
Sales	+14.6%	−2.7%
Net profit	+19.5%	+45.2%
Investment	+22.2%	+3.6%
ROCE	−2.3%	+40.1%
Actual sales/target sales	+6.7% (1990)	+8.8% (1990)
	+1.9% (1991)	0 (1991)

Assuming that the actual results for 1991 conform with the budgeted results, the general manager of region 3 will exceed his sales target but the ROCE will decline. However, capital employed increases from £1.85m to £2.26m, and thus the ROCE is multiplied by 3% of £2.26m instead of 2% of £1.85m.

The general manager of region 7 is expected to just meet his sales target for 1991. However, ROCE increases from 5.93% in 1990 to 8.3% in 1991. There is a small increase in capital employed (3.6% compared with 22.2% for region 3).

The manager of region 3 receives an increase in remuneration of £1197 (5.5%) if we ignore the service increment, whereas there is a very slight decrease in remuneration of the manager of region 7. In view of the fact that ROCE is normally considered to be the key financial performance measure, it would seem that the manager of region 7 ought to be better rewarded for a 40% increase in ROCE. This inadequate reward has arisen because the increase in ROCE bonus does not offset the decline in the sales bonus arising from a static sales performance in 1991.

The present system provides for a 5.5% increase in the remuneration (excluding the service element) of the manager of region 3 because he is controlling a larger investment and has significantly exceeded his sales target.

(c) The present service element is ten increments of £1000 and is based entirely on length of service. This can lead to situations where a long-serving manager who is managing a smaller, less important division is paid significantly more than a young dynamic manager who is managing a larger, more important division. It is recommended that the service element be reduced from £10 000 to £5000 (5 × £1000 increments or 10 × £500 increments). Part or all of the £5000 that is removed from the service element could be used to remunerate managers according to the size of the investment in each division: for example £x increment for each £0.5 increase in capital employed (suitably adjusted to remove inflationary increases).

The bonus based on sales revenue does not take into account the differing profit margins on the various activities. Managers might therefore be motivated to pursue activities that generate high sales revenues with low contribution margins. It is therefore recommended that the sales bonus be based on a target contribution from sales rather than target sales revenues.

The present ROCE bonus may incorrectly encourage managers to invest, in order to increase capital employed, and thus obtain a greater bonus. For example, the present system of applying a different percentage rate to investments above and below £2m is too drastic and may encourage unnecessary investment just to get above this figure. This differential should be removed. It is recommended that the ROCE bonus should be based on a target residual income (that is, profit after charging interest on capital) rather than ROCE. Targets should be based on the residual incomes of similar firms (adjusted for size) operating in the same industry. For a comparison of ROCE and residual income see 'Return on investment' and 'Residual income' in Chapter 26.

Thus, under the proposed system, managers would be rewarded by:

1. A basic salary based on length of service to reward loyalty plus a reward related to the level of responsibility based on the total assets that managers have under their control.
2. A bonus based on:
   (a) achieving above target sales contribution;
   (b) achieving above target residual income.

(a) (i) Return on capital employed and residual income should be considered as **Question 26.21** potential measures. The superiority of residual income over return on capital employed (see Chapter 26) should be discussed. The objective is to select a performance measure that is consistent with the NPV rule. Residual income is the long-run counterpart of the NPV rule, but it may lead to decisions that are not consistent with the NPV rule if managers base their decisions on short-term measures. Problems occur with both return on capital employed and residual income in terms of bases that should be used for asset valuations. Current values are preferable to historical costs.

(ii) Ideally, market performance measures should indicate sales achievement in relation to the market, competitors and previous performance. Target market shares or unit sales should be established for each product or product range. Actual market shares and unit sales should be compared with targets and previous periods. Trends in market shares should be compared with overall market trends and product life cycles.

(iii) Productivity is concerned with the efficiency of converting physical inputs into physical outputs. Therefore the performance measure should be a physical one. Possible performance measures include output per direct labour hour and output per machine hour. Where divisions produce a variety of products, output could be expressed in standard hours. If monetary measures are used then changes in price levels should be eliminated. In addition to *total* measures of output for each division, performance measures should also be computed for individual products. Output measures should be compared with targets, previous periods and with other divisions.

(iv) Possible measures of the ability of divisions to offer up-to-date product ranges include:
   1. number of new products launched in previous periods;
   2. expenditure on product development.
   Quality and reliability might be measured in terms of:
   1. percentage of projects rejected;
   2. comparison of target and actual market shares;
   3. comparisons with competitors' products;
   4. customer surveys.
   The performance measures should be compared with previous periods, targets and competitors (if this is possible). Some of the measures may be difficult to express in quantitative terms, and a subjective evaluation may be necessary.

(v) Responsibility towards employees might be reflected by the following measures:
   1. rate of labour turnover;
   2. level of absenteeism.
   Additional information is also necessary to explain the reasons for high labour turnover and absenteeism. Possible reasons might be identified by regularly undertaking attitude surveys on such issues as:
   1. payment systems;
   2. management style;
   3. degree of participation;

4. working conditions.

Other proxy measures that might be used include:

1. number of promotions to different employee and management grades;
2. number of grievance procedures processed;
3. number of applications received per vacancy;
4. training expenditure per employee;
5. number of accidents reported per period.

The above measures should be compared with previous periods and targets.

(vi) It is extremely difficult to assess whether a firm is considered to be a socially responsible citizen within the community. Possible areas of inter-action between the firm and the local community include:

1. employment;
2. environmental effects;
3. involvement in community affairs;
4. provision of recreational and social facilities.

Surveys should be undertaken locally in order to assess the attitude of the population to each of the above areas. Possible quantitative measures include:

1. amount of financial support given to charities, sports organizations and educational establishments;
2. amounts spent on anti-pollution measures;
3. number of complaints received from members of the local community.

(vii) Possible growth measures include comparisons over time (in absolute terms and percentage changes) of the following:

1. total sales revenue;
2. profit (expressed in terms of residual income);
3. total assets;
4. total employees;
5. total market share.

Price changes should be removed where appropriate. Comparisons should be made with other divisions, comparable firms and the industry as a whole.

Survival in the long term depends on an acceptable level of profitability. Therefore appropriate profitability measures should be used. The degree of divisional autonomy might be measured in terms of an assessment of the central controls imposed by central headquarters. (For example: what are the limits on the amounts of capital expenditure decisions that divisions can determine independently?)

(b) A single performance measure underestimates the multi-faceted nature of organizational goals. It might be claimed that a profitability measure is sufficiently general to incorporate the other goals. For example, maintaining high market shares, increasing productivity, offering an up-to-date product range, being a responsible employee, and growth tend to result in increased profitability. To this extent a profitability measure might best capture the multi-faceted nature of organizational goals. Nevertheless the profitability goal alone cannot be expected to capture the complexity of organizational goals. Firms pursue a variety of goals, and for this reason there are strong arguments for using multiple performance measures when evaluating organizational performance. For a further discussion of organizational goals see 'Decision-making process' in Chapter 1.

Question 26.25 (a) *Calculation of written-down values (WDVs) and capital employed*

Year	1	2	3	4	5
	(£m)	(£m)	(£m)	(£m)	(£m)
Opening WDV	1.5	1.2	0.9	0.6	0.3
Depreciation (straight line)	0.3	0.3	0.3	0.3	0.3
Closing WDV	1.2	0.9	0.6	0.3	—
Opening capital employed (opening WDV + WC)	2.0	1.7	1.4	1.1	0.8

Calculation of residual income and ROCE

Year	1	2	3	4	5
	(£m)	(£m)	(£m)	(£m)	(£m)
Sales	2.0				
Operating costs	(1.35)				
Depreciation	(0.30)				
Net profit	0.35	0.35	0.35	0.35	0.35
Imputed interest (20%)	0.40	0.34	0.28	0.22	0.16
Residual income	(0.05)	0.01	0.07	0.13	0.19
ROCE	17.5%	20.6%	25%	31.8%	43.7%

CP's management would be unlikely to undertake the project if they are evaluated on the basis of ROCE, since it yields a return of less than 30% for each of the first three years. Consequently, the total ROCE will be less than 30% during the first three years. Residual income is negative in the first year and positive for the remaining four years. If the management of CP place more emphasis on the impact on the performance measure on the first year, they may reject the project. On the other hand, if they adopt a longer-term perspective, they will accept the project.

(b) *Calculation of annuity depreciation*

Year	(1) Annual repayment (£m)	(2) 20% interest on capital outstanding (£m)	(3) = (1) − (2) Capital repayment (£m)	(4) = (4) − (3) Capital outstanding (£m)
0				1.5
1	0.5016	0.3	0.2016	1.2984
2	0.5016	0.2597	0.2419	1.0565
3	0.5016	0.2113	0.2903	0.7662
4	0.5016	0.1532	0.3484	0.4178
5	0.5016	0.0838	0.4178	—

For an explanation of the calculations see 'Annuity depreciation' in Appendix 26.1. Note that the annual repayment is determined by referring to the capital recovery table in Appendix D of the text for 5 years at 20%. The capital recovery factor is 0.3344, and this is multiplied by the capital outlay to give an annual repayment of £0.5016m.

Calculation of residual income and ROCE

Year	1	2	3	4	5
	(£m)	(£m)	(£m)	(£m)	(£m)
Opening WDV	1.50	1.30	1.06	0.77	0.42
Annuity depreciation	0.20	0.24	0.29	0.35	0.42
Closing WDV	1.30	1.06	0.77	0.42	—
Total opening capital employed	2.0	1.80	1.56	1.27	0.92
Operating earnings	0.65	0.65	0.65	0.65	0.65
Depreciation	0.20	0.24	0.29	0.35	0.42
Net profit	0.45	0.41	0.36	0.30	0.23
Imputed interest	0.40	0.36	0.31	0.25	0.18
Residual income	0.05	0.05	0.05	0.05	0.05
ROCE	22.5%	22.8%	23.1%	23.6%	25%

Since the projected ROCE is less than 30%, CP's management are likely to reject the project if performance is evaluated on the basis of ROCE. If performance is evaluated on the basis of residual income, the project is likely to be accepted, since it has a positive residual income for all five years.

(c) The calculation of NPV is as follows:

	(£m)
PV of net cash inflows (£0.65m × 2.991 discount factor)	1.944
Working capital released at the end of the project (0.5m × 0.4019)	0.201
Initial outlay	(2.000)
NPV	0.145

The project should be accepted, since it has a positive NPV. The objective is to design a performance measurement system that is consistent with the NPV rule. The ROCE measure may not encourage goal congruence, because managers of divisions with a ROCE in excess of the cost of capital may incorrectly reject projects with positive NPVs. Alternatively, managers of divisions with a ROCE that is less than cost of capital may incorrectly accept projects with negative NPVs. This situation arises because managers who are evaluated on the basis of ROCE may base their investment decisions on the impact on ROCE and use the existing ROCE as the cut-off rate.

The project outlined in the question has a positive NPV, but the ROCE is less than 30% for the first three years in (a), where straight-line depreciation is used. If annuity depreciation is used, the project has a ROCE of less than 30% for each year of the project's life. The manager is therefore unlikely to accept the investment, since it will result in a decline in the overall ROCE of the division.

In the long run, the residual income method produces a calculation that is consistent with the NPV rule. The short-term residual income calculation may not, however, motivate managers to select projects that are consistent with applying the NPV rule. In the case of constant cash flows the problem can be resolved by using the annuity method of depreciation, but when annual cash flows fluctuate, this method of depreciation does not ensure that the short-term residual income measure is consistent with the NPV rule. For a discussion of how this problem might be resolved see 'Reconciling short-term and long-term residual income measures' in Appendix 26.1 to Chapter 26. You can see that, for the project outlined in the question, residual income is positive for all years where the annuity method of depreciation is used, but it is negative in the first year and positive for the remaining years where straight-line depreciation is used.

Question 26.26 (a)

Summary statement 1 (Straight-line depreciation)

Year	1	2	3	4	5
	(£000)	(£000)	(£000)	(£000)	(£000)
Investment at start of year	600	480	360	240	120
Net cash flow (40% of sales)	200	200	200	200	200
Less: depreciation	120	120	120	120	120
Net profit	80	80	80	80	80
Less: interest on capital[a]	96	76.8	57.6	38.4	19.2
Residue income	(16)	3.2	22.4	41.6	60.8
ROCE[b]	13.3%	16.7%	22.2%	33.3%	66.7%

Notes
[a]16% of investment at the start of the year.
[b]Net profit expressed as a percentage of the investment at the start of the year.

Calculation of annuity depreciation

Year	(1) Annual repayment (£000)	(2) 16% interest on capital outatanding (£000)	(3) = (1) − (2) Capital repayment (£000)	(4) = (4) − (3) Capital outstanding (£000)
0				600.0
1	183.24	96.0	87.24	512.76
2	183.24	82.04	101.20	411.56
3	183.24	65.85	117.39	294.17
4	183.24	47.07	136.17	158.00
5	183.24	25.28	158.00	—

For an explanation of the calculations see 'Annuity depreciation' in Appendix 26.1. Note that the annual repayment is determined by referring to the capital recovery table in Appendix D of the text for 5 years at 16%. The capital recovery factor is 0.3054 and this is multiplied by the capital outlay to give an annual repayment of £183 240. Alternatively, the annual repayment could have been calculated by dividing the investment of £600 000 by the cumulative discount factor for 5 years at 16% (3.274 shown in Appendix B).

Summary Statement 2 (Annuity depreciation)

Year	1 (£000)	2 (£000)	3 (£000)	4 (£000)	5 (£000)
Investment at start of year	600	512.76	411.56	294.17	158.00
Net cash flow	200	200	200	200	200
Depreciation	87.24	101.20	117.39	136.17	158.00
Net profit	112.76	98.80	82.61	63.83	42.0
Imputed interest	96.00	82.04	65.85	47.07	25.28
Residual income	16.76	16.76	16.76	16.76	16.72
ROCE	18.8%	19.3%	20.1%	21.7%	26.6%

(b) (i) Management are motivated to focus only on the outcomes of the first year for any new project because of the criterion used for performance measurement and investment decisions. When straight-line depreciation is used residual income is negative and the ROCE of 13.3% is less than the target return of 20%. Therefore if the focus is only on the performance measures for the first year the project will be rejected even though residual income and ROCE rise steadily throughout the five-year period.

When annuity depreciation is used residual income is positive and constant for each year of the project's life and therefore the proposal would be accepted if the residual income method is used. ROCE is 18.8% and this is less than the target return of 20% and the project would be rejected using this method. However, ROCE ranges from 18.8% to 26.6% when annuity depreciation is used, compared with 13.3% to 66.7% with straight-line depreciation. Therefore, when compared with straight-line depreciation annuity depreciation does not distort ROCE to the same extent.

(ii)

NPV = £200 000 × cumulative discount factor for 5 years at 16% (3.274)
     − Investment outlay (£600 000)
    = £54 800

The project has a positive NPV and should be accepted. Residual income is the long-run counterpart of NPV. The present value of residual income of

£16 760 per year for 5 years discounted at 16% is approximately £54 800. When cash flows are constant and the annuity method of depreciation is used residual income will also be constant. For a more detailed discussion of the relationship between residual income and NPV see the Appendix to Chapter 26.

(c) (i)

	Year 1 (straight-line depreciation) (£000)	Year 1 (annuity depreciation) (£000)
Investment at beginning of year	600	600
Net cash flow (40% × £700 000)	280	280
Less:		
Depreciation (see part (a))	(120)	(87.3)
Profit	160	192.7
Less:		
Interest on capital	(96)	(96)
Residual income	64	96.7
ROCE	26.7%	32.1%

(ii) *Discounted cash flow approach*:

Year	Physical (£000)	Discount factor at 16%	DCF (£000)
0	(600)	1.000	(600)
1	280	0.862	241.36
2	200	0.743	148.60
3	200	0.641	128.20
4	120	0.552	66.24
5	80	0.476	38.08
		NPV	22.48

(iii) Adopting the criteria used by management both projects yield a positive residual income and a ROCE in excess of the target return in the first year using either straight-line or annuity methods of depreciation. The project therefore will be accepted. The project also has a positive NPV and, in this situation, the criteria used by management will be consistent with the NPV decision model. The decline in NPV reflects the fact that sales revenue has declined over the five-year period.

Transfer pricing in divisionalized companies

Solutions to Chapter 27 questions

Question summary

27.1–27.6   Various discussion questions relevant to Chapter 27.

27.7   Calculation and comparison of divisional and group profits based on various transfer prices.

27.8   Resolving a transfer pricing conflict.

27.9   Make or buy decisions involving inter-group trading.

27.10   Calculation of the profit contribution for various departments where conflicts arise as to what should be the appropriate transfer price.

27.11   Computation of an optimal transfer price range based on competitive market prices.

27.12   Construction of profit statements illustrating sub-optimality when a cost-plus transfer price is applied. This question is similar to the self-assessment question at the end of Chapter 27.

27.13   Computation of cost-plus and market-based transfer prices and comments on the extent to which they encourage goal congruence.

27.14   Calculation of divisional profits where market-based transfer prices are used, and a recommendation of a transfer price that avoids sub-optimal decisions arising from using market based pricing system.

27.15   A discussion of the optimal transfer price where there is a perfect market for the intermediate product but the buying price includes additional transportation costs. The second part of the question involves the setting of an optimal transfer price when there is an imperfect market for the intermediate product.

27.16   Calculation of optimal output and transfer price when there is an imperfect market for the intermediute product: Part (c) requires a discussion of international aspects of transfer pricing.

27.17, 27.18   Calculation of the optimum selling price using calculus and the impact of using the imperfect market price as the transfer price.

27.19   Calculating optimal transfer prices and profits using differential calculus.

27.20   Calculation of transfer prices using shadow prices when the capacity of the supplying division is restricted and the intermediate product has alternative uses.

27.21   The application of linear programming to set transfer prices.

Question 27.1

(a) *Advantages of absorption cost*

Provides an indication of the long-run production costs of the supplying division. Therefore the receiving department will be charged at the long-run cost of production.

Disadvantages of absorption cost
- (i) Cannot be guaranteed to motivate a divisional manager to make sound decisions. Transfer prices based on absorption cost are not consistent with the optimum transfer price rule outlined in Chapter 27.
- (ii) Transfer prices are imposed, resulting in divisional autonomy being undermined.
- (iii) Ignores market prices.
- (iv) Inefficiencies will be passed on to the receiving division if actual cost is used.
- (v) Zero profits will be earned by the supplying division. Therefore this measure will not be a reasonable measure of the economic performance of the division.

(b) *Advantages of marginal cost*

Will motivate sound decisions if set at the marginal cost of supplying division for the output at which marginal cost equals the sum of the receiving division's net marginal revenue from using the intermediate product and the marginal revenue from the sale of the intermediate product.

Disadvantages of marginal cost
- (i) Imposed transfer prices.
- (ii) May not provide a meaningful performance measure. If variable cost is constant then the supplying division will make a loss equal to the total amount of the fixed costs.
- (iii) Inefficiencies will be passed on to the receiving division if actual cost is used.

(c) *Advantages of cost-plus*

Provides an indication of the long-run production costs of the company and may provide a reasonable measure of economic performance of the supplying and receiving divisions since transfer prices might approximate a fair market price when no external market exists.

Disadvantages of cost-plus

See absorption cost disadvantages.

(d) *Advantages of standard cost*

Ensures that inefficiencies are charged to the supplying division and are not passed on to the receiving division.

Disadvantages of standard cost

Depends on whether standard absorption, marginal or absorption-plus is used. See (a)−(c) above for their respective disadvantages.

Question 27.2 A sound transfer pricing system should accomplish the following objectives:
- (i) It should motivate the divisional manager to make *sound decisions* and it should communicate information that provides a reliable basis for such decisions. This will happen when actions that divisional managers take to improve the reported profit of their divisions also improve the profit of the company as a whole.
- (ii) It should result in a report of divisional profits that is a reasonable measure of the *managerial performance* of the division.
- (iii) It should ensure that divisional *autonomy* is not undermined.

It can be shown that full-cost transfer prices may not meet any of the above objectives. Full-cost transfer prices contain unitized fixed costs, which can easily be misinterpreted as variable costs. This will result in incorrect pricing and output decisions. See 'Effect of cost-plus transfer prices' in Chapter 27 for an explanation of how full-cost based transfer prices can lead to incorrect decisions.

When *actual* full-cost transfer prices are used, objectives (ii) and (iii) will not be met since inefficiencies of the supplying division will be passed on to the receiving division. This will mean that actual results will not represent a reasonable measure of divisional performance, and divisional autonomy will be undermined. If standard costs are used and there is no external market for the intermediate then objective (ii) above may be satisfied if the transfer price represents the long-run cost of supplying the intermediate product.

Question 27.4 (a) With cost-based transfer price systems, transfers are made either at actual cost or standard cost. Where actual costs are used, there is no incentive for the supplying centre to control costs because any inefficiencies arising in the supplying centre will be passed on to the receiving centre. Consequently, the receiving centre will be held accountable for the inefficiencies of the supplying division. Transfers at actual cost are therefore inappropriate for responsibility accounting.

Where cost-based transfer pricing systems are used, transfers should be at standard cost and not actual cost. This will result in the supplying centre being held accountable for the variances arising from the difference between standard and actual cost of the transfers. The managers of the supplying centres are therefore motivated to minimize their costs. When transfers are made at standard cost, any inefficiencies of the supplying centre are not passed on to the receiving centre. The receiving centre should be held accountable for usage of resources at the standard price, thus ensuring that the manager of the receiving centre is held accountable only for excessive usage of resources.

Where cost-based transfer prices are used, there is still a danger that inappropriate transfer prices are set that will not provide an appropriate basis for allocating profits between divisions. Where there is a competitive market for intermediate products, the current market price is the most suitable basis for setting the transfer price. When transfers are recorded at market prices, profit centre performance is likely to represent the real economic contribution of the profit centre to total company profits. If the supplying centre did not exist, the intermediate product would have to be purchased on the outside market at the current market price. Alternatively, if the receiving centre did not exist, the intermediate product would have to be sold on the outside market at the current market price. Responsibility centre profits are therefore likely to be similar to the profits that would be calculated if the centres were separate independent businesses. Therefore transfers based on selling prices will represent a more appropriate basis for meeting the requirements of a responsibility accounting system.

(b) When the supplying division does not have sufficient capacity to meet all the demands placed upon it, linear programming can be used to determine the optimum production level. The transfer price that will induce the supplying division to produce the optimum output level can be derived from the linear programming model. The transfer price is determined by adding the shadow prices of the scarce resources (as indicated by the output from the linear programming model) to the variable cost of the resources consumed by the intermediate product. For an explanation of this approach see 'The use of linear programming to establish optimum transfer prices' in Chapter 27. This section indicates that the transfer price will result in the supplying division being credited with all of the contribution arising from the transfers and the receiving division earning a zero contribution. The allocation of zero contribution to the receiving division will have a negative motivational influence, and result in a loss of divisional autonomy and a reported performance that does not reflect the economic performance of the division.

(a) The variable costs per unit of output for sales *outside* the company are £11 for the intermediate product and £49 [£10(A) + £39(B)] for the final product. Note that selling and packing expenses are not incurred by the supplying division for the transfer of the intermediate product. It is assumed that the company has sufficient capacity to meet demand at the various selling prices. **Question 27.7**

Optimal output of intermediate product for sale on external market

Selling price (£)		20	30	40
Unit contribution (£)		9	19	29
Demand (units)	15 000	10 000	5000
Total contribution (£)	135 000	190 000	145 000

Optimal output is 10 000 units at a selling price of £30.

Optimal output for final product

Selling price (£)	80	90	100
Unit contribution (£)	31	41	51
Demand (units)	7 200	5 000	2 800
Total contribution (£)	223 200	205 000	142 800

Optimal output is 7200 units at a selling price of £80.

Optimal output of Division B based on a transfer price of £29
Division B will regard the transfer price as a variable cost. Therefore total variable cost per unit will be £68 (£29 + £39), and Division B will calculate the following contributions:

Selling price (£)	80	90	100
Unit contribution (£)	12	22	32
Demand (units)	7 200	5 000	2 800
Total contribution (£)	86 400	110 000	89 600

The manager of Division B will choose an output level of 5000 units at a selling price of £90. This is sub-optimal for the company as a whole. Profits for the *company as a whole* from the sale of the final product are reduced from £223 200 (7200 units) to £205 000 (5000 units). The £205 000 profits would be allocated as follows:

Division A £95 000 [5000 units at (£29 − £10)]
Division B £110 000

(b) At a transfer price of £12, the variable cost per unit produced in Division B will be £51 (£12 + £39). Division B will calculate the following contributions:

Selling price (£)	80	90	100
Unit contribution (£)	29	39	49
Demand (units)	7 200	5 000	2 800
Total contribution (£)	208 800	195 000	137 200

The manager of Division B will choose an output level of 7200 units and a selling price of £80. This is the optimum output level for the company as a whole. Division A would obtain a contribution of £14 400 [7200 × (£12 − £10)] from internal transfers of the intermediate product, whereas Division B would obtain a contribution of £208 800 from converting the intermediate product and selling as a final product. Total contribution for the company as a whole would be £223 200. Note that Division A would also earn a contribution of £190 000 from the sale of the intermediate product to the external market.

Question 27.9 (a) *Preliminary comments*

The answer to this question requires that we compare the relevant costs for each of the three alternatives. Relevant costs will include incremental costs plus any lost contribution where a division has no spare capacity. Only RR is working at full capacity. Therefore the relevant costs are as follows:

Work undertaken by RP, RS and RT: Relevant cost equals incremental cost for the group as a whole.

Work undertaken by RR: Relevant cost equals incremental cost plus lost contribution from the displaced work. (This is equivalent to the lost sales revenue.)

Relevant cost of company A quote	£33 000

Relevant cost of company B quote	(£)
Cost of quote	35 000
Less benefits to group of subcontract work[a]	2 420
Relevant cost	32 580

Note

[a]It is assumed that the £13 000 RS charge to Company B includes 25% on the cost of its own work but no additional margin is added to the £7500 market price for the parts purchased from RR. Therefore the price of £13 000 by RS to Company B is assumed to include £7500 in respect of RR work plus the balance of £5500 for RS work. The total cost of RS work is £4400 (the question indicates that RS expects to earn a profit of 25% on its *own* work). Therefore the group contribution from subcontract work is as follows:

	(£)	(£)
Selling price of special unit		13 000
Less incremental cost to group of RR's own work (70% × £4400)	3080	
Relevant cost of RR's work (market price)	7500	10 580
Contribution to group		2 420

Relevant cost of RS quote

The following diagram illustrates the inter-group transfers:

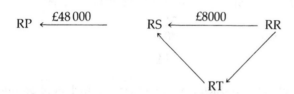

From the above information, it is necessary to ascertain the relevant cost of the *group* from producing the electronic control system. The relevant cost of RR work is the market price of £19 000 (£11 000 + £8000). The relevant cost of RS and RT work is the variable cost (excluding the cost of transfers within the group). The calculations are as follows:

RS conversion cost:	(£)
RS total cost	42 000
Less costs transferred from other members of the group (£30 000 + £8000)	38 000
Cost of RS conversion work	4000
Variable cost of RS conversion work (70% of £4000)	2 800

RT conversion cost:	(£)
Price charged by RT to RS	30 000
Less profit margin (20% on total cost)	5 000
Total cost of RS work (including transfer from RR)	25 000
Less transfer price of parts purchased from RR	11 000
Total cost of work added by RT	14 000
Variable cost of work added by RT (65% × £14 000)	9 100

Therefore the relevant cost to the group is as follows:

	(£)
Work undertaken by RR	19 000
Variable costs of conversion work by RT	9 100
Variable costs of conversion work by RS	2 800
Relevant cost	30 900

The order should be awarded to RS because this is the lowest relevant cost alternative.

(b) The following assumptions have been made in part (a):

   (i) Incremental costs are represented by variable costs, and no additional fixed costs will be incurred for each alternative.

   (ii) Variable costs are linear with respect to output changes.

   (iii) RS and RT have sufficient spare capacity to accept the work. Hence no orders will be turned away and opportunity costs are assumed to be zero.

   (iv) RP is not free to select its own source of supply. If RP has complete independence then it is likely to accept the quote that will minimize its costs (i.e. the Company A quote).

Question 27.11 (a) The calculation of selling price for product X based on the cost-plus pricing system operated by L Ltd is calculated as follows:

	(£)
Direct materials	18
Direct wages	15
Variable overhead (1 hour × £10)	10 (£70 000/7000 hours)
	43
Fixed overhead (1 hour × £8)	8 (£56 000/7000 hours)
Total cost	51
Profit (60% of total cost)	30.6
Selling price	81.6

Since the company is committed to producing Y, any internal transfers of product X will not reduce capacity that could be used for producing product Y. If product X is not sold externally, there will be an opportunity cost to the group of £81.60 representing the lost sales revenue. Assuming that the transfer price is set at £81.60 market price, K Ltd will make a profit of £1.4 per kg of product Z [£100 − (£15 + £2 + £81.60)]. The total profit on the order is £2800 (2000 kg × £1.40).

It is therefore profitable for K Ltd to produce product Z. The transfer price reflects the opportunity cost from the lost sales revenue from product X. Each division and the group as a whole should be indifferent to whether K Ltd acquires product X internally or purchases it on the external market. If the product is purchased on the external market at £81.60, additional costs of £81.60 are incurred, but this will enable additional revenue of £81.60 to be obtained from sales by L Ltd. The transfer price should therefore be set at £81.60. If K Ltd can purchase product X on the external market at a price below £81.60, it should do so, since this would be in the best interests of the group as a whole.

The above recommendation assumes that L Ltd will not save any selling costs if the product is transferred internally. If, for example, variable selling overheads of £3 per unit could be saved then the transfer price should be reduced by £3 + 60% to reflect the variable cost savings. Without further information, the potential transfer price range would be between £76.80 (£81.60 − £4.80) and £81.60.

(b) The question specifies that K Ltd is working at full capacity. If additional units of product X could be produced by working overtime and this output could not be sold on the external market then the incremental cost per unit of the additional output would represent the appropriate transfer price.

Alternatively, if product X is in short supply, L Ltd should be instructed to supply 2000 kg to K Ltd and use the balance of its capacity for sales on the external market.

(a) (i) *Monthly profits at present sales level*

	(£000)
L Ltd: Sales (10 000 drums[a] at £20 per drum)	200
Costs: Raw materials (£9 per drum)	(90)
Other costs	(30)
Contribution	80
Fixed costs	40
Profit	40
M Ltd: Sales (750 000 kilolitres at £9 per 25 litres)	270
Costs: Variable	(150)
Fixed	(60)
Profit	60

Note
[a] Sales of L Ltd = 250 000 kilolitres internal transfers/25 000 litres per drum.

(ii) *Monthly profits at higher sales level*

	(£000)
L Ltd: Sales (18 000 drums at £16 per drum)	288
Costs: Raw materials (£9 per drum)	(162)
Other expenses	(54)
Contribution	72
Fixed costs	40
Profit	32
M Ltd: Sales (950 000 kilolitres[a] at £9 per 25 litres)	342
Costs: Variable	(190)
Fixed	(60)
Profit	92

Note
[a] Internal transfers (18 000 drums at 25 litres per drum) plus 500 000 kilolitres external sales.

(b) (i) The use of a market price as the transfer price produces difficulties because L Ltd is not motivated to reduce the selling price, in order to increase volume, because its profits decline from £40 000 to £32 000. However, the profits of M Ltd increase from £60 000 to £92 000. Thus the profits for the company as a whole increase by £24 000. Hence the transfer price does not encourage goal congruence in this particular situation.

(ii) In order to overcome the above difficulties, there is a need to offer some inducement to L Ltd such that its profits will increase as a result of lowering the selling price in order to increase volume. Factors to consider are the following:

1. The significance of the loss in profits arising from the difference between profits at the optimum output level and profits based on the output using the current transfer pricing system.

2. Savings in selling and distribution costs arising from internal transfers compared with external sales. The savings per unit should be deducted from the market price.

3. The probability of divisional managers selecting optimal output levels if they are allowed to negotiate the prices of transfers between the divisions.
4. The extent to which divisional autonomy will be undermined if corporate headquarters determines the transfer prices that will motivate divisional managers to produce at the optimum output level.

(c) M Ltd has spare production capacity, and any transfer price in excess of variable cost, for output in excess of the present transfers of 250 kilolitres, would increase the profits of M Ltd. The profits of L Ltd will increase if the transfer price on the extra output of 8000 drums is reduced by more than £1 (£8000 loss in profits/ 8000 drums) per drum. The variable cost per kilolitre of M Ltd is £200. Thus the variable cost per 25 kilolitres (i.e. the raw materials required for 1 drum) is £5. If the transfer price for output in excess of 10 000 drums is set at above £5 and less than £8 per drum then both divisions will gain if the selling price of the final product is reduced by 20% and volume is increased by 80%.

Question 27.15 (a) The answer to this question can be found in the section headed 'A perfect market for the intermediate product with different buying and selling prices' in Appendix 27.1 to Chapter 27.

(b) *Schedule 1: Calculation of marginal cost, marginal revenue and net marginal revenue*

Output of Alpha (units)	Alpha marginal cost (£000)	Alpha marginal revenues[a,b] (£000)	Beta net marginal revenue[a] (£000)
0–10	<28	65 (1)	57 (3)
10–20	<28	60 (2)	55 (4/5)
20–30	<28	55 (4/5)	53 (6)
30–40	<28	50 (8)	51 (7)
40–50	<28	45 (11/12)	49 (9)
50–60	<28	40	47 (10)
60–70	28	35	45 (11/12)
70–80	30	30	43 (13)
80–90	33	25	40
90–100	35	20	36
100–110	37	15	33
110–120	40	10	30
120–130	44	5	25

Notes
[a]The numbers in parentheses represent the descending order of ranking of marginal revenue/net marginal revenue for Alpha and Beta.
[b]The question indicates that the marginal revenue function for Alpha decreases in increments of £5000 for each 10 units increase in sales value of Alpha for output levels from 60 to 130 units. This implies that the total revenue and marginal revenue function of Alpha can be computed from this information on the basis of a £5000 decline in marginal revenue for each 10 units of output.
[c]The marginal cost per 10 units of Alpha increases as output expands. This implies that the marginal cost per 10 units of Alpha is less than £28 000 for output of less than 60 units.
[d]The NMR of Beta declines as output rises, thus suggesting an imperfect final product market. The implication of this is that NMR is in excess of £47 000 for increments of 10 units sales of Beta at less than 50 units. The NMR for the first 50 units sales of Beta has been estimated based on the information given in the question. We shall see that the accuracy of the estimates for output levels below 60 units is not critical for calculating the optimum transfer price and activity level.

The output of Alpha is allocated between the sale of the intermediate product on the external market and the transfer of the intermediate product for sale as a final product on the basis of the ranking indicated in Schedule 1. The allocation is presented in the following schedule:

Schedule 2: Allocation of output of Alpha

(1) Output of Alpha (units)	(2) Alpha marginal cost (£000)	(3) Allocation per ranking in Schedule 1[a]	(4) Marginal revenue or NMR[b]
0–10	<28	Alpha	65
10–20	<28	Alpha	60
20–30	<28	Beta	57
30–40	<28	Beta	55
40–50	<28	Alpha	55
50–60	<28	Beta	53
60–70	28	Beta	51
70–80	30	Alpha	50
80–90	33	Beta	49
90–100	35	Beta	47
100–110	37	Beta	45
110–120	40	Alpha	45
120–130	44	no allocation (MR/NMR < MC)	43

Notes
[a] Alpha refers to sale of Alpha as an intermediate product. Beta refers to the transfer of Alpha internally for conversion to Beta and sale in the final product market.
[b] Appropriate MR/NMR per ranking in Schedule 1.

Conclusions
The optimal output level is 120 units. Below this output level MR > MC, but beyond 120 units MC > MR. To induce the output of 120 units, the transfer price should be set at £44 so as to prevent the receiving division from requesting a further 10 units, which will yield an NMR of £43. Examination of Schedule 2 indicates that 70 units should be transferred internally for sale as a final product and 50 units of the intermediate product sold externally. A transfer price of £44 will result in both divisions arriving at this production plan independently. Therefore, the optimal transfer price is the marginal cost of the supplying division for that output at which marginal cost equals the sum of the receiving division's net marginal revenue from using the intermediate product and the marginal revenue from the sale of the intermediate product – in other words, where column 2 equals column 4 in Schedule 2.

Question 27.17

(a) The starting point to answering this question is to ascertain whether the capacity of the supplying division is sufficient to meet the demand from both the external market and the receiving division. To increase demand by one unit of Aye the selling price must be reduced by £0.04 (£1/25 units). Thus the maximum selling price for an output of x units is:

SP $= £1000 - £0.04x$
Total revenue for an output of x units $= £1000x - £0.04x^2$
Marginal revenue $= dTR/dx = £1000 - £0.08x$
Marginal cost $=$ variable cost $= £280$

At the optimum output level where MR $=$ MC:
£1000 $- 0.08x = £280$
$x = 9000$ units

The highest selling price at which the optimum output can be sold is: SP = £1000 − £0.04 (9000) = £640. This leaves 21 000 units spare capacity for Division A. Therefore Division A can meet the maximum output for Bee of 18 000 units without restricting sales and a forgone contribution from Aye. The maximum selling price for Bee for output of x units is:

$$SP = £4000 − £0.10x$$
Total revenue for an output of x units $= £4000x − £0.10x^2$
Marginal revenue $= dTR/dx = £4000 − £0.20x$
Marginal costs $= £280 + £590 = £870$
At the optimum output level where MR = MC:
$£4000 − £0.20x = £870$
$$x = 15\,650 \text{ units}$$

The highest selling price at which the optimum output can be sold is: SP = £4000 − 0.10 (15 650) = £2435. The contributions at the optimal selling prices are:

Division A = £ 3 240 000 [9 000 × (£640 − £280)]
Division B = £24 492 250 [15 650 × (£2435 − £870)]
Group = £27 732 250

(b) If Division A sets the transfer price at the optimum selling price of £640 the variable cost per unit of output for producing Bee will be £1230 (£640 + £590).

MR of Division B $= £4000 − £0.20x$ (See part (a))

The optimn output level is where:

$$£4000 − £0.20x = £1230$$
$$x = 13\,850 \text{ units}$$

The optimum selling price is: £4000 − £0.10 (13 850) = £2615
(c) The revised contributions if the transfer price is set at £640 will be as follows:

	(£)
Division A : External sales [9000 × (£640 − £280)]	3 240 000
Internal transfers [13 850 × (£640 − £280)]	4 986 000
Division B : External sales [13 850 × (£2615 − £1230)]	19 182 250
Total contribution	27 408 250

Setting the transfer price at the market price results in an increase in total contribution of Division A and a decline in the total contribution of Division B. The contribution for the group as a whole declines by £324 000.

As a result of the increase in the transfer price Division B's marginal cost increases and it will therefore restrict output and set a higher selling price. Where the market for the intermediate product is imperfect, the optimal transfer price is the marginal cost of producing the intermediate product at the optimum output level for the group as a whole. Since marginal cost per unit is constant and equal to variable cost, the optimum transfer price is variable cost. If the transfer price is set at variable cost the receiving division will have a cost function identical to that specified in (a) and will set the selling price at the optimum output for the group as a whole.

Question 27.19 (a) (i) Profits for the group as a whole will be maximized where the marginal cost of Chem is equal to the net marginal revenue of Drink.

Price $= £45 − £0.0008Q_D$

Therefore

Total revenue
$$= Q_D (45 - 0.0008Q_D)$$
$$= 45Q_D - 0.0008Q_D^2$$

Therefore

$$MR = \frac{dTR}{dQ_D} = 45 - 0.0016Q_D$$

$$MC_D = \frac{dTC_D}{dQ_D} = 11 + 0.002Q_D$$

$$NMR_D = MR_D - MC_D = 34 - 0.0036Q_D$$

$$MC_C = \frac{dTC_C}{dQ_C} = 5.50 + 0.004Q_C$$

So profits are maximized where

$$5.50 + 0.004Q_C = 34 - 0.0036Q_D$$

Because there is no intermediate market, both divisions must agree on the output level. Therefore $Q_C = Q_D = Q$, and so

$$0.0076Q = 28.50$$
$$Q = 3750 \text{ (i.e. optimum monthly output is 3750 units)}$$

(ii) The optimum transfer price is the marginal cost of Chem for that output at which the marginal cost equals Drink's net marginal revenue from processing the intermediate product (i.e. at an output level of 3750 units as calculated in (i)). The marginal cost of Chem at an output level of 3750 units is:

$$5.50 + 0.004 \times 3750 = £20.50$$

At 3750 units the price that Drink would charge for selling the final product is:

$$45 - 0.0008 \times 3750 = £42$$

The resulting profits for each division would be:

Chem	(£)	Drink	(£)
Revenues (3750 × £20.50 TP)	76 875	Revenues (3750 × £42)	157 500
Costs (W1)	(58 750)	Conversion costs (W2)	(70 312)
Profit	18 125	Transferred costs	(76 875)
		Profit	10 313

Group profit = £28 438 (£18 125 + £10 313)

Workings
(W1) $TC_C = £10\,000 + £5.50 \times 3750 + £0.002 \times (3750)^2 = £58\,750$
(W2) $TC_D = £15\,000 + £11 \times 3750 + £0.001 \times (3750)^2 = £70\,312$

(b) (i) In (a) the marginal cost for Chem at different output levels was equated to the NMR of Drink. It is assumed that the question implies that Chem would quote transfer prices based on its marginal cost at given output levels, so that Drink would regard these transfer prices ($5.5 + 0.004Q_C$) to be constant per unit for all output levels. Drink's net profit (NP) will be as follows:

$$NP = [(45Q - 0.0008Q^2) - (15\,000 + 11Q + 0.001Q^2) - Q(5.5 + 0.004Q)]$$
$$= 28.5Q - 0.0058Q^2 - 15\,000$$

Profit is maximized where $dNP/dQ = 0$; that is, where

$$28.5 - 0.0116Q = 0$$
$$Q = 2457 \text{ units}$$

An alternative approach is to equate the net marginal revenue with the marginal cost of the transfers. Chem will transfer out at a marginal cost of $5.5 + 0.004Q_C$, and Drink will treat this price at a constant sum per unit. Therefore the total cost of transfers to Drink will be:

$$Q_C(5.5 + 0.004Q_C) = 5.5Q_C + 0004Q_C{}^2$$

Therefore the marginal cost of transfers will be:

$$5.5 + 0.008Q_C$$

The transfer price for Drink that maximizes its profits is where NMR = MC, i.e. where

$$34 - 0.0036Q = 5.5 + 0.008Q$$
$$Q = 2457 \text{ units}$$

(ii) The level that maximizes profit for Drink determines the transfer price. At an output level of 2457 units the transfer price will be:

$$5.5 + (0.004 \times 2457) = £15.33$$

At 2457 units the price that Drink would charge for selling the final product is:

$$45 - (0.0008 \times 2457) = £43.034$$

Chem	(£)	Drink	(£)
Revenues (2457 × £15.33)	37 666	Revenues (2457 × £43.034)	105 735
Cost (W1)	(35 587)	Conversion costs (W2)	(48 064)
		Transferred costs	(37 666)
Profit	2 079	Profit	20 005

Group profit = £22 084

Workings
(W1) $TC_C = £10\,000 + (£5.50 \times 2457) + [£0.002 \times (2457)^2]$
(W2) $TC_D = £15\,000 + (£11 \times 2457) + [£0.001 \times (2457)^2]$

(c) A sound transfer pricing system should accomplish the following objectives:
  (i) It should motivate divisional managers to make sound decisions that will lead to maximization of group profits.
  (ii) It should enable a report to be made of divisional profits that is a reasonable measure of the management performance of the division.
  (iii) It should ensure that divisional autonomy is not undermined.
  When there is a perfect market for the intermediate product, the correct transfer price is the market price, and it will be possible to achieve all the above objectives. However, when there is no market price, it is unlikely that all the above objectives can be achieved. The result in (a) achieves the first objective and possibly the second, depending upon the managers' attitudes to the relative profits. However, to achieve the first objective, it has been necessary to set the transfer price centrally, and this means that the prices of internal inputs and outputs are not

set by the divisional managers. Therefore divisional autonomy is undermined.

In (b) the output and transfer pricing decision has been delegated to the divisions. Drink determines its own optimum output level based on Chem's marginal cost, and thus sets the transfer price. This approach does not result in maximizing group profits and fails to provide a reasonable measure of each divisions contribution to total group profit. Central management is likely to regard the solution as unacceptable, because of the loss of profits, and the management of Chem will have to accept the transfer price determined by Drink and the resulting low profitability and spare capacity. The end result is likely to be intervention by central management. The implications for Megacorp are that, in order to achieve goal congruence, transfer pricing decisions cannot be made independently by either division.

(d) The answer should include a discussion of market-based transfer prices, cost-plus transfer prices, transfer prices based on linear programming methods and negotiated transfer prices. See Chapter 27 for a discussion of each of these methods.

Question 27.20

(a)

	Blackalls			Brownalls	
	(£)	(£)	(£)		(£)
Selling price		45			54
Component costs: Alpha	18 (3 × £6)		12 (2 × £6)		
Beta	8 (2 × £4)		16 (4 × £4)		
Processing cost	12	38	14		42
Contribution		7			12

Group contribution:	(£)
Blackalls 200 × £7	1400
Brownalls 300 × £12	3600
	5000

(b) Transfer price = variable cost + shadow price

Alpha	=	£6	+	£0.50	= £6.50
Beta	=	£4	+	£2.75	= £6.75

(i)

	Division A	Division B
	(£)	(£)
Transfer price	6.50	6.75
Variable cost	6.00	4.00
Contribution/unit	0.50	2.75

(ii)

	Black division		Brown division	
	(£)	(£)	(£)	(£)
Selling price		45		54
Component cost:				
Alpha	19.50 (3 × £6.50)		13.00 (2 × £6.50)	
Beta	13.50 (2 × £6.75)		27.00 (4 × £6.75)	
Processing cost	12.00	45	14.00	54
Contribution/unit		nil		nil

(c) When the supplying division does not have sufficient capacity to meet all the demands placed upon it, linear programming can be used to determine the optimum production level. The transfer price that will induce the supplying division to produce the optimum output level can be derived from the linear programming model. The transfer price is determined by adding the shadow prices of the scarce resources to the variable cost of the resources consumed by the intermediate product. The transfer price that induces the supplying division to transfer the optimum output to the receiving division results in the supplying division being credited with all of the contribution arising from the transfers and the receiving division earning a zero contribution. This is illustrated in part (b) of the answer.

The managers of the receiving divisions will be indifferent about producing the final products, since they yield a zero contribution, but the group as a whole will be worse off if the final products are not produced. To ensure that the optimal output of the final products is produced, it will be necessary for head office to instruct the receiving divisions to convert all the output that the supplying divisions are prepared to transfer (at the transfer prices derived from the linear programming model). This will have a negative motivational influence on the managers of the receiving division, and will result in a loss of divisional autonomy. In addition, the reported performance of the divisions will not reflect their contribution to group profits. Therefore the transfer prices will not be acceptable to the managers of the receiving divisions, whereas the managers of the supplying divisions (A and B) will be satisfied since they will be allocated with the full amount of the contribution.

(d) (i) The transfer price should reflect the opportunity cost of producing the intermediate products. The transfer prices are calculated as follows:

$$\text{variable cost} + \text{opportunity cost}$$
$$\text{Alpha} = £6 + (5\% \times £6) = £6.30$$
$$\text{Beta} = £4 + (£3.50 - £0.50) = £7$$

Note that the above transfer prices reflect the selling prices (or net sales revenue) from using the capacity of the supplying divisions to produce other products (A division) or sell the intermediate product on the external market (B division).

(ii) The contributions per unit for Blackalls and Brownalls are as follows:

| | Black division | | Brown division | |
	(£)	(£)	(£)	(£)
Selling price		45.00		54.00
Component costs:				
Alpha (at £6.30)	18.90		12.60	
Beta (at £7)	14.00		28.00	
Processing cost	12.00	44.90	14.00	54.60
Contribution/unit		0.10		(0.60)

Brown division will not produce Brownalls, because they yield a negative contribution, but Black division will wish to maximize production of Blackalls. The production capacity of Alpha and Beta is as follows:

Alpha 2400 units (restricts maximum production of Blackalls to 800 units)
Beta 3200 units (restricts maximum production of Blackalls to 1600 units)

Production of Blackalls is therefore restricted to 800 units, thus using all of the available Alpha capacity. Production of 800 units of Blackalls requires 1600 units of Beta (800 × 2 units). The unused Beta capacity of 1600 units (3200 − 1600) will be sold on the external intermediate market. Therefore the optimal output is as follows:

Brownalls zero
Blackalls 800 units
Alpha   2400 units transferred to Black division
Beta   3200 units (1600 units transferred to Black division and 1600 units sold externally)

The resulting maximum group contribution is:

		(£)
Blackalls (800 × £7)		5 600
Beta	[1600 × (£7 − £4)]	4 800
		10 400

Past, current and future developments in management accounting practice

Solutions to Chapter 28 questions

Question summary

This chapter contains questions relating to the impact of the changing manufacturing and competitive environment on management accounting. Questions 28.1–28.9 are essay questions and Question 28.10 requires the calculation of costs before and after the introduction of a quality management programme.

Question 28.3 (a) Physical measures are quantitative measures that do not use monetary measurements as a common denominator. Non-financial indices are ratios that are used to compare the trend in physical measures.

(b) (i)
$$\frac{\text{processing time}}{\text{processing time} + \text{inspection time} + \text{wait time} + \text{move time}}$$

This ratio gives an indication of the proportion of manufacturing cycle time which is engaged on value-added activities. Of the activities outlined above, only processing time adds value.

(ii)
$$\frac{\text{number of deliveries not on time}}{\text{total number of deliveries}}$$

This is a measure of the extent to which a company is failing to meet customer quality requirements in terms of late deliveries.

(iii)
$$\frac{\text{closing stocks}}{\text{average production output per day}}$$

This measure provides an indication of the average number of days production in inventory. This performance measure should be analysed by inventory category and location. It provides an indication of the extent to which the objectives of a just-in-time philosophy of minimizing stock levels is being achieved.

(c) For the answer to this question see 'Non-financial performance measures' in Chapter 18 and 'Criticisms of management accounting' in Chapter 28.

Question 28.6 Benchmarking is a continuous process that involves comparing business processes and activities in an organization with those in other companies that represent world-class best practices in order to see how processes and activities can be improved. The comparison involves both financial and non-financial indicators.

Two different approaches are adopted in most organizations. Cost-driven benchmarking involves applying the principles of benchmarking from a distance and comparing some aspects of performance with those of competitors, usually using intermediaries such as consultants. The outcome of the exercise is cost reduction. The second approach involves process-driven benchmarking. It is a process involving the philosophy of continuous improvement. The focus is not necessarily on competitors but on a benchmarking partner. The aim is to obtain a better understanding of the processes and questions the reason why things take place, how they take place and how often they take place. The outcome should be superior performance through the strengthening of processes and business behaviour.

Inter-firm comparisons place much greater emphasis on the use of financial data and mostly involve comparisons at the company or strategic business unit level rather than at the business process or activity level. Inter-firm comparisons tend to compare data derived from published financial accounts whereas benchmarking also makes use of both internal and external data.

Benchmarking contributes to cost reduction by highlighting those areas where performance is inferior to competitors and where opportunities for cost reduction exist (e.g. Elimination of non-value added activities or more efficient ways of carrying out activities).

Activity-based budgeting (ABB) is an extension of ABC applied to the preparation of budgets. It focuses on the costs of activities necessary to produce and sell products and services by assigning costs to separate activity cost pools. The cause and effect criterion based on cost drivers is used to establish budgets for each cost pool.

ABB involves the following stages:
1. Determining the budgeted cost (i.e. the cost driver rate) of performing each unit of activity for all major activities.
2. Determine the required resources for each individual activity to meet sales and production requirements.
3. Computing the budgeted cost for each activity.

Note that ABB focuses on budgets for the cost of activities rather than functional departments.

Zero-base budgeting tends to be used more as a one-off cost reduction programme. The emphasis is on functional responsibility areas, rather than individual activities, with the aim of justifying all costs from a zero base.

Activity analysis is required prior to implementing ABB. This process can help to identify non-value added activities that may be candidates for elimination or performing the activities in different ways with less resources. Activity performance measures can be established that enable the cost per unit of activity to be monitored and used as a basis for benchmarking. This information should highlight those activities where there is a potential for performing more efficiently by reducing resource consumption and future spending.

See 'Target costing' in Chapter 13 for an explanation of the objectives and workings of target costing.

Continuous cost improvement is a process whereby a firm gradually reduces costs without attempting to achieve a specific target. Target costing is emphasized more at a product's design and development stage whereas continuous cost improvement occurs throughout a product's life. The principles of target costing can also be applied to cost reduction exercises for existing products. Where this approach is applied there is little difference between the two methods. Both approaches clearly focus on reducing costs throughout a product's life cycle but target costing emphasizes cost reduction at the design and development stage. At this stage there is a greater potential for reducing costs throughout the product life cycle.

(a) Total quality management (TQM) is a term that is used to describe a situation **Question 28.7** where all business functions are involved in a process of continuous quality improvement. The critical success factors for the implementation of TQM are:
　　(i) The focus should be on customer needs. This should not just represent the

final customer. All sections within a company should be seen as a potential customer of a supplying section and a potential supplier of services to other sections.

(ii) Everyone within the organization should be involved in TQM. Senior management should provide the commitment that creates the culture needed to support TQM.

(iii) The focus should be on continuous improvement. Continuous improvement seeks to eliminate non-value activities, produce products and provide services with zero defects and simplify business processes. All employees, rather than just management, should be involved in the process since employees involved in the processes are often the source of the best ideas.

(iv) The aim should be to design quality into the product and the production process. This requires a close working relationship between sales, production, distribution and research.

(v) Senior management should promote the required culture change by promoting a climate for continuous improvement rather than imposing blame for a failure to achieve static targets.

(vi) An effective performance measurement system that measures continuous improvement from the customer's perspective should be introduced. Simple non-financial measures involving real time reporting should be seen as a vital component of the performance measurement system.

(vii) Existing rewards and performance measurements should be reviewed to ensure that they encourage, rather than discourage, quality improvements.

(viii) Appropriate training and education should be given so that everyone is aware of the aims of TQM.

(b) For the answer to this question you should refer to 'Total quality management' in Chapter 28. In particular the answer should describe the different categories of cost that are included in a Cost of Quality Report and indicate how the report can be used to draw management's attention to the possibility of reducing total quality costs by a wiser allocation of costs between the different categories.

Question 28.10 (a) (i) *Total production units (pre-inspection)*

	Existing situation		Revised situation
Total sales requirements	5000		5000
Specification losses (5%)	250	(2.5%)	125
	5250		5125
Downgrading at inspection (12.5/87.5 × 5250)	750	(7.5/92.5 × 5125)	416
Total units before inspection (100/87.5 × 5250)	6000	(100/92.5 × 5125)	5541

(ii) *Purchase of material X (m²)*

Materials required to meet pre-inspection production requirements (6000 × 8 m²)	48 000	(5541 × 8 m²)	44 328
Processing losses (4/96 × 48 000)	2000	(2.5/97.5 × 44 328)	1137
Input to the process (100/96 × 48 000)	50 000		45 465
Scrapped materials (5/95 × 50 000)	2632	(3/97 × 45 465)	1406
Total purchases (100/95 × 50 000)	52 632	(100/97 × 45 465)	46 871

(iii) *Gross machine hours*

Initial requirements (6000 × 0.6)	3600	(5541 × 0.5 hrs)	2771
Rectification units (80% × 250 × 0.2 hrs)	40	(80% × 125 × 0.2 hrs)	20
	3640		2791
Idle time (20/80 × 3460)	910	(12.5/87.5 × 2791)	399
Gross machine hrs (100/80 × 3640)	4550	(100/87.5 × 2791)	3190

(b) *Profit and Loss Accounts*

	Existing situation (£)		Revised situation (£)
Sales revenue:			
First quality 5000 × £100	500 000	5000 × £100	500 000
Second quality 750 × £70	52 500	416 × £70	29 120
Third quality 200 × £50	10 000	100 × £50	5000
Scrap sales 50 × £5	250	25 × £5	125
	562 750		534 245
Costs			
Material X (52 632 × £4)	210 528	46 871 × £4	187 484
Insp/storage costs (52 632 × £0.10)	5263	46 871 × £0.10	4 687
Machine costs (4550 × £40)	182 000	3190 × £40	127 600
Delivery of replacements (250 × £8)	2 000	125 × £8	1 000
Inspection and other costs	25 000	60% × £25 000	15 000
Product liability (3% × £500 000)	15 000	1% × 500 000	5000
Sundry fixed costs	60 000	90% × £60 000	54 000
Prevention programme costs	20 000		60 000
	519 791		454 771
Net profit	42 959		79 474

(c) A cost of quality report is a major feature of a quality control programme. The report should indicate the total cost to the organization of producing products that do not conform to quality requirements. The cost of quality report should analyse costs by prevention costs, appraisal costs, internal failure costs and external failure costs. You should refer to Chapter 28 for a description of each of these cost categories.

The cost of quality report can be used as an attention-directing device to make top management aware of how much is being spent on quality-related costs. The report can be used to draw management's attention to the possibility of reducing total quality costs by a wiser allocation of costs among the four quality categories. For example, by spending more on prevention costs, the amount of spending in the internal and external failure categories can be substantially reduced, and therefore total spending can be lowered.

Examples of each of the four cost categories for Calton Ltd are as follows:

Internal failure costs: Incoming materials scrapped due to poor receipt and storage organization, and downgrading products at the final inspection stage.

External failure costs: Free replacement of goods, product liability claims, loss of customer goodwill.

Appraisal costs: Inspection checks of incoming materials and completed output.

Prevention costs: Training costs in quality prevention and preventative maintenance.

New questions for 1999

Question 3.1
intermediate

If actual output is lower than budgeted output, which of the following costs would you expect to be lower than the original budget?

A Total variable costs
B Total fixed costs
C Variable costs per unit
D Fixed costs per unit

ACCA Foundation Paper 3 –
Sample Question

Question 3.2
intermediate

The following data relate to two output levels of a department:

Machine hours	17 000	18 500
Overheads	£246 500	£251 750

The variable overhead rate per hour is £3.50. The amount of fixed overheads is:

A £5250
B £59 500
C £187 000
D £246 500

CIMA Stage 1

Question 3.3
intermediate

Prime cost is:

A all costs incurred in manufacturing a product;
B the total of direct costs;
C the material cost of a product;
D the cost of operating a department.

CIMA Stage 1

Question 3.4
intermediate

Direct costs are:

A costs which can be identified with a cost centre but not identified to a single cost unit;
B costs which can be identified with a single cost unit;
C costs incurred as a direct result of a particular decision;
D costs incurred which can be attributed to a particular accounting period;
E none of the above.

CIMA Stage 2

Question 3.5
intermediate

A direct cost is a cost which:

A is incurred as a direct consequence of a decision;
B can be economically identified with the item being costed;
C cannot be economically identified with the item being costed;
D is immediately controllable;
E is the responsibility of the board of directors.

CIMA Stage 2

Distinguish between, and provide an illustration of:
(i) 'avoidable' and 'unavoidable' costs;
(ii) 'cost centres' and 'cost units'.

8 marks
ACCA Foundation Paper 3

Item (B) will be constant within the relevant range of output.
Item (C) will be constant per unit.
If output declines fixed cost per unit will decrease.
Total variable cost will fall in line with a decline in output and therefore item A is the correct answer.

Total variable overheads = 17 000 × £3.50 = £59 500.
Total variable overhead (£59 500) + Total fixed overhead = Total overhead (£246 500).
Total fixed overhead = £246 500 − £59 500 = £187 000.
Answer = C

Answer = B

Answer = B

Answer = B

See Chapter 3 for an explanation of the terms avoidable costs, unavoidable costs and cost centres. A cost unit is a unit of product or service for which costs are ascertained. In a manufacturing organization a cost unit will be a unit of output produced within a cost centre. In a service organization, such as an educational establishment, a cost unit might be the cost per student.

Using the first in, first out (FIFO) system for pricing stock issues means that when prices are rising:
A   product costs are overstated and profits understated;
B   product costs are kept in line with price changes;
C   product costs are understated and profits understated;
D   product costs are understated and profits overstated.

CIMA Stage 1

Stores pricing and preparation of the stores control account
(a) Explain the meaning of:
   (i) continuous stocktaking and
   (ii) perpetual inventory
   in the context of a material control system.   5 marks
(b) A company operates an historic batch costing system, which is not integrated with the financial accounts, and uses the weighted average method of pricing raw material issues. A weighted average price (to three decimal places of a pound £) is calculated after each purchase of material.
Receipts and issues of Material X for a week were as follows:

	Receipts into stock			Issues to production	
Day	kg	£	Day	kg	
1	1400	1092.00	2	1700	
4	1630	1268.14	5	1250	

At the beginning of the week, stock of material X was 3040 kg at a cost of £0.765 per kg. Of the issues of material on day 2, 60 kg were returned to stock on day 3. Of the receipts of material on day 1, 220 kg were returned to the supplier on day 4. Invoices for the material receipts during the week remained unpaid at the end of the week.

Required:

(i) Prepare a tabulation of the movement of stock during the week, showing the changes in the level of stock, its valuation per kilogram, and the total value of stock held.

(ii) Record the week's transactions in the material X stock account in the cost ledger, indicating clearly in each case the account in which the corresponding entry should be posted.

9 marks
Total 14 marks
ACCA Foundation Paper 3

Answer 4.1 Answer = D

Answer 4.2 (a) (i) See Chapter 4 for an explanation of continuous stocktaking.

(ii) Perpetual inventory is a system of entering details of receipts and issues for each individual item of materials onto a record card. A separate record is maintained for each individual item of material. Therefore the quantity of stock on hand can be ascertained at any point in time. In most organizations stock records are maintained in a computerized format.

(b) (i)

Date	Receipts Quantity	Price £	Value £	Issues Quantity	Price £	Value £	Balance Quantity	Price £	Value £
Day 1							3 040	0.765	2 325.60
1	1 400	0.780	1 092				4 440	0.770	3 417.60
2				1 700	0.770	1 309	2 740	0.770	2 108.60
3	60	0.770	46.20				2 800	0.770	2 154.80
4				220	0.780	171.60	2 580	0.769	1 983.20
4	1 630	0.778	1 268.14				4 210	0.772	3 251.34
5				1 250	0.772	965	2 960	0.772	2 286.34

Material X Account

	£		£
Opening stock	2 325.60	Work-in-progress	1 309.00
Cost ledger control	1 092.00	Cost ledger control	171.60
Work-in-progress	46.20	Work-in-progress	965.00
Cost ledger control	1 268.14	Closing stock	2 286.34
	4 731.94		4 731.94

Question 5.1
intermediate

A company uses a predetermined overhead recovery rate based on machine hours. Budgeted factory overhead for a year amounted to £720 000, but actual factory overhead incurred was £738 000. During the year, the company absorbed £714 000 of factory overhead on 119 000 actual machine hours.

What was the company's budgeted level of machine hours for the year?

A 116 098
B 119 000
C 120 000
D 123 000

ACCA Foundation Paper 3 –
Specimen Question

Question 5.2
intermediate

A company absorbs overheads on machine hours which were budgeted at 11 250 with overheads of £258 750. Actual results were 10 980 hours with overheads of £254 692.

Overheads were:
  A under-absorbed by £2152
  B over-absorbed by £4058
  C under-absorbed by £4058
  D over-absorbed by £2152

CIMA Stage 1

The following data are to be used for sub-questions (i) and (ii) below:

Budgeted labour hours	8 500
Budgeted overheads	£148 750
Actual labour hours	7 928
Actual overheads	£146 200

(i) Based on the data given above, what is the labour hour overhead absorption rate?
  A £17.50 per hour
  B £17.20 per hour
  C £18.44 per hour
  D £18.76 per hour
(ii) Based on the data given above, what is the amount of overhead under/over-absorbed?
  A £2550 under-absorbed
  B £2529 over-absorbed
  C £2550 over-absorbed
  D £7460 under-absorbed

CIMA Stage 1 – Specimen Paper

A firm makes special assemblies to customers' orders and uses job costing. The data for a period are:

	Job no. AA10 (£)	Job no. BB15 (£)	Job no. CC20 (£)
Opening WIP	26 800	42 790	–
Material added in period	17 275	–	18 500
Labour for period	14 500	3 500	24 600

The budgeted overheads for the period were £126 000.
  (i) What overhead should be added to job number CC20 for the period?
    A £24 600
    B £65 157
    C £72 761
    D £126 000
 (ii) Job no. BB15 was completed and delivered during the period and the firm wishes to earn $33\frac{1}{3}$% profit on sales.
    What is the selling price of job number BB15?
    A £69 435
    B £75 521
    C £84 963
    D £138 870
(iii) What was the approximate value of closing work in progress at the end of the period?
    A £58 575
    B £101 675
    C £147 965
    D £217 323

CIMA Stage 1

Overhead analysis, calculation of overhead rates and a product cost

Knowing that you are studying for the CIMA qualification, a friend who manages a small business has sought your advice about how to produce quotations in response to the enquiries which her business receives. Her business is sheet metal fabrication – supplying ducting for dust extraction and air conditioning installations. She believes that she has lost orders recently through the use of a job cost estimating system which was introduced, on the advice of her auditors, seven years ago. You are invited to review this system.

Upon investigation, you find that a plant-wide percentage of 125% is added to prime costs in order to arrive at a selling price. The percentage added is intended to cover all overheads for the three production departments (Departments P, Q and R), all the selling, distribution and administration costs, and the profit.

You also discover that the selling, distribution and administration costs equate to roughly 20% of total production costs, and that to achieve the desired return on capital employed a margin of 20% of sales value is necessary.

You recommend that an analysis of overhead cost items be undertaken with the objective of determining a direct labour hour rate of overhead absorption for each of the three departments work passes through. (You think about activity-based costing but feel this would be too sophisticated and difficult to introduce at the present time.)

There are 50 direct workers in the business plus 5 indirect production people.

From the books, records and some measuring, you ascertain the following information, which will enable you to compile an overhead analysis spreadsheet and to determine overhead absorption rates per direct labour hour for departmental overhead purposes:

Cost/expense	Annual amount (£)	Basis for apportionment where allocation not given
Repairs and maintenance	62 000	Technical assessment: P £42 000, Q £10 000 R £10 000
Depreciation	40 000	Cost of plant and equipment
Consumable supplies	9 000	Direct labour hours
Wage-related costs	87 000	12.5% of direct wages costs
Indirect labour	90 000	Direct labour hours
Canteen/rest/smoke room	30 000	Number of direct workers
Business rates and insurance	26 000	Floor area

Other estimates/information:

	Department P	Department Q	Department R
Estimated direct labour hours	50 000	30 000	20 000
Direct wages costs	£386 000	£210 000	£100 000
Number of direct workers	25	15	10
Floor area in square metres	5 000	4 000	1 000
Plant and equipment at cost	£170 000	£140 000	£90 000

Required:
(a) Calculate the overhead absorption rates for each department, based on direct labour hours.   *9 marks*
(b) Prepare a sample quotation for job 976, utilizing information given in the question, your answer to (a) above, and the following additional information:

Estimated direct material cost: £800
Estimated direct labour hours: 30 in department P
                                  10 in department Q
                                  5 in department R

3 marks

(c) Calculate what would have been quoted for job 976 under the 'auditors' system' and comment on whether your friend's suspicions about lost business could be correct.

3 marks
Total 15 marks
CIMA Stage 2 Cost Accounting

Overhead analysis, calculation of overhead rates and a product cost

ABC Limited is preparing its departmental budgets and product cost estimates for the year ending 31 December 1995. The company has three manufacturing departments – machining, assembly and finishing – together with a production maintenance department.

The following costs and related data have been estimated for the year to 31 December 1995:

Costs:	Machining	Assembly	Finishing	Maintenance	Total
Direct wages	60	32	72	30	194
Indirect wages	10	6	8	–	24
Direct materials	80	10	4	–	94
Indirect materials	15	4	8	20	47
Power					102
Light and heat					10
Depreciation					7
Rent and rates					25
Personnel					63
Other data:					
Direct labour hours	12 000	8 000	16 000	6 000	42 000
Machine hours	40 000	5 000	6 000	–	51 000
Employees	6	4	8	3	21
Floor area (sq. metres)	1 000	400	300	300	2 000
Net book value of fixed assets	20 000	8 000	3 000	4 000	35 000

The maintenance department is expected to spend 60% of its time working for the machining department, with the remainder of its time being shared equally between assembly and finishing.

Required:

(a) Prepare an overhead analysis sheet for ABC Limited for its year ending 31 December 1995. *8 marks*

(b) Calculate appropriate overhead absorption rates for the machining, assembly and finishing departments.

6 marks

(c) Prepare a cost estimate, based on the following data, for a product which is to be manufactured in January 1995:

	Machining	Assembly	Finishing
Direct materials (£)	2500	400	200
Direct labour hours	800	350	1140
Machine hours	1400	100	80

4 marks

(d) Prepare the fixed production overhead control account for the machining department, assuming that:
   (i) all the overhead costs budgeted are fixed costs;
   (ii) the actual fixed overhead costs incurred amounted to £128 000;
   (iii) the actual direct labour and machine hours were 10 500 and 39 000, respectively. *3 marks*

(e) Analyse the causes of the under/over-absorption shown in your answer to (d) above.

4 marks
Total 25 marks
CIMA Stage 1 Accounting

Question 5.7 Job cost calculation

intermediate A printing and publishing company has been asked to provide an estimate for the production of 100 000 catalogues, of 64 pages (32 sheets of paper) each, for a potential customer.

Four operations are involved in the production process: photography, set-up, printing and binding.

Each page of the catalogue requires a separate photographic session. Each session costs £150.

Set-up would require a plate to be made for each page of the catalogue. Each plate requires 4 hours of labour at £7 per hour and £35 of materials. Overheads are absorbed on the basis of labour hours at an hourly rate of £9.50.

In printing, paper costs £12 per thousand sheets. Material losses are expected to be 2% of input. Other printing materials will cost £7 per 500 catalogues. 1000 catalogues are printed per hour of machine time. Labour and overhead costs incurred in printing are absorbed at a rate of £62 per machine hour.

Binding costs are recovered at a rate per machine hour. The rate is £43 per hour and 2500 catalogues are bound per hour of machine time.

A profit margin of 10% of selling price is required.

You are required to:

(a) determine the total amount that should be quoted for the catalogue job by the printing and publishing company.

11 marks

(b) calculate the additional costs that would be charged to the job if the labour efficiency ratio achieved versus estimate in set-up is 90%.

4 marks
15 marks
ACCA Foundation Stage – Paper 3

Answer 5.1

Overhead absorbed (£714 000)   =   Actual hours (119 000) × Pre-determined overhead rate.

Pre-determined overhead rate   =   £714 000/119 000 = £6.

Budgeted overheads (£720 000)   =   Budgeted machine hours × Budgeted overhead rate (£6).

Budgeted machine hours = £720 000/£6 = 120 000 hours.

Answer = C

Answer 5.2

Budgeted overhead rate = £258 750/11 250 hours = £23 per machine hour.

Overheads absorbed = £23 × 10 980 Actual hours = £252 540.

Overheads incurred = £254 692

Overheads absorbed = £252 540

Under-absorbed overheads = £2 152

Answer = A

Answer 5.3(i)

Budgeted overhead rates and not actual overhead rates should be used as indicated in Chapter 4.

Overhead rate = £148 750/8 500 hours = £17.50 per hour.

Answer = A

	£
Actual overheads incurred	146 200
Overheads absorbed (7 928 × £17.50)	138 740
Under-absorbed overheads	7 460

Answer = D

It is assumed that labour cost is to be used as the allocation base.
Total labour cost = £14 500 + £3 500 + £24 600 = £42 600.
Overhead recovery rate = £126 000/£42 600 = £2.9578 per £1 of labour.
Overhead charged to Job CC20 = £24 600 × £2.9578 = £72 761.

Answer = C

	£
Opening WIP	42 790
Direct labour	3 500
Overhead (£3 500 × £2.9578)	10 352
	56 642
Selling price (£56 642/0.667)	84 921
or £56 642 divided by $\frac{2}{3}$ =	£84 963

Answer = C

closing WIP = Total cost of AA10 and CC20

	Total	AA10	CC20
	£	£	£
Opening WIP		26 800	0
Materials in period		17 275	18 500
Labour in period		14 500	24 600
Overheads in period:			
2.9577465 × £14 500		42 887	
2.9577465 × £24 600			72 761
	217 323	101 462	115 861

Answer = D

(a) Calculation of department overhead rates

	Department P	Department Q	Department R
	£	£	£
Repairs and maintenance	42 000	10 000	10 000
Depreciation	17 000[a]	14 000	9 000
Consumable supplies	4 500[b]	2 700	1 800
Wage related costs	48 250	26 250	12 500
Indirect labour	45 000	27 000	18 000
Canteen/rest/smoke room	15 000[c]	9 000	6 000
Business rates and insurance	13 000[d]	10 400	2 600
	184 750	99 350	55 900
Direct labour hours	50 000	30 000	20 000
Overhead absorption rate	£3.70	£3.31	£3.00

Notes:
The calculations for Department P are:
[a]Depreciation = £170 000/£400 000 × £40 000.
[b]Consumable supplies = 50 000/100 000 × £9 000.

^{c}Canteen = 25/50 × £30 000.
^{d}Business rates insurance = 5 000/10 000 × £26 000.

(b) Job 976: Sample quotation

		£	£
Direct materials			800.00
Direct labour	P (30 × £7.72^a)	231.60	
	Q (10 × £7.00^b)	70.00	
	R (5 × £5.00^c)	25.00	326.60
Overhead absorbed	P (30 × £3.70)	111.00	
	Q (10 × £3.31)	33.10	
	R (5 × £3.00)	15.00	159.10
Production cost			1 285.70
Selling, distribution and administration costs (20% × £1 285.70)			257.14
Total cost			1 542.84
Profit margin (20% of selling price)			385.71
Selling price (£1 542.84 × 100/800)			1 928.55

Notes:
^{a}£386 000/50 000.
^{b}£210 000/30 000.
^{c}£100 000/20 000.

(c)

	£
Direct materials	800.00
Direct labour	326.60
Prime cost	1 126.60
Overhead applied (125%)	1 408.25
Total cost	2 534.85

The auditor's system results in a higher cost for this quotation. However, other jobs will be overcosted with the previous system. The auditor's system will result in the reporting of more accurate job costs with some job costs being higher, and others being lower, than the present system. For a more detailed answer see the section on blanket overhead rates in Chapter 5.

Answer 5.6 (a) Overhead analysis sheet for ABC Limited for the year ending 31 December 1995

Expense	Machining £000	Assembly £000	Finishing £000	Maintenance £000	Total £000	Basis of apportionment
Indirect wages	10	6	8	30	54	Allocation
Indirect material	15	4	8	20	47	Allocation
Power	80	10	12	–	102	Machine hours
Light and heat	5	2	1.5	1.5	10	Area
Depreciation	4	1.6	0.6	0.8	7	Book value
Rent and rates	12.5	5	3.75	3.75	25	Area
Personnel	18	12	24	9	63	No. of employees
	144.5	40.6	57.85	65.05	308	
Reallotment of maintenance	39.03	13.01	13.01	(65.05)	–	
	183.53	53.61	70.86	–	308	

(b)
Machining $\dfrac{£183\ 530}{40\ 000\ \text{hours}}$ £4.59 per machine hour

Assembly $\dfrac{£53\ 600}{8\ 000\ \text{hours}}$ £6.70 per direct labour hour

Finishing $\dfrac{£70\ 860}{16\ 000\ \text{hours}}$ £4.43 per direct labour hour

Note that assembly and Finishing Department overheads are recovered on the basis of direct labour hours, since direct labour hours represent the predominant activity. In the Machining Department overheads are likely to be most closely related to machine hours.

(c) Cost estimate:

			£	£
Direct material (2 500 + 400 + 200)				3 100

Direct labour: Machining $\left(800 \text{ hrs} \times \dfrac{£60\,000}{12\,000 \text{ hours}}\right)$ 4 000

Assembly $\left(350 \text{ hrs} \times \dfrac{£32\,000}{8\,000 \text{ hours}}\right)$ 1 400

Finishing $\left(140 \text{ hrs} \times \dfrac{£72\,000}{16\,000 \text{ hours}}\right)$ 630 6 030

Production overheads:

		£	£
Machining	1400 × 4.59	6 426	
Assembly	350 × 6.70	2 345	
Finishing	140 × 4.43	620.20	9 391.20
			18 521.20

(d) Machining department – fixed production overhead control account

	£		£
Creditors	128 000	WIP^a	179 010
Profit & Loss A/C (Over-recovery of overheads)	51 010		
	179 010		179 010

Note:
^{a}39 000 machine hours × £4.59 per hour = £179 010.

(e)

	£		
Expenditure	55 530	favourable	[Budgeted cost (£183 530 − actual cost £128 000)]
Volume	4 520	adverse	(Balancing figure)
	51 010	favourable	

(a)

	£	£	**Answer 5.7**
Photography: 64 pages at £150 per page		9 600	
Set-up:			
Labour – 64 plates × 4 hours per plate			
= 256 hours at £7 per hour	1 792		
Materials – 64 plates at £35 per plate	2 240		
Overhead – 256 labour hours at £9.50 per hour	2 432		
		6 464	

Printing:
Materials (paper):

$100\,000 \text{ catalogues} \times 32 \text{ sheets} \times \dfrac{£12}{1\,000} \times \dfrac{100}{98}$ 39 184

Materials (other):

$\dfrac{100\,000}{500} \times £7$ 1 400

Labour and Overheads –
$$\frac{100\,000}{1\,000} \text{ m/c hours at £62 per hour} \qquad\qquad 6\,200$$

46 784

Binding:
Labour and Overheads –
$$\frac{100\,000}{2\,500} \text{ m/c hours at £43 per hour} \qquad\qquad \underline{1\,720}$$

Total costs   64 568

Selling price – $£64\,568 \times \dfrac{100}{90}$ 71 742

(b) Estimated hours = 256

Actual hours = $256 \times \dfrac{100}{90}$

= 284.4

Additional costs = $(284.4 - 256) \times £16.50$ (£7 labour rate + £9.50 overhead rate)
= £469.3

Question 6.1
intermediate

A construction company has the following data concerning one of its contracts:

Contract price	£2 000 000
Value certified	£1 300 000
Cash received	£1 200 000
Costs incurred	£1 050 000
Cost of work certified	£1 000 000

The profit (to the nearest £1000) to be attributed to the contract is:
A £250 000
B £277 000
C £300 000
D £950 000
E £1 000 000

CIMA Stage 2 Specimen Paper

Question 6.2
intermediate

The profit shown in the financial accounts was £158 500 but the cost accounts showed a different figure. The following stock valuations were used:

Stock valuations	Cost accounts (£)	Financial accounts (£)
Opening stock	35 260	41 735
Closing stock	68 490	57 336

What was the profit in the cost accounts?
A £163 179
B £140 871
C £176 129
D £153 821

CIMA Stage 1 Specimen Paper

Question 6.3
intermediate

Calculation and analysis of gross wages and preparation of wages and overhead control accounts

The finishing department in a factory has the following payroll data for the month just ended:

	Direct workers	Indirect workers
Total attendance time (including overtime)	2640 hours	940 hours
Productive time	2515 hours	–
Non-productive time:		
Machine breakdown	85 hours	–
Waiting for work	40 hours	–
Overtime	180 hours	75 hours
Basic hourly rate	£5.00	£4.00
Group bonuses	£2840	£710
Employers' National Insurance contributions	£1460	£405

Overtime, which is paid at 140% of basic rate, is usually worked in order to meet the factory's general requirements. However, 40% of the overtime hours of both direct and indirect workers in the month were worked to meet the urgent request of a particular customer.

Required:
(a) Calculate the gross wages paid to direct workers and to indirect workers in the month. *4 marks*
(b) Using the above information, record the relevant entries for the month in the finishing department's wages control account and production overhead control account. (You should clearly indicate the account in which the corresponding entry would be made in the company's separate cost accounting system. Workings must be shown.)

10 marks
Total 14 marks
ACCA Foundation Paper 3

Where substantial costs have been incurred on a contract and it is nearing completion the following formula is often used to determine the attributable profit to date: **Answer 6.1**

$$2/3 \times \text{Notional profit} \times \frac{\text{cash received}}{\text{value of work certified}}$$

$= 2/3 \times (£1.3 \text{ m} - £1 \text{ m}) \times £1.2 \text{ m}/£1.3 \text{ m} = £276\,923$

Answer = B

	Cost accounts	Financial accounts	Difference	**Answer 6.2**
Stock increase	£33 230	£15 601	£17 629	

The stock increase shown in the cost accounts is £17 629 more than the increase shown in the financial accounts. Closing stocks represent expenses to be deferred to future accounting periods. Therefore the profit shown in the cost accounts will be £176 129 (£158 500 + £17 629).

Answer = C

(a) *Calculation of gross wages:* **Answer 6.3**

	Direct workers		Indirect workers		Total
		£		£	£
Attendance time	2 640 × 5.00 =	13 200	940 × 4.00 =	3 760	
Overtime premium	180 × 200 =	360	75 × 1.60 =	120	
Group bonuses		2 840		710	
Gross wages		16 400		4 590	20 990

(b) *Analysis of gross wages:*

	Direct charge (to WIP)		Indirect charge to production overhead		Total
		£		£	£
Attendance time:					
Direct workers	2 515 × 5.00 =	12 575	125 × 5.00 =	625	
Indirect workers			940 × 4.00 =	3 760	
Overtime premium:					
Direct workers	72 × 2.00 =	144	108 × 2.00 =	216	
Indirect workers	30 × 1.60 =	48	45 × 1.60 =	72	
Group bonuses					
Direct workers				2 840	
Indirect workers				710	
		12 767		8 223	20 990

Wages control account

	£		£
Cost ledger control	20 990	Work in progress	12 767
(Gross wages)		Production overhead	8 223
	20 990		20 990

Production overhead control account:

	£
Wages control	8 223
Cost ledger control	1 865
(Employers' employment costs)	

Question 7.1
intermediate

AK Chemicals produces high-quality plastic sheeting in a continuous manufacturing operation. All materials are input at the beginning of the process. Conversion costs are incurred evenly throughout the process. A quality control inspection occurs 75% through the manufacturing process, when some units are separated out as inferior quality. The following data are available for December.

Materials costs	£90 000
Conversion costs	£70 200
Units started	£40 000
Units completed	£36 000

There is no opening or closing work in progress. Past experience indicates that approximately 7.5% of the units started are found to be defective on inspection by quality control.

What is the cost of abnormal loss for December?

A £3 600
B £4 050
C £4 680
D £10 800

ACCA Paper 3 Specimen Question

Question 7.2
intermediate

KL Processing Limited has identified that an abnormal gain of 160 litres occurred in its refining process last week. Normal losses are expected and have a scrap value of £2.00 per litre. All losses are 100% complete as to material cost and 75% complete as to conversion costs.

The company uses the weighted average method of valuation and last week's output was valued using the following costs per equivalent unit:

| Materials | £9.40 |
| Conversion costs | £11.20 |

The effect on the profit and loss account of last week's abnormal gain is:
- A Debit   £2 528
- B Debit   £2 828
- C Credit   £2 528
- D Credit   £2 848
- E Credit   £3 168

CIMA Stage 2

In process costing, if an abnormal loss arises the process account is generally:
- A debited with the scrap value of the abnormal loss units;
- B debited with the full production cost of the abnormal loss units;
- C credited with the scrap value of the abnormal loss units;
- D credited with the full production cost of the abnormal loss units;
- E credited with the full production cost less the scrap value of the abnormal loss units.

CIMA Stage 2

The following details relate to the main process of W Limited, a chemical manufacturer:

Opening work in progres	2000 litres, fully complete as to materials and 40% complete as to conversion
Material input	24 000
Normal loss is 10% of input	
Output to process 2	19 500 litres
Closing work in progress	3000 lites, fully complete as to materials and 45% complete as to conversion

The number of equivalent units to be included in W Limited's calculation of the cost per equivalent unit using a FIFO basis of valuation are:

	Materials	Conversion
A	19 400	18 950
B	20 500	20 050
C	21 600	21 150
D	23 600	20 750
E	23 600	21 950

CIMA Stage 2

Process B had no opening stock. 13 500 units of raw material were transferred in at £4.50 per unit. Additional material at £1.25 per unit was added in process. Labour and overheads were £6.25 per completed unit and £2.50 per unit incomplete.

If 11 750 completed units were transferred out, what was the closing stock in process B?
- A £77 625.00
- B £14 437.50
- C £141 000.00
- D £21 000.00

CIMA Stage 1 Specimen Paper

Losses in process (weighted average)
Chemical Processors manufacture Wonderchem using two processes, mixing and distillation. The following details relate to the distillation process for a period.

No opening work in progress (WIP)
Input from mixing   36 000 kg at a cost of   £166 000
Labour for period   £43 800
Overheads for period   £29 200

Closing WIP of 8000 kg, which was 100% complete for materials and 50% complete for labour and overheads.

The normal loss in distillation is 10% of fully complete production. Actual loss in the period was 3600 kg, fully complete, which were scrapped.

Required:
(a) Calculate whether there was a normal or abnormal loss or abnormal gain for the period.   *2 marks*
(b) Prepare the distillation process account for the period, showing clearly weights and values.   *10 marks*
(c) Explain what changes would be required in the accounts if the scrapped production had a resale value, *and* give the accounting entries.   *3 marks*
Total marks 15
CIMA Stage 1 Cost Accounting

Answer 7.1

	Cost £	Units completed	Normal loss equiv. units	Abnormal loss equiv. units	Total equiv. units	Cost per unit £
Materials	90 000	36 000	3 000 (100%)	1 000 (100%)	40 000	2.25
Conversion cost	70 200	36 000	2 250 (75%)	750 (75%)	39 000	1.80
						4.05

Cost of abnormal loss:
Materials $1\,000 \times £2.25 = £2\,250$
Conversion cost $750 \times £1.80 = £1\,350$
                                         £3 600

Answer = A

Answer 7.2

Abnormal gain debited to process account and credited to abnormal gain account:

	£	£
Materials ($160 \times £9.40$)	1 504	
Conversion cost ($160 \times 0.75 \times £11.20$)	1 344	
		2 848
Lost sales of scrap ($180 \times £2$)		(360)
Net cost credited to profit and loss account		2 528

Answer = C

Answer 7.3

Answer = D

Answer 7.4

Input   = Opening WIP (2 000 units) + Material input (24 000) = 26 000
Output = Completed units (19 500) + Closing WIP (3 000) + Normal Loss (2 400) = 24 900
Abnormal Loss = 1 100 units (Balance of 26 000 − 24 900)

Equivalent units (FIFO)

	Completed units less Opening WIP equiv. units	Closing WIP equiv. units	Abnormal loss equiv. units	Total equiv. units
Materials	17 500 (19 500 − 2 000)	3 000 (100%)	1 100 (100%)	21 600
Conversion	18 700 (19 500 − 800)	1 350 (45%)	1 100 (100%)	21 150

It is assumed that losses are detected at the end of the process and that the answer should adopt the short-cut method and ignore the normal loss in the cost per unit calculations.

Answer = C

Answer 7.5

Closing stock = Opening stock (Nil) + Input (13 500) − Completed units (11 750)
= 1 750 units

It is assumed that materials are fully complete (£5.75) and labour and overheads are partly complete (£2.50)

Value of closing stock = (1 750 × £5.75) + (1 750 × £2.50) = £14 437.50

Answer = B

Answer 7.6

(a) Fully complete production = Input (36 000) − Closing WIP (8 000)
= 28 000 kg

Normal loss	= 2 800 (10% × 28 000 kg)
Abnormal loss	= 800 (Actual loss (3 600) − 2 800)
Good output	= 24 400 (28 000 − 3 600)

(b)

	Completed units £	Normal loss	Abnormal loss	Closing WIP	Total equiv. units	Cost per unit £
Previous process cost	166 000	24 400	2 800	800	8 000	36 000	4.61111
Conversion cost	73 000	24 400	2 800	800	4 000	32 000	2.28125
	239 000						6.89236

		£	£
Completed units (24 400 × £6.89236)		168 174	
Add normal loss (2 800 × £6.89236)		19 298	
			187 472
Abnormal loss (800 × £6.89236)			5 514
WIP: Previous process cost	(8 000 × £4.61111)	36 889	
Conversion cost	(4 000 × £2.28125)	9 125	
			46 014
			239 000

The above computations assume that losses are detected at the end of the process when the units are fully complete. Therefore none of the normal loss is allocated to partly completed units (WIP). There is an argument for allocating the normal loss between completed units and the abnormal loss (See the section on equivalent units and abnormal losses in Chapter 7) but it is unlikely to make a significant difference to the answer. Also examination questions are unlikely to require such sophisticated answers.

An alternative approach is to adopt the short-cut method described in Chapter 7. This method allocates the normal loss between completed units, WIP and the abnormal loss. Because the units actually lost are fully complete it is likely that losses are detected on completion. Therefore the short-cut method is not theoretically correct. Nevertheless the computations suggest that it was the examiner's intention that the question should be answered using the short-cut method. The revised answer is as follows:

	£	Completed units	Abnormal loss	WIP	Total equiv. units	Cost per unit £	WIP £
Previous process cost	166 000	24 400	800	8 000	33 200	5.00	40 000
Conversion cost	73 000	24 400	800	4 000	29 200	2.50	10 000
	239 000					7.50	50 000

Completed units (24 400 × £7.50)	183 000
Abnormal loss (800 × £7.50)	6 000
	239 000

Distillation Process Account

	kg	£		kg	£
Input from mixing	36 000	166 000	Finished goods	24 400	183 000
Labour		43 800	Abnormal loss	800	6 000
Overheads		29 200	Normal loss	2 800	–
			Closing WIP	8 000	50 000
	36 000	239 000		36 000	239 000

(c) If the scrapped production had a resale value the resale value would be credited to the process account (thus reducing the cost of the process account). The accounting entries would be as follows:

Dr Cash
Cr Process Account (with sales value of normal loss)
Cr Abnormal Loss Account (with sales value of abnormal loss)

Question 8.1
intermediate

A company operates a process which produces three joint products – K, P and Z. The costs of operating this process during September 1993 amounted to £117 000. During the month the output of the three products was:

K	2000 litres
P	4500 litres
Z	3250 litres

P is further processed at a cost of £9.00 per litre. The actual loss of the second process was 10% of the input which was normal. Products K and Z are sold without further processing.
    The final selling prices of each of the products are:

K	£20.00 per litre
P	£25.00 per litre
Z	£18.00 per litre

Joint costs are attributed to products on the basis of output volume.
    The profit attributed to product P was:

A £6750
B £12 150
C £13 500
D £16 200
E £18 000

CIMA Stage 2 Specimen Paper

Preparation of joint product account and a decision of further processing

Question 8.2
intermediate

PQR Limited produces two joint products – P and Q – together with a by-product R, from a single main process (process 1). Product P is sold at the point of separation for £5 per kg, whereas product Q is sold for £7 per kg after further processing into product Q2. By-product R is sold without further processing for £1.75 per kg.

Process 1 is closely monitored by a team of chemists, who planned the output per 1000 kg of input materials to be as follows:

Product P	500 kg
Product Q	350 kg
Product R	100 kg
Toxic waste	50 kg

The toxic waste is disposed of at a cost of £1.50 per kg, and arises at the end of processing.

Process 2, which is used for further processing of product Q into product Q2, has the following cost structure:

Fixed costs	£6000 per week
Variable costs	£1.50 per kg processed

The following actual data relate to the first week of accounting period 10:

Process 1
Opening work in process	Nil
Materials input 10 000 kg costing	£15 000
Direct labour	£10 000
Variable overhead	£4 000
Fixed overhead	£6 000

Outputs:
Product P	4800 kg
Product Q	3600 kg
Product R	1000 kg
Toxic waste	600 kg
Closing work in progress	Nil

Process 2
Opening work in process	Nil
Input of product Q	3600 kg
Ouput of product Q2	3300 kg
Closing work in progress	300 kg, 50% converted

Conversion costs were incurred in accordance with the planned cost structure.

Required:
(a) Prepare the main process account for the first week of period 10 using the final sales value method to attribute pre-separation costs to joint products. *12 marks*
(b) Prepare the toxic waste accounts and process 2 account for the first week of period 10. *9 marks*
(c) Comment on the method used by PQR Limited to attribute pre-separation costs to its joint products. *4 marks*

(d) Advise the management of PQR Limited whether or not, on purely financial grounds, it should continue to process product Q into product Q2:
  (i) if product Q could be sold at the point of separation for £4.30 per kg; *and*
  (ii) if 60% of the weekly fixed costs of process 2 were avoided by not processing product Q further.

5 marks
Total marks 30
CIMA Stage 2
Operational Cost Accounting

Answer 8.1

	£
Joint costs apportioned to P (4 500/9 750 × £117 000) =	54 000
Further processing costs (4 500 × £9) =	40 500
Total cost	94 500
Sales revenues (4 050 × £25)	101 250
Profit	6 750

Answer = A

Answer 8.2

(a) Normal loss (toxic waste) = 50 kg per 1 000 kg of input (i.e. 5%)
Actual input = 10 000 kg
Abnormal loss = Actual toxic waste (600) less normal loss (500) = 100 kg

By-product R net revenues of £1 750 are credited to the joint (main) process account and normal and abnormal losses are valued at the average cost per unit of output:

$$\frac{\text{Net cost of production (£35 750} - \text{£1 750)}}{\text{Expected output of the joint products (8 500 kg)}} = £4$$

The cost of the output of the joint products is £33 600 (8 400 kg × £4) and this is to be allocated to the individual products on the basis of final sales value (i.e. 4 800 kg × £5 = £24 000 for P and 3 600 kg × £7 = £25 200 for Q):
P = £24 000/£49 200 × £33 600 = £16 390
Q = £25 200/£49 200 × £33 600 = £17 210

The main process account is as follows:

Main process account

	kg	£		kg	£
Materials	10 000	15 000	P Finished goods	4 800	16 390
Direct labour	–	10 000	Q Process 2	3 600	17 210
Variable overhead	–	4 000	By-product R	1 000	1 750
Fixed overhead	–	6 000	Normal toxic waste	500	–
Toxic waste disposal a/c	–	750	Abnormal toxic waste	100	400
	10 000	35 750		10 000	35 750

(b)

Toxic waste disposal (Creditors' Account)

	£		£
Bank	900	Main process account	750
		Abnormal toxic waste	150
	900		900

Abnormal toxic waste account

	£		£
Main process account	400	Profit and Loss Account	550
Toxic waste disposal account	150		
(100 × £1.50)			
	550		550

Process 2 account

	kg	£		kg	£
Main process Q	3 600	17 210	Finished goods Q[b]	3 300	26 465
Fixed cost		6 000	Closing work-in-progress[b]	300	1 920
Variable cost		5 175[a]			
	3 600	28 385		3 600	28 385

Notes:

[a] $3\,300 + (50\% \times 300) \times £1.50 = £5\,175$

[b]

	£	Completed units	WIP equiv. units	Total equiv. units	Cost per unit
Previous process cost	17 210	3 300	300	3 600	£4.78
Conversion cost	11 175	3 300	150	3 450	£3.24
					£8.02

	£
Completed units (3 300 units × £8.02)	26 465
WIP (300 × £4.78) + (150 × £3.24)	1 920
	28 385

(c) See the section on methods of apportioning joint costs to joint products in Chapter 8 for the answer to this question.

(d)

	£
Incremental sales revenue per kg from further processing (£7 − £4.30)	2.70
Incremental (variable) cost per kg of further processing	1.50
Incremental contribution per kg from further processing	1.20

	£
At an output of 3 600 kg the incremental contribution is	4 320
Avoidable fixed costs	3 600
Net benefit	720

$$\text{Break-even point} = \frac{\text{Avoidable fixed costs (£3 600)}}{\text{Incremental unit contribution (£1.20)}} = 3\,000 \text{ kg}$$

Further processing should be undertaken if output is expected to exceed 3 000 kg per week.

Z Limited manufactures a single product, the budgeted selling price and variable cost details of which are as follows:

Question 9.1
intermediate

	(£)
Selling price	15.00
Variable costs per unit:	
Direct materials	3.50
Direct labour	4.00
Variable overhead	2.00

Budgeted fixed overhead costs are £60 000 per annum, charged at a constant rate each month. Budgeted production is 30 000 units per annum.

In a month when actual production was 2400 units and exceeded sales by 180 units the profit reported under absorption costing was:

A £6660
B £7570
C £7770
D £8200
E £8400

CIMA Stage 2

Question 9.2
intermediate

A company made 17 500 units at a total cost of £16 each. Three-quarters of the costs were variable and one-quarter fixed. 15 000 units were sold at £25 each. There were no opening stocks.

By how much will the profit calculated using absorption costing principles differ from the profit if marginal costing principles had been used?

A The absorption costing profit would be £22 000 less.
B The absorption costing profit would be £10 000 greater.
C The absorption costing profit would be £135 000 greater.
D The absorption costing profit would be £10 000 less.

CIMA Stage 1 Specimen Paper

Question 9.3
intermediate

Preparation of variable and absorption costing profit statements for FIFO and AVECO methods

The following information relates to product J, for quarter 3, which has just ended:

	Production (units)	Sales (units)	Fixed overheads (£000)	Variable costs (£000)
Budget	40 000	38 000	300	1800
Actual	46 000	42 000	318	2070

The selling price of product J was £72 per unit.

The fixed overheads were absorbed at a predetermined rate per unit.

At the beginning of quarter 3 there was an opening stock of product J of 2000 units, valued at £25 per unit variable costs and £5 per unit fixed overheads.

Required:
(a)   (i)   Calculate the fixed overhead absorption rate per unit for the last quarter, and present profit statements using FIFO (first in, first out) using:
       (ii) absorption costing;
       (iii) marginal costing; and
       (iv) reconcile and explain the difference between the profits or losses.   *12 marks*
(b) Using the same data, present similar statements to those required in part (a), using the AVECO (average cost) method of valuation, reconcile the profit or loss figures, and comment briefly on the variations between the profits or losses in (a) and (b).   *8 marks*

Total 20 marks
ACCA Paper 8 Managerial Finance

Answer 9.1

Fixed overhead = £2 per unit (£60 000/30 000 units)

Because production exceeded sales by 180 units a sum of £360 (180 × £2) is included in the stock valuation and not charged as an expense of the current period. Fixed overheads of £4 640 (£5 000 monthly cost − £360) are therefore charged as an expense for the period.

	£
Contribution (2 220 units sales × £5.50)	12 210
Fixed overheads charged as an expense	4 640
Profit	7 570

Answer = B

Closing stock = 2 500 units (17 500 − 15 000)

With absorption costing fixed overheads of £10 000 (£2 500 units × £4) are deferred as a future expense whereas marginal costing treats fixed overheads as a period expense. Therefore absorption costing will be £10 000 greater.

Answer = B

(a)
$$\text{Fixed overhead rate per unit} = \frac{\text{Budgeted fixed overheads (£300 000)}}{\text{Budgeted production (40 000 units)}} = £7.50$$

Absorption Costing (FIFO) Profit Statement:

		£000
Sales (42 000 × £72)		3 024
Less cost of sales:		
Opening stock (2 000 × £30)	60	
Add production (46 000 × £52.50[a])	2 415	
	2 475	
Less closing stock (6 000 × £52.50)	315	2 160
		864
Add over-absorption of overheads[b]		27
Profit		891

Notes:

[a] Variable cost per unit = £2 070/46 000 = £45

Total cost per unit = £45 + £7.50 Fixed overhead = £52.50

[b] Overhead absorbed (46 000 × £7.50) = £345 000

Actual overhead incurred = £318 000

Over-recovery = £27 000

Marginal Costing (FIFO) Profit Statement:

	£000	£000
Sales		3 024
Less Cost of Sales:		
Opening stock (2 000 × £25)	50	
Add Production (46 000 × £45)	2 070	
	2 120	
Less closing stock (6 000 × £45)	270	1 850
Contribution		1 174
Less fixed overheads incurred		318
Profit		856

Reconciliation:

Absorption profit exceeds marginal costing profit by £35 000 (£891 000 − £856 000). The difference is due to the fixed overheads carried forward in the stock valuations:

	£
Fixed overheads in closing stocks (6 000 × £7.50)	45 000
Less fixed overheads in opening stocks (2 000 × £5)	10 000
Fixed overheads included in stock movement	35 000

Absorption costing gives a higher profit because more of the fixed overheads are carried forward into the next accounting period than were brought forward from the last accounting period.

(b) *Absorption costing (AVECO) Profit Statement:*

	£000	£000
Sales		3 024
Opening stock plus production		
(48 000 × £51.56[a])	2 475	
Less closing stock (6 000 × £51.56)	309	2 166
		858
Add over-absorption of overheads		27
Profit		885

Marginal Costing (AVECO) Profit Statement:

	£000	£000
Sales		3 024
Less cost of sales		
Opening stock plus production		
(48 000 × £44.17[b])	2 120	
Less closing stock (6 000 × £44.17)	265	1 855
Contribution		1 169
Less fixed overheads		318
Profit		851

Notes:
[a] With the AVECO method the opening stock is merged with the production of the current period to ascertain the average unit cost:
Opening stock (2 000 × £30) + Production cost (£2 415 000) = £2 475 000
Average cost per unit = £2 475 000/48 000 units
[b] Average cost = (Production cost (£2 070 000) + Opening stock (50 000))/48 000 units.

Reconciliation:

	£000s
Difference in profits (£885 − £851)	34
Fixed overheads in closing stocks (309 − 265)	44
Less fixed overheads in opening stock (2 000 × £5)	10
Fixed overheads included in stock movement	34

The variations in profits between (a) and (b) are £6 000 for absorption costing and £5,000 for marginal costing. With the FIFO method all of the lower cost brought forward from the previous period is charged as an expense against the current period. The closing stock is derived only from current period costs. With the AVECO method the opening stock is merged with the units produced in the current period and is thus allocated between cost of sales and closing stocks. Therefore some of the lower cost brought forward from the previous period is incorporated in the closing stock at the end of the period.

Question 10.1
intermediate

A company manufactures and sells two products, X and Y. Forecast data for a year are:

	Product X	Product Y
Sales (units)	80 000	20 000
Sales price (per unit)	£12	£8
Variable cost (per unit)	£8	£3

Annual fixed costs are estimated at £273 000

What is the break-even point in sales revenue with the current sales mix?

A £570 000

B £606 667

C £679 467

D £728 000

ACCA Foundation Paper 3 –
Sample Question

H Limited manufactures and sells two products, J and K. Annual sales are expected to be in the ratio of J : 1, K : 3. Total annual sales are planned to be £420 000. Product J has a contribution to sales ratio of 40%, whereas that of product K is 50%. Annual fixed costs are estimated to be £120 000.

Question 10.2
intermediate

The budgeted breakeven sales value (to the nearest £1000):

A £196 000

B £200 000

C £253 000

D £255 000

E cannot be determined from the above data.

CIMA Stage 2

The following details relate to product R:

Question 10.3
intermediate

Level of activity (units)	1000	2000
	(£/unit)	(£/unit)
Direct materials	4.00	4.00
Direct labour	3.00	3.00
Production overhead	3.50	2.50
Selling overhead	1.00	0.50
	11.50	10.00

The total fixed cost and variable cost per unit are:

	Total fixed cost (£)	Variable cost per unit (£)
A	2000	1.50
B	2000	7.00
C	2000	8.50
D	3000	7.00
E	3000	8.50

CIMA Stage 2

Z plc currently sells products Aye, Bee and Cee in equal quantities and at the same selling price per unit. The contribution to sales ratio for product Aye is 40%; for product Bee it is 50% and the total is 48%. If fixed costs are unaffected by mix and are currently 20% of sales, the effect of changing the product mix to:

Question 10.4
intermediate

Aye   40%

Bee   25%

Cee   35%

is that the total contribution/total sales ratio changes to:

A 27.4%

B 45.3%

C 47.4%

D 48.4%

E 68.4%

CIMA Stage 2

Question 10.5
intermediate

E plc operates a marginal costing system. For the forthcoming year, variable costs are budgeted to be 60% of sales value and fixed costs are budgeted to be 10% of sales value.

If E plc increases its selling prices by 10%, but if fixed costs, variable costs per unit and sales volume remain unchanged, the effect on E plc's contribution would be:

A a decrease of 2%;
B an increase of 5%;
C an increase of 10%;
D an increase of 25%;
E an increase of $66\frac{2}{3}$%.   *CIMA Stage 2*

Question 10.6
intermediate

A Limited has fixed costs of £60 000 per annum. It manufactures a single product which it sells for £20 per unit. Its contribution to sales ratio is 40%.

A Limited's breakeven point in units is:

A 1200
B 1800
C 3000
D 5000
E 7500

CIMA Stage 2 Specimen Paper

Question 10.7
intermediate

The following data relate to the overhead expenditure of a contract cleaners at two activity levels:

Square metres cleaned	12 750	15 100
Overheads	£73 950	£83 585

What is the estimate of the overheads if 16 200 square metres are to be cleaned?

A £88 095
B £89 674
C £93 960
D £98 095

CIMA Stage 1

Question 10.8
intermediate

Separation of fixed and variable costs and construction of a break-even chart

Z plc operates a single retail outlet selling direct to the public. Profit statements for August and September 1996 are as follows:

	August (£)	September (£)
Sales	80 000	90 000
Cost of sales	50 000	55 000
Gross profit	30 000	35 000
Less:		
Selling and distribution	8 000	9 000
Administration	15 000	15 000
Net profit	7 000	11 000

Required:

(a) Use the high- and low-points technique to identify the behaviour of:
  (i) cost of sales;
  (ii) selling and distribution costs;
  (iii) administration costs.   *4 marks*

(b) Using the graph paper provided, draw a contribution break-even chart and identify the monthly break-even sales value and area of contribution.   *10 marks*

(c) Assuming a margin of safety equal to 30% of the break-even value, calculate Z plc's annual profit.   *2 marks*

(d) Z plc is now considering opening another retail outlet selling the same products. Z plc plans to use the same profit margins in both outlets and has estimated that the specific fixed costs of the second outlet will be £100 000 per annum.

Z plc also expects that 10% of its annual sales from its existing outlet would transfer to this second outlet if it were to be opened.

Calculate the annual value of sales required from the new outlet in order to achieve the same annual profit as previously obtained from the single outlet.

5 marks

(e) Briefly describe the cost accounting requirements of organizations of this type.

4 marks
Total marks 25
Chartered Institute of Management
Accountants Operational Cost Accounting –

Calculation of break-even points and limiting factor decision-making

Question 10.9
intermediate

You are employed as an accounting technician by Smith, Williams and Jones, a small firm of accountants and registered auditors. One of your clients is Winter plc, a large department store. Judith Howarth, the purchasing director for Winter plc, has gained considerable knowledge about bedding and soft furnishings and is considering acquiring her own business.

She has recently written to you requesting a meeting to discuss the possible purchase of Brita Beds Ltd. Brita Beds has one outlet in Mytown, a small town 100 miles from where Judith works. Enclosed with her letter was Brita Beds' latest profit and loss account. This is reproduced below.

Brita Beds Ltd
Profit and loss account – year to 31 May 1997

Sales	(units)	(£)
Model A	1 620	336 960
Model B	2 160	758 160
Model C	1 620	1 010 880
Turnover		2 106 000
Expenses	(£)	
Cost of beds	1 620 000	
Commission	210 600	
Transport	216 000	
Rates and insurance	8 450	
Light heat and power	10 000	
Assistants' salaries	40 000	
Manager's salary	40 000	2 145 050
Loss for year		39 050

Also included in the letter was the following information:
- Brita Beds sells three types of bed, models A to C inclusive.
- Selling prices are determined by adding 30% to the cost of beds.
- Sales assistants receive a commission of 10% of the selling price for each bed sold.
- The beds are delivered in consignments of 10 beds at a cost of £400 per delivery. This expense is shown as 'Transport' in the profit and loss account.
- All other expenses are annual amounts.
- The mix of models sold is likely to remain constant irrespective of overall sales volume.

Task 1
In preparation for your meeting with Judith Howarth, you are asked to calculate:
(a) the minimum number of beds to be sold if Brita Beds is to avoid making a loss;
(b) the minimum turnover required if Brita Beds is to avoid making a loss.

At the meeting, Judith Howarth provides you with further information:
- The purchase price of the business is £300 000
- Judith has savings of £300 000 currently earning 5% interest per annum, which she can use to acquire Brita Beds.
- Her current salary is £36 550.

To reduce costs, Judith suggests that she should take over the role of manager as the current one is about to retire. However, she does not want to take a reduction in income. Judith also tells you that she has been carrying out some market research. The results of this are as follows:
- the number of households in Mytown is currently 44 880.
- Brita Beds Ltd is the only outlet selling beds in Mytown.
- According to a recent survey, 10% of households change their beds every 9 years, 60% every 10 years and 30% every 11 years.
- The survey also suggested that there is an average of 2.1 beds per household.

Task 2
Write a letter to Judith Howarth. Your letter should:
(a) identify the profit required to compensate for the loss of salary and interest;
(b) show the number of beds to be sold to achieve that profit;
(c) calculate the likely maximum number of beds that Brita Beds would sell in a year;
(d) use your answers in (a) to (c) to justify whether or not Judith Howarth should purchase the company and become its manager;
(e) give *two* possible reasons why your estimate of the maximum annual sales volume may prove inaccurate.

On receiving your letter, Judith Howarth decides she would prefer to remain as the purchasing director for Winter plc rather than acquire Brita Beds Ltd. Shortly afterwards, you receive a telephone call from her. Judith explains that Winter plc is redeveloping its premises and that she is concerned about the appropriate sales policy for Winter's bed department while the redevelopment takes place. Although she has a statement of unit profitability, this had been prepared before the start of the redevelopment and had assumed that there would be in excess of 800 square metres of storage space available to the bed department. Storage space is critical as customers demand immediate delivery and are not prepared to wait until the new stock arrives.

The next day, Judith Howarth sends you a letter containing a copy of the original statement of profitability. This is reproduced below:

Model	A	B	C
Monthly demand (beds)	35	45	20
	(£)	(£)	(£)
Unit selling price	240.00	448.00	672.00
Unit cost per bed	130.00	310.00	550.00
Carriage inwards	20.00	20.00	20.00
Staff costs	21.60	40.32	60.48
Departmental fixed overheads	20.00	20.00	20.00
General fixed overheads	25.20	25.20	25.20
Unit profit	23.20	32.48	(3.68)
Storage required per bed (square metres)	3	4	5

In her letter, she asks for your help in preparing a marketing plan which will maximize the profitability of Winter's bed department while the redevelopment takes place. To help you, she has provided you with the following additional information:
- Currently storage space available totals 300 square metres.
- Staff costs represent the salaries of the sales staff in the bed department. Their total cost of £3780 per month is apportioned to units on the basis of planned turnover.

- Departmental fixed overhead of £2000 per month is directrly attributable to the department and is apportioned on the number of beds planned to be sold.
- General fixed overheads of £2520 are also apportioned on the number of beds planned to be sold. The directors of Winter plc believe this to be a fair apportionment of the store's central fixed overheads.
- The cost of carriage inwards and the cost of beds vary directly with the number of beds purchased.

Task 3
(a) Prepare a recommended monthly sales schedule in units which will maximize the profitability of Winter plc's bed department.
(b) Calculate the profit that will be reported per month if your recommendation is implemented.

Association of Accounting Technicians –
Technician's Stage

Analysis of change in profit arising from changes in volume and production methods plus sales revenue required to achieve a desired profit

Question 10.10
intermediate

A company has the following summary trading statement reflecting performance over two accounting periods:

	Period 1 (£000)	Period 2 (£000)
Sales	902.0	1108.1
Variable costs	360.8	398.9
Contribution	541.2	709.2
Fixed costs	490.5	549.0
	50.7	160.2

In period 2 selling prices were 5% higher than in period 1 and cost inflation (affecting both variable and fixed costs) was also 5%.

At the start of period 2 production methods were reorganized. This was the only other factor affecting costs between the two periods (apart from inflation and volume).

Required:
(a) Calculate the percentage increase in sales volume in period 2 compard with period 1.   *2 marks*
(b) Calculate the increase in net profit in period 2 compared with period 1, due to:
    (i) volume
    (ii) reorganization of production methods.
    (Calculations should be done at year 1 prices.   *6 marks*
(c) Calculate the sales (to the nearest £000) that were required in period 2 in order to achieve the same net profit as period 1.   *3 marks*
(d) State, and explain, the formula for the calculation of the break-even sales revenue for a period (figures are not required).   *3 marks*
Total 14 marks
ACCA Foundation Paper 3

	Product X	Product Y	Total
Budgeted sales volume (units)	80 000	20 000	
Budgeted contribution per unit	£4	£5	
Budgeted total contribution	£320 000	£100 000	£420 000
Budgeted sales revenue	£960 000	£160 000	£1 120 000

Answer 10.1

Average contribution per unit = £420 000/100 000 units = £4.20

$$\text{Break-even point} = \frac{\text{Fixed costs (£273 000)}}{\text{Average contribution per unit (£4.20)}} = 65\,000 \text{ units}$$

Average selling price per unit = £1 120 000/100 000 units = £11.20

Break-even point in sales revenue = 65 000 units × £11.20 = £728 000

Answer = D

Answer 10.2

$$\text{Average contribution to sales ratio} = \frac{(40\% \times 1) + (50\% \times 3)}{4} = 47.5\%$$

Break-even point is at the point where 47.5% of the sales equal the fixed costs (i.e. £120 000/0.475 = £252 632).

$$\text{In other words, the break-even point} = \frac{\text{Fixed costs}}{\text{PV ratio}}$$

Answer = C

Answer 10.3

	Total cost (1 000 units) £	Total cost (2 000 units) £
Production overhead	3 500 (£3.50 × 1 000)	5 000 (£2.50 × 2 000)
Selling overhead	1 000 (£1 × 1 000)	1 000 (£0.5 × 2 000)

$$\text{Variable cost per unit} = \frac{\text{Change in cost}}{\text{Change in activity}}$$

Production overhead = £1 500/1 000 units = £1.50
Selling overhead = Fixed cost since total costs remain unchanged.
The unit costs of direct materials are constant at both activity levels and are therefore variable.
Production overheads fixed cost element = Total cost (£3 500) − Variable cost
(1 000 × £1.50) = £2 000

Total fixed cost = £2 000 + £1 000 = £3 000
Unit variable cost £4 + £3 + £1.50 = £8.50

Answer = E

Answer 10.4

Contribution/sales (%) = (0.33 × 40% Aye) + (0.33 × 50% Bee) + (0.33 × ? Cee) = 48%
Cee = 54% (Balancing figure)
The total contribution/sales ratio for the revised sales mix is:
(0.40 × 40% Aye) + (0.25 × 50% Bee) + (0.35 × 54% Cee) = 47.4%

Answer = C

Answer 10.5

Sales	100	110 (100 + 10%)
Variable cost	60	60
Contribution	40	50
Increase = 25%		

Answer = D

Answer 10.6

Contribution per unit = 40% × £20 = £8

$$\text{Break-even point} = \frac{\text{Fixed costs (£60 000)}}{\text{Contribution per unit (£8)}} = 7\,500 \text{ units}$$

Answer = E

Change in activity = 2 350 m^2
Change in costs = £9 635
Variable cost per metre = £4.10 (£9 635/2 350)
Fixed costs at 15 100 m^2 = £21 675 (£83 585 − (15 100 × £4.10))
Total cost at 16 200 m^2 = £88 095 (£21 675 + (16 200 × £4.10))

Answer = A

(a)

	August £	September £	Change £
Sales	80 000	90 000	10 000
Cost of sales	50 000	55 000	5 000
Selling and distribution	8 000	9 000	1 000
Administration	15 000	15 000	Nil

The only activity measure that is given is sales revenue. An increase in sales of £10 000 results in an increase in cost of sales of £5 000 and an increase in selling and distribution costs of £1 000. It is therefore assumed that the increase is attributable to variable costs and variable cost of sales is 50% of sales and variable selling and distribution costs are 10% of sales.

Fixed costs are derived by deducting variable costs from total costs for either month. The figures for August are used in the calculations below:

	Total cost £	Variable cost £	Fixed cost (Balance) £
Cost of sales	50 000	40 000	10 000
Selling and distribution	8 000	8 000	Nil
Administration	15 000	Nil	15 000
			25 000

Total cost = £25 000 fixed costs + variable costs (60% of sales)

(b) The following items are plotted on the graph:

	Variable cost	Total cost
Zero sales	Nil	£25 000 fixed cost
£80 000 sales	£48 000 (60%)	£73 000
£90 000 sales	£54 000 (60%)	£79 000
£50 000 sales	£30 000 (60%)	£55 000
£100 000 sales	£60 000	£85 000

$$\text{Break-even point} = \frac{\text{Fixed costs (£25 000)}}{\text{Contribution to sales ratio (0.40)}} = £62\,500 \text{ sales}$$

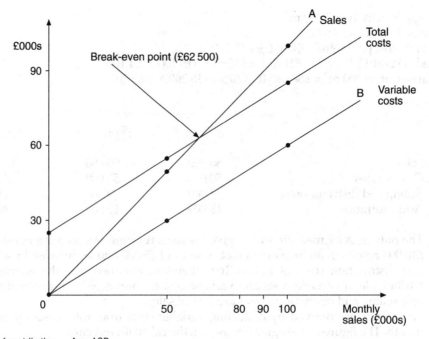

Area of contribution = Area AOB
Figure Q10.8 *Contribution break-even graph.*

(c)
		£
Actual sales = 1.3 × Break-even sales (£62 500)	=	81 250
Contribution (40% of sales)	=	32 500
Fixed costs	=	25 000
Monthly profit	=	7 500
Annual profit	=	90 000

(d)
		£
Annual contribution from single outlet (£32 500 × 12)	=	390 000
Contribution to cover lost sales (10%)	=	39 000
Specific fixed costs	=	100 000
Total contribution required		529 000

Required sales = £529 000/0.4 = £1 322 500

(e) The answer should draw attention to the need for establishing a sound system of budgeting and performance reporting for each of the different outlets working in close conjunction with central office. The budgets should be merged together to establish a master budget for the whole company.

Answer 10.9 *Task 1*

	£	£
Sales		2 106 000
Less variable cost of sales:		
Cost of beds	1 620 000	
Commission	210 600	
Transport	216 000	2 046 600
Contribution		59 400

Average contribution per bed sold = £59 400/5 400 = £11
Fixed costs (£8 450 + £10 000 + £40 000 + £40 000) = £98 450

$$\text{Break-even point (units)} = \frac{\text{Fixed costs (£98 450)}}{\text{Contribution per unit (£11)}} = 8\,950 \text{ beds}$$

Average selling price per unit (£2 106 000/5 400 beds) = £390
Break-even point (sales revenue) = 8 950 beds at £390 = £3 490 500

Task 2
The letter should include the items listed in (a) to (e) below:

(a) Required contribution: £
    Salary   36 550
    Interest lost   15 000
    Fixed costs shown in Task 1   98 450
                                           150 000
    Less manager's salary saved   40 000
    Total contribution   110 000

The minimum profit required to compensate for loss of salary and interest is £11 550 (£110 000 − £98 450 fixed costs).

(b) Required volume = Required contribution (£110 000)/Contribution per unit (£11)
    = 10 000 beds

(c) Average life of a bed = (9 years × 0.10) + (10 years × 0.60) + (11 years × 0.3) = 10.2 years

Total bed population = 44 880 households × 2.1 beds per market = 94 248

$$\text{Estimated annual demand} = \frac{94\ 248 \text{ beds}}{\text{Average replacement period (10.2 years)}}$$
$$= 9\ 240 \text{ beds}$$

(d) The proposal will not achieve the desired profit. Estimated annual sales are 9 240 beds but 10 000 beds must be sold to achieve the desired profit. The shortfall of 760 beds will result in profit being £8 360 (760 × £11) less than the desired profit.

(e) The estimate of maximum annual sales volume may prove to be inaccurate because of the following reasons:
    (i) The population of Mytown may differ from the sample population. For example the population of Mytown might contain a greater proportion of elderly people or younger people with families. Either of these situations may result in the buying habits of the population of Mytown being different from the sample proportion.
    (ii) The data is historic and does not take into account future changes such as an increase in wealth of the population, change in composition or a change in buying habits arising from different types of beds being marketed.

Task 3
This question requires a knowledge of the material covered in Chapter 11. Therefore you should delay attempting this question until you have understood the content of Chapter 11.

	A	B	C	Total
	£	£	£	
Selling price	240	448	672	
Unit purchase cost	130	310	550	
Carriage inwards	20	20	20	
Contribution	90	118	102	
Square metres per bed	3	4	5	
Contribution per square metre	£30	£29.50	£20.40	
Ranking	1	2	3	
Maximum demand	35	45	20	
Storage required (square metres)	105	180	100	385

Monthly sales schedule and statement of profitability:

	£	£
Contribution from sales of A (35 × £90)		3 150
Contribution from sales of B (45 × £118)		5 310
Contribution from sales of C (3^a × £102)		306
		8 766
Less specific avoidable fixed costs:		
Staff costs	3 780	
Departmental fixed overheads	2 000	5 780
Contribution to general fixed overheads		2 986
Less general fixed overheads		2 520
Departmental profit		466

Note:
[a] The balance of storage space available for Model C is 300 square metres less the amount allocated to A and B (285 metres) = 15 metres. This will result in the sales of 3 beds (15 metres/5 metres per bed).

Answer 10.10

(a)

		£000s
Period 2 sales volume at period 1 prices (1 108.1 × 100/105)	=	1 055.333
Period 1 sales volume at period 1 prices	=	902.000
Increase in sales attributable to sales volume		153.333
% increase in sales volume (153.333/902 × 100)	=	17%

(b) (i)

	£000s
Increase in sales attributable to sales volume	153.333
Contribution based on period 1 cost structure (60% of sales)	92.000
Fixed costs are assumed to be unaffected by volume changes	
Increase in profit attributable to volume	92.000

(b) (ii)

	Period 2 sales volume at period 1 prices and period 1 production methods	Period 2 sales volume at period 1 prices and period 2 production methods
	£000s	£000s
Sales	1 055.333	1 055.333
Variable costs	422.133[a]	379.905[b]
Contribution	633.200	675.428
Fixed costs	490.500[c]	522.857[d]
Net profit	142.700	152.571

	£000
Reduction in variable costs arising from reorganization in production methods	42.228
Increase in fixed costs arising from reorganization in production methods	(32.357)
	9.871

Notes:
[a] Sales × period 1 contribution to sales ratio of 60%
[b] £398.9 × 100/105
[c] Fixed costs are assumed to be unaffected by changes in sales volume
[d] £549.0 × 100/105

(c) Required contribution = Period 2 fixed costs (£549 000) + Period 1 profit (£50 700) = £599,700. The contribution/sales ratio (profit–volume ratio) for period 2 is 64% (£709.2/£1 108.1). In other words each £1 sale generates £0.64 contribution. To generate a contribution of £599 700 sales revenue of £937 031 is required (£599 700/0.64).

(d) The formula for the break-even point in sales revenue is:

$$\frac{\text{Fixed costs}}{\text{Contribution/sales ratio}} \text{ or Fixed costs} \times \frac{\text{Sales}}{\text{Contribution}}$$

When sales revenue generates a contribution that is exactly equal to fixed costs break-even point is achieved. To determine this level of sales revenue fixed costs must be divided by the rate at which contribution is made per £1 of sales.

Z Limited manufactures three products, the selling price and cost details of which are given below:

Question 11.1
intermediate

	Product X	Product Y	Product Z
	(£)	(£)	(£)
Selling price per unit	75	95	95
Costs per unit:			
Direct materials (£5/kg)	10	5	15
Direct labour (£4/hour)	16	24	20
Variable overhead	8	12	10
Fixed overhead	24	36	30

In a period when direct materials are restricted in supply, the most and the least profitable uses of direct materials are:

	Most profitable	Least profitable
A	X	Z
B	Y	Z
C	X	Y
D	Z	Y
E	Y	X

CIMA Stage 2

Your company regularly uses material X and currently has in stock 600 kg, for which it paid £1500 two weeks ago. If this were to be sold as raw material it could be sold today for £2.00 per kg. You are aware that the material can be bought on the open market for £3.25 per kg, but it must be purchased in quantities of 1000 kg.

Question 11.2
intermediate

You have been asked to determined the relevant cost of 600 kg of material X to be used in a job for a customer. The relevant cost of the 600 kg is:

A £1200
B £1325
C £1825
D £1950
E £3250

CIMA Stage 2

Q plc makes two products – Quone and Qutwo – from the same raw material. The selling price and cost details of these products are as shown below:

Question 11.3
intermediate

	Quone	Qutwo
	(£)	(£)
Selling price	20.00	18.00
Direct material (£2.00/kg)	6.00	5.00
Direct labour	4.00	3.00
Variable overhead	2.00	1.50
	12.00	9.50
Contribution per unit	8.00	8.50

The maximum demand for these products is:

Quone   500 units per week
Qutwo   unlimited number of units per week

If materials were limited to 2000 kg per week, the shadow price of these materials would be:

   A nil;
   B £2.00 per kg;
   C £2.66 per kg;
   D £3.40 per kg;
   E none of these

CIMA Stage 2

Question 11.4
intermediate

BB Limited makes three components: S, T and W. The following costs have been recorded:

	Component S Unit cost	Component T Unit cost	Component W Unit cost
	(£)	(£)	(£)
Variable cost	2.50	8.00	5.00
Fixed cost	2.00	8.30	3.75
Total cost	4.50	16.30	8.75

Another company has offered to supply the components to BB Limited at the following prices:

	Component S	Component T	Component W
Price each	£4	£7	£5.50

Which component(s), if any, should BB Limited consider buying in?

   A Buy in all three components.
   B Do not buy any.
   C Buy in S and W.
   D Buy in T only

CIMA Stage 1 Specimen Paper

M plc makes two products – M1 and M2 – budgeted details of which are as follows:

	M1	M2
	(£)	(£)
Selling price	10.00	8.00
Costs per unit:		
Direct materials	2.50	3.00
Direct labour	1.50	1.00
Variable overhead	0.60	0.40
Fixed overhead	1.20	1.00
Profit per unit	4.20	2.60

Budgeted production and sales for the year ended 31 December 1998 are:

Product M1   10 000 units
Product M2   12 500 units

The fixed overhead shown above comprises both general and specific fixed overhead costs. The general fixed overhead cost has been attributed to units of M1 and M2 on the basis of direct labour cost.
The specific fixed cost totals £2500 per annum and relates to product M2 only.
(a) Both products are available from an external supplier. If M plc could purchase only one of them, the maximum price which should be paid per unit of M1 or M2 instead of internal manufacture would be :

	M1	M2
	(£)	(£)
A	4.60	4.40
B	4.60	4.60
C	5.80	4.40
D	5.80	4.60
E	5.80	5.60

(b) If only product M1 were to be made, the number of units to be sold to achieve a profit of £50,000 per annum (to the nearest unit) would be:
A 4074;
B 4537;
C 13 333;
D 13 796
E none of the above

CIMA Stage 2

A company is considering accepting a one-year contract which will require four skilled employees. The four skilled employees could be recruited on a one-year contract at a cost of £40 000, per employee. The employees would be supervised by an existing manager who earns £60 000 per annum. It is expected that supervision of the contract would take 10% of the manager's time.

Instead of recruiting new employees, the company could retrain some existing employees who currently earn £30 000 per year. The training would cost £15 000 in total. If these employees were used they would need to be replaced at a total cost of £1 000 000.
The relevant labour cost of the contract is:
A £100 000
B £115 000

C £135 000
D £141 000
E £166 000

CIMA Stage 2

Question 11.7
intermediate

Z plc manufactures three products which have the following selling prices and costs per unit:

	Z1 (£)	Z2 (£)	Z3 (£)
Selling price	15.00	18.00	17.00
Costs per unit:			
Direct materials	4.00	5.00	10.00
Direct labour	2.00	4.00	1.80
Overhead:			
Variable	1.00	2.00	0.90
Fixed	4.50	3.00	1.35
	11.50	14.00	14.05
Profit per unit	3.50	4.00	2.95

All three products use the same type of labour.
  In a period in which labour is in short supply, the rank order of production is:

	Z1	Z2	Z3
A	First	Second	Third
B	Third	Second	First
C	Second	First	Third
D	First	Third	Second
E	Second	Third	First

CIMA Stage 2

Question 11.8
intermediate

calculation of minimum selling price

You have received a request from EXE plc to provide a quotation for the manufacture of a specialized piece of equipment. This would be a one-off order, in excess of normal budgeted production. The following cost estimate has already been prepared:

		Note	(£)
Direct materials			
Steel	10m² at £5.00 per sq. metre	1	50
Brass fittings		2	20
Direct labour:			
Skilled	25 hours at £8.00 per hour	3	200
Semi-skilled	10 hours at £5.00 per hour	4	50
Overhead	35 hours at £10.00 per hour	5	350
Estimating time		6	100
			770
Administration overhead			
at 20% of production cost		7	154
			924
Profit at 25% of total cost		8	231
Selling price			1155

Notes

1. The steel is regularly used, and has a current stock value of £5.00 per sq. metre. There are currently 100 sq. metres in stock. The steel is readily available at a price of £5.50 per sq. metre.

2. The brass fittings would have to be bought specifically for this job: a supplier has quoted the price of £20 for the fittings required.
3. The skilled labour is currently employed by your company and paid at a rate of £8.00 per hour. If this job were undertaken it would be necessary either to work 25 hours overtime which would be paid at time plus one half or to reduce production of another product which earns a contribution of £13.00 per hour.
4. The semi-skilled labour currently has sufficient paid idle time to be able to complete this work.
5. The overhead absorption rate includes power costs which are directly related to machine usage. If this job were undertaken, it is estimated that the machine time required would be ten hours. The machines incur power costs of £0.75 per hour. There are no other overhead costs which can be specifically identified with this job.
6. The cost of the estimating time is that attributed to the four hours taken by the engineers to analyse the drawings and determine the cost estimate given above.
7. It is company policy to add 20% on to the production cost as an allowance against administration costs associated with the jobs accepted.
8. This is the standard profit added by your company as part of its pricing policy.

Required:
(a) Prepare, on a relevant cost basis, the lowest cost estimate that could be used as the basis for a quotation. Explain briefly your reasons for using each of the values in your estimate.   *12 marks*
(b) There may be a possibility of repeat orders from EXE plc which would occupy part of normal production capacity. What factors need to be considered before quoting for this order?   *7 marks*
(c) When an organization identifies that it has a single production resource which is in short supply, but is used by more than one product, the optimum production plan is determined by ranking the products according to their contribution per unit of scarce resource.
    Using a numerical example of your own, reconcile this approach with the opportunity cost approach used in (a) above.   *6 marks*
                                                                                              Total marks 25
                                                                          CIMA Stage 2 Operation Cost Accounting

Key/limiting factor decision-making

BVX Limited manufactures three garden furniture products – chairs, benches and tables. The budgeted unit cost and resource requirements of each of these items is detailed below:

	Chair	Bench	Table
	(£)	(£)	(£)
Timber cost	5.00	15.00	10.00
Direct labour cost	4.00	10.00	8.00
Variable overhead cost	3.00	7.50	6.00
Fixed overhead cost	4.50	11.25	9.00
	16.50	43.75	33.00
Budgeted volumes			
per annum	4000	2000	1500

These volumes are believed to equal the market demand for these products.
The fixed overhead costs are attributed to the three products on the basis of direct labour hours.
    The labour rate if £4.00 per hour.
    The cost of the timber is £2.00 per square metre.

The products are made from a specialist timber. A memo from the purchasing manager advises you that because of a problem with the supplier it is to be assumed that this specialist timber is limited in supply to 20 000 square metres per annum.

The sales director has already accepted an order for 500 chairs, 100 benches and 150 tables, which if not supplied would incur a financial penalty of £2000. These quantities are included in the market demand estimates above.

The selling prices of the three products are:

Chair	£20.00
Bench	£50.00
Table	£40.00

Required:

(a) Determine the optimum production plan *and* state the net profit that this would yield per annum.   *10 marks*

(b) Calculate *and* explain the maximum prices which should be paid per sq. metre in order to obtain extra supplied of the timber.   *5 marks*

(c) The management team has accused the accounts of using too much jargon.

Prepare a statement which explains the following terms in a way that a multi/disciplinary team of managers would understand. The accountant will use this statement as a briefing paper at the next management meeting. The terms to be explained are:

- variable costs;
- relevant costs;
- avoidable costs;
- opportunity costs.

10 marks
Total 25 marks
CIMA
Stage 2 Operation Cost Accounting

Question 11.10 Price/output and key factor decisions

intermediate You work as a trainee for a small management consultancy which has been asked to advise a company, Rane Limited, which manufactures and sells a single product. Rane is currently operating at full capacity, producing and selling 25 000 units of its product each year. The cost and selling price structure for this level of activity is as follows:

	At 25 000 units output	
	£ per unit	£ per unit
Production costs:		
Direct material	14	
Direct Labour	13	
Variable production overhead	4	
Fixed production overhead	8	
Total production cost		39
Selling and distribution overhead:		
Sales commission –		
10% of sales value	6	
Fixed	3	
		9
Administration overhead:		
Fixed		2
Total cost		50
Mark up – 20%		10
Selling price		60

A new managing director has recently joined the company and he has engaged your organization to advise on his company's selling price policy. The sales price of £60 has been derived as above from a cost-plus pricing policy. The price was viewed as satisfactory because the resulting demand enabled full capacity operation.

You have been asked to investigate the effect on costs and profit of an increase in the selling price. The marketing department has provided you with the following estimates of sales volumes which could be achieved at the three alternative sales prices under consideration.

Selling price per unit	£70	£80	£90
Annual sales volume (units)	20 000	16 000	11 000

You have spent some time estimating the effect that changes in output volume will have on cost behaviour patterns and you have now collected the following information:

Direct material: The loss of bulk discounts means that the direct material cost per unit will increase by 15% for all units produced in the year if activity reduces below 15 000 units per annum.

Direct labour: Savings in bonus payments will reduce labour costs by 10% for all units produced in the year if activity reduces below 20 000 units per annum.

Sales commission: This would continue to be paid at the rate of 10% of sales price.

Fixed production overhead: If annual output volume was below 20 000 units, then a machine rental cost of £10 000 per annum could be saved. This will be the only change in the total expenditure on fixed production overhead.

Fixed selling overhead: A reduction in the part-time sales force would result in a £5000 per annum saving if annual sales volume falls below 24 000 units. This will be the only change in the total expenditure on fixed selling and distribution overhead.

Variable production overhead: There would be no change in the unit cost for variable production overhead.

Administration overhead: The total expenditure on administration overhead would remain unaltered within this range of activity.

Stocks: Rane's product is highly perishable, therefore no stocks are held.

Task 1
(a) Calculate the annual profit which is earned with the current selling price of £60 per unit.
(b) Prepare a schedule to show the annual profit which would be earned with each of the three alternative selling prices.

Task 2
Prepare a brief memorandum to your boss; Chris Jones. The memorandum should cover the following points:
(a) Your recommendation as to the selling price which should be charged to maximize Rane Limited's annual profits.
(b) *Two* non-financial factors which the management of Rane Limited should consider before planning to operate below full capacity.

Another of your consultancy's clients is a manufacturing company, Shortage Limited, which is experiencing problems in obtaining supplies of a major component. The component is used in all of its four products and there is a labour dispute at the supplier's factory, which is restricting the component's availability.

Supplies will be restricted to 22 400 components for the next period and the company wishes to ensure that the best use is made of the available components. This is the only component used in the four products, and there are not alternatives and no other suppliers.

The components cost £2 each and are used in varying amounts in each of the four products.

Shortage Limited's fixed costs amount to £8000 per period. No stocks are held of finished goods or work in progress.

The following information is available concerning the products.

	Product A	Product B	Product C	Product D
Maximum demand per period	4000 units	2500 units	3600 units	2750 units
	£ per unit	£ per unit	£ per unit	£ per unit
Selling price	14	12	16	17
Component costs	4	2	6	8
Other variable costs	7	9	6	4

Task 3
(a) Prepare a recommended production schedule for next period which will maximize Shortage Limited's profit.
(b) Calculate the profit that will be earned in the next period if your recommended production schedule is followed.

Association of Accounting Technicians –
Technicians Stage

Question 11.11
intermediate

Limiting factor optimum production and the use of simultaneous equations where more than one scarce factor exists

A company manufactures two products (X and Y) in one of its factories. Production capacity is limited to 85 000 machine hours per period. There is no restriction on direct labour hours.

The following information is provided concerning the two products:

	Product X	Product Y
Estimated demand (000 units)	315	135
Selling price (per unit)	£11.20	£15.70
Variable costs (per unit)	£6.30	£8.70
Fixed Costs (per unit)	£4.00	£7.00
Machine hours (per 000 units)	160	280
Direct labour hours (per 000 units)	120	140

Fixed costs are absorbed into unit costs at a rate per machine hour based upon full capacity.

Required:
(a) Calculate the production quantities of products X and Y which are required per period in order to maximize profit in the situation described above. *5 marks*
(b) Prepare a marginal costing statement in order to establish the total contribution of each product, and the net profit per period, based on selling the quantities calculated in (a) above. *4 marks*
(c) Calculate the production quantities of products X and Y per period which would fully utilize both machine capacity and direct labour hours, where the available direct labour hours are restricted to 55 000 per period. (The limit of 85 000 machine hours remains.) *5 marks*

Total 14 marks
ACCA Foundation Paper 3

	X	Y	Z	**Answer 11.1**
Contribution per unit	£41	£54	£50	
Kg used (Limiting factor)	2 (£10/5)	1	3	
Contribution per kg	£20.5	£54	£16.67	
Ranking	2	1	3	

Answer = B

The material is in regular use and if used will have to be replaced at a cost of £1,950 **Answer 11.2** (600 × £3.25). The cash flow consequences are £1,950.
Answer = D

The shadow price is the opportunity cost or contribution per unit of a scarce **Answer 11.3** resource.

	Quone	Qutwo
Contribution per unit	£8	£8.50
Kg per unit	3 (£6/£2)	2.50 (£5/£2)
Contribution per kg	£2.67	£3.40

Scarce materials will be used to make Qutwos and will yield a contribution of £3.40 per kg. Therefore the opportunity cost is £3.40 per kg.

Answer = D

Assuming that fixed costs will remain unchanged whether or not the company **Answer 11.4** makes or buys the components the relevant cost of manufacture will be the variable cost. Under these circumstances the company should only purchase components if the purchase price is less than the variable cost. Therefore the company should only purchase component T.

Answer = D

(i) General fixed overheads are recovered at a rate of 80% of direct labour cost **Answer 11.5** (£1.20/£1.50). Therefore general fixed overheads for Product M2 are £0.80 (80% × £1 Direct Labour Cost). The balance of £0.20 represents specific fixed costs for Product M2. The incremental costs of manufacturing are:

	Product M1	Product M2
	£	£
Direct costs	4.60	4.40
Specified fixed costs		0.20
Maximum purchase price	4.60	4.60

Answer = B
(ii) General fixed overheads = £12 000 allocated to M1 (10 000 × £1.20)
           = £10 000 allocated to M2 (12 500 × £1 less
               £2 500 specific fixed costs)
         £22 000

$$\text{Number of units to be sold} = \frac{\text{Fixed costs (£22 000) + Desired profit (£50 000)}}{\text{Unit contribution (£5.40)}}$$

         = 13 333 units

Answer = C

Answer 11.6

Incremental cost of new employees = £40 000 × 4 = £160 000
Supervision is not an incremental cost.
Incremental costs of retraining
  = £15 000 + £100 000 replacement cost = £115 000
Retraining is the cheaper alternative and therefore the relevant cost of the contract is
£115 000.

Answer = B

Answer 11.7

	Z1	Z2	Z3
Product contributions	£8	£7	£4.30
Contribution per £1 of labour	£4 (£8/£2)	£1.75	£2.40
Ranking	1	3	2

Answer = D

Answer 11.8

(a) *Calculation of minimum selling price:*

	£
Direct materials: Steel[a]	55.00
Brass Fittings[b]	20.00
Direct Labour: Skilled[c]	300.00
Semi-skilled[d]	–
Overhead[e]	7.50
Estimating time[f]	–
Administration[g]	–
Relevant cost of the order	382.50

Notes:

[a] Using the materials for the order will result in them having to be replaced. Therefore future cash outflows will increase by £55.

[b] Future cash outflows of £20 will be incurred.

[c] The required labour hours can be obtained by reducing production of another product involving a lost contribution before deducting the labour cost of £21 (£13 + £8) per hour (note that the labour cost will be incurred for all alternatives and therefore is not an incremental cash flow). Alternatively, the company can pay additional wages involving overtime of £300 (25 hours × £12). Therefore the latter course of action is the most economical and the incremental cash flows from undertaking the order will be £300.

[d] No incremental cost is involved since the alternative is paid idle time.

[e] The only incremental cost is power consisting of 10 hours at £0.75 per hour.

[f] Estimating time is a sunk cost.

[g] Administration does not involve any incremental cash flows.

(b) Factors to be considered include:
  (i) time period for repeat orders, the number of repeat orders and the likely demand;
  (ii) the cash flows generated from the alternative use of the capacity;
  (iii) competition to obtain future orders from Exe plc;
  (iv) estimated price quotations from competitors.

(c) *Limiting factor presentation:*

	Product X	Product Y
Product contribution	£10	£20
Kg of material used per product	1	4
Contribution per kg	£10	£5

Thus scarce materials should be allocated to Product X since it yields a contribution of £5 per kg in excess of the contribution derived from Product Y.

Opportunity cost approach:

	Product X	Product Y
Product contribution at acquisition cost	£10	£20
Lost contribution from alternative use:		
1 kg allocated to Y at £5 per kg	(£5)	
4 kg allocated to X at £10 per kg		£40
Cash flow impact per product	+£5	−£20
Cash flow impact per kg	+£5 (£5/1 kg)	−£5 (£20/4 kg)

The above analysis shows that X yields a contribution of £5 per kg when taking alternative uses of the materials into consideration. Producing Product Y results in the contribution being reduced by £5 per kg taking into account the alternative use of the materials. This is consistent with the limiting factor approach which indicates that the company is £5 per kg better off using the materials for X or £5 per kg worse off from using the materials for Y.

(a)

	Chairs	Benches	Tables	Total
Timber required per unit (m²)	2.5(£5/£2)	7.5(£15/£2)	5(£10/£2)	
Budgeted sales volume (units)	4 000	2 000	1 500	
Total timber required (m²)	10 000	15 000	7 500	32 500

Production requirements exceed the available supply of materials by 12 500 m²

	Chairs	Benches	Tables
Unit contributions (£)	8	17.50	16
Timber requirements (m²)	2.5	7.5	5
Contribution per m² (£)	3.2	2.33	3.20
Ranking	1	3	1

The scarce materials should be allocated as follows:

	Materials used	Balance unused
Chairs (4 000 units × 2.5)	10 000	10 000
Tables (1 500 units × 5)	7 500	2 500
Benches (2 500/7.5 = 333 units)	2 500	–

The above production plan is sufficient to meet the order that has already been accepted. The profit arising from the above production plan is calculated as follows:

	£
Chairs (4 000 units × £8 contribution)	32 000
Tables (1 500 units × £16 contribution)	24 000
Benches (333 units × £17.50 contribution)	5 827
Total contribution	61 827
Fixed overheads (4 000 × £4.50) + (2 000 × £11.25) + (1 500 × £9)	54 000
Profit	7 827

(b) The above production plan indicates that maximum sales demand for chairs and tables has been met but there is unutilized demand for benches. Therefore any additional materials purchased will be used to make benches yielding a contribution per unit sold of £17.50 and contribution per metre of material used of

£2.33 (see part (a) for calculation). The company should not pay above £2.33 in excess of the acquisition cost of materials. The maximum purchase price is £4.33 (£2 + £2.33).

(c) See Chapter 3 for an explanation of each of the items listed in the question.

Answer 11.10 *Task 1*

(a) and (b)

Selling price	£60	£70	£80	£90
Sales volume (units)	25 000	20 000	16 000	11 000
	£ per unit	£ per unit	£ per unit	£ per unit
Direct material	14.00	14.00	14.00	16.10 (£14 × 115/100)
Direct labour	13.00	13.00	11.70 (90%)	11.70
Variable production overhead	4.00	4.00	4.00	4.00
Sales commission (10% of selling price)	6.00	7.00	8.00	9.00
Total variable cost per unit	37.00	38.00	37.70	40.80
Contribution per unit	23.00	32.00	42.30	49.20
	£000	£000	£000	£000
Total contribution	575	640	676.8	541.2
Fixed costs:				
production overhead (25 000 × £8)	200	200	190	190
selling and distribution (25 000 × £3)	75	70	70	70
administration (25 000 × £2)	50	50	50	50
Total fixed costs	325	320	310	310
Total annual profit	250	320	366.8	231.2

Task 2

(a) A selling price of £80 maximizes company profits at £366 800 per annum.
(b) Factors to be considered include:
  (i) The effect on morale arising from a large reduction in direct labour and the resulting redundancies.
  (ii) If competitors do not increase their prices customers may migrate to competitors in the long term and long-term annual profits may be considerably less than the profits predicted in the above schedule. The migration of customers may also enable competitors to reap the benefits of economies of scale thus resulting in their having lower unit costs than Rane Ltd.

Task 3

(a) The products should first he ranked according to their contribution per component used.

	Product A	Product B	Product C	Product D
	£ per unit	£ per unit	£ per unit	£ per unit
Selling price	14	12	16	17
Variable costs	11	11	12	12
Contribution	3	1	4	5
Number of components used per unit	2 (£4/£2)	1 (£2/£2)	3 (£6/£2)	4 (£8/£2)
Contribution per component	£1.50	£1.00	£1.33	£1.25
Ranking	1	4	2	3

The scarce components should be allocated as follows:

Product	Units	Components used	Balance unused
A	4 000	8 000	14 400
C	3 600	10 800	3 600
D	900	3 600	–
		22 400	

(b) Profit to be earned next period:

Product	Units	Contribution per unit	Total
		£	£
A	4 000	3	12 000
C	3 600	4	14 400
D	900		4 500
Total contribution			30 900
Fixed costs			8 000
Profit			22 900

(a)

Answer 11.11

	Product X	Product Y	Total
(1) Estimated demand (000 units)	315	135	
(2) Machine hours required (per 000 units)	160	280	
(3) Machine hours required to meet demand (1 × 2)	50 400	37 800	88 200

The machine hours required to meet demand are in excess of the machine hours that are available. Therefore machine hours are the limiting factor and the company should allocate capacity according to contribution per machine hour.

	Product X	Product Y
	£	£
Selling price	11.20	15.70
Variable cost	6.30	8.70
Contribution	4.90	7.00
Machine hours required per unit[a]	0.16	0.28
Contribution per machine hour	£30.625	£25

Note:
a Product X = 160/1 000   Product Y = 280/1 000

The company should concentrate on maximizing output of Product X. Meeting the maximum demand of Product X will require 50 400 machine hours and this will leave 34 600 hours (85 000 hrs − 50 400 hrs) to be allocated to Product Y. Therefore 123 571 units (34 600 hrs/0.28 hrs) of Y and 315 000 units of X should be produced.

(b)

	Product X	Product Y	Total
	£	£	£
Contribution per unit	4.90	7.00	
Sales volume	315 000	123.571	
Contribution (£000s)	1 543.5	864.997	2 408.497
Less fixed costs[a]			2 124.997
Profit			283.500

^{a} Fixed costs: Product X = 315 000 units $\times$ £4 per unit   = £1 260 000

               Product Y = 123 571 units $\times$ £7 per unit   =   £864 997

                                                        2 124 997

(c) There are now two limiting factors and linear programming techniques must be used.

Let   X = Number of units of X produced (in 000s of units)

        Y = Number of units of Y produced (in 000s of units)

$160X + 280Y = 85\,000$ Machine hours   (1)

$120X + 140Y = 55\,000$ Labour hours   (2)

Multiply equation (2) by 2 and equation (1) by 1

$160X + 280Y = 85\,000$ (1)

$240X + 280Y = 110\,000$ (2)

Subtract equation (2) from equation (1)

$- 80X = -25\,000$

     X = 312.5 (i.e. 312 500 units)

Substitute for X in equation (1)

$160\,(312.5) + 280Y = 85\,000$

$50\,000 + 280Y = 85\,000$

$280Y = 35\,000$

$Y = 125$ (i.e. 125 000)

Therefore the optimal output to fully utilize both labour and machine capacity is 312 500 units of Product X and 125 000 units of Product Y.

Question 12.1 Preparation of conventional costing and ABC profit statements

intermediate   The following budgeted information relates to Brunti plc for the forthcoming period:

		Products	
	XYI	YZT	ABW
	(000)	(000)	(000)
Sales and production (units)	50	40	30
	(£)	(£)	(£)
Selling price (per unit)	45	95	73
Prime cost (per unit)	32	84	65
	Hours	Hours	Hours
Machine department (machine hours per unit)	2	5	4
Assembly department (direct labour hours per unit)	7	3	2

Overheads allocated and apportioned to production departments (including service cost centre costs) were to be recovered in product costs as follows:

Machine department at   £1.20 per machine hour

Assembly department at   £0.825 per direct labour hour

You ascertain that the above overheads could be re-analysed into 'cost pools' as follows:

Cost pool	£000	Cost driver	Quantity for the period
Machining services	357	Machine hours	420 000
Assembly services	318	Direct labour hours	530 000
Set-up costs	26	Set-ups	520
Order processing	156	Customer orders	32 000
Purchasing	84	Supplier's orders	11 200
	941		

You have also been provided with the following estimates for the period:

	Products		
	XYI	YZT	ABW
Number of sales	120	200	200
Customer orders	8 000	8 000	16 000
Suppliers' orders	3 000	4 000	4 200

Required:
(a) Prepare and present profit statements using:
    (i) conventional absorption costing;   *5 marks*
    (ii) activity-based costing;   *10 marks*
(b) Comment on why activity-based costing is considered to present a fairer valuation of the product cost per unit.   *5 marks*
           Total 20 marks
           ACCA Paper 8 Managerial Finance

(a) (i) *Conventional Absorption Costing Profit Statement:*   **Answer 12.1**

		XYI	YZT	ABW
(1)	Sales volume (000 units)	50	40	30
		£	£	£
(2)	Selling price per unit	45	95	73
(3)	Prime cost per unit	32	84	65
(4)	Contribution per unit	13	11	8
(5)	Total contribution in £000s (1 × 4)	650	440	240
(6)	Machine department overheads[a]	120	240	144
(7)	Assembly department overheads[b]	288.75	99	49.5
	Profit (£000s)	241.25	101	46.5

Total profit = £388 750

Notes:
[a] XYI = 50 000 × 2 hrs × £1.20, YZT = 40 000 × 5 hrs × £1.20
[b] XYI = 50 000 × 7 hrs × £0.825, YZT = 40 000 × 3 hrs × £0.825

(ii) *Cost pools:*

	Machining services	Assembly services	Set-ups	Order processing	Purchasing
£000	357	318	26	156	84
Cost drivers	420 000 machine hours	530 000 direct labour hours	520 set-ups	32 000 customer orders	11 200 suppliers' orders
Cost driver rates	£0.85 per machine hour	£0.60 direct labour hour	£50 per set-up	£4.875 per customer order	£7.50 per suppliers' order

ABC Profit Statement:

	XYI £000s	YZT £000s	ABW £000s
Total contribution	650	440	240
Less overheads:			
Machine department at £0.85 per hour	85	170	102
Assembly at £0.60 per hour	210	72	36
Set-up costs at £50 per set-up	6	10	10
Order processing at £4.875 per order	39	39	78
Purchasing at £7.50 per order	22.5	30	31.5
Profit (Loss)	287.5	119	(17.5)

Total profit = £389 000

(b) See the section on a comparison of ABC and traditional product costs in Chapter 12 for the answer to this question.

Question 16.1

intermediate

Computation of NPV and tax payable

Sound Equipment Ltd was formed five years ago to manufacture parts for hi-fi equipment. Most of its customers were individuals wanting to assemble their own systems. Recently, however, the company has embarked on a policy of expansion and has been approached by JBZ plc, a multinational manufacture of consumer electronics. JBZ has offered Sound Equipment Ltd a contract to build an amplifier for its latest consumer product. If accepted, the contract will increase Sound Equipment's turnover by 20%.

JBZ's offer is a fixed price contract over three years, although it is possible for Sound Equipment to apply for subsequent contracts. The contract will involve Sound Equipment purchasing a specialist machine for £150 000. Although the machine has a 10-year life, it would be written off over the three years of the initial contract as it can only be used in the manufacture of the amplifier for JBZ.

The production director of Sound Equipment has already prepared a financial appraisal of the proposal. This is reproduced below. With a capital cost of £150 000 and total profits of £60 300, the production director has calculated the return on capital employed as 40.2%. As this is greater than Sound Equipment's cost of capital of 18%, the production director is recommending that the board accepts the contract.

Proposal to build amplifier for JBZ plc

	Year 1 (£)	Year 2 (£)	Year 3 (£)	Total (£)
Turnover	180 000	180 000	180 000	540 000
Materials	60 000	60 000	60 000	180 000
Labour	40 000	40 000	40 000	120 000
Depreciation	50 000	50 000	50 000	150 000
Pre-tax profit	30 000	30 000	30 000	90 000
Corporation tax at 33%	9 900	9 900	9 900	29 700
After-tax profit	20 100	20 100	20 100	60 300

You are employed as the assistant accountant to Sound Equipment Ltd and report to John Green, the financial director, who asks you to carry out a full financial appraisal of the proposed contract. He feels that the production director's presentation is inappropriate. He provides you with the following additional information:

- Sound Equipment pays corporation tax at the rate of 33%;
- the machine will qualify for a 25% writing-down allowance on the reducing balance;

- the machine will have no further use other than in manufacturing the amplifier for JBZ;
- on ending the contract with JBZ, any outstanding capital allowances can be claimed as a balancing allowance;
- the company's cost of capital is 18%;
- the cost of materials and labour is forecast to increase by 5% per annum for years 2 and 3.

John Green reminds you that Sound Equipment operates a just-in-time stock policy and that production will be delivered immediately to JBZ, who will, under the terms of the contract, immediately pay for the deliveries. He also reminds you that suppliers are paid immediately on receipt of goods and that employees are also paid immediately.

Write a report to the financial director. Your report should:
(a) use the net present value technique to identify whether or not the initial three-year contract is worthwhile;
(b) explain your approach to taxation in your appraisal;
(c) identify *one* other factor to be considered before making a final decision.

Notes:

For the purpose of this task, you may assume the following:

- the machine would be purchased at the beginning of the accounting year;
- there is a one-year delay in paying corporation tax;
- all cash flows – other than the purchase of the machine – occur at the end of each year;
- Sound Equipment has no other assets on which to claim capital allowances.

Association of Accounting Technicians –
Technicians Stage

The report should include the information contained in items (a) to (c) below:

Answer 16.1

(a) Depreciation is not a cash flow. The operating net cash inflows (before tax) therefore consist of sales less materials and labour costs. The NPV calculation is as follows:

Year	0	1	2	3	4
	£	£	£	£	£
Net cash inflows before tax		80 000	75 000	69 750	
Tax^a			(14 025)	(15 469)	4 826
Investment outlay	(150 000)				
Net cash flow	(150 000)	80 000	60 975	54 281	4 826
Discount factor (18%)	1.000	0.847	0.718	0.609	0.516
Present value	(150 000)	67 760	43 780	33 057	2 490

NPV = −£2 913

Note:

The tax computation is as follows:

Year	1	2	3
	£	£	£
Net cash inflows before tax	80 000	75 000	69 750
Writing down allowances	37 500	28 125	84 375
Taxable profit	42 500	46 875	(14 625)
Tax at 33%	14 025	15 469	(4 826)
Writing down allowances:			
Opening WDV	150 000	112 500	84 375

Writing down allowances (25%)	37 500	28 125	
Closing WDV	112 500	84 375	Nil
Balancing allowance			84 375

(b) Because corporation taxes are payable on taxable profits and not accounting profits depreciation has been replaced by the Inland Revenue's allowable depreciation (known as written-down allowances). The net cost of the asset is £150 000 and written-down allowances received amounted to £65 625 (£37 500 + £28 125). Therefore a balancing allowance is available at the end of the asset's life of £84 375 (£150 000 − £65 625). The Inland Revenue allows the net cost of the asset to be claimed over its life with a balancing adjustment in the final year. Because taxation is normally payable 9 months after the company's accounting year end the taxation cash flows are shown to be delayed by one year. This is a simplification of the actual situation but is normally sufficiently accurate for appraising investments.

(c) Other factors to be considered include:

(i) The probability of obtaining a subsequent contract. There would be no need to purchase a further machine and the project would therefore yield a positive NPV.

(ii) The negative NPV is very small and if the company has other profitable activities it may be worthwhile accepting in order to have the chance of obtaining a second contract and establishing long-term relationships with a large multinational customer.

(iii) Capacity that is available. If other profitable opportunities have to be forgone to undertake the contract because of shortage of capacity then the opportunity cost should be included in the financial analysis.

Question 17.1
intermediate

When preparing a production budget, the quantity to be produced equals:

A sales quantity + opening stock + closing stock
B sales quantity − opening stock + closing stock
C sales quantity − opening stock − closing stock
D sales quantity + opening stock − closing stock
E sales quantity

CIMA Stage 2

Question 17.2
intermediate

A fixed budget is:

A a budget for a single level of activity;
B used when the mix of products is fixed in advance of the budget period;
C a budget which ignores inflation;
D used only for fixed costs;
E an overhead cost budget.

CIMA Stage 2

Question 17.3
intermediate

BDL plc is currently preparing its cash budget for the year to 31 March 1998. An extract from its sales budget for the same year shows the following sales values:

	(£)
March	60 000
April	70 000
May	65 000
June	65 000

40% of its sales are expected to be for cash. Of its credit sales, 70% are expected to pay in the month after sale and take a 2% discount; 27% are expected to pay in the second month after the sale, and the remaining 3% are expected to be bad debts.

The value of sales receipts to be shown in the cash budget for May 1997 is:

A £38 532
B £39 120
C £60 532
D £64 220
E £65 200

CIMA Stage 2

A flexible budget is:

A a budge of variable production costs only;
B a budget which is updated with actual costs and revenues as they occur during the budget period;
C a budget which shows the costs and revenues at different levels of activity;
D a budget which is prepared using a computer spreadsheet model;
E a budget which is prepared for a period of six months and reviewed monthly; following such review a further one month's budget is prepared.

CIMA Stage 2

Question 17.4
intermediate

A master budget comprises:

A the budgeted profit and loss account;
B the budget cash flow, budgeted profit and loss account and budgeted balance sheet;
C the budgeted cash flow;
D the capital expenditure budget;
E the entire set of budgets prepared.

CIMA Stage 2

Question 17.5
intermediate

Preparation of cash budgets

The following data and estimates are available for ABC Limited for June, July and August.

Question 17.6
intermediate

	June (£)	July (£)	August (£)
Sales	45 000	50 000	60 000
Wages	12 000	13 000	14 500
Overheads	8 500	9 500	9 000

The following information is available regarding direct materials:

	July (£)	July (£)	August (£)	September (£)
Opening stock	5 000	3 500	6 000	4 000
Material usage	8 000	9 000	10 000	

Notes:

1. 10% of sales are for cash, the balance is received the following month. The amount received in June for May's sales is £29 500.
2. Wages are paid in the month they are incurred.
3. Overheads include £1 500 per month for depreciation. Overheads are settled the month following. £6 500 is to be paid in June for May's overheads.
4. Purchases of direct materials are paid for in the month purchased.
5. The opening cash balance in June is £11 750.
6. A tax bill of £25 000 is to be paid in July.

Required:
(a) Calculate the amount of direct material purchases in *each* of the months of June, July and August. *3 marks*
(b) Prepare cash budgets for June, July and August. *9 marks*
(c) Describe briefly the advantages of preparing cash budgets. *3 marks*

Total marks 15

CIMA Stage 1 Cost Accounting

Question 17.7
intermediate

Budget preparation and comments on sales forecasting methods

You have recently been appointed as the management accountant to Alderley Ltd, a small company manufacturing two products, the Elgar and the Holst. Both products use the same type of material and labour but in different proportions. In the past, the company has had poor control over its working capital. To remedy this, you have recommended to the directors that a budgetary control system to be introduced. This proposal has, now, been agreed.

Because Alderley Ltd's production and sales are spread evenly over the year, it was agreed that the annual budget should be broken down into four periods, each of 13 weeks, and commencing with the 13 weeks ending 4 April 1997. To help you in this task, the sales and production directors have provided you with the following information:

1. Marketing and production data

	Elgar	Holst
Budgeted sales for 13 weeks (units)	845	1235
Material content per unit (kilograms)	7	8
Labour per unit (standard hours)	8	5

2. Production labour
   The 24 production employees work a 37-hour, five-day week and are paid £8 per hour. Any hours in excess of this involve Alderley in paying an overtime premium of 25%. Because of technical problems, which will continue over the next 13 weeks, employees are only able to work at 95% efficiency compared to standard.

3. Purchasing and opening stocks
   The production director believes that raw material will cost £12 per kilogram over the budgeted period. He also plans to revise the amount of stock being kept. He estimates that the stock levels at the commencement of the budget period will be as follows:

Raw materials	Elgar	Holst
2328 kilograms	163 units	361 units

4. Closing stocks
   At the end of the 13-week period closing stocks are planned to change. On the assumption that production and sales volumes for the second budget period will be similar to those in the first period:

   - raw material stocks should be sufficient for 13 days' production;
   - finished stocks of the Elgar should be equivalent to 6 days' sales volume;
   - finish stocks of the Holst should be equivalent to 14 days' sales volume.

Task 1
Prepare in the form of a statement the following information for the 13-week period to 4 April 1997:
(a) the production budget in units for the Elgar and Holst;
(b) the purchasing budget for Alderly Ltd in units;
(c) the cost of purchases for the period;
(d) the production labour budget for Alderley Ltd in hours;
(e) the cost of production labour for the period.

Note: Assume a five-day week for both sales and production.

The managing director of Alderley Ltd, Alan Dunn, has also only recently been appointed. He is keen to develop the company and has already agreed to two new products being developed. These will be launched in eighteen months' time. While talking to you about the budget he mentions that the quality of sales forecasting will need to improve if the company is to grow rapidly. Currently, the budgeted sales figure is found by initially adding 5% to the previous year's sales volume and then revising the figure following discussions with the marketing director. He believes this approach is increasingly inadequate and now requires a more systematic approach.

A few days later, Alan Dunn sends you a memo. In that memo, he identifies three possible strategies for increasing sales volume. They are:

- more sales to existing customers;
- the development of new markets;
- the development of new products.

He asks for your help in forecasting likely sales volumes from these sources.

Task 2
Write a brief memo to Alan Dunn. Your memo should:
(a) identify *four* ways of forecasting future sales volume;
(b) show how each of your four ways of forecasting can be applied to *one* of the sales strategies identified by Alan Dunn and justify your choice.
(c) give *two* reasons why forecasting methods might not prove to be accurate.

Association of Accounting Technicians –
Technicians Stage

Answer = B   **Answer 17.1**

Answer = A   **Answer 17.2**

	£	£	**Answer 17.3**
Cash sales		22 000	
Credit sales:			
April (70% × 0.6 × 0.98 × £70 000)	28 812		
March (27% × 0.6 × £60 000)	9 720	38 532	
		60 532	

Answer = C

Answer = C   **Answer 17.4**

Answer = B   **Answer 17.5**

Answer 17.6 (a)

	June £	July £	August £
Closing stock	3 500	6 000	4 000
Material usage	8 000	9 000	10 000
	11 500	15 000	14 000
Less: Opening stock	5 000	3 500	6 000
Direct material purchases	6 500	11 500	8 000

(b) *Cash budgets for June, July and August:*

	June £	July £	August £
Receipts			
Sales cash (10%)	4 500	5 000	6 000
credit	29 500	40 500	45 000
	34 000	45 500	51 000
Payments			
Wages	12 000	13 000	14 500
Overheads (less depreciation)	6 500	7 000	8 000
Direct materials	6 500	11 500	8 000
Taxation	–	25 000	–
	25 000	56 500	30 500
Opening balance	11 750	20 750	9 750
Receipts	34 000	45 500	51 000
Payments	25 000	56 500	30 500
Closing balance	20 750	9 750	30 250

(c) See the section on cash budgets in Chapter 17 for the answer to this question.

Answer 17.7 *Task 1*

Alderley Ltd Budget Statements 13 weeks to 4 April 1997

(a) Production Budget

	Elgar units	Holst units
Budgeted sales volume	845	1 235
Add closing stock[a]	78	1 266
Less Opening stock	(163)	(361)
Units of production	760	1 140

(b) Material Purchases Budget

	Elgar kg	Holst kg	Total kg
Material consumed	5 320 (760 × 7)	9 120 (1 140 × 8)	14 440
Add raw material closing stock[b]			2 888
Less raw material opening stock			(2 328)
Purchases (kg)			15 000

(c) Purchases (£) (1 500 × £12) — £180 000

(d) Production Labour Budget

	Elgar hours	Holst hours	Total hours
Standard hours produced[c]	6 080	5 700	11 780
Productivity adjustment (5/95 × 11 780)			620
Total hours employed			12 400
Normal hours employed[d]			11 544
Overtime hours			856

(e) Labour cost   £

	£
Normal hours (11 544 × £8)	92 352
Overtime (856 × £8 × 125%)	8 560
Total	100 912

Notes:

[a] Number of days per period = 13 weeks × 5 days = 65
Stock: Elgar = (6/65) × 845 = 78, Holst = (14/65) × 1 235 = 266

[b] (13/65) × (5 320 + 9 120) = 2 888

[c] Elgar 760 × 8 hours = 6 080, Holst 1 140 × 5 hours = 5 700

[d] 24 employees × 37 hours × 13 weeks = 11 544

Task 2

(a) Four ways of forecasting future sales volume are:
   (i) Where the number of customers is small it is possible to interview them to ascertain what their likely demand will be over the forecasting period.
   (ii) Produce estimates based on the opinion of executives and sales personnel. For example, sales personnel may be asked to estimate the sales of each product to their customers, or regional sales managers may estimate the total sales for each of their regions.
   (iii) Market research may be necessary where it is intended to develop new products or new markets. This may involve interviews with existing and potential customers in order to estimate potential demand.
   (iv) Estimates involving statistical techniques that incorporate general business and market conditions and past growth in sales.

(b) Interviewing customers and basing estimates on the opinions of sales personnel are likely to be more appropriate for existing products and customers involving repeat sales. Market research is appropriate for new products or markets and where the market is large and anticipated revenues are likely to be sufficient to justify the cost of undertaking the research.

   Statistical estimates derived from past data are likely to be appropriate where conditions are likely to be stable and past demand patterns are likely to be repeated through time. This method is most suited to existing products or markets where sufficient data is available to establish a trend in demand.

(c) The major limitation of interviewing customers is that they may not be prepared to divulge the information if their future plans are commercially sensitive. There is also no guarantee that the orders will be placed with Alderley Ltd. They may place their orders with competitors.

   Where estimates are derived from sales personnel there is a danger that they might produce over-optimistic estimates in order to obtain a favourable performance rating. Alternatively, if their future performance is judged by their ability to achieve the budgeted sales they may be motivated to underestimate sales demand.

   Market research is expensive and may produce unreliable estimates if inexperienced researchers are used. Also small samples are often used which may not be indicative of the population and this can result in inaccurate estimates.

   Statistical estimates will produce poor demand estimates where insufficient past data is available, demand is unstable over time and the future environment is likely to be significantly different from the past. Statistical estimates are likely to be inappropriate for new products and new markets where past data is unavailable.

Preparation of flexible budgets

The Arcadian Hotel operates a budgeting system and budgets expenditure over eight budget centres as shown below. Analysis of past expenditure patterns indicates that

Question 18.1
intermediate

variable costs in some budge centres vary according to occupied room nights (ORN), while in others the variable proportion of costs varies according to the number of visitors(V).

The budgeted expenditures for a period with 2000 ORN and 4300V were as follows:

Budget centre	Variable costs vary with	Budgeted expenditure	Partial cost analysis Budget expenditure includes
		(£)	
Cleaning	ORN	13 250	£2.50 per ORN
Laundry	V	15 025	£1.75 per V
Reception	ORN	13 100	£12 100 fixed
Maintenance	ORN	11 100	£0.80 per ORN
Housekeeping	V	19 600	£11 000 fixed
Administration	ORN	7 700	£0.20 per ORN
Catering	V	21 460	£2.20 per V
General overheads	–	11 250	all fixed

In period 9 with 1850 ORN and 4574 V, actual expenditures were as follows:

Budget Centre	Actual expenditure
	(£)
Cleaning	13 292
Laundry	14 574
Reception	13 855
Maintenance	10 462
Housekeeping	19 580
Administration	7 930
Catering	23 053
General overheads	11 325

Required:
(a) Prepare a flexible budget for period 9.   *7 marks*
(b) Show the individual expenditure variables for each budget centre.   *5 marks*
(c) Discuss briefly the advantages that a budgeting system brings to the Arcadian Hotel.   *3 marks*

Total marks 15
CIMA State 1 Cost Accounting

Question 18.2
intermediate

Preparation of a flexible budget performance report

The Viking Smelting Company established a division, called the reclamation division, in April 1995, to extract silver from jewellers' waste materials. The waste materials are processed in a furnace, enabling silver to be recovered. The silver is then further processed into finished products by three other divisions within the company.

A performance report is prepared each month for the reclamation division which is then discussed by the management team. Sharon Houghton, the newly appointed financial controller of the reclamation division, has recently prepared her first report for the four weeks to 31 May 1997. This is shown below:

Performance Report – Reclamation Division
– 4 weeks to 31 May 1997

	Actual	Budget	Variance		Comments
Production (tonnes)	200	250	50	(F)[a]	
	(£)	(£)	(£)		
Wages and social security costs	46 133	45 586	547	(A)[a]	Overspend
Fuel	15 500	18 750	3 250	(F)	
Consumables	2 100	2 500	400	(F)	
Power	1 590	1 750	160	(F)	
Divisional overheads	21 000	20 000	1 000	(A)	Overspend
Plant maintenance	6 900	5 950	950	(A)	Overspend
Central services	7 300	6 850	450	(A)	Overspend
Total	100 523	101 386	863	(F)	

[a](A) = adverse, (F) = favourable

In preparing the budgeted figures, the following assumptions were made for May:

- the reclamation division was to employ four teams of six production employees;
- each employee was to work a basic 42-hour week and be paid £7.50 per hour for the four weeks of May;
- social security and other employment costs were estimated at 40% of basic wages;
- a bonus, shared amongst the production employees, was payable if production exceeded 150 tonnes. This varied depending on the output achieved.
  1. if output was between 150 and 199 tonnes, the bonus was £3 per tonne produced;
  2. if output was between 200 and 249 tonnes, the bonus was £8 per tonne produced;
  3. if output exceeded 249 tonnes the bonus was £13 per tonne produced;
- the cost of fuel was £75 per tonne;
- consumables were £10 per tonne;
- power comprised a fixed charge of £500 per four weeks plus £5 per tonne for every tonne produced;
- overheads directly attributable to the division were £20 000;
- plant maintenance was to be apportioned to divisions on the basis of the capital values of each division;
- the cost of Viking's central services was to be shared equally by all four divisions.

You are the deputy financial controller of the reclamation division. After attending her first monthly meeting with the board of the reclamation division, Sharon Houghton arranges a meeting with you. She is concerned about a number of issues, one of them being that the current report does not clearly identify those expenses and variances which are the direct responsibility of the reclamation division.

Task 1
Sharon Houghton asks you to prepare a flexible budget report for the reclamation division for May 1997 in a form consistent with responsibility accounting.

On receiving your revised report, Sharon tells you about the other questions raised at the management meeting when the original report was presented. These are summarized below:
  (i) Why are the budget figures based on 2-year-old data taken from the proposal recommending the establishment of the reclamation division?
  (ii) Should the budget data be based on what we were proposing to do or what we actually did do?
  (iii) Is it true that the less we produce the more favourable our variances will be?
  (iv) Why is there so much maintenance in a new division with modern equipment

and why should we be charged with the actual costs of the maintenance department even when they overspend?
(v) Could the comments, explaining the variances, be improved?
(vi) Should all the variances be investigated?
(vii) Does showing the cost of central services on the divisional performance report help control these costs and motivate the divisional managers?

Task 2
Prepare a memo for the management of the reclamation division. Your memo should:
(a) answer their queries and justify your comments;
(b) highlight the main objective of your revised performance report developed in Task 1 and give two advantages of it over the original report.

Association of Accounting Technicians –
Technicians Stage

Question 18.3
intermediate

Sales forecasting removing seasonal variations, flexible budgets and budget preparation

You work as the assistant to the management accountant for Henry Limited, a medium-sized manufacturing company. One of its products, product P, has been very successful in recent years, showing a steadily increasing trend in sales volumes. Sales volumes for the four quarters of last year were as follows:

	Quarter 1	Quarter 2	Quarter 3	Quarter 4
Actual sales volume (units)	420 000	450 000	475 000	475 000

A new assistant has recently joined the marketing department and she has asked you for help in understanding the terminology which is used in preparing sales forecasts and analysing sales trends. She has said: 'My main problem is that I do not see why my boss is so enthusiastic about the growth in product P's sales volume. It looks to me as though the rate of growth is really slowing down and has actually stopped in quarter 4. I am told that I should be looking at the deseasonalized or seasonally adjusted sales data but I do not understand what is meant by this.'
You have found that product P's sales are subject to the following seasonal variations:

	Quarter 1	Quarter 2	Quarter 3	Quarter 4
Seasonal variations (units)	+25 000	+15 000	0	-40 000

Task 1
(a) Adjust for the seasonal variations to calculate deseasonalized or seasonally adjusted sales volume (i.e. the trend figures) each quarter of last year.
(b) Assuming that the trend and seasonal variations will continue, forecast the sales volumes for each of the four quarters of next year.

Task 2
Prepare a memorandum to the marketing assistant which explains:
(a) what is meant by seasonal variations and deseasonalized or seasonally adjusted data?;
(b) how they can be useful in analysing a time series and preparing forecasts?
Use the figures for product P's sales to illustrate your explanations.

Task 3
Using the additional data below, prepare a further memorandum to the marketing assistant which explains the following:

(a) why fixed budgets are useful for planning but flexible budgets may be more useful to enable management to exercise effective control over distribution costs;

(b) *two* possible activity indicators which could be used as a basis for flexing the budget for distribution costs;

(c) how a flexible budget cost allowance is calculated and used for control purposes. Use your own examples and figures where appropriate to illustrate your explanations.

Additional data:

The marketing assistant has now approached you for more help in understanding the company's planning and control systems. She has been talking with the distribution manager, who has tried to explain how flexible budgets are used to control distribution costs with Henry Limited. She makes the following comment. 'I thought that budgets were supposed to provide a target to plan our activities and against which to monitor our costs. How can we possibly plan and control our costs if we simply change the budgets when activity levels alter?'

Product Q is another product which is manufacture and sold by Henry Limited. In the process of preparing budgetary plans for next year the following information has been made available to you.

1. Forecast sales units of product Q for the year = 18 135 units.

2. Closing stocks of finished units of product Q at the end of next year will be increase by 15% from their opening level of 1 200 units.

3. All units are subject to a quality control check. The budget plans are to allow for 1% of all units checked to be rejected and scrapped at the end of the process. All closing stocks will have passed this quality control check.

4. Five direct labour hours are to be worked for each unit of product Q processed, including those which are scrapped after the quality control check. Of the total hours to be paid for, 7.5% are budgeted to be idle time.

5. The standard hourly rate of pay for direct employees is £6 per hour.

6. Material M is used in the manufacture of product Q. One finished unit of product Q contains 9 kg of M but there is a wastage of 10% of input of material M due to evaporation and spillage during the process.

7. By the end of next year stocks of material M are to be increased by 12% from their opening level of 8 000 kg. During the year a loss of 1 000 kg is expected due to deterioration of the material in store.

Task 4

Prepare the following budgets for the forthcoming year;

(a) production budget for product Q, in units;

(b) direct labour budget for product Q, in hours and in £;

(c) material usage budget for material M, in kg;

(d) material purchases budget for material M, in kg.

Task 5

The supplier of material M was warned that available supplies will be below the amount indicated in your budget for Task 4 part (d) above. Explain the implications of this shortage and suggest *four* possible actions which could be taken to overcome the problem. For each suggestion, identify any problems which may arise.

Association of Accounting Technicians –
Technicians Stage

(a) The question only provides a partial cost analysis. To ascertain the cost formula for each item of expense it is necessary to ascertain the missing information for the activity level given in the question (2 000 ORN and 4 300V):

Answer 18.1

Item of expense	Budgeted expenditure £	Variable cost		£	Fixed cost £
Cleaning	13 250	2 000 × £2.50	=	5 000	8 250
Laundry	15 025	4 300 × £1.75	=	7 525	7 500
Reception	13 100	£1 000/2 000 × 2 000	=	1 000	12 100
Maintenance	11 100	2 000 × £0.80	=	1 600	9 500
Housekeeping	19 600	£8 600/4 300 × 4 300	=	8 600	11 000
Administration	7 700	2 000 × £0.20	=	400	7 300
Catering	21 460	4 300 × £2.20	=	9 460	12 000
General overheads	11 250		=	0	11 250

Note that the variable cost or the fixed cost is the balancing figure in the above calculations. We can now compute the flexible budget for period 9.

Flexible budget for period 9 (Activity = 1 850 ORN and 4 575V):

	Variable cost		£	Fixed cost £	Total cost £
Cleaning	1 850 × £2.50	=	4 625	8 250	12 875
Laundry	4 575 × £1.75	=	8 006	7 500	15 506
Reception	1 850 × £0.50	=	925	12 100	13 025
Maintenance	1 850 × £0.80	=	1 480	9 500	10 980
Housekeeping	4 575 × £2	=	9 150	11 000	20 150
Administration	1 850 × £0.20	=	370	7 300	7 670
Catering	4 575 × £2.20	=	10 065	12 000	22 065
General overheads		=	0	11 250	11 250
					113 521

(b)

	Flexed budget £	Actual £	Variance £	Favourable/ adverse
Cleaning	12 875	13 292	(417)	ADV
Laundry	15 506	14 574	932	FAV
Reception	13 025	13 855	(830)	ADV
Maintenance	10 980	10 462	518	FAV
Housekeeping	20 150	19 580	570	FAV
Administration	7 670	7 930	(260)	ADV
Catering	22 065	23 053	(988)	ADV
General overheads	11 250	11 325	(75)	ADV
	113 521	114 071	(550)	

(c) See the section on why do we produce budgets in Chapter 17 for the answer to this question.

Answer 18.2 Task 1

Reclamation Division Performance Report – 4 weeks to 31 May 1997:
Original budget   250 tonnes
Actual output   200 tonnes

	Budget based on 200 tonnes	Actual	Variance	Comments
Controllable expenses:				
Wages and social security costs[a]	43 936	46 133	2 197A	
Fuel[b]	15 000	15 500	500A	
Consumables[c]	2 000	2 100	100A	
Power[d]	1 500	1 590	90A	
Directly attributable overheads[e]	20 000	21 000	1 000A	
	82 436	86 323	3 887A	
Non-controllable expenses:				
Plant maintenance[e]	5 950	6 900	950A	
Central services[e]	6 850	7 300	450A	
	12 800	14 200	1 400A	
Total	95 236	100 523	5 287A	

Notes:
[a] 6 employees $\times$ 4 teams $\times$ 42 hours per week $\times$ £7.50 per hour $\times$ 4 weeks = £30 240.
[b] 200 tonnes $\times$ £75
[c] 200 tonnes $\times$ £10
[d] £500 + (£5 $\times$ 200) = £1 500
[e] It is assumed that directly attributable expenses, plant maintenance and central services are non-variable expenses.

Task 2
(a) (i) Past knowledge can provide useful information on future outcomes but ideally budgets ought to be based on the most up-to-date information. Budgeting should be related to the current environment and the use of past information that is two years old can only be justified where the operating conditions and environment are expected to remain unchanged.

(ii) For motivation and planning purposes budgets should represent targets based on what we are proposing to do. For control purposes budgets should be flexed based on what was actually done so that actual costs for actual output can be compared with budgeted costs for the actual output. This ensures that valid comparisons will be made.

(iii) For variable expenses the original budget should be reduced in proportion to reduced output in order to reflect cost behaviour. Fixed costs are not adjusted since they are unaffected in the short-term by output changes. Flexible budgeting ensures that like is being compared with like so that reduced output does not increase the probability that favourable cost variances will be reported. However, if less was produced because of actual sales being less than budget this will result in an adverse sales variance and possibly an adverse profit variance.

(iv) Plant maintenance costs are apportioned on the basis of capital values and therefore newer equipment (with higher written-down values) will be charged with a higher maintenance cost. Such an approach does not provide a meaningful estimate of maintenance resources consumed by departments since older equipment is likely to be more expensive to maintain. The method of recharging should be reviewed and ideally based on estimated usage according to maintenance records. The charging of the overspending by the maintenance department to user departments is questionable since this masks inefficiencies. Ideally, maintenance department costs should be recharged based on actual usage at budgeted cost and the maintenance department made accountable for the adverse spending (price) variance.

(v) The comments do not explain the causes of the variances and are presented in a negative tone. No comments are made, nor is any praise given, for the favourable variances.

(vi) Not all variances should be investigated. The decision to investigate should depend on both their absolute and relative size and the likely benefits arising from an investigation.

(vii) Central service costs are not controllable by divisional managers. However, even though the divisional manager cannot control these costs there is an argument for including them as non-controllable costs in the performance report. The justification for this is that divisional managers are made aware of central service costs and may put pressure on central service staff to control such costs more effectively. It should be made clear to divisional managers that they are not accountable for any non-controllable expenses that are included in their performance reports.

Answer 18.3

Task 1

(a)

	Quarter 1 units	Quarter 2 units	Quarter 3 units	Quarter 4 units
Actual sales volume	420 000	450 000	475 000	475 000
Seasonal variation	+25 000	+15 000	–	240 000
Deseasonalized sales volumes	395 000	435 000	475 000	515 000

(b) The trend is for sales volume to increase by 40,000 units each quarter:

Forecast for next year	Quarter 1 units	Quarter 2 units	Quarter 3 units	Quarter 4 units
Trend projection	555 000	595 000	635 000	675 000
Seasonal variation	+25 000	+15 000	–	−40 000
Forecast sales volumes	580 000	610 000	635 000	635 000

Task 2

(a) Seasonal variations represent consistent patterns in sales volume that occur throughout each year. For example, the seasonal variation of +25 000 for Quarter 1 indicates that sales volume in the first quarter tends to be 25 000 units higher than the underlying trend in sales. In contrast, the seasonal variation of −40 000 in Quarter 4 indicates that sales in this quarter tend to be 40 000 units lower than the underlying trend in sales.

To derive the deseasonalized data the seasonal variations must be removed so that a trend can be observed. The above figures indicate an increase of 40,000 units per quarter. This trend is concealed when the actual data is observed because of the distorting effects of seasonal variations. Observations of the actual data suggests that the rate of increase in sales is declining.

(b) Provided that the observed trend in deseasonalized data continues the deseasonalized data can be used to project the trend in future sales. The trend values are adjusted by seasonal variations in each quarter to predict actual sales.

Task 3

(a) A fixed budget is a budget for the planned level of activity and budgeted costs are not adjusted to the actual level of activity. A fixed budget is used at the planning stage because an activity level has to be initially determined so that all department activities can be coordinated to meet the planned level of activity. However, it is most unlikely that actual activity will be the same as the planned level of activity. For example, if the actual level of activity is greater than budgeted level of activity then those costs that vary with the level of activity will be greater than the budgeted costs purely because of changes in activity. It is clearly inappropriate for variable costs to compare actual costs at one level of activity with budgeted costs at another level of activity. The original fixed budget must be adjusted to reflect the budgeted expenditure at the actual level of activity. This procedure is called flexible budgeting. The resulting comparison of actual costs with a flexible budget is more meaningful for cost control because the effect of the change in the activity level has been eliminated.

(b) Possible activity indicators include number of deliveries made, miles travelled and journeys made.

(c) See the section on budget formula in Chapter 18 for the answer to this question.

Task 4

(a) Production budget for product Q

	units
Forecast sales for year	18 135
Increase in stock (15% × 1 200)	180
Finished units required	18 315
Quality control loss (1/99)	185
Total units input to production	18 500

(b) Direct labour budget for product Q

	hours
Active labour hours required (18 500 × 5)	92 500
Idle time allowance (7.5/92.5)	7 500
Total hours to be paid for	100 000
Standard hourly rate	£6
Budgeted labour cost	£600 000

(c) Material usage budget for material M

	kg
Material required for processing	
18 500 units (× 9 kg)	166 500
Wastage (10/90)	18 500
Material usage for year	185 000

(d) Material purchases budget for material M

	kg
Material required for production input	185 000
Increase in material stocks (12%)	960
Expected loss in stores	1 000
Material purchases required	186 960

Task 5

The implications of the shortage is that the budget plans cannot be achieved and the availability of material is the limiting factor. If the limiting factor cannot be removed the materials purchase budget should be the first budget to be prepared and all the other budgets coordinated to ensure the most efficient usage of materials. The following four possible actions could be taken to overcome the problem:

(i) Seek alternative supplies for material M. Possible problems include the reliability and quality of materials delivered by new suppliers. New suppliers should be carefully vetted prior to entering into any contracts or making company plans dependent on deliveries from new suppliers.

(ii) Reduce the budgeted sales of product Q. This will lead to loss in profits and the possible permanent loss of customers to competitors if the competitors are able to meet customer demand.

(iii) Reduce the stock levels for product Q and material M. The danger with this course of action is that stocks may not be available when required which could lead to disruptions in production and lost sales.

(iv) Reduce the wastage of material M and the defective output of product Q. This course of action will cause problems if quality standards are reduced resulting in inferior quality output. This could have a harmful effect on future sales. Problems will not be caused if quality standards are maintained and improved working practices result in a reduction of waste and defective output.

Question 19.1
intermediate

During a period of 175 000 labour hours were worked at a standard cost of £6.50 per hour. The labour efficiency variance was £7800 favourable.

How many standard hours were produced?

A   1 200
B   16 300
C   17 500
D   18 700

CIMA Stage 1

Question 19.2
intermediate

T plc uses a standard costing system, which is material stock account being maintained at standard costs. The following details have been extracted from the standard cost card in respect of direct materials:

8 kg at £0.80/kg = £6.40 per unit
Budgeted production in April 1995 was 850 units.

The following details relate to actual materials purchased and issued to production during April 1995, when actual production was 870 units:

Materials purchased   8200 kg costing £6888
Materials issued to production   7150 kg

Which of the following correctly states the material price and usage variances to be reported?

	Price	Usage
A	£286 (A)	£152 (A)
B	£286 (A)	£280 (A)
C	£286 (A)	£294 (A)
D	£328 (A)	£151 (A)
E	£328 (A)	£280 (A)

CIMA Stage 2

Question 19.3
intermediate

PQ Limited operates a standard costing system for its only product. The standard cost card is as follows:

Direct materials (4 kg at £2/kg)	£8.00
Direct labour (4 hours at £4/hour)	£16.00
Variable overheads (4 hours at £3/hour)	£12.00
Fixed overheads (4 hours at £5/hour)	£20.00

Fixed overheads are absorbed on the basis of labour hours. Fixed overhead costs are budgeted at £12 000 per annum, arising at a constant rate during the year.

Activity in period 3 of 1995 is budgeted to be 10% of total activity for the year.

Actual production during period 3 was 500 units, with actual fixed overhead costs incurred being £9800 and actual hours worked being 1970.

The fixed overhead expenditure variance for period 3 of 1995 was:

A £2200 (F)
B £200 (F)
C £50 (F)
D £200 (A)
E £2200 (A)

CIMA Stage 2

QR Limited uses a standard absorption costing system. The following details have been extracted from its budget for April 1997:

Fixed production overhead cost   £48 000
Production (units)   4 800

In April 1997 the fixed production overhead cost was under-absorbed by £8000 and the fixed production overhead expenditure variance was £2000 adverse.
The actual number of units produced was:

A 3800
B 4000
C 4200
D 5400
E 5800

CIMA Stage 2

Question 19.4
intermediate

F Limited has the following budget and actual data:

Budget fixed overhead cost   £100 000
Budget production (units)   20 000
Actual fixed overhead cost   £110 000
Actual production (units)   19 500

The fixed overhead volume variance:

A is £500 adverse;
B is £2500 adverse;
C is £10 000 adverse;
D is £17 500 adverse;
E cannot be calculated from the data given.

CIMA Stage 2 Specimen Paper

Question 19.5
intermediate

J Limited operates a standard cost accounting system. The following information has been extracted from its standard cost card and budgets:

Budgeted sales volume   5000 units
Budgeted selling price   £10.00 per unit
Standard variable cost   £5.60 per unit
Standard total cost   £7.50 per unit

If it used a standard marginal cost accounting system and its actual sales were 4500 units at a selling price of £12.00, its sales volume variance would be:

A £1250 adverse
B £2200 adverse
C £2250 adverse
D £3200 adverse
E £5000 adverse

CIMA Stage 2 Specimen Paper

Question 19.6
intermediate

Question 19.7
intermediate

In a period, 11 280 kg of material were used at a total standard costs of £46 248. The material usage variance was £492 adverse.
What was the standard allowed weight of material for the period?

    A   11 520 kg
    B   11 280 kg
    C   11 394 kg
    D   11 160 kg

CIMA Stage 1 Specimen Paper

Question 19.8
intermediate

S plc has the following fixed overhead cost data for October 1997:

Budgeted cost	£100 000
Actual cost	£101 400
Budget output	10 000 standard hours
Actual output	9 000 standard hours
Actual efficiency	96%

The values of over-absorption/under-absorption caused by volume and expenditure effects are:

	Volume	Expenditure
A	£7 650	£1 400 under
B	£7 650	£7 650 under
C	£10 000	£1 400 under
D	£10 000	£7 650 under
E	£10 000	£11 400 under

CIMA Stage 2

Question 19.9
intermediate

The following information relates to R plc for October 1997.

    Bought 7800 kg of material R at a total cost of £16 380
    Stocks of material R increased by 440 kg
    Stocks of material R are valued using standard purchase price
    Material price variance was £1170 adverse

The standard price per kg for material R is:

    A   £1.95
    B   £2.10
    C   £2.23
    D   £2.25
    E   £2.38

CIMA Stage 2

Question 19.10
intermediate

P Limited has the following data relating to its budgeted sales for October 1997:

Budgeted sales	£100 000
Budgeted selling price per unit	£8.00
Budgeted contribution per unit	£4.00
Budgeted profit per unit	£2.50

During October 1997 actual sales were 11 000 units for a sales revenue of £99 000.
    P Limited uses an absorption costing system.
    The sales variances reported for October 1997 were:

	Price	Volume
A	£11 000 F	£3 750 A
B	£11 000 F	£6 000 A
C	£11 000 A	£6 000 A
D	£12 500 F	£12 000 A
E	£12 500 A	£12 000 A

CIMA Stage 2

The following details have been extracted from a standard cost card of X plc:

Product X
Direct labour   4 hours at £5.40 per hour

During October 1997 the budgeted production was 5000 units of product X and the actual production was 4650 units of product X. Actual hours worked were 19 100 and the actual direct labour cost amounted to £98 350.
The labour variances reported were:

	Rate	Efficiency
A	£9650 F	£4860 F
B	£9650 F	£2700 A
C	£4790 F	£2575 A
D	£4790 F	£4860 F
E	£4790 F	£2700 A

CIMA Stage 2

In a period, 5792 units were made with a standard labour allowance of 6.5 hours per unit at £5 per hour. Actual wages were £6 per hour and there was an adverse efficiency variance of £36 000.

How many labour hours were actually worked?

A   30 448
B   31 648
C   43 648
D   44 848

CIMA Stage 1

Computation of labour and material variances for a hotel
You work as the assistant to the management accountant for a major hotel chain, Stately Hotels plc. The new manager of one of the largest hotels in the chain, the Regent Hotel, is experimenting with the use of standard costing to plan and control the costs of preparing and cleaning the hotel bedrooms.

Two of the costs involved in this activity are cleaning labour and the supply of presentation soap packs.

Cleaning labour:
Part-time staff are employed to clean and prepare the bedrooms for customers. The employees are paid for the number of hours that they work, which fluctuates on a daily basis depending on how many rooms need to be prepared each day.

The employees are paid a standard hourly rate for weekday work and a higher hourly rate at the weekend. The standard cost control system is based on an average of these two rates, at £3.60 per hour.

The standard time allowed for cleaning and preparing a bedroom is fifteen minutes.

Presentation soap packs:

A presentation soap pack is left in each room every night. The packs contain soap, bubble bath, shower gel, hand lotion etc. Most customers use the packs or take them home with them, but many do not. The standard usage of packs used for planning and control purposes is one pack per room night.

The packs are purchased from a number of different suppliers and the standard price is £1.20 per pack. Stocks of packs are valued in the accounts at standard price.

Actual results for May:

During May 8400 rooms were cleaned and prepared. The following data was recorded for cleaning labour and soap packs.

Cleaning labour paid for:

Weekday labour	1850	hours at £3 per hour
Weekend labour	700	hours at £4.50 per hour
	2550	

Presentation soap packs purchased and used:

6530	packs at £1.20 each
920	packs at £1.30 each
1130	packs at £1.40 each
8580	

Task

(a) Using the data above, calculate the following cost variances for May:
    (i)   soap pack price;
    (ii) soap pack usage;
    (iii) cleaning labour rate;
    (iv) cleaning labour utilization or efficiency.
(b) Suggest one possible cause for each of the variances which you have calculated, and outline any management action which may be necessary.

Association of Accounting Technicians –
Technicians Stage

Question 19.14

intermediate

Calculation of labour and material variances and a reconciliation statement

You are employed as the assistant management accountant to Albion Ltd. Albion Ltd manufactures a single product, the Xtra, an ingredient used in food processing. The basic raw material in Xtra production is material X. The average unit prices for material X in each quarter last year, and the seasonal variations based on several years' observations, are reproduced below:

	Quarter 1	Quarter 2	Quarter 3	Quarter 4
Average unit price of X	£10	£11	£16	£19
Seasonal variations	−£1	−£2	+£1	+£2

Task 1

(a) Calculate the seasonally adjusted unit price of material X for each of the four quarters of last year.
(b) Assuming a similar pattern of price movements in the future, forecast the likely purchase price for the four quarters of the current year.

Albion Ltd operates a standard absorption costing system. Standards are established at the beginning of each year. Each week the management accounting section prepares a statement for the production director reconciling the actual cost of production with its standard cost. Standard costing data for week 8 of quarter 4 in the current year is given below:

Standard costing and budget data for week 8 of quarter 4

	Quantity	Unit price	Cost per unit
Material (kilograms)	3	£23.00	£69
Labour (hours)	2	£20.00	£40
Fixed overheads (hours)	2	£60.00	£120
Standard unit cost			£229

Budgeted production for week 8	Budgeted units	Standard cost per unit	Standard cost of production
	10 000	£229	£2 290 000

During week 8 production of Xtra totalled 9000 units and the actual costs for that week were:

Inputs	Units	Total cost
Materials (kilograms)	26 500	£662 500
Labour (hours)	18 400	£349 600
Fixed overheads (hours)	18 400	£1 500 000

Using this data, a colleague has already calculated the fixed overhead variances. These were as follows:

Fixed overhead expenditure (or price) variances	£300 000 adverse
Efficiency (or usage) variance	£24 000 adverse
Capacity variance	£96 000 adverse

Task 2
Your colleague asks you to:
(a) calculate the following variances:
    (i) material price;
    (ii) material usage;
    (iii) labour rate;
    (iv) labour efficiency (sometimes called utilization).
(b) Prepare a statement reconciling the actual cost of production with the standard cost of actual production.

The production director of Albion Ltd is concerned that the material price variance may not accurately reflect the efficiency of the company's purchasing department.

Task 3
You have been asked by your finance director to write a *brief* memorandum to the production director. Your note should:
(a) explain what variances are attempting to measure*;
(b) list *three* general ways production variances arise other than through errors*;
(c) identify *three* general reasons why there might be errors in reporting variances*;
(d) use your solution to task 1 to suggest why the production director's concern might be justified.

Note: In parts (a), (b) and (c) of this task, you should restrict your comments to variances in general and not address issues arising from particular types of variances.

> *Association of Accounting Technicians –*
> *Technicians Stage*

Computation of labour and material variances and reconciliation statements

Question 19.15
intermediate

Malton Ltd operates a standard marginal costing system. As the recently appointed management accountant to Malton's Eastern division, you have responsibility for the preparation of that division's monthly cost reports. The standard cost report uses variances to reconcile the actual marginal cost of production to its standard cost.

The Eastern division is managed by Richard Hill. The division only makes one product, the Beta. Budgeted Beta production for May 1997 was 8000 units, although actual production was 9500 units.

In order to prepare the standard cost report for May, you have asked a member of your staff to obtain standard and actual cost details for the month of May. This information is reproduced below:

| | Unit standard cost | | | | Actual details for May | |
	Quantity	Unit price	Cost per Beta (£)		Quantity	Total cost (£)
Material	8 litres	£20	160	Material	78 000 litres	1 599 000
Labour	4 hours	£6	24	Labour	39 000 hours	249 600
			184	Total Cost		1 848 600

Task 1
(a) Calculate the following:
   (i) the material price variance;
   (ii) the material usage variance;
   (iii) the labour rate variance;
   (iv) the labour efficiency variance (sometimes called the utilization variance);
(b) Prepare a standard costing statement reconciling the actual marginal cost of production with the standard marginal cost of production.

After Richard Hill has received your standard costing statement, you visit him to discuss the variances and their implications. Richard, however, raises a number of queries with you. He makes the following points:

- An index measuring material prices stood at 247.2 for May but at 240.0 when the standard for the material price was set.
- The Eastern division is budgeted to run at its normal capacity of 8000 units of production per month, but during May it had to manufacture an additional 1500 Betas to meet a special order agreed at short notice by Malton's sales director.
- Because of the short notice, the normal supplier of the raw material was unable to meet the extra demand and so additional materials had to be acquired from another supplier at a price per litre of £22.
- This extra material was not up to the normal specification, resulting in 20% of the special purchase being scrapped *prior* to being issued to production.
- The work force could only produce the special order on time by working overtime on the 1500 Betas at a 50% premium.

Task 2
(a) Calculate the amounts within the material price variance, the material usage variance and the labour rate variance which arise from producing the special order.
(b) (i) Estimate the revised standard price for materials based on the change in the material price index.
   (ii) For the 8000 units of normal production, use your answer in (b) (i) to estimate how much of the price variance calculated in Task 1 is caused by the general change in prices.
(c) Using your answers to parts (a) and (b) of this task, prepare a revised standard costing statement. The revised statement should subdivide the variances prepared in Task 1 into those elements controllable by Richard Hill and those elements caused by factors outside his divisional control.

(d) Write a *brief* note to Richard Hill justifying your treatment of the elements you believe are outside his control and suggesting what action should be taken by the company.

Association of Accounting Technicians –
Technicians Stage

Computation of variable overhead variances

The following details have been extracted from the standard cost card for product X:

		(£/unit)
Variable overhead		
4 machine hours at	£8.00/hour	32.00
2 labour hours at	£4.00/hour	8.00
Fixed overhead		20.00

During October 1997, 5450 units of the product were made compared to a budgeted production target of 5500 units. The actual overhead costs incurred were:

Machine-related variable overhead	£176 000
Labour-related variable overhead	£42 000
Fixed overhead	£109 000

The actual number of machine hours was 22 000 and the actual number of labour hours was 10 800.

Required:
(a) Calculate the overhead cost variances in as much detail as possible from the data provided.   *12 marks*
(b) Explain the meaning of, and give possible causes for, the variable overhead variances which you have calculated.   *8 marks*
(c) Explain the benefits of using multiple activity bases for variable overhead absorption.   *5 marks*

Total marks 25
CIMA Stage 2 – Operational Cost Accounting

Variance analysis and reconciliation of budgeted and actual profit

The Perseus Co. Ltd, a medium-sized company, produces a single product in its one overseas factory. For control purposes, a standard costing system was recently introduced and is now in operation.

The standards set for the month of May were as follows:

Production and sales	16 000 units
Selling price (per unit)	£140
Materials	
Material 007	6 kilos per unit at £12.25 per kilo
Material XL90	3 kilos per unit at £3.20 per kilo
Labour	4.5 hours per unit at £8.40 per hour

Overheads (all fixed) at £86 400 per month are not absorbed into the product costs.
The actual data for the month of May, is as follows:

Produced 15 400 units, which were sold at £138.25 each
Materials
   Used 98 560 kilos of material 007 at a total cost of £1 256 640
   Used 42 350 kilos of material XL90 at a total cost of £132 979

Labour
Paid an actual rate of £8.65 per hour to the labour force. The total amount paid out
amounted to £612 766
Overheads (all fixed) £96 840

Required:
(a) Prepare a standard costing profit statement, and a profit statement based on
actual figures for the month of May   *6 marks*
(b) prepare a statement of the variances which reconciles the actual with the standard profit or loss figure.   *9 marks*
(c) Explain briefly the possible reasons for interrelationships between material variances and labour variances.   *5 marks*
Total 20 marks
ACCA Paper 8 Managerial Finance

Question 19.18   **Calculation of actual quantities working backwards from variances**
intermediate   The following profit reconciliation statement summarizes the performance of one of
SEW's products for March 1997.

	(£)
Budgeted profit	4250
Sales volume variance	850A
Standard profit on actual sales	3400
Selling price variance	4000A
	(600)

Cost variances:	Adverse	Favourable	
	(£)	(£)	
Direct material price		1000	
Direct material usage	150		
Direct labour rate	200		
Direct labour efficiency	150		
Variable overhead expenditure	600		
Variable overhead efficiency	75		
Fixed overhead efficiency		2500	
Fixed overhead volume		150	
	1175	3650	2475F
Actual profit		1875	

The budget for the same period contained the following data:

Sales volume		1 500	units
Sales revenue	£20 000		
Production volume		1 500	units
Direct materials purchased		750	kg
Direct materials used		750	kg
Direct material cost	£4 500		
Direct labour hours		1 125	
Direct labour cost	£4 500		
Variable overhead cost	£2 250		
Fixed overhead cost	£4 500		

Additional information:
- Stocks of raw materials and finished goods are valued at standard cost.
- During the month the actual number of units produced was 1550.

- The actual sales revenue was £12 000.
- The direct materials purchased were 1000 kg.

Required:
(a) Calculate
 (i) the actual sales volume;
 (ii) the actual quantity of materials used;
 (iii) the actual direct material cost;
 (iv) the actual direct labour hours;
 (v) the actual direct labour cost;
 (vi) the actual variable overhead cost. *19 marks*
(b) Explain the possible causes of the direct materials usage variance, direct labour
 rate variance and sales volume variance. *6 marks*

Total marks 25
Chartered Institute of Management Accounts
Operational Cost Accounting Stage 2

Comparison of absorption and marginal costing variances

You have been provided with the following data for S plc for September 1996:

Question 19.19
intermediate

Accounting method:	Absorption	Marginal
Variances:	(£)	(£)
Selling price	1900 (A)	1900 (A)
Sales volume	4500 (A)	7500 (A)
Fixed overhead expenditure	2500 (F)	2500 (F)
Fixed overhead volume	1800 (A)	n/a

During September 1996 production and sales volumes were as follows:

	Sales	Production
Budget	10 000	10 000
Actual	9 500	9 700

Required:
(a) Calculate:
 (i) the standard contribution per unit;
 (ii) the standard profit per unit;
 (iii) the actual fixed overhead cost total. *9 marks*
(b) Using the information presented above, explain why different variances are calculated depending upon the choice of marginal or absorption costing. *8 marks*
(c) Explain the meaning of the fixed overhead volume variance and its usefulness to
 management. *5 marks*
(d) Fixed overhead absorption rates are often calculated using a single measure of
 activity. It is suggested that fixed overhead costs should be attributed to cost
 units using multiple measures of activity (activity-based costing).
 Explain 'activity-based costing' and how it may provide useful information to
 managers.
 (Your answer should refer to both the setting of cost driver rates and subsequent overhead cost control.) *8 marks*

Total marks 30
Chartered Institute of Management Accountants
Operational Cost Accounting – Stage 2

Answer 19.1 A favourable labour efficiency variance indicates that actual hours used were less than the standard hours produced. The favourable variance was £7 800. Therefore the standard hours produced were 18 700 (17 500 + £7 800/£6.50).

Answer = D

Answer 19.2

Materials price variance	= (Standard price − Actual price) × Actual quantity	
	= (Actual quantity × Standard price) − Actual cost	
	= (8 200 × £0.80) − £6 888	
	= £328 Adverse	
Material usage variance	= (Standard quantity − Actual quantity) × Standard price	
	= (870 × 8 kg = 6 960 − 7 150) × £0.80	
	= £512 Adverse	

Answer = D

Answer 19.3 Fixed overhead variance = Budgeted cost (not flexed) − Actual cost
= £10 000 per month − £9 800
= £200 Favourable

Answer = B

Answer 19.4

$$\text{Standard fixed overhead rate} = \frac{\text{Budgeted cost (£48 000)}}{\text{Budgeted output (4 800 units)}} = £10$$

Overheads incurred = Budgeted cost + Expenditure variance (£2 000) = £50 000
Overheads absorbed = £50 000 − Under-absorption (£8 000) = £42 000
Actual number of units produced = £42 000/£10 = 4 200

Answer = C

Answer 19.5 Volume variance
= (Actual production − Budgeted production) × Fixed overhead rate
= (19 500 − 20 000) × (£100 000/20 000)
= £2 500A

Answer = B

Answer 19.6 Sales volume variance = (Actual sales volume − Budgeted sales volume) × Standard contribution margin
= (4 500 − 5 000) £4.40
= £2 200 Adverse

Answer = B

Answer 19.7 Standard price per kg = £46 248/11 280 = £4.10
Usage variance (kg) = £492/£4.10 = 120 kg
Actual usage exceeds standard usage by 120 kg
Standard usage = 11 280 − 120 = 11 160 kg

Answer = D

Budgeted overhead rate = £10 per hour
Actual volume was 1 000 standard hours less than budget thus causing an under-absorption of £10 000. Actual expenditure was £1 400 more than budget thus resulting in an under-absorption of £1 400.

Answer = C

	£
Actual cost	16 380
Less adverse price variance	1 170
Actual purchases at standard price	15 210

Standard price = £15 210/7 800 kg = £1.95

Answer = A

Sales volume variance = (Actual sales volume − Budgeted sales volume) × Standard profit margin
= (11 000 − £100 000/£8)£2.50 = £3 750A
Sales price variance = (Actual price − Budgeted price) × Actual sales volume
= (£9 − £8) × 11 000 = £11 000F

Answer = A

Efficiency variance = (Standard hours − Actual hours) Standard rate
= (4 650 × 4 hrs = 18 600 − 19 100) £5.40
= £2 700A
Rate variance = (Standard rate − Actual rate) Actual hours
= (£5.40 − £98 350/19 100) 19 100
= £4 790F

Answer = E

Efficiency variance = (Standard hours − Actual hours) × Standard rate
= (Standard hours × Standard rate) − (Actual hours −
= Standard rate)
− £36,000A = (5 792 × 6.5 hrs × £5 = £188 240) − (AH × £5)
5AH = £188 240 + £36 000
AH = 44 848

Answer = D

Task
(a) Soap pack price variance = (Standard price − Actual price) Actual quantity
= (£1.20 − £1.30) 920 = £92A
= (£1.20 − £1.40) 1 130 = £226A
£318A

Soap pack usage variance = (Standard quantity − Actual quantity) Standard price
= (8 400 − 8 580) £1.20
= £216A

$$\text{Cleaning labour rate variance} = (\text{Standard rate} - \text{Actual rate}) \text{ Actual hours}$$
$$= (£3.60 - £3) \, 1{,}850 = £1\,110\text{F}$$
$$= (£3.60 - £4.50) \, 700 = \underline{£630\text{A}}$$
$$\underline{£480\text{F}}$$

Cleaning labour efficiency

$$\text{variance} = (\text{Standard hours} - \text{Actual hours}) \text{ Standard rate}$$
$$= (8\,400 \times 0.25 \text{ hours} = 2\,100 - 2\,550) \, £3.60$$
$$= £1\,620\text{A}$$

(b) (i) The soap price variance could be due to inflation and a general increase in the market price. In such circumstances the standard price should be altered to reflect the current standard price.

    (ii) The adverse soap usage variance could be due to theft or excess issues. Managers should check that stocks are securely locked away and that only the standard quantity is issued each day.

    (iii) The labour rate variance may have arisen because proportionately less weekend work was undertaken than that allowed for in the standard. It may be appropriate to maintain separate standards for weekend and non-weekend work and separate records so that variances can be reported for both categories of labour.

    (iv) The standard time may represent an inappropriate standard that must be changed. Alternatively, excessive idle time may have occurred because of rooms not being vacated when the cleaners are being paid. Working practices and vacation procedures should be investigated to ensure that vacation is synchronized with when the cleaners are employed for cleaning the rooms.

Answer 19.14 *Task 1*

(a) To ascertain the seasonally adjusted price it is necessary to remove the seasonal variations from the observed price:

	Quarter 1	Quarter 2	Quarter 3	Quarter 4
	£	£	£	£
Actual price	10	11	16	19
Seasonal variations	−1	−2	+1	+2
Seasonally adjusted price	11	13	15	17

(b) The seasonally adjusted price shows a trend of prices increasing by £2 per quarter. To ascertain the forecast price it is necessary to adjust the seasonally adjusted forecast by incorporating the seasonally adjusted price variations:

	Quarter 1	Quarter 2	Quarter 3	Quarter 4
	£	£	£	£
Seasonally adjusted forecast	19	21	23	25
Seasonal variations	−1	−2	+1	+2
Forecast price	18	19	24	27

Task 2

$$\text{Material price variances} = (\text{Standard price} - \text{Actual price}) \text{ Actual quantity}$$
$$= (\text{Actual quantity} \times \text{standard price}) - \text{Actual cost}$$
$$= (26\,500 \times £23) - £662\,500$$
$$= £609\,500 - £662\,500$$
$$= £53\,000\text{A}$$

Material usage variance = (Standard quantity − Actual quantity) Standard price
= (9 000 × 3 kg = 27 000 kg − 26 500) £23
= £11 500F

Labour rate = (Standard price − Actual price) Actual hours
= (Actual hours × Standard price) − Actual cost
= (18 400 × £20) − £349 600
= £18 400F

Labour efficiency = (Standard hours − Actual hours) Standard price
= (9 000 × 2 = 18 000 − 18 400) £20
= £8 000A

Reconciliation Statement:

	£	£
Standard cost of actual production (9 000 units × £229)		2 061 000
Material variances:		
Price	53 000A	
Usage	11 500F	41 500A
Labour variances:		
Rate	18 400F	
Efficiency	8 000A	10 400F
Fixed overhead variances		
Expenditure	300 000A	
Capacity	96 000A	
Efficiency	24 000A	420 000A
Actual cost (£662 500 + £349 600 + £1 500 000)		2 512 100A

Task 3
(a) Variances attempt to measure the cost of deviations from planned results. Significant variances should be investigated and remedial action taken where inefficiencies are identified. Alternatively, the investigation may signal the need for replanning if there has been a permanent change in the production process or environment. For a more detailed answer see the section on comparing actual and planned outcomes and responding to divergences from plan in Chapter 1.
(b) Variances can arise because of changes in prices of inputs, changes in quantities of inputs and actual production or sales volume deviating from budgeted volume.
(c) (i) Variances arising from measurement errors where the recorded amounts for actual costs or actual usage differ from the actual amounts. For example, labour hours for a particular operation might be incorrectly added up.
(ii) Variances arising from out of date standards. For example, where frequent changes in prices of inputs occur there is a danger that prices may be out of date.
(iii) Variances arising from random or uncontrollable factors. These occur when a particular process is performed by the same worker under the same conditions, yet performance varies. When no known cause is present to account for this variability, it is said to be due to random or uncontrollable factors. A standard is determined from a series of observations. It is most unlikely that repeated observations of this operation will yield the same result, even if the operation consists of the same worker completing the same task under identical conditions. The approach is to choose a representation reading from these observations to determine a standard. Frequently the representative reading that is chosen is the average. One summary reading is chosen to represent the standard when in reality a range of outcomes is possible when the process is *under control*. Any observation that differs from the chosen

standard when the process is under control can be described as a random uncontrollable variation around the standard.

(d) The standard price is £23 but the forecast price was £27. The actual price paid was £25 (£662 500/26 500). However, if the £27 represents the current market price the actual price is less than the current market price and the purchasing department has bought efficiently. The reported adverse variance reflects the fact that the standard has not been updated to reflect market changes.

Answer 19.15 *Task 1*

(a) Material price variance = (Standard price − Actual price) × Actual quantity
   = (Standard price × Actual quantity) − Actual cost
   = (78 000 × £20) − £1 599 000
   = £1 560 000 − £1 599 000
   = £39 000A

Material usage
   variance = (Standard quantity − Actual quantity) × Standard price
   = (9 500 × 8 = 76 000 litres − 78 000 litres) × £20
   = £40 000 Adverse

Wage rate variance = (Standard price − Actual price) × Actual hours
   = (Standard price × Actual hours) − Actual cost
   = (£6 × 39 000 = £234 000) − £249 600
   = £15 600A

Labour efficiency variance = (Standard hours − Actual hours) × Standard rate
   = (9 500 × 4 = 38 000 − 39 000) × £6
   = £6 000A

(b)

	£	£
Standard cost of production (9 500 × £184)		1 748 000
Add adverse variances: Material price	39 000	
Material usage	40 000	
Wage rate	15 600	
Labour efficiency	6 000	100 600
Actual cost		1 848 600

Task 2

(a) Material used in standard quantities
   (1 500 × 100/80 × 8 litres) = 15 000
   Standard usage for special order (1 500 × 8) = 12 000
   Material usage variance arising from special order
   (3 000 kg × £20) = £60 000A
   Material price variance arising from special order
   (15 000 kg × (£22 − £20)) = £18 000A
   Wage rate variance arising from special order
   (1 500 × 4 hrs × £6 × 50%) = £18 000A

(b) Revised standard price (247.2/240 × £20)   £20.60
   Increase over original standard   £0.60
   Material used excluding special order (78 000 − 15 000)   63 000 litres
   Price variance arising from price increase (63 000 × £0.60)   £37 800A

(c)

	£	£
Standard cost of production		1 748 000
Add non-controllable variances		
Special order material usage variance	60 000A	

Special order material price variance	30 000A	
Special order wage rate variance	18 000A	
Material price variance due to increase in market price	37 800A	145 800A
Add controllable variances:		
Material price (£39 000 − £30 000 − £37 800)	28 800F	
Material usage (£40 000 − £60 000)	20 000F	
Wage rate (£15 600 − £18 000)	2 400F	
Labour efficiency	6 000A	45 200F
Actual cost		1 848 600

(d) The answer should draw attention to the fact that the divisional total variance was £100 600 but £145 800 was not controllable by the manager. This consisted of £37 800 arising from an increase in market prices and £108 000 arising from the special order. The manager should be congratulated on the favourable controllable variances.

If the index of material prices was applicable to the type of materials used by the division then the standard should be altered to reflect the price change. The profitability of the special order should be recalculated after taking into account the extra cost arising from the adverse variances and the sales director informed. The sales director should also be requested to provide details of special orders to the relevant managers so that steps can be taken to ensure that the materials can be obtained from the normal supplier.

(a) Because some variable overheads vary with machine hours and other variable **Answer 19.16** overheads vary with direct labour hours separate variable overhead efficiency and expenditure variances should be computed for machine-related and labour-related variable overheads.

Variable overhead efficiency variance:
(Standard hours − Actual hours) × Standard rate
Machine related = (5 450 × 4 hours = 21 800 − 22 000) × £8 = £1 600A
Labour related = (5 450 × 2 hours = 10 900 − 10 800) × £4 = £400F

Variable overhead expenditure variance:
(Actual hours × Standard rate) − Actual variable overheads incurred
Machine related = 22 000 × £8 = £176 000 − £176 000 = Nil
Labour related = 10 800 × £4 = £43 200 − £42 000 = £1 200F

Fixed overhead expenditure variance
$$= \text{Budgeted cost} - \text{Actual cost}$$
$$= 5\ 500 \text{ units} \times £20 = £110\ 000 - £109\ 000$$
$$= £1\ 000F$$

Fixed overhead volume $= (\text{Actual production} - \text{Budgeted production}) \times \text{Standard rate}$
$$= (5\ 450 - 5\ 500) \times £20 = £1\ 000A$$

(b) The variable overhead machine-related efficiency variance arises because machine hours exceeded target (standard) hours that should have been used for the actual output. Because it is assumed that some variable overheads vary with machine hours the excess usage has resulted in additional spending on variable overheads. Failure to maintain machinery may have resulted in the use of hours in excess of standard.

The variable overhead labour-related variance arises because actual direct labour hours were less than the hours that should have been used for the actual output. This has resulted in reduced expenditure on those variable overheads that vary with direct labour hours. An improvement in the efficiency of direct labour has resulted in the favourable variance.

The variable overhead labour-related expenditure variance arises because actual spending was less than budgeted spending flexed to the actual level of activity. Prices paid for variable overhead items (e.g. indirect materials) may have been lower than the figures used to derive the budgeted expenditure. For a more detailed answer see the section on variable overhead expenditure variance in Chapter 19.

(c) See an illustration of ABC and traditional product costing systems in Chapter 19 for the answer to this question. In particular, the answer should demonstrate how the use of multiple cost drivers should result in the reporting of more accurate product costs than when a single cost driver is used. In order to understand and manage costs more effectively there is a need to measure overhead resource consumption using cost drivers that are the causes of overhead expenditure. Different cost drivers, rather than a single cost driver, provide a better explanation of cost behaviour. Thus multiple cost drivers should also result in better cost management (see the section on activity-cost management in Chapter 12 for a more detailed explanation of this point).

Answer 19.17 (a) It is assumed that the term 'standard costing profit statement' means budgeted profit statement (i.e. budgeted sales less standard cost of budgeted sales). Alternatively, the term 'standard costing profit statement' can be interpreted as actual sales less standard cost of actual sales. Adopting this interpretation will mean that a sales volume variance will not be reported.

Budgeted profit statement:

		£
Sales (16 000 units × £140)		2 240 000
Materials		
007 (16 000 × 6 kg × £12.25)	1 176 000	
XL90 (16 000 × 3 kg × £3.20)	153 600	
Labour		
16 000 × 4.5 hours × £8.40	604 800	
Overheads		
All fixed (given)	86 400	1 882 560
Profit		219 200

Actual profit statement:

		£
Sales (15 400 units × £138.25)		2 129 050
Materials		
007	1 256 640	
XL90	132 979	
Labour	612 766	
Overheads	96 840	2 099 225
Profit		29 825

Note that the above statements are prepared on a marginal costing basis.

(b) Material price variance = (Standard price − Actual price) × Actual quantity
= (Actual quantity × Standard price) − Actual cost
Material 007 = (98 560 kg × £12.25) − £1 256 640 = £49 280A
Material XL90 = (42 350 kg × £3.20) − £132 979 = £2 541F
Material usage variance = (Standard quantity − Actual quantity) × Standard price
Material 007 = (15 400 × 6 kg = 92 400 − 98 560) × £12.25 = £75 460

Material XL90	$= (15\,400 \times 3\text{ kg} = 46\,200 - 42\,350) \times £3.20 = £12\,320$F
Wage rate variance	= (Standard price − Actual price) × Actual hours
	$= (£8.40 - £8.65) \times £612\,766/£8.65 = £17\,710$A
Labour efficiency variance	= (Standard hours − Actual hours) × Standard price
	$= (15\,400 \times 4.5\text{ hrs} = 69\,300 - 70\,840^a) \times £8.40 = £12\,936$A
Fixed overhead expenditure	= Budgeted cost − Actual cost
	$= £86\,400 - £96\,840 = £10\,440$A
Sales margin price	= (Actual price − Budgeted price) × Actual volume
	$= (£138.25 - £140) \times 15\,400 = £26\,950$A
Sales margin volume	= (Actual volume − Budgeted volume) × Standard margin
	$= (15\,400 - 16\,000) \times £19.10^b - £11\,460$A

Notes:
[a] Actual hours = £612 766/£8.65 = 70 840

	£
[b] Budgeted contribution margin = Selling price	140.00
Less Direct materials $(6 \times £12.25) + (3 \times £3.20)$	83.10
Direct labour $(4.5 \times £8.40)$	37.80
	19.10

Reconciliation statement:	£
Budgeted profit	219 200
Add favourable variances (£2,541 + £12,320)	14 861
	234 061
Less adverse variances (£49 280 + £75 460 + £17 710 + £12 936)	
(+ £10 440 + £26 950 + £11 460)	204 236
Actual profit	29 825

(c) The purchase of cheap, poor quality materials below standard price will result in a favourable price variance but may be the cause of an adverse material usage and labour efficiency variance. Similarly, the use of unskilled instead of skilled labour will result in a favourable wage rate variance and may be the cause of an adverse material usage variance arising from spoilt work and excessive usage of materials. The use of less skilled labour may also result in an adverse labour efficiency variance if the workers are not as efficient as skilled workers.

Answer 19.18

(a) (i) A fixed overhead volume variance only occurs with an absorption costing system. The question indicates that a volume variance has been reported. Therefore the company must operate an absorption costing system and report the sales volume variance in terms of profit margins, rather than contribution margins.

Budgeted profit margin = Budgeted   profit   (£4 250)/Budgeted   volume (1 500 units)
= £2.83

Adverse sales volume variance in units = £850/£2.83 = 300 units
Therefore actual sales volume was 300 units below budgeted sales volume
Actual sales volume = 1 200 units (1 500 units − 300 units)

(ii) Standard quantity of material used per units of output:
Budgeted usage (750 kg)/Budgeted production (1 500 units) = 0.5 kg
Standard price = Budgeted material cost (£4 500)/Budgeted usage (750 kg) = £6

Material usage variance = (Standard quantity − Actual Quantity) Standard
price
£150A = (1 550 × 0.5 kg = 775 kg − AQ) £6
− £150 = 4 650 − 6AQ
6AQ = 4 800
Actual quantity used = 800 kg

(iii) Material price variance = (Standard price − Actual price) × Actual purchases

£1 000F = (£6 − Actual price) × 1 000 kg
£1 000F = £6 000 − 1 000AP
1 000AP = £5 000
AP = £5 per kg
Actual material cost = 1 000 kg × £5 = £5 000

(iv) Standard hours per unit of output = $\dfrac{\text{Budgeted hours (1 125)}}{\text{Budgeted output (1 500 units)}}$
= 0.75 hours

Standard wage rate = Budgeted labour cost (£4 500)/Budgeted hours (1 125)
= £4

Labour efficiency variance = (Standard hours − Actual hours) × Standard
rate

£150A = (1 550 × 0.75 = 1 162.5 − Actual hours) × £4
− £150 = £4 650 − 4AH
4AH = £4 800
Actual hours = 1 200

(v) Total labour variance = Standard cost − Actual cost
(£200A + £150A) = (1 550 × 0.75 hrs × £4) − Actual cost
£350A = £4 650 − Actual cost
Actual cost = £5 000

(vi) Standard variable overhead cost per unit
= $\dfrac{\text{Budgeted variable overheads (2 250)}}{\text{Budgeted output (1 500 units)}}$
= £1.50

Total variable overhead variance = Standard cost − Actual cost
(£600A + £75A) = (1 550 × £1.50 = £2 325) − Actual cost
£675A = £2 325 − Actual cost
Actual cost = £3 000

(vii) Fixed overhead expenditure variance = Budgeted cost − Actual cost
£2 500F = £4 500 2 Actual cost
Actual cost = £2 000

(b) See Chapter 19 for an explanation of the causes of the direct material usage,
direct labour rate and sales volume variances

Answer 19.19 (a) (i) *Sales margin volume variance (Marginal costing):*
(Actual volume − Budgeted volume) × Standard contribution margin per
unit
(9 500 − 10 000) × Standard margin (SM) = £7 500A
500,SM = 7 500
Standard margin = £15

(ii) *Sales margin volume variance (Absorption costing):*
(Actual volume − Budgeted volume) × Standard profit margin per unit
(9 500 − 10 000) × Standard margin (SM) = £4 500A
500,SM = £4 500
Standard profit margin per unit = £9

(iii) *Fixed overhead volume variance:*
(Actual production − Budgeted production) × Standard rate
(9 700 − 10 000) × Standard rate = £1 800A
Standard fixed overhead rate per unit = £6
Budgeted fixed overheads = 10 000 units × £6 = £60 000
Fixed overhead expenditure variance   = £2 500F
Actual fixed overheads (£60 000 − £2 500)   = £57 500

(b) Absorption costing unitizes fixed overheads and treats them as product costs whereas marginal costing does not charge fixed overheads to products. Instead, the total amount of fixed overheads is charged as an expense (period cost) for the period. A fixed overhead volume variance only occurs with an absorption costing system. Because marginal costing does not unitize fixed costs product margins are expressed as contribution margins whereas absorption costing expresses margins as profit margins. For a more detailed answer you should refer to the section on standard absorption costing in Chapter 19.

(c) See the section on volume variance in Chapter 19 for the answer to this question.

(d) See an illustration of ABC and traditional product costing systems and the section on activity-based cost management in Chapter 12 for the answer to this question.

New ACCA questions

Question 1
(relating to Chapter 7)

Equivalent production with no losses (FIFO method)

A company operates a manufacturing process where six people work as a team and are paid a weekly group bonus based upon the actual output of the team compared with output expected.

A basic 37 hour week is worked during which the expected output from the process is 4 000 equivalent units of product. Basic pay is £5.00 per hour and the bonus for the group, shared equally, is £0.80 per unit in excess of expected output.

In the week just ended, basic hours were worked on the process. The following additional information is provided for the week:

Opening work in process (1 000 units):
  Materials £540 (100% complete)
  Labour and overheads £355 (50% complete).

During the week:
  Materials used £2 255
  Overheads incurred £1 748
  Completed production 3 800 units

Closing work in process (1 300 units):
  Materials (100% complete)
  Labour and overheads (75% complete).

There are no process losses.

The FIFO method is used to apportion costs.

Required

(a) Prepare the process account for the week just ended. *(10 marks)*

(b) Explain the purpose of the following documents which are used in the control of, and accounting for, the materials used in the process described in part (a)
  (i) purchase requisition
  (ii) materials (stores) requisition. *(4 marks)*
  (14 marks)
  ACCA Foundation Stage – Paper 3

Answer (a)

Cost element	Current period costs £	Completed units less opening WIP equiv. units	Closing WIP equiv. units	Current total equiv. units	Cost per unit £
Materials	2 255	2 800	1 300	4 100	0.55
Conversion cost (1)	3 078	3 300	975	4 275	0.72
	5 333				

	£	£
Completed production:		
Opening WIP (£540 + £355)	895	
Materials (2 800 × £0.55)	1 540	
Conversion cost (3 300 × £0.72)	2 376	
		4 811

Closing work in progress:
Materials (1 300 × £0.55)   715
Conversion cost (975 × £0.72)   702
                                         1 417
                                         6 228

Note
(1) Bonus = Current total equivalent units (4 275) − Expected output (4 000)
            = 275 units × £0.80 = £220
    Labour cost = 6 men × 37 hours = £5 = £1 110 + Bonus (£220) = £1 330
    Conversion cost = £1 748 overhead + £1 330 labour = £3 078

	Process Account		
	£		£
Opening WIP	895	Completed output	4 811
Materials	2 255	Closing WIP	1 417
Labour and overhead	3 078		
	6 228		6 228

(b) See 'Materials control procedure' in Chapter 4 for an explanation of the documents.

Calculation of sales by individual products to achieve a target contribution

Question 2
(relating to Chapter 10)

A company manufactures and sells three products which currently have the following annual trading performance:

		Product	
(£000)	A	B	C
Sales	1 794	3 740	2 950
Production cost of sales	1 242	2 860	1 888
Gross provis	552	880	1 062
Non-production overheads	460	770	767
Net profit	92	110	295
Sales units (000)	1 150	2 200	2 360

For each product, units produced and sold were the same in the period.

Fixed product overheads are absorbed at a rate of £0.30 per unit for each product. Non-production overheads include certain costs which vary with activity at a rate of 10% of sales value. The remaining non-production overheads are fixed costs.

Required
(a) **Prepare a statement, in marginal costing format, showing the sales, costs, and profit contribution of each product expressed both in £ per unit (to three decimal places) and also as a % of sales (to one decimal place)** (*8 marks*)
(b) **Calculate, based upon the current mix of sales, the sales requied of each product (to the nearest £000) in order to generate a total contribution of £3.75m per annum.** (*6 marks*)
                                                                          (*14 marks*)
                                              ACCA Foundation Stage – Paper 3

Answer (a)

	Product A		Product B		Product C	
	£/unit	% of sales	£/unit	% of sales	£/unit	% of sales
Sales[1]	1.560	100.0	1.700	100.0	1.250	100.0
Variable production cost[2]	0.780	50.0	1.000	58.8	0.500	40.0
Variable non-production cost[3]	0.156	10.0	0.170	10.0	0.125	10.0
Total variable cost	0.936	60.0	1.170	68.8	0.625	50.0
Contribution	0.624	40.0	0.530	31.2	0.625	50.0

Notes
1. Total sales revenue/units sold (Product A = £1 794 000/1 150 000 units = £1.56).
2. Production cost of sales/units sold − £0.30 fixed overheads.
3. 10% of selling price.

(b)

	A	B	C	Total
1. Units sold	1 150	2 200	2 360	5 710
2. Sales mix[1]	20.14%	38.53%	41.33%	
3. Unit contribution (a)	£0.624	£0.530	£0.625	
4. Total contribution (1 × 3)	£717.6	£1 166	£1 475	3 358.6
5. Sales revenues	1 794	3 740		

Note
1. Product A = 1 150 units/5 170 units, B = 2 200/5 710, C = 2 360/5 170
   Average contribution per unit sold = £3 358.6/5 170 units = £0.5882
   Total units sold to generate a contribution of £3.75m = £3.75m/£0.5882
   = 6 375 383 units

Total sales of 6,375 units at the current sales mix is:
   Product A = 20.14% × 6 375 383 units = 1 284 002 units
           B = 38.53% × 6 375 383 units = 2 456 435 units
           C = 41.33% × 6 375 383 units = 2 634 946 units
Answer in sales revenues:
   Product A = 1 284 002 units × £1.560 unit selling price = £2 003 043
           B = 2 456 435 units × £1.70 unit selling price = £4 175 940
           C = 2 634 946 units × £1.25 unit selling price = £3 293 683
   Total sales   £9 472 663

Question 3
(relating to Chapter 15)

An investment project has the following expected cash flows over its economic life of three years:

	£
Year 0	(142 700)
1	51 000
2	62 000
3	73 000

Required
(i) Calculate the net present value (NPV) of the project at discount rates of 0%, 10% and 20% respectively.
(ii) Draw a graph of the project NPVs calculated in (i) and use the graph to estimate, and clearly indicate, the project internal rate of return (IRR) to the nearest integer percentage. *(8 marks)*

ACCA Foundation Stage – Paper 3

(i) Net present values: **Answer**

Year	0% NPV £	10% Discount Factor	NPV £	20% Discount Factor	NPV £
0	(142 700)	1.000	(142 700)	1.000	(142 700)
1	51 000	0.909	46 59	0.833	42 483
2	62 000	0.826	51 212	0.694	43 028
3	73 000	0.751	54 823	0.579	42 267
	43 300		9 694		(14 922)

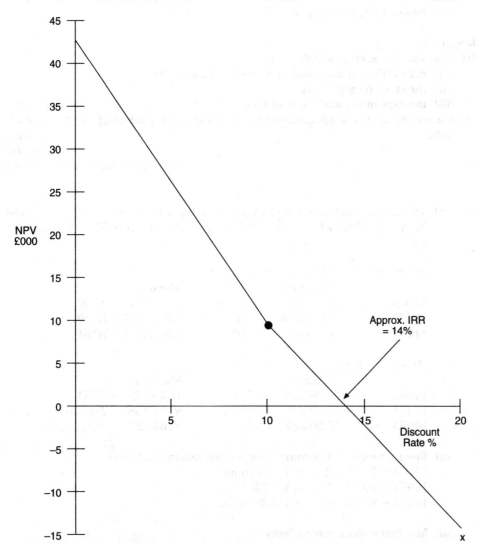

Calculation of re-order and maximum stock levels

Question 4
(relating to Chapter 15)

(a) A retail company has been reviewing the adequacy of its stock control systems and has identified three products for investigation. Relevant details for the three products are set out below:

Item code	EOQ (000 units)	Stock (warehouse and stores) (000 units)	(£/unit at cost)	Weekly sales (£000) minimum	normal	maximum	Gross* margin (% of sales)
14/363	25	32.5	2.25	26	28	30	42
11/175	500	422.7	0.36	130	143	160	46
14/243	250	190	0.87	60	96	128	37

*Gross margin = sales − purchase cost of product.

Outstanding order: Item code 14/243 − order for 250 000 units placed 2 trading days ago.

There are 6 trading days per week.

All orders are delivered by suppliers into the retailer's central warehouse. The lead time is one week from placement of order. A further week is required by the retailer in order to transfer stock from central warehouse to stores. Both of these lead times can be relied upon.

Required:
(a) Calculate for each product:
  (i) the minimum and maximum weekly sales units
  (ii) the stock re-order level
  (iii) the maximum stock control level. *(9 marks)*
(b) Comment upon the adequacy of the existing stock control of the three products. *(5 marks)*
(14 marks)
ACCA Foundation Stage − Paper 3

Answer (a) (i) The cost of sales expressed as a percentage of total sales is 100 − Gross Margin %. Product A = 58% (100 − 42%), Product B = 54%, Product C = 63%.

Weekly cost of sales (£000s)

	Minimum		Maximum	
14/363	26 × 0.58	= 15.08	30 × 0.58	= 17.40
11/175	130 × 0.54	= 70.20	160 × 0.55	= 86.40
14/243	60 × 0.63	= 37.80	128 × 0.63	= 80.64

Weekly sales (units)

	Minimum		Maximum	
14/363	15.08/2.25	= 6 702	17.40/2.25	= 7 733
11/175	70.20/0.36	= 195 000	86.40/0.36	= 240 000
14/243	37.80/0.87	= 43 448	80.64/0.87	= 92 690

(ii) Re-order level = Maximum usage × maximum lead time
14/363 = 7 733 × 2   = 15 466 units
11/175 = 240 000 × 2   = 480 000 units
14/243 = 92 000 × 2   = 185 380 units

(iii) Maximum stock control level
= Re-order level + EOQ (Minimum usage in minimum lead time)
14/363 = 15 466 + 25 000 − (6 702 × 2)   = 27 062 units
11/175 = 480 000 + 500 000 − (195 000 × 2) = 590 000 units
14/243 = 185 380 + 250 000 − (43 448 × 2) = 348 484 units

(b) 1. Excessive stocks of item 14/363 are being held since stock exceeds the maximum stock level;
2. Stock is below the re-order level for item 11/175 and there are no outstanding orders. An order should have been raised;
3. The order for item 14/243 has been placed too early since stock exceeds the re-order level.